Care-giving in Dementia

```
WITHDRAWN
FROM
STOCK
```

Research and applications, Volume 4

Edited by Bère M.L. Miesen and Gemma M.M. Jones

D0270611

Routledge
Taylor & Francis Group

LONDON AND NEW YORK

First published 2006 by Routledge
27 Church Road, Hove, East Sussex BN3 2FA

Simultaneously published in the USA and Canada
by Routledge
270 Madison Ave, New York, NY 10016

Routledge is an imprint of the Taylor & Francis Group, an informa business

Typeset in Times by
RefineCatch Limited, Bungay, Suffolk
Printed and bound in Great Britain by
MPG Books Ltd, Bodmin, Cornwall
Paperback cover design by Sandra Heath

This publication has been produced with paper manufactured to strict environmental standards and with pulp derived from sustainable forests.

British Library Cataloguing in Publication Data
A catalogue record for this book is available from the British Library

Library of Congress Cataloging-in-Publication Data
Care-giving in dementia : research and applications / edited by Gemma M. M. Jones and Bére M. L. Miesen. – 4th vol.
 p. cm.
 Includes bibliographical references and index.
 ISBN 1–58391–190–7 (hardback : alk. paper) –
ISBN 1–58391–191–X (pbk. : alk. paper)
 1. Senile dementia. 2. Psychotherapy in old age. 3. Senile dementia – Patients – Care. 4. Community mental health services. I. Jones, Gemma M. M., 1957– II. Miesen, Bére M. L., 1946– III. Title.
RC524.C37 2004
618.97′683 – dc22
                    2003024917

ISBN13: 978–1–58391–190–7 (hbk)
ISBN13: 978–1–58391–191–4 (pbk)

ISBN10: 1–58391–190–7 (hbk)
ISBN10: 1–58391–191–X (pbk)

This volume is dedicated to our families, especially Ries Kleijnen and Ian Jones, who have often stepped out of their own family roles and busy careers to listen to, help reflect upon and patiently support us in our desire to open up a new arena of awareness about the many issues surrounding the care given to persons with dementing illnesses.

Contents

List of contributors   xi
Preface   xvii

PART I
Models and theories   1

1 Visuoperceptual-cognitive deficits in Alzheimer's disease:
   adapting a dementia unit   3
   GEMMA JONES, WILLIAM VAN DER EERDEN-REBEL AND
   JEREMY HARDING

2 Visual phenomena in Alzheimer's disease: distinguishing
   between hallucinations, illusions, misperceptions and
   misidentifications   59
   GEMMA JONES, JEREMY HARDING AND WILLIAM
   VAN DER EERDEN-REBEL

3 Attachment in dementia. Bound from birth?   105
   BÈRE MIESEN

4 Awareness and people with early-stage dementia   133
   LINDA CLARE, IVANA MARKOVÁ, BARBARA ROMERO, FRANS
   VERHEY, MICHAEL WANG, ROBERT WOODS AND JOHN KEADY

PART II
Interventions in care facilities   153

5 The role of humour in dementia   155
   WILL BLAKE, MARIE MILLS AND PETER COLEMAN

6 Occupational therapy use of sensory stimulation techniques to
   enhance engagement in later stage dementia care   175
   LESLEY ANN WAREING

7 Building Community through Arts (BCA). Cooperative inquiry
   using arts media with people with dementia   199
   JILL ANDERSON, KITTY LLOYD-LAWRENCE AND HILDA FLINT

8 Medical care for chronically ill elderly people: nursing home
   medicine as *functional geriatrics*   219
   CEES HERTOGH

9 Dementia and spiritual care   241
   PETER SPECK

PART III
Topics related to care-giving issues   257

10 Psychotherapeutic groups for people with dementia: the
   Dementia Voice group psychotherapy project   259
   RIK CHESTON, KERRY JONES AND JANE GILLIARD

11 Experiential support groups for people in the early to moderate
   stages of dementia   271
   MARIE MILLS AND ELIZABETH BARTLETT

12 Qualitative evaluation of an Alzheimer Café as an ongoing
   supportive group intervention   291
   AMY THOMPSON

PART IV
Family and professional care-givers   313

13 The Meeting Centres Support Programme model for persons
   with dementia and their carers: aims, methods and research   315
   ROSE-MARIE DRÖES, FRANKA MEILAND AND
   WILLEM VAN TILBURG

14   Couples group (psycho)therapy (CGT) in dementia   341
     BÈRE MIESEN

PART V
Education and ethics   363

15   Improving end-of-life care for people with dementia – the
     benefits of combining UK approaches to palliative care and
     dementia care   365
     NEIL SMALL, MURNA DOWNS AND KATHERINE FROGGATT

16   Death comes in the end. A palliative perspective of caring
     for people with dementia   393
     MARINUS VAN DEN BERG

17   Care-giving in dementia: moving ahead together. Review and
     perspectives   409
     BÈRE MIESEN

     Index   423

Contributors

Jill Anderson, BCA Consultant, trainer and supervisor for BCA since 1996, introduced cooperative inquiry into the structure, a process originated by John Heron, with whom she worked at Surrey University. She is a therapist in private practice, a group facilitator and mediator, and teaches an Advanced Counselling Course at Kensington Further Education College.

Elizabeth Bartlett is trained as a social worker and a Relate counsellor. She is now a counsellor and approved trainer with the Salisbury Branch of the Alzheimer's Society. She has recently developed her work with people diagnosed with dementia, adapting counselling techniques to meet their needs and participating in a Mental Health Foundation project on psycho-therapy groups for people with dementia.

Will Blake RMN, BSc (Hons.), is a Senior Clinical Nurse who manages the Older Adult In-Patient Services in the Amblescroft unit in Salisbury, England. He has over 25 years of clinical experience within mental health, the majority of this being associated with the care of people with dementia. He lectures and educates on aspects of dementia care and clinical nurse leadership and is involved in the development of in-service training on dementia care for professional carers within his organization.

Rik Cheston works as a consultant psychologist for Avon and Wiltshire Mental Health Partnership. He has been leading and also carrying out research into psychotherapy groups for people with dementia for 12 years.

Linda Clare, senior lecturer at the University of Wales Bangor, is a chartered clinical psychologist and neuropsychologist. Her research interests focus primarily on the theoretical and clinical issues surrounding awareness, the impact of progressive cognitive impairment on self-concept and the potential of rehabilitation for people with early-stage dementia.

Peter Coleman is Professor of Psychogerontology at the University of South-ampton, Head of the Health Psychology Research Group and Convenor of the Ageing Research Network of the same university. His research interests include 'Self and identity in advanced old age and dementia' and 'well-being'. He has published extensively on these and other topics.

Murna Downs is Professor in Dementia Studies and Head of the Bradford Dementia Group at the University of Bradford, UK. Professor Downs' research interests relate to quality of life and quality of care for people with dementia and their families.

Rose-Marie Dröes, PhD and human movement scientist, is Associate Professor in Psychogeriatrics at the VU medical centre in Amsterdam. She developed the Meeting Centres Support Programme and is chair of the Quality of Life in Dementia working group of the Leo Cahn Foundation and member of the Interdem group for timely diagnosis and psychosocial interventions in dementia. She is (co)author of several books and many (inter)national publications on psychosocial care and support for people with dementia and their carers, e.g. in Meeting Centres.

Hilda Flint worked with BCA from 1994, training as a facilitator. She submitted 'Spirituality and dementia' as her dissertation for her MA (London). She is a Lay Reader in the Church of England and a chaplaincy visitor in a hospital for continuing care for South West London & St George's Mental Health Trust.

Katherine Froggatt currently holds a postdoctoral research fellowship, funded by The Health Foundation, at the School of Nursing and Midwifery at the University of Sheffield, UK. The focus of this work is to develop end-of-life care in care homes involving older people, their relatives and staff.

Jane Gilliard, Professor, first worked as a medical social worker, then with children and families and finally with older people, especially people with dementia. In 1990, Jane established an innovative service supporting the carers of people attending the Bristol Memory Disorders Clinic. In the mid-1990s she set up Dementia Voice, a regional dementia services development centre for the South-West. Jane now works as part of the Health and Social Care Change Agent Team.

Jeremy W. Harding graduated in medicine from Leeds University in 1975 and did his Senior Registrarship in Oxford. He is a Consultant Old Age Psychiatrist in East Berkshire based at Heatherwood Hospital. Ascot, UK since 1987. He received an award from the Alzheimer Society for services to local branches in 2000 and is a founding member of the Slough, Windsor, Ascot, Bracknell Alzheimer Café. His research interests include visuoperceptual difficulties in Alzheimer's dementia as they pertain to care-giving issues.

Cees Hertogh is an MD geriatrician and has a PhD in philosophy. He is

Senior Researcher at the Institute for Research in Extramural Medicine of the Free University Medical Centre, Amsterdam, and a geriatrician at the Naarderheem Centre for geriatric rehabilitation and long-term care. He is (co)author of several books and articles on nursing home medicine and medical ethics, and is also a member of the editorial board of the Dutch *Journal of Gerontology and Geriatric Medicine*. His research is presently focused on the relationship between awareness and competence in persons with dementia and on 'end of life' decisions in dementia.

Gemma M.M. Jones (nee: van Amelsvoort) has Canadian undergraduate degrees in Zoology/Cell Biology and Nursing, and a PhD in the Neuropsychology of Alzheimer's Disease (Institute of Psychiatry, London, UK; University of London). She currently works as a freelance educator and consultant about care-giving in dementia issues and the design of care facilities for persons with dementia. She is a guest lecturer in psychogeriatrics at the Hague University and a founding member of the first Alzheimer Café in the UK, in Farnborough.

Kerry Jones, formerly a Research Officer for Dementia Voice, which is the Dementia Services Development Centre (DSDC) for South-West England and is part of a national network of DSDCs across the UK, is also currently involved with 'For Dementia Training', an organization linked to the Admiral Nurse (specialist training for dementia care nursing) Programme.

John Keady is Professor of Admiral Nursing at Northumbria University. This is a jointly funded post with the national charity 'For Dementia' and the first chair of dementia care nursing in the UK. He is founding and co-editor of *Dementia: the International Journal of Social Research and Practice*.

Kitty Lloyd-Lawrence, a graphic designer, founded a community-based arts studio (Kew Studio) in 1980. She pioneered BCA as its outreach programme from 1993 to the present. Since 1996, coordinating a company and charity partnership programme in Westminster, she is currently bringing her experience together in an MA study: 'The gifts of difference: reciprocal learning through creative community partnerships'.

Ivana Marková is a senior lecturer in psychiatry, University of Hull, UK. Her clinical work is based in neuropsychiatry with special interest in younger people with dementia and Huntington's disease. Her research is focused on descriptive psychopathology and her main interest is concentrated on the concept of insight in psychiatry.

Franka Meiland, PhD, MSc and Health Psychologist, works as a senior researcher in the regional mental health care institute GGZ-Buitenamstel, Valerius Clinic in Amsterdam. She wrote her PhD thesis on the management of waiting lists for nursing home placement and the consequences on persons with dementia and their carers. She worked as a post-doctorate in the project Implementation of the Model of Meeting Centres, on which she published several articles. She is a member of the Interdem group for timely diagnosis and psychosocial interventions in dementia.

Bère M.L. Miesen, PhD, is a registered Clinical Psycho(geronto)logist NIP and HealthCare Psychologist who has been working with people with dementia, their families and professionals since 1970. He is clinician, therapist, researcher, teacher, author and poet. Today he is Professor of PsychoGeriatrics at the Hague University, affiliated with the Department of Clinical and Health Psychology at the Leiden University, and consultant in psychogeriatrics at the WZH De Strijp-Waterhof nursing home in the Hague. He has received several awards for his efforts in emancipating all 'parties' involved in the field of care-giving in dementia. In 1997 he started the first Alzheimer Café in The Netherlands.

Marie Mills is a chartered health psychologist and counsellor. She is Visiting Fellow in the Centre for Research in Health Psychology at the University of Southampton. Her current research interests include meaning and spiritual beliefs in later life, particularly with regard to bereavement. Other important interests are mental health issues in later life, including the counselling needs of older depressed people with and without dementia. She has lectured and presented her work both in the UK and abroad.

Barbara Romero, PhD, is Research Chief of the Alzheimer Therapy Centre, Neurological Clinic Bad Aibling, Germany. She developed the concept of self-maintenance therapy for persons with dementia and the Alzheimer Therapy Centre programme for patients with dementia and care-giving relatives. She is involved in research projects, clinical practice and education.

Neil Small is Professor of Health Research in the School of Health Studies, Bradford University, UK. He combines research interests in chronic illness, end-of-life care and service organization and evaluation.

Peter Speck, Reverend Prebendary, worked for the last 30 years as a full-time healthcare chaplain and as a senior lecturer in medical ethics. A previous member of the editorial board of *Palliative Medicine* and the editorial board producing *Guidance on Supportive Care in Palliative Care within the UK* (NICE), he has authored several peer-reviewed publications and books and is Honorary Visiting Fellow at Southampton University.

Amy Thompson is a trainee clinical psychologist at Coventry and Warwick Universities. Prior to starting a doctoral programme she completed a degree in psychology at Northumbria University, thereafter gaining 4 years of experience as an assistant psychologist in learning disabilities and child and adolescent mental health. Her involvement with the Alzheimer Cafés began following a 6-month placement in older adult psychology.

Marinus van den Berg has been working as a Roman-Catholic Minister in several Dutch nursing homes during the last 30 years: at present in Antonius Ijsselmonde nursing home, Rotterdam. He is a regular guest (speaker) in the Dutch Alzheimer Cafés. One of his topics is counselling family members on what dementia means to them. In the last 7 years he has become more and more involved in palliative terminal care and recently he published several books on this theme.

William J. van der Eerden-Rebel took a Doctorate in Neurobiology in 1980 and became a Medical Doctor in 1988 at the Free University, Amsterdam. Specializations: neuroanatomy (1980–1984), neuro-rehabilitation (1994–1998) and geriatric medicine (2001–2003). Special interests: hippocampus (aging effects), neuromechanics (how the brain creates functional movements) and the brain's ability to make representations in all modalities. He is chairman of the Geriatric Department of the (Combi-Care) Residential/Nursing Home 'De Drie Hoven', Antaris, Amsterdam and Head of its Stroke Unit.

Willem van Tilburg is Professor of Clinical Psychiatry at the department of Psychiatry of the VU medical centre in Amsterdam and medical director of the regional mental healthcare institute GGZ-Buitenamstel in Amsterdam. He was chairman of the steering group of the project Implementation of the Model of Meeting Centres.

Frans Verhey is Professor of Old Age Psychiatry and Neuropsychiatry in the University Hospital of Maastricht, The Netherlands. The topics of his current research projects include: clinical aspects of preclinical Alzheimer's; behavioural disturbances in dementia; predictors of vascular dementia; the course of depression after stroke; and the efficacy of a psychogeriatric day hospital.

Michael Wang is Professor of Clinical Psychology in the Postgraduate Medical Institute, University of Hull, and holds honorary consultant appointments with local hospital and community NHS Trusts. He is experienced in the neuropsychological examination of brain impairment, is a registered cognitive-behavioural psychotherapist and has worked as a clinical psychologist for more than 25 years.

Lesley Ann Wareing has worked as an Occupational Therapist in Dorset HealthCare NHS Trust since 1988. She collaborated on research with colleagues in The Netherlands, Sweden and USA. As well as teaching, she obtained an MSc in Rehabilitation Research. This led to interest in studying sensory stimulation as 'occupation' for people in late-stage dementia. She is currently completing a doctorate on the contribution that occupational therapists' philosophy of occupational performance can make to dementia care.

Bob Woods is Professor of Clinical Psychology of Older People at the University of Wales Bangor and co-Director of the Dementia Services Development Centre, Wales. He has been a clinical psychologist working with older people for 30 years and his current research is on psychosocial interventions, awareness and care-giving.

Preface

This fourth volume is a milestone. For 20 years now we (the editors) have been working together between the UK and The Netherlands to contribute to the laying down of a knowledge base for the newly developing field of 'Care-giving in Dementia'.

The paradoxes evident in preparing these volumes have been many: what a long/short 20 years; what relief at the progress/frustration with the difficulties involved in change; what constancy in vision maintenance/ how numerous the hidden differences in perception and assumptions between us. How difficult/ easy it is to define 'ideal care' with one's head/heart.

Trying to establish the cause and treatment/cure for dementing illnesses has proved to be one of the most difficult things ever undertaken by researchers. This search has been ongoing for over a century now; causation and cure still elude a quick, easy answer and treatment approaches have been more modest than hoped for. Diagnosis and research becomes more complex as some dementing illnesses are being found to lie on a continuum rather than be discrete entities (e.g. Alzheimer's disease, Lewy body dementia and Parkinson's disease with dementia).

However, research is increasingly delving into areas that have other practical implications for professional care-givers, namely those of: spared cognitive and sensory abilities (which can be worked with and focused on and used to compensate for declining abilities); the degree of preservation of some types of affected abilities (recall, learning ability and emotional functioning). What do the visuoperceptual changes in specific dementing illnesses mean for how a person perceives what is happening in their 'visual' and 'thought' worlds, and how can useful visual adaptations be made to compensate for these changes. New research is also being directed towards increased understanding of the order of progression of deficits in language ability, time perception and mobility/gait difficulties as a consequence of visuoperceptual difficulties.

Interpersonal and group interventions for persons with dementia and their families/carers continue to be adapted, expanded and refined. (A new 'café' approach to supporting professional care-givers is being piloted as this is being written.) Simultaneously, more interest is being focused on the latter stages of the illness through to death and on communication and sensory stimulation methods through to adapted palliative care.

Such research efforts increasingly require an accurate shared vocabulary and shared 'core concepts' to replace older notions of dementia (which were mostly borrowed from other disciplines and brought along with them the 'not always appropriate' assumptions of those disciplines).

Ten years ago the figure was quoted somewhere that there were over 20 000 research papers a year published in the field of dementia but with little practical information about support or care-giving. A quick tap into the World Wide Web today with the search word 'dementia' would reveal no less than 11 900 000 entries, and many of these are carer support sites.

But this expanding knowledge is as much use to us as knowing about an expanding universe if we do not find what binds this knowledge and try to elucidate the patterns within the seemingly endless expansion of questions and information. For our purposes, this binding has begun with (1) interdisciplinary and international cooperation in trying to study 'phenomena' and 'patterns of illness' and (2) to continue answering difficult questions about their causation, progression and possible slowing or amelioration. However, the binding is not complete without an understanding of how dementia affects a person at all levels of their being and how to 'sustain' care for persons and their family members/carers. All seem to agree that only a multi-disciplinary approach to dementia care makes it 'sustainable'.

Multi-disciplinary research cooperation too, is essential but difficult to practise for obvious reasons; learning the specialized vocabularies of new disciplines is a significant and conspicuous impediment. But there are other, subtler ones, such as learning to understand the 'tools' and 'metaphorical lenses' that are inherent within the knowledge base of a given field, which may not be obvious or logical (or useful) to someone trying to look at something with a new eye. The difficulty can then spread, from taking on a specific question, to questioning the bedrock 'foundation assumptions' of a field that is not one's own. Sometimes new ideas can grate with one's own personal, cultural or professional (even habitual) way of working.

Several chapters in this volume are noteworthy for their attempt to look at old questions in a new, interdisciplinary way. For example, to a lay reader, it may seem incredulous that so little is known about 'perception', 'awareness context' or even 'palliative care' in dementia, and yet . . . this is our current reality.

The official goals of care are to minimize the deleterious effects of an illness, to compensate for deficits and maximize comfort, regardless of the stage of illness or other concomitant changes. The field of 'care-giving' is about trying to be "present to" and "with the other", in whatever ways that is possible, verbally or otherwise. The unofficial goal of care-giving is to remain aware of the significance of one's own presence to another, so that one offers it willingly, whenever possible, not just for the mandatory tasks required by the job description. With the discovery that fear is present for many persons for large amounts of the time, the most important care-giving message to communicate to another to alleviate fear would seem to be 'you are not alone'. Fortunately, that message can be delivered in many ways and throughout the illness.

New attitudes make a new 'care-giving culture' possible. It is difficult to give words to just how things are changing because there are many axes of influence upon 'an attitude', and 'attitude change' is usually a slow, only semi-conscious process. However, one example of such change is particularly relevant. Twenty-five years ago, persons with dementia were assumed to 'be deluded' (a term borrowed directly from psychiatry) if they said 'crazy-sounding things that weren't intelligible'. Nursing students like myself were told not to encourage the person to 'speak nonsense' (collude with delusion) because that would only make 'them worse'. One tutor even frowned upon reminiscing with persons with dementia 'because it will make it more difficult for them to come back to and stay in reality'. Today, we find ourselves having to look afresh at the very assumption about delusion (and other so-called neuropsychiatric symptoms such as hallucinations) in dementia because of the complex interaction between perception, declining memory, attention, logical reasoning ability and language difficulties. (It does not make sense to try to reason with a person who cannot follow the steps and links within your persuasion/ argument; neither does it make sense to tell someone 'the facts' repeatedly when their short-term memory and 'ability to store new facts' are severely damaged.)

How indeed does one know whether someone is deluded and/or hallucinatory if one does not first speak with a person and find out what their perception is like or what their story is (though expressed with difficulty)? When one observes and listens (understanding the visuoperceptual, attentional, reasoning and linguistic difficulties), things that at first glance seem 'a bit crazy' can often seem very human, even downright clever, despite their limitations. Humans remain problem-solving creatures despite sustaining brain damage. It is easier to sustain care for persons when you are interested, unafraid, have a sense of understanding of what is happening to them and are respectful of a person's efforts and attempts to cope, however inadequately.

The societal provision of care for persons with dementia and their families (statutory, voluntary and collaborative) is complex. New attempts to provide support, from the beginning to the end of this illness and beyond into the healing of completed grieving, are very welcome. So too is the increasing acknowledgement that there is a positive side to caring for a person with dementia, as a carer or care-giver.

It is our hope that this volume will give you a flavour of how this field of *Care-giving in Dementia* is growing, whether that be to enhance your own practice, educate others or give you ideas for further new exploration and developments.

In the first volume we pleaded for a multi-disciplinary core curriculum for all involved in dementia care, in addition to their own professional specialty education.

Among other issues that we would like to plead for again, this one would take priority. As this volume will show, there is a great deal to know and be able to speak with each other about in planning ongoing, supportive care to those living with dementia (the person *per se* and their family/carers). It will help all involved in care-giving if a way can be found to educate all concerned to speak the same 'core language' and think with the same 'core concepts' and tools of service. The newly developed SPECTRUM framework sets out to introduce such a multidisciplinary core for care-giving.

In this volume we again acknowledge the difficulties inherent in translation work. For example, what is the best way to refer to '*a person with dementia*'? The terms for this in other languages do not always have English equivalents, or, if translated literally, they sound 'politically incorrect' when they are not in the original language. (This also applies to names of healthcare disciplines and to dementia services in different countries.) Mostly 'person with dementia' will be used, but alternatives (e.g. patient) are also present in discussing the history of care-giving services and legal/ethical issues.

Such difficulties also apply to the word '*care*'. In other languages, it is understood that the focus of this word is implicitly directed to the person in need of care. The currently popular British term '*person-centred care*' is puzzling to some professionals in other countries, who now wonder what the word 'care' means here.

Lastly, the term '*carer*' usually refers to a family, friend or neighbour who is not paid or under contractual obligations to provide care for the person with dementia; they may or may not live with them. The term '*care-giver*' refers to persons within the healthcare professions who are paid to provide care and services to a person with dementia and/or their family.

Gemma M. M. Jones
April 2005

Part I

Models and theories

Visuoperceptual-cognitive deficits in Alzheimer's disease: adapting a dementia unit

Gemma Jones, William van der Eerden-Rebel and Jeremy Harding

Overview

This chapter presents Alzheimer's disease (AD) as a simultaneous visuoperceptual and cognitive illness, with a view to educating care-givers about the types of visual deficits and resultant difficulties that persons can experience. Typical visuo-cognitive errors made by persons with AD throughout the illness process are presented to illustrate the ever-changing nature of the visual world to a person with AD. This chapter also provides possible ways of making care environment adaptations to aid in the perception of key visual information.

Research findings about pathological changes to the visual system in AD and the resulting perceptual deficits are numerous and have many implications for assessment and care. Clinicians have been slow to respond to this information because the link between vision and cognition in AD was not well understood (nor detectable with conventional sight tests measuring primarily acuity and visual fields), even though it was known that the brain areas for control of memory and detailed visual perception (which lie next to each other in the medial temporal lobe) are the first structures damaged in AD. The presence of additional visual pathology and/or age-related visual deficits (which may be present before, simultaneous with, or later on in the AD process, depending on the age of onset) has also contributed to the difficulty in establishing the link between visuoperceptive and cognitive deficits in AD.

The progressive visuoperceptual deficits in AD require specials tests to measure them. Tests to detect visual deficits in AD measure contrast sensitivity, visual attention, object and facial recognition, colour and depth perception, figure/background discrimination and the eye movements needed for scanning moving and stationary items in the environment and for reading, among others. Eventually, visual phenomena in AD include 'looking but not seeing' and Balint's sign. These deficits cannot be corrected simply by prescribing glasses, but require a more practical range of interventions, starting with improved lighting levels, increased figure background contrasts and colour saturation for important visual cues.

The neurofibrillary tangle and beta-amyloid plaque pathology, which characterize AD, slowly damage many structures in the visual system (retina, optic nerve, lateral geniculate nucleus, inferior colliculus, the primary visual cortex and associative visual cortices). Damage extends to both the 'conscious Primary Visual Pathway' and the less understood 'unconscious (automatic seeing) Tectal Pathway'; the latter is providing new explanations for early, but complex visuoperceptual symptoms that include difficulty in shifting visual attention and guiding responses to events.

A pilot study is presented to show the effects of making visual environmental changes to an 11-bed dementia unit; parameters included increasing ambient light levels, increasing the saliency of familiar cues, providing a variety of familiar seating options and arrangements, enhanced figure background contrast of key environmental features and lowering signs and new decorations to within the visual field of residents. An immediate decrease in 'lost-wandering' and 'wanting to go home' behaviour was observed in conjunction with an increase in social interactions with other residents and caregivers, and engagement with familiar household objects and activities was observed. The changes also provided family visitors with more sociable seating and activity options.

Initial examples of visuo-cognitive difficulties in Alzheimer's disease

Below are examples of visual errors made by persons with AD. Note how pervasive and frustrating such events can be during the course of a day, and their potential impact on a person's emotional state.

Mouse in the bin

Mrs T, 85, said to staff in the care home 'There is a mouse in the bin'. They checked and told her that there was none. She pointed to the bin again saying 'There it is'. A care-giver checked again, and seeing none, reassuringly told Mrs T that 'this is a clean place and no one has ever reported seeing mice'. Mrs T remained insistent and continued repeating herself. Finally, someone sat next to her and noticed the image in Figure 1.1A. They realized that Mrs T was reporting literally what she was seeing, unable to say 'the distorted image in the highly reflective cylindrical surface is causing an illusion that makes the doorstop and tile line-curvature look just like a mouse'.

Mrs T would likely have felt understood, though still repeated herself, if staff had replied 'You're right! It looks just like a mouse in the bin. No wonder you were surprised.' In this instance, Mrs T was not afraid of mice, and did not seem distressed, but had she been, she may have started screaming and become agitated. (She may even have been thought to be hallucinating.) Had she been frightened, removing the bin from sight, changing her

(A) The distorted and duplicated reflection of the doorstop in the bin looked like a 'Mouse in the bin' to a lady.

(B) These photos are all taken from the top of staircases. Note the difficulty of seeing where the bottom rung is when carpeting is dark and the lighting poor. Note the size and depth illusion effects caused by the step edging.

(C) Mirrors and reflective or glare-producing surfaces can easily cause visual illusions (mistakes) such as thinking that there is someone else in or approaching the lift, or that it is a corridor or contains a window.

Figure 1.1 Visual challenges for persons with Alzheimer's disease.

seating and getting a non-reflective bin are three immediate options for removing the possibly offending stimulus from her sight.

Mr D always jumps from the third step when coming downstairs

Mr D, 67, could go upstairs effortlessly. His family could not understand why he made such a nuisance of himself when coming downstairs. He literally hurled himself from the third to bottom step, as if jumping from an enormous height, and sometimes fell onto the darkly carpeted landing on his hands and knees (see Figure 1.1B).

When his family realized he was having difficulty seeing and could no longer accurately interpret the shadows on the stairs and the illusions of different lengths and heights of steps, they increased the lighting over the staircase. They also came to help hold his hand more often to guide him when he was going downstairs instead of becoming frustrated by his 'strange' behaviour.

He also became aggressive and resistant when his wife tried to get him to sit accurately on the toilet. He hesitated and resisted her help to sit down (being nudged/pushed backward), as if he thought he would fall. His wife also tried to get him to sit on the toilet to urinate because he was often missing the toilet. She had recently discovered several bowel movements just in front of or beside the base of the toilet (suggesting he had not seated himself). She thought he was becoming incontinent. However, installing extra-length extended handrails on either side of the toilet (painted in a bright colour) helped for a number of months. He still needed help at times to position himself correctly in front of the toilet and to make sure he could feel the rim of the toilet against the back of his legs. However, seeing and holding the handrails himself seemed to make him feel safer and more in control than having his wife push him backwards.

The elevator is always full to Mr W

Mr W, 84, was standing in a sheltered accommodation building, waiting for the elevator so that he could return to his room. The corridor was poorly lit and the carpeting dark. When the elevator arrived and the door opened, he mistook his reflection (visible from the three surfaces of highly polished metal inside) for an elevator full of people (see Figure 1.1C). He politely announced that they could go ahead and he would wait for the next elevator. This happened several times in succession and he could not be persuaded to enter the elevator. He began looking for the stairs, but became increasingly flustered angry and lost. (This difficulty could have been helped by removing or covering-over the mirrors, improving the lighting in the lift and putting a lighter coloured flooring in the lift.)

Mr D could not find his yellow fleece jacket

Mr D, 55, is aware of his diagnosis of early-onset AD and welcomes opportunities to discuss how it affects his life. He told of looking for the yellow fleece jacket that was hanging in the wardrobe. After looking back and forth along the length of the clothes-rail several times he became upset that he could not find it and called his wife. She found it immediately and handed it to him. From that point onwards, Mr D told others that he was 'missing bits of vision' and explained it as: 'I feel like I'm going crazy. I know things are there but I cannot see or find them. It's like someone is following me around with an "invisible gun". They disappear everything I need.'

He was afraid to tell the doctor about this, fearing to be thought 'crazy'. His wife had not found any references to visuoperceptual problems in the AD literature she had.

Changing the lighting brings back a war memory

Mr P, 74, had been diagnosed with AD for 2 years. In recent weeks he had become distressed each evening near dusk. It started after his wife closed the living room curtains and put the hall lights and table-lamps on in the living room as she was preparing to watch TV. Mr P had started hiding behind the chairs and couch in the living room, would not come out with his wife's prompting and had even urinated there, although during the daytime he used the toilet by himself. Eventually, a connection was made between the change in lighting conditions and his recently worsening 'disorientation in time' (he sometimes thought he was back in the war again).

At one point, as an escaping prisoner of war, he had hidden himself in a large-diameter water tunnel for several weeks (hiding and vigilant by day, and leaving briefly to steal food by night). The lighting changes his wife made at dusk produced a comparatively strong glare of light coming through the opened double doors into the [now] dimly lit lounge. This lighting condition must have reminded him again somehow of the (comparatively) strong light at the entrance of the dark tunnel, and passing shadows meaning potential danger. It is also possible that he was not resolving his wife's image correctly against the glare, and hence hid and resisted her efforts to come out from behind the furniture. This could account for his urinating there too.

It seems that his wife had unknowingly re-created similar lighting conditions to a past traumatic event. After realizing that her husband's recent behaviour changes might be linked to misperceiving his environment and re-living a traumatic memory, she tried leaving the overhead lights on in the living room (as opposed to the small table lamps, which produced little light) and kept the hall and toilet well lit. Mr P's seeming 'perceived fear' behaviours ceased.

Background

Vision is defined as the process referred to as 'seeing with our eyes', which gives us a representation of the world around and the possibility of interacting with it through movement. 'Perception' is the process that allows us to provide meaning to the things we see (and otherwise sense, and feel emotionally). Perception enables our building upon and evaluation of memories, and the making of inner models of our surroundings. In this sense our many thinking/cognitive abilities are inseparable from perception.

Already in 1956, Williams, after studying perceptual ability in persons with dementia, noted: 'It is not so much that he [the person with dementia] is unable to receive information through his senses, but that he is unable to select or abstract from all the information available that which is relevant.' Current understanding indicates that this inability to find and select is directly caused by visuoperceptual deficits, which indeed affect ability to abstract.

Persons with AD experience significant numbers of 'visual mistakes' that are linked to their 'thinking errors', which is why we can speak of a combined 'seeing-thinking' illness or 'visuoperceptual-cognitive' illness (visuo-cognitive for short). Such deficits impinge upon many aspects of Activities of Daily Living (ADLs) and behaviour, but this is a different way to understand AD than most carers, care-givers or other healthcare professionals were taught.

What is the nature of such visual mistakes? At what point in the illness process do they occur? What is their influence on behaviour? How can they be better understood with a view to optimizing care interventions for persons with AD?

There are different ways of trying to answer these questions: describing specific visual deficits during ongoing neuropsychological, opthalmological testing and various types of scan and treatment interventions; from complex tests of visual/thinking/reaction time (like simulated driving tests) that simultaneously examine eye/head movement, judgment, reaction time and steering motor responses (Rizzo et al, 2001); determining the extent of visual AD pathology at autopsy; and from observing recurrent patterns of behaviour common to persons with AD in a variety of care settings. Some of the answers to these questions will seem readily explainable; many lie beyond our current abilities. Box 1.1 illustrates the way in which these difficulties are conceived for the purpose of this chapter.

Seeing and perceiving abilities are dependent on the health of the individual and joint components of the visual system (pupil, muscles, lens, each retinal layer, the optic nerve, etc.; the visual areas of the occipital, temporal and parietal cortices; and access routes to visual and other memory storage sites connecting these areas). Perception is also dependent on one's overall health, attentional ability, the significance of a given visual experience,

---

Box 1.1 Compounding types of visual difficulties change the perceived world in Alzheimer's disease

What we see and perceive is what we take to be real outside ourselves; this affects our beliefs and expectations about the world around us, and our reactions to it.

Normal age-related visual changes (with related difficulties)
+
Possible visual pathology or illness affecting vision
+
Possible visual effects of medication
+
Visual pathology specific to AD (or other types of dementia)
+
Decreased cognitive ability to name/understand/interpret/remember what is being perceived
↓
Predictable types of ADL difficulties and behavioural responses to a poorly seen environment

---

alertness, mood, state of consciousness and, very importantly, on the motivation and expectations of 'what should be seen'. Perceiving therefore is not just 'seeing-in-good-focus', recognizing and attributing meaning, but it also involves the complexities of synchronizing every aspect of our cognitive and response abilities.

Reference points with regard to other literature on vision deficits in Alzheimer's disease

There are variations in the order of development of symptoms and severity that have been reported for various sub-types of AD. The most common type is late-onset AD (LOAD; diagnosed after age 65). Early-onset AD is far less common (EOAD; diagnosed before age 65). Some have reported a rare 'posterior occipital visual form of AD' (Bouras et al, 1989; Mendez et al, 1990, 2002; Croisile, 2004). Also, increasingly, AD, Lewy body dementia (LBD) and Parkinson's disease dementia (PDD) have been found to show overlap in neuropathology, neurochemistry, clinical findings and pharmacological responses (Serby and Almiron, 2005). (Discussions about visual difficulties may also apply to persons with ADD and LBD; see Chapter 2 about errors in identifying visual phenomena in this group.)

The examples presented in this chapter are intended to help the reader be familiar with the range of possible visual-cognitive difficulties typically seen in LOAD. This chapter treats EOAD visual deficits as similar to LOAD, but progressing more quickly than those in LOAD, and without the age-related visual deficits accompanying LOAD. This concurs with work of Galton et al (2000), showing that there may be a posterior-occipital visual neuropathology shift in EOAD, earlier than is normally seen in LOAD.

For those doing further reading in this subject, Cronin-Golomb and Hof (2004) have edited an extensive book about visual changes in AD and its sub-types: it is useful to know that sometimes there are several names for a given phenomenon, e.g. posterior cortical atrophy is also known as Benson's syndrome, a visual variant of AD and progressive agnosias and apraxia (Hof et al, 1997); the term Balint's syndrome (also called psychic paralysis and optic ataxia) is sometimes also used to refer to the fixed gaze occurring in behavioural stage 3 AD, where persons can hold only one item in view (Rizzo and Vecera, 2002).

Assumptions about the link between vision, perception, language and thinking

Normally, despite whatever changes and distortions that happen to vision with aging, persons appear to be able to continue to function fairly accurately in a visual world. Doubtless, experience and expectation from memory of 'how things ought to look' assist us. Our expectations seem to provide some stability to the perceived environment, which means that compensation and learning to adjust to the visual changes are taking place. Most persons without cognitive difficulties could learn or 'accurately problem solve' their way through the examples already given.

For persons with AD, it seems as though such problem solving, compensation and remembering are limited and often fairly 'literal' to the most salient cue they are seeing/perceiving, though their efforts are unmistakable. Unless we can discover our visual mistakes, what we perceive is what we think is really happening or present around us (regardless of objective reality to others or their attempts to persuade us tactfully, logically or otherwise), therefore such mistakes have cognitive and behavioural consequences.

Figure 1.2 shows photos of everyday situations that can be difficult for older persons, and especially persons with AD, to interpret visually. Unless we understand how commonplace such 'obstacles' are, we cannot design environments that will try to compensate for them; neither can we assist in solving more complex mistakes such as that of Mr P's situation in the first examples given.

Common difficulties include situations with: reflections and glare (from mirrors, glass and TVs); shadows and dark surfaces or floors; patterned

Patterned carpeting appears to move and have objects on it.

Shadows on carpeting cause depth perception illusions.

Is there a step down here or not? (Not!) Note that one's own shadow on this area would make it even darker.

With peripheral vision and hearing reduced, little social contact is possible with this seating arrangment.

Background glare; faces and persons left in shadow.

Paintings are lost in pattern and mirror reflections.

Dark floors and patterns obscure two care-givers present.

Which room? Doors all white, signs above visual field.

Figure 1.2 Common visual difficulties in care facilities.

surfaces, which make it difficult to distinguish figure from background (including seeing pictures and signs on walls, or seeing persons when there is strong light behind them), estimating depth of field (where the floor is, and how far to lower one's foot to make contact) and reduced contrast sensitivity between objects (finding cauliflower and cheese on a white plate). The work of Van Rhijn et al (2004) has shown how AD pathology corresponds to difficulties with ADL tasks that include visual perception tasks. Laatu et al (2003) have looked at how 'increasing language difficulties' relate to visual phenomena, and Watson et al (1999) have been looking for the neural basis of such impairments.

The position of this chapter is that visual mistakes start to occur early in AD, and continue throughout the duration of the illness. Box 1.2 provides a listing of visuo-cognitive mistakes that have been made by persons in progressive stages of the illness (behavioural stages: Jones, 1997, 2004a,b).

Box 1.2 Examples of visuo-cognitive difficulties in Alzheimer's disease		
Behavioural stage	Observed behaviour	Additional explanation
1	Gentleman bought more watches in the past year, & was now wearing an **armful of watches**.	Noticing that he was having difficulty remembering appointments & following time, this was his solution to make sure he noticed the time.
1	Lady carrying **two handbags** having lost the first one several times over.	This was her way of making sure she would always have her 'survival kit' with her.
1	Gentleman had **two torches** in his pockets to illumine what he was looking at.	He told his family that he knew that he wasn't 'seeing things properly' and this would help him.
1	Man who emptied his filing cabinet of **files, laying them out in rows on the living room floor**, with yellow notes on the files about when to pay	He realized that he was having difficulty with checking his files & paying his bills. He couldn't bear the thought of not being conscientious, as he had

invoices. Yet, he neglected to open his daily mail, which was accumulating in boxes in the kitchen.

always been, and found this solution (which was visually helpful, but not logical in that it lost him the use of a whole room in a small apartment).

1

Lady, who covered with newspaper, the long horizontal **mirror in the lounge**. It was startling her & giving her the sense of people around when there weren't.

Walking past the mirror often 'made her jump' & think that others were in the house. She still had the insight to understand it was caused by the mirror, & solved the problem herself.

Low 1

A gentleman got down on his knees & **tried to pick up small pieces of black carpet-repair tape** from the floor thinking they were 'After Eight' mints.

It took him a long while to notice they weren't mints. The ability to test reality & interpret the results accurately was done 'literally' instead of testing with his foot (& was slowed down significantly).

Low 1

Many persons look down towards the floor increasingly to see where to plant their feet, **taking 'high steps' over carpet-joining rails**, changes in colour & shadows on the floor.

This also happens in trying to avoid dark colours on carpeting or in mosaic floor tiling, stepping in lifts, crossing thresholds.

Low 1

A gentleman thought there were **strangers using his toilet**. He yelled at them to leave, but when he went in to check, there was still someone in there. He did not turn on the lights for himself, being familiar with his own apartment.

A mirror was hung above the toilet, on the wall directly opposite the door. The dark reflection of himself, looked 'as if' someone was in the toilet. He explained that they were rude, since when he asked if they were finished they did not reply.

Box 1.2 Continued

Behavioural stage	Observed behaviour	Additional explanation
Low 1	Persons with AD often had **difficulty in visually locating & pointing to a target stimulus** on a computer touch-sensitive screen for neuropsychological testing of visual attention.	Some took up to tens of seconds to locate an object before the test commenced. In later stages of the illness, there were 'gap times' when they lost the sense of the task briefly. Later still, some tapped the screen seemingly randomly & repetitively (Jones, 1990; Jones and Burns, 1992)
Low 1	A lady's husband was angry because he thought she was being lazy; she had not finished **preparing the salad** for the BBQ while he had done all the other work. Only lettuce & onion had been cut up. The tomato was in another room, the celery was still in the fridge.	On realizing that she was getting 'visually lost' in her environment & memory, he tried again. He laid out everything she needed to cut up, already washed, on a tray & got the cutting board & knife ready for her beside it. She was able to complete this, but slowly. (Laying her clothes out in order so she could dress herself didn't work: her problems arose when she put things behind her back – blouse/bra/sweater – & lost sight/position of them.)
Transitional 1–2	A lady **did not eat the yogurt in the half of the pot that was covered in shadow**. After putting it aside, on a flat surface, the shadow	She missed the cues of feeling the remaining yogurt with the spoon, or testing to see if the shadow moved if she moved the

disappeared; when she reached for it again, the shadow was present again. She was perturbed & pushed it far away from her.

pot. She responded only to the presence of the shadow. It seemed as if she thought someone was nearby, playing tricks on her. After looking around her, not seeing anyone, she sat, arms folded, looking downward.

T1→2   Lady who said **her bedroom was not her room**, that it looked like it, but was different somehow. She thought she'd been drugged overnight, that her family had found an identical room, painted it & moved all her things.

She said the room didn't feel 'as it should', even though everything was there. It was the bedroom she had used most of her life, in a house she had lived in all her life. What she said indicates that something 'didn't look & feel right' to her, consistent with having perceptual difficulties.

T1→2   A lady insisted that her husband was not her husband but **some sort of a double** or a phony stooge imposter.

He looked the same usually, but like a chameleon changed himself when others didn't notice & then changed back again. (These words seem to indicate fluctuations in perception & recognition.)

T1→2   A community nurse observed that a lady had put a square slice of **ham onto the handle of her tea-pot**, instead of her usual square pot holder.

It looked like the pinkish pot-holder she normally used. She did this using some visual cues of similarity, missing other sensory information about the texture and wetness.

T1→2   A lady was turned slightly, speaking to a resident

Staff asked her why she was eating someone else's food. She denied it, saying

Box 1.2 Continued

Behavioural stage	Observed behaviour	Additional explanation
	seated next to her at lunchtime. She ate **the food from her neighbour's plate** whilst ignoring her own (decreased peripheral visual field).	that someone must have switched plates. (The adjacent lady, who also had memory difficulties, didn't notice.)
T1→2	A wife was indignant that she awoke to a **smoke-filled kitchen**, although her husband was oblivious, trying to surprise her by making breakfast.	He had not cooked in over 2 years prior to this. He remembered that she liked prunes, had found them in the cupboard, put the oven on, laid them on the grill, but still in their plastic bag. He got no thanks!
T1→2	A gentleman pulled the **red Emergency Bar** on the underground suddenly, causing the crowded train to stop.	He was standing up & the sign was in front of him. He told his wife that it said 'PULL' . . . he had not read 'in case of emergencies only'.
2	Numerous instances of watching persons hold **conversations with images in televisions and mirrors** as if they were real (some became distressed, others not).	One lady was convinced she was speaking with her twin sister in the mirror, and was obviously contented.
2	A lady **would not cross a shadow on the corridor floor** whilst trying to get to the toilet late one evening. She urinated on the floor despite staff prompts to call her towards the toilet.	Staff were unaware that the shadow probably looked like a steep drop-off that was unsafe to cross. They missed the chance to walk backwards, in front of her, obscuring her view of the shadow.
2	Two ladies did not use the opened white	They did not appear to recognize what the

commodes next to their beds. One **used the large planter in the corridor to urinate** into. The other used the bin in her room.

commode was, & went in search of a toilet. Not being able to find one (since the doors were all painted white), they used the next most available similar/discreet thing.

2   A husband noticed muddy dog prints on the kitchen floor. He got towels & **wiped the floor**, but continued to wipe mud from the walkway **& driveway**.

His wife was furious since he had used & ruined the new 'guest towels' in the bathroom instead of using the proper cleaning cloths from the utility cupboard. He said he could not find them; she doubted this.

2   A gentleman did not use the (white) toilet in a white bathroom but **urinated in the bin**, on the radiator grill & in the sink each night.

The bin was more visible in the dark, against pastel walls, than the toilet was; the radiator grill & sinks looked like urinals, and had better visibility than the toilet.

2   Lady who **pulled the (red) emergency help pull-cord in the toilet every night**, instead of the (white against white wall) flush & light pull-cords.

The red cord was the only one visible against the light coloured walls at night. She did not remember making this mistake; and endured staff chastisements each time as a result.

2   A gentleman **turning in circles in front of his bed (& chairs)**, was unable to sit down on it to get into it the normal way; dived in head first (holding it & climbing over it).

He explained that the bed would 'not disappear' this way. (Persons trying to get into chairs; held them with both arm-supports, climbing on & over top still holding on & lowered themselves down.)

Box 1.2 Continued

Behavioural stage	Observed behaviour	Additional explanation
2	A lady started **straddling the toilet, like a horse**, face forwards.	This behaviour change happened after a number of 'accidents' where she couldn't sit on the toilet seat properly and was very embarrassed & upset.
2	Staff on two dementia units complained that **persons with AD were not using the new toilets**, but were urinating in the floor-grill at the entrance of the toilet, or in the bins.	There was a full-length mirror on the right wall of the entrance to one set of toilets, and, in the other, a full length mirror in the wall next to the toilet, in which one's own reflection (or appearing to be someone else) could be seen whilst on the toilet.
2	A gentleman in a wheelchair would not let staff **push him face-forwards into the elevator**. He dug his heels into the ground, kicked, held doors open with his hands & became angry.	It was eventually discovered that he had poor peripheral visual fields; he did not see the elevator doors start to close initially; when he finally saw them, he startled, assumed they would squeeze him, & tried to keep them prized open.
2	A lady sat in her chair, apparently **blowing in the air** most of a morning.	She said she was trying to blow the floor dry before getting up, in case she fell, but that it was staying wet a long time. The polished floor did look wet.
2	**A lady did not recognize her husband** anymore when he visited; she was polite but quiet. Staff tried in vain to persuade her they were married.	In the end, she stared at him but said humorously, 'If we're married, somebody should have told me . . . my husband doesn't have white hair!'.

2	A lady was often pacing the corridors & **getting lost in the dead-ends** of them; sometimes found crying & distraught.	When asked why she didn't return to the lounge, she said 'There's no lounge where it's dark and lost' (which is likely how the 'world' seemed to her).
Trans. 2→ 3	A lady **tried to grab & eat the patterned objects on the tablecloth,** ignoring the plate of food before her.	**Figure/background contrast problem**: the pasta & cheese sauce on a white plate was not as visually salient as the colours on the tablecloth.
3	A lady **could not find/see her handbag, even though it was in front of her** & pointed to by staff.	She appeared to be looking right through it; her distress continued until it was handed to her directly to feel and look at.
3	A man **picked lint from his pullover,** & kept picking until he had made a large hole in it, seemingly unaware.	He also repetitively picked biscuit crumbs off the table & continued when there were none left. He noticed only one visual aspect of this task.
3	Ladies **lifting up & rolling their dress,** & using them variously as polishing cloths, tablecloths & folding the edges of them like towels & nappies.	No other textiles were available. When engaged in conversation, they said they were busy 'tidying & helping'. It seems that they used simple cues & stored visual images to help substitute for & enhance what they could not see clearly.
3	Lady being helped by a 'feeding assistant' sitting beside her at the table, startles, & becomes **combative at attempts to place the spoon near her mouth**.	Her behaviour stopped when the feeding assistant was located directly opposite, or adjacent to her, at a corner of the table. From here she could see the spoon being filled & moving towards her.

Box 1.2 Continued

Behavioural stage	Observed behaviour	Additional explanation
3	A husband entered a room to visit his wife & **started speaking to her before getting eye-contact** with her.	She appeared to panic; her eyes were wide open. She tried to find him in her visual field with glances in all directions, but was unable to locate him.
3	A lady could not read or write anymore, but shouted 'STOP' on being pushed past a **stop-sign** in a wheelchair.	It was a large, new sign, within her field of view. The red attracted her attention; she reacted to the signal by feeling that it was wrong not to 'stop'.
3	A lady, seated for breakfast, was found by staff, smiling, with **two pairs of glasses on**; they had just cleaned four others.	She no longer wore glasses & her eyesight was not testable. She couldn't have seen through them clearly, but seemed to enjoy the feel of them.
3	A lady was trying to **eat brightly coloured plastic Xmas ornaments**.	They did look like sweets, and though they were the wrong texture & taste, she persisted.
3→4	A bedridden lady **looked round in all directions** trying to find the visitor who was singing to her.	The lady smiled & tried to speak (jumbled) only while the visitor remained very close by, directly in front of her. At 1 m distance visual contact was lost.
3→4	A lady (who normally did not make eye contact & only repeated expletive/swear words), reached out to touch & speak to someone near wearing **bright lipstick**.	This lady was seen/heard to suddenly say something that sounded like: 'That's the one, the simey the red the best' and to grab the person's hand to kiss it.

A summary of the behavioural staging model of AD, linked to overall visual difficulties and the presumed underlying neuropathological stage, is given in Figure 1.3.

Backtracking: understanding visual aging, pathology and changes in Alzheimer's disease

Now that additional examples of visuo-cognitive errors over the course of AD have been provided, how can we start to understand how and why vision is changing in conjunction with cognitive abilities? The following sections build upon one another in an attempt to understand how visual difficulties, ranging from blurring, loss of colour, missing the edges of images, through to missing parts of the visual field, arise in the perceptual world of a person with AD.

Baseline summary of normal age-related visual loss and change

Normal aged-related changes need to be understood as a baseline against which to gauge the presence of other visual difficulties. Key findings about normal age-related visual changes are summarized in Table 1.1, along with some of the practical consequences of these changes and their causes. Such 'wear and tear' changes are distinct from, but often co-exist with, visual pathology.

Many visual aging changes happen slowly, almost imperceptibly; persons may not be aware of how much their vision has changed or of what adaptations they have been making to 'normalize' what they see. They may also be blaming their change in vision on other things. (One lady was sure that electricity companies were trying to increase their profits and not sending as much power through the wires thinking the public would not notice; but she knew her light bulbs were not as bright as they should be!)

Common visual pathologies in old age

The most common visual pathologies in old age are cataracts, glaucoma, macular degeneration and retinal complications from diabetes. In the UK, for those over age 65 and registered blind or partially sighted, 53% result from macular degeneration, 12% from glaucoma and 8% from cataract (Weddell, 2003). These conditions can result in all gradations of change from blurring, partial loss of visual field, through to genuine visual hallucinations and complete blindness. It is estimated that about 60% of persons will experience some degree of cataract as they age.

Campbell (2005) goes on to make the link between vision deficits and falls, reporting that: 'Visual impairment affects about 10% of people aged 65–75

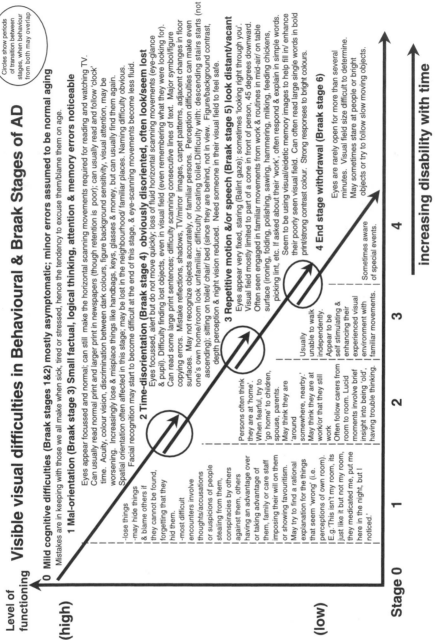

Figure 1.3 Eye movement in behavioural and Braak stages of Alzheimer's disease. (Behavioural stages adapted & expanded from Jones, 1997, 2004a, b; Braak & Braak, 1998; Braak et al, 1998.)

Table 1.1 Normal age-related visual changes: some variables interact with each other

Feature	Change	Behavioural/other adaptation	Reason
Colour vision	Bright colours seen best, blue to purple vision reduced, dark colours difficult to distinguish between, light pastel shades not saturated enough to be obvious	Difficulty matching colours, frequent preference for brighter colours, heavier application of make-up, bright hues on TVs, easy to confuse coloured pills	Fixed lens discolours to yellow/brown with age; the effect can be thought of like wearing sunglasses indoors. This filters out the blue/purple making it look grey-dull. Red, orange, yellow seen best (Haegerstrom-Portnoy et al, 1999)
Reduced acuity (ability to resolve details)	Nearby images become blurred, especially fine detail & reading material. Difficulty seeing position of dials on appliances, small print. Viewing things/ reading without corrective lenses causes eye strain	Moving reading material further away from eyes, the area of optimal focus; later, using reading glasses, then bi-focals, seven vari-focals, increased size (or print size) of objects & the figure/back- ground contrast	The cornea (first lens) thickens making light scatter inside the eye & reducing the fixed lens' focusing power (Oberlink, 1997). Fixed lens becomes less flexible throughout life making first near, then distance focusing increasingly difficult (Spector, 1982)
Blurring from floaters (clumps of cellular debris)	Irritation from unclear vision	Wondering if one is 'seeing things' or has a serious eye problem	Vitreous humour gel thins with age. Floaters do not settle and stay at bottom of the eye as well (Balazas and Denlinger, 1982)
Momentary intrusions from posterior vitreous detachment	Intrusions may be like light flashes or distortions of images	Wondering if one is 'seeing things' or has a serious eye problem	The thinning 'vitreous' begins to pull slowly away from the retina (Balazas and Denlinger, 1982)

Continued overleaf

Table 1.1 Continued

Feature	Change	Behavioural/other adaptation	Reason
Ambient light levels required to see	Increased light required	In care homes, the seats most occupied are the ones near the best lighting conditions & near exits	Only 30% of the light reaches the retina at age 60 compared to age 20 due to pupil diameter reduction & lens transparency changes (Ordy et al, 1982)
Increased effect of glare from strong light sources, reflective surfaces & back-lighting	E.g. extra light reflecting in bathroom mirror, morning sun shining face on, in large window, difficult to be in strong outdoor light	Avoid sitting in areas that are visually uncomfortable. Increased use of sunglasses and sunhats to enjoy being outside in bright light	The pigmented surface layer behind the retina becomes irregular, less able to absorb excess light & control light scatter in the eye. Retinal thinning at peripheral edges changes cellular orientation & angle of light hitting the photo-receptors (Marmor, 1982; Sekuler and Owsley, 1982; Oberlink, 1997)
Night vision or response time adaptation to large light level changes	Difficulty moving from darkness into light, or vice versa. Darkness looks darker. Strong light from a point source can temporarily blind	Driving at night is limited. Increased difficulty finding things in the dark, or in dark spaces such as handbags & drawers. Difficulty moving from dark to light rooms or vice versa	Pupil size decreases with age; less light reaches retina. Lens changes increase light scatter, reducing contrast (light/dark) of an image
Peripheral vision	Reduced by up to 35° on each side by age 80–85	Startle reflex when approached quickly from behind or the side. Difficulty seeing/ talking to persons seated next to you. When driving,	Foveal vision decreased. Sensitivity of visual field decreased twice as rapidly at 30° eccentric than at centre field (Jaffe et al, 1986)

		not seeing cars motorbikes approaching. Difficulty locating traffic signs & lights. Not seeing elevator doors start to close, startling when they suddenly appear to be closing. Not noticing contents on upper or lower shelves	
Contrast sensitivity (ability to detect boundaries between objects)	Decreased ability to detect boundaries, edges of objects, text and backgrounds	Choose a larger sized text, more resolvable figure–background combinations (e.g. black text on white paper, or a strong hue against a pale, contrasting one)	Combination of above factors (Pastalan, 1982)
Decreased eye (saccadic) movement for tracking still & moving objects	Slowing, affects a variety of tasks including reading	Use of larger, clearer print and increased light levels	Decreased visual reaction time (short-term memory changes in normal aging also affect ability to organize incoming visual stimuli (Leigh, 1982; Lott et al, 2001)
Depth perception	Decreased	More care in placing feet, reaching for object accurately	A combination of the above reasons
Decreased critical flicker fusion (CFF) effect	Rapidly flashing light looks like a constant sooner than for younger persons. Strobe/disco flashing light effects may be less. General visual slowing of visual responses	Affects the quality of what is seen in diverse ways	CFF indicates reactivity of visual photo-receptors. It is slowed in normal elderly, and significantly more in persons with AD (Jones, 1990; Jones and Burns, 1992)

and 20% of those aged 75 and older. It is estimated that about a third of people aged 65 and over will fall at least once a year. That figure rises to approximately half of those aged 85 and over. Older people with sight problems are not only more likely to fall, but are at a greater risk of multiple falls, compared to their fully sighted peers.'

Physical pathology and medication that can affect vision in old age

Sometimes the medication that a person is taking can cause or contribute to visual difficulties (a summary of medication that can affect vision is given in Appendix 2.1 of Chapter 2). A few specific examples of difficulties that some medications can cause to vision are listed in Box 1.3.

Box 1.3 Medications known to affect vision (from Patel, 1994; Gherghel, 2003)

Cardiac drugs

Digoxin, digitoxin, ouabain (visual effects: chloropsia, xanthopsia, red/green colour defects)

Diuretics may additionally cause 'dry eye' in elderly patients whose tear production is already naturally reduced

Minoxidil users need surveillance for optic nerve toxicity

Beta-blocker ocular effects include reduced tear secretion, diplopia, oedema of eyelids, non-specific conjunctivitis & loss of accommodation

Anti-arrhythmics

Quinidine may cause clouding, flickering of vision through to complete blindness

Disopyramide (Rythmodan) may cause acute angle closure glaucoma, blurred vision, papillary paralysis, photophobia

Mexiletine (Mexitil) may cause visual hallucinations

Flecainide & encainide may cause corneal deposits

Amiodarone (CordaroneX) may cause corneal epithelial deposits, blurred vision, haloes around lights & coloured vision

Eye medications

Timlol (for glaucoma): 10% of patients experience fatigue, depression, dissociative behaviour, memory loss, paranoia, confusion, hallucinations & psychosis (Gherghel, 2003)

Anticholinergic eyedrops (atropine, homatropine, scopolamine, cyclopentolate): reported side effects include visual & auditory hallucinations, irritability restlessness, insomnia, confusion, memory loss, delirium & paranoia (Gherghel, 2003)

Medications that can cause blurring, spots and halos
Anticholinergics
Antihistamines
Clomiphene
Chloroquine
Cycloplegic
Digitalis derivatives (temporary)
Ethambutol
Guanethidine
Indomethacin
Methanol toxicity (permanent)
Phenothiazines
Phenylbutazone
Quinine sulfate
Reserpine
Thiazide diuretics

Understanding visuoperceptual damage in Alzheimer's disease

The 'Primary Visual Pathway' and the spread of plaque and tangle damage in Alzheimer's disease

The major hallmarks of Alzheimer-type damage consist of neurofibrillary tangles (NFT, caused by tau protein 'folding problems' within cells) and beta-amyloid (or neuritic) plaques (BAP, caused by an abnormal accumulation of this matter around cells). This AD damage starts in the middle of the temporal lobe of the brain around the areas linked to memory and vision and usually spreads in a particular direction (Braak and Braak, 1998; Braak et al, 1998; Yilmazer-Hanke and Hanke, 1999).

This 'direction of spread' of NFTs and BAPs gives an indication of the order in which the visual areas of the brain are most commonly disrupted. Yet this 'localization of damage' knowledge is not as helpful as might be supposed because current understanding of the visual system is very incomplete and many areas within the visual system are interlinked.

Dorsal (object recognition) and ventral (spatial localization) paths

Most of us were taught about a 'main visual pathway' (also called the primary visual or retino-calcarine pathway), starting at the retina and ending in the primary visual cortex (occipital lobe) area at the back of the head (Figure 1.4) but that explanation was too simple. Information reaching the primary

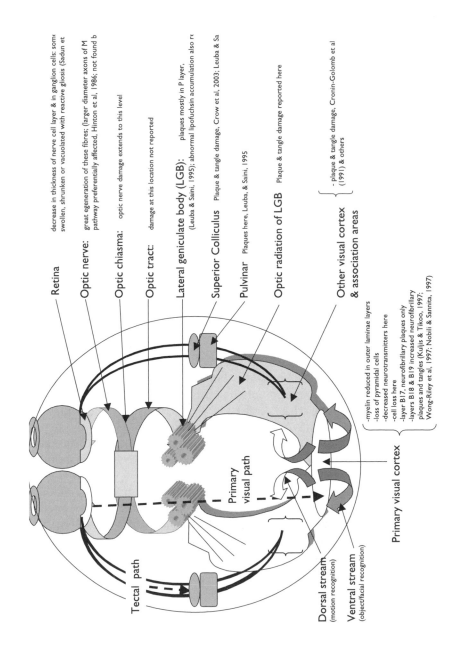

Retina   decrease in thickness of nerve cell layer & in ganglion cells: som(
swollen, shrunken or vacuolated with reactive gliosis (Sadun et

Optic nerve: great degeneration of these fibres; (larger diameter axons of M
pathway preferentially affected, Hinton et al, 1986; not found b

Optic chiasma: optic nerve damage extends to this level

Optic tract: damage at this location not reported

Lateral geniculate body (LGB):   plaques mostly in P layer,
(Leuba & Saini, 1995); abnormal lipofuchsin accumulation also r(

Superior Colliculus   Plaque & tangle damage, Crow et al, 2003; Leuba & Sa

Pulvinar   Plaques here, Leuba, & Saini, 1995

Optic radiation of LGB   Plaque & tangle damage reported here

Other visual cortex
& association areas   - plaque & tangle damage, Cronin-Golomb et al
(1991) & others

Tectal path

Primary
visual path

Dorsal stream
(motion recognition)

Ventral stream
(object/facial recognition)

Primary visual cortex

-myelin reduced in outer laminae layers
-loss of pyramidal cells
-decreased neurotransmitters here
-cell loss here
-layer B17, neurofibrillary plaques only
-layers B18 & B19 increased neurofibrillary
plaques and tangles (Kuljis & Tikoo, 1997;
Wong-Riley et al, 1997; Nobili & Sannita, 1997)

Figure 1.4 Visual pathology in Alzheimer's disease (adapted from Armstrong, 1991; Armstrong and Syed, 1992).

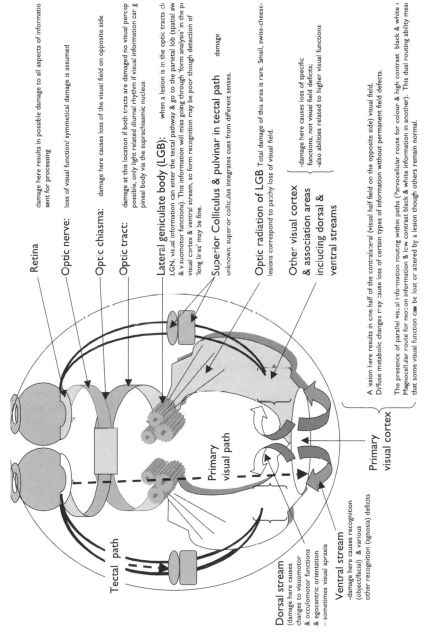

Figure 1.5 Ophthalmic implications of visual pathology (adapted from Hyvärinen, 2005a,b).

visual cortex undergoes additional elaborate processing in what are called dorsal and ventral paths or streams (Ungerleider and Mishkin, 1982) (Figure 1.4). The ventral (lower) stream is associated with 'object recognition' and is also called the 'What' path. It involves our ability for colour discrimination and contrast sensitivity. The dorsal (upper) stream is associated with the 'spatial localization' of things and is also called the 'Where' path. It allows us to detect the movement of objects.

The naming of these two paths is only a simplification to 'get a handle' on very complex exchange and analysis of signals between linked brain areas providing additional details that enrich our perception. 'We need recognition of the environment to orient in it although during the movement we do not analyze in detail the structure of the body part moving or the environment. The two main types of vision combine their functions and support them with information from visual memory' (Hyvarinen, 2005a).

Both paths damaged in Alzheimer's disease, but the ventral path first

Both ventral and dorsal stream areas have shown NFT and BAP damage (Haxby et al, 1991, 1994; Leuba and Saini, 1995). Researchers have been using various visual tests (and sometimes scans simultaneously) to try to establish if one of these pathways is damaged more than the other in AD. Some have found that 'object recognition' is more impaired than 'spatial localization' in AD (Arnold et al, 1991; Fujimori et al, 2000). In addition, others have found that contrast sensitivity is especially affected in persons with AD, and that it affects object and facial recognition (Mendola et al, 1995; Cronin-Golomb and Gilmore, 2003). The findings of the ventral stream being affected first are consistent with the spread of AD damage described by Braak et al (1998). Such findings comprise the rationale for trying to develop new visual tests/tasks to detect AD earlier (Lindeboom et al, 2002).

What does damage to particular areas do?

It is difficult to know how the effect of progressive damage to increasing numbers of visual regions makes the world look to someone with AD. The examples already listed provided clues, but it is still difficult to imagine it directly. Current research often examines abilities in a piecemeal fashion, which does not help to convey the overall effects of visual deficits. Figure 1.5 tries to address this question circumspectly by describing what the effects of lesions along both pathways do, from the opthalmological point of view in persons with non-AD damage to these sites.

Facial recognition problems linked to reduced contrast sensitivity functioning in ventral path

Faces are objects, but it seems that the brain has a special sub-area for processing them that is distinct from other objects. This facial processing sub-area for faces has been named the Fusiform Face Area. It is located within the temporal lobe although its exact location is still being debated (fusiform gyrus or ventral temporal and middle inferotemporal areas: Haxby et al, 1994; Clark et al, 1996; Van Rhijn et al, 2004).

Persons with AD can lose the ability to recognize their own face in the mirror (Breen et al, 2004), as well as having difficulty recognizing familiar faces. This difficulty usually becomes evident in behavioural stage 2 (obvious time disorientation). An important aspect of professional care-giving is to explain to family carers that this part of the brain can become damaged, and that persons with AD can still have a sense of being connected to someone even though they may lose the ability to recognize them (and because of the language function changes, lose the ability to identify them by name accurately).

The mysterious and little known Tectal Pathway

There is also another, less known, visual pathway called the Tectal Pathway (or retinotectal, retino-collicular or extrageniculate) (Figures 1.4 and 1.5). It is a more primitive evolutionary visual pathway and has been largely disregarded because it was thought to be a vestigial visual system. Its workings in humans are not very well understood, but renewed interest for such things as 'blindsight' (where persons with visual field deficits perform at an 'above-chance level' on visual discrimination tasks, despite being unaware of the visual stimuli), 'partial sight' and agnosia phenomena are showing it to be responsible for some of our most advanced types of visual abilities. Studies are showing that the Tectal Pathway may be the key to understanding our automatic (without awareness) visually guided behaviour (Ro et al, 2004).

Two key structures in this Tectal Pathway – the Superior Colliculus (SC, involved in sensory encoding and generating saccadic eye movements) and the Pulvinar (P, thought to play a role in our orienting to peripheral stimuli reflex; Lewis and Maurer, 1986 – are shown in Figure 1.4.

Ro (in press) has demonstrated that much of the information we are confronted with is processed without awareness either early on in the visual cortex or in the Tectal Pathway. Ro et al (2004) have shown that the SC mediates the unconscious processing of visual distractors (which influence the generation of saccadic eye movements), and implicates the Tectal Pathway in many blindsight phenomena. Others are also studying this pathway, as the meeting place for our attentional and visual abilities. In fish, amphibians and reptiles, the SC is the most important visual processing centre; it is also critically involved in the fast eye movements that primates incessantly engage in. The SC signals the difference between where the eyes are pointed now, and where they will go to next. This information is directly processed and goes to the P nuclei of the thalamus and to brainstem oculomotor areas controlling eye muscles. Seeing is not done through the eyes, but with the brain in fact (Koch, 2004).

Leuba and Saini (1995) and Crow et al (2003) found extensive AD pathology throughout the regions of both primary and tectal pathways. In conjunction with what is known about the spread of AD damage from the the Braak neuropathological staging model (1998), it seems that the Tectal system may be sustaining damage even before the primary visual pathway. This may be the reason why, to outside observers, the earliest detectable symptoms of dementia are vague ones starting with decreased visual attention, slowed responses to sudden confrontations or problem-solving situations and, eventually, difficulties with object recognition (but not usually anything as obvious as visual acuity: Cormack et al, 2000).

Some of the early visual errors and difficulties that persons with AD experience could also be described as a loss of 'automatic visual behaviour' (recall previous examples in Box 1.2). An increasing loss of automaticity fits in with the deficits that are prominent as the illness progresses, including 'looking but not seeing' (Traub and Baucer, 1986; Rizzo and Hurtig, 1987) and Balint's sign (staring or gazing right through a person at one fixed point, unable to shift gaze normally).

The order of loss and progression of visual deficits and symptoms in Alzheimer's disease

Most agree that the higher order visual abilities (see Box 1.4) are affected early in AD. There is no agreement yet on order of damage to primary and intermediate level visual abilities, in part because most studies do not compare early versus late-onset AD, let alone separate the various age decades contained within the late-onset group, to help determine the role of visual age deficits. Most researchers do not simplify and titrate tests to continue to study persons into behavioural stages 2 and 3, because of language and comprehension difficulties (except Jones et al, 1992). Yet, such observations are needed to build a better picture.

It seems obvious that age-related visual deficits will very adversely affect the progression of AD in someone starting to show signs of this illness in very old age, there being a tremendous overlap in deficits (such as colour vision) reported in both normal visual aging and AD (Mendola et al, 1995; compare also Table 1.1, Figure 1.4 and Box 1.3).

What has not been linked to AD yet is the contribution of the even higher, automatic visual and attentional functioning systems facilitated by the Tectal

Box 1.4 Summary descriptions of visual system changes in Alzheimer's disease

Disturbances of visual functioning can include:

Agraphia: loss of the ability to write (includes difficulties in copying pictures or figures)

Agnosia: severe deficit in recognizing objects, faces, sometimes persons (Sacks, 1985)

Simultanagnosia: looking but not seeing; stationary objects reported as disappearing (Rizzo and Hurtig, 1987)

Anomia: loss of the ability to name what is being seen

Apperceptive agnosia: unable to see a coherent picture of the structure of an object

Associative agnosia: can see an object but cannot recognize it

Gerstmann's syndrome: left/right disorientation, finger agnosia, agraphia/acalculia

Balint's syndrome: inability to shift gaze to object of interest; difficulty locating objects in space, groping for objects as if blind (though vision is spared), unable to pay attention to two points in space simultaneously

Alexia: loss of the ability to read (words & music) with/without agraphia

Proposagnosia: inability to recognize faces (different types of & aspects to this disability)

Achromatopsia or other colour perception impairment

Ocular dysmetria: a lack of symmetry of eye movements (saccades) in voluntarily looking at something. The eyes appear to slowly move back and forth about the visual target-point with increasingly smaller movements as the eyes fixate on the object

Apraxia: the inability to make voluntary movements

Hemianopsia: a visual field deficit (many sizes and areas possible)

Saccades: rapid eye movements allowing a voluntarily shift of the line of sight between objects of interest (all directions)

A – Deficits in lower order primary ocular function (Armstrong, 1991; Armstrong and Syed, 1996)
- initial reception & encoding of visual stimuli seem intact in early AD
- visual acuity: research controversial; seems normal in early stages for some persons; decreased acuity has been linked to extra difficulty in contrast sensitivity
- increased contrast sensitivity thresholds (Cronin-Golomb and Gilmore, 2003)
- colour vision deficits in up to 50% of persons; mostly blue/violet range; Cronin-Golomb, 2001

- visual field abnormalities: decreased sensitivity throughout visual field but most pronounced in inferior field; progressive visual field loss throughout illness (Armstrong and Syed, 1996) stereoacuity deficits (Cronin-Golomb et al, 1991)
- depth perception – particularly in those who have decreased acuity (Mendez et al, 1996)
- motion perception affected (only 4.72°/second of motion detection, Wong Riley et al, 1997; Tetewsky and Duffy, 1999; Rizzo et al, 2001)
- reduced Critical Flicker Fusion thresholds (Jones, 1990; Jones and Burns, 1992) (not found by others)

B – Intermediate level functions (see Wong-Riley et al, 1997; Kurylo et al, 2003)
- decreased perceptual organization
- decreased ability to group objects visually
- decreased ability to discriminate textures
- decreased figure/background separation (also distinguishing objects on patterned surfaces)
- decreased identification of fragmented pictures
- ability to integrate visual elements into global images
- improper use of discrete visual elements; identifying/describing & segregating individual objects
- inability to process multiple elements to interpret an image

C – Eye movement problems
- saccadic latency, velocity, accuracy and initiation
- decreased ability to fixate upon a target (Hutton et al, 1984)

D – Complex visual functions (Armstrong, 1991; Armstrong and Syed, 1996)
- visuospatial: 40–50% of persons exhibit troubles
- reading: eye movements needed to follow lines (aside from comprehension problems)
- object recognition: 50% of persons have problems with object and facial recognition

Resulting effect on behaviour
- increased difficulty in identifying what & who is in the environment & whether it remains stable/present
- increased difficulty in being able to check one's surrounding environment/locate others, to be/feel safe
- decreased ability to focus & hold gaze on more than one object at a time leads to decreased participation with environment

Pathway, which likely accounts for some of the most difficult to describe visual dysfunctions that occur earliest.

Future research on AD will need to take into account the changing relationships between aging vision, visual deficits specific to AD and the decline to cognition and language ability; these changes have undoubted consequences for mobility/motion in the AD population, which are as yet unexplored. These factors are shown overlapping increasingly with time in Figure 1.6.

Evidence that aiding specific visual functions can help persons with Alzheimer's disease

Lighting, life and falls

'If you do not advise on lighting properly, work on enhancement of acuity is essentially a waste of time. Improved lighting is the single best low-vision aid of all.' (Rumney, 1992).

'It has been estimated that more than half of British homes have insufficient light even for ordinary visual purposes.' (Whitfield Grundy, 1992). Extrapolating from these comments to the lighting conditions in environments for the elderly is a much needed endeavour.

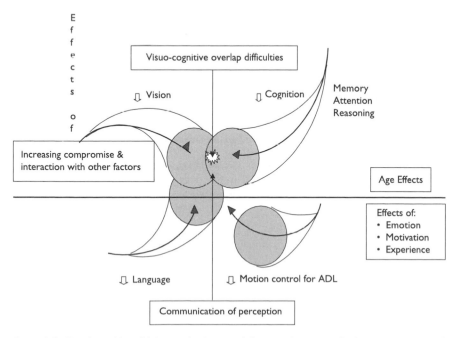

Figure 1.6 Overlap of key Alzheimer's disease deficits with time: multi-factor causation of disability.

Increasingly, researchers have started pointing out the need for better lighting conditions for the general population (Klernan, 1994), the elderly, persons with visual conditions such as Charles Bonnet syndrome with dementia (Eperjesi and Akbarali, 2003) and persons with AD (Cormack et al, 2000). Vision is important in maintaining postural stability in the elderly (Milner and Goodale, 1995), and decreased acuity and contrast sensitivity have been shown to predict falls in the elderly (Lord and Ward, 1994). (Other studies have found that the risk of hip fractures [which are all too familiar in persons with dementia] was significantly related to all measures of visual function, but that for low-vision patients spatial contrast sensitivity has more influence on orientation-mobility than visual acuity.) Increased lighting has been shown to reduce hallucinations in some circumstances (Pankow, 1996).

Colour cues

Cernin et al (2003) found that using specific vivid colour cues in the environment can help short-term memory recall in persons with AD, e.g. colour-coding bedroom doors. Some have found that enhancing contrast sensitivity (by using special yellow lenses) helped a person with AD who had trouble with 'apperceptive agnosia' (the inability to make a coherent picture of an object being looked at) (Sakai et al, 2002). Increasing light intensity, and providing 'high contrast dishes and eating utensils' were among the recommendations made in the above studies to maximize visual contrast ability. The strongest effect shown by such interventions so far has been by Dunne et al (2004), who found that using high-contrast red dishes to replace the white ones led to a 25% increase in food and an 84% increase in liquid consumption in persons with AD.

Past misunderstandings of visual phenomena

Some Care Home designers (not understanding the visual deficits of AD, nor making the link between 'being lost' in one's environment and being fearful) incorporate 'Wandering Circuits' in effect to let the 'wanderers' (as they are often called) pace aimlessly, so as not to be a disturbance to other residents. With our current understanding, it seems preferable to create care environments that look and feel like home, i.e. a place of safety, which would encourage a different set of behaviours in persons experiencing disorientation resultant from visual-cognitive changes.

Some persons have unwittingly used visual difficulties in AD to try to control 'problematic behaviour'. The use of full-length mirrors placed at entrances to care facilities to startle persons away from the doorway is such an example (Mayer and Darby, 1991). Dark carpets and carpets with a spiral pattern on them (visual obstacles creating the illusion of a drop-off) have also been used in some homes to deter disoriented residents from approaching the exit. (This goes against the line of help that we are recommending, in that it can further adversely affect the emotional state of an 'already emotionally fragile' person.)

The study presented hereafter is an attempt to intervene by making very deliberate changes to an environment containing many visuoperceptual hindrances to feeling 'at home'.

Study of effects of environmental changes on a dementia unit to enhance key visual cues

Background

This study is reporting on the first phase of changes made to an 11-bed dementia unit. A housing charity wanted to adapt a dementia unit, located within a 1960s-built, 45-bed residential home for the elderly. The adaptations chosen were intended to help overcome some of the behavioural effects of visuo-cognitive difficulties of persons with dementia on the unit.

The dementia unit was on the first floor of a residential home, which had originally been built for use by older persons who were becoming fragile but not having dementia or serious physical difficulties. As with most residential facilities in the UK, there are increasing numbers of persons with dementia who either develop the illness whilst in residence or who, because of a short-age of specialist dementia facilities, are still placed in residential homes. Over the past 5 years, persons with dementia in this residence were gradually moved to rooms closer to one another; several years ago this part of the residence became known as the dementia unit.

There were no possibilities for structural changes to the existing building, so decorative and environmental layout changes were made to reflect the 'vision of dementia care' that the housing charity wished to promote in their homes. This vision included providing an adapted environment (and staff education about these changes) to compensate for the known visuopercep-tual deficits in dementia, with a view to creating strong visual cues that would orient a person to the feeling of a cozy, home-like living room/dining/kitchen area.

The existing building layout posed a number of difficulties for a dementia unit. The unit comprised a dining room and kitchenette at one end of a long corridor and a lounge/kitchen area at the other end. Bedrooms, bathrooms, utility rooms and storage areas were spread along the length of a corridor. The first of these difficulties was that, three times a day, persons were being moved to a formal dining room and then back to the lounge area, traversing a long mirror-lined corridor each time. This seemed to make it difficult for residents to settle after they were moved. The dining room and lounge areas gave the impression of something like a hotel foyer and formal dining room (some residents even becoming distressed thinking they had to leave tips and unable to find their handbags) rather than a 'home-like' one.

This lack of a 'visual anchor of home' was identified as a key item for change, as well as trying to increase other important visual handles to help interpret and navigate the environment.

The purpose of this study was to see if changes in key environmental variables could change some of the distressed behaviour of persons with dementia on the unit, to help contribute to making residents feel more 'at home', a place where familiar activities were happening and could be participated in, instead of a place to get lost in or try to leave to 'go home'. It was also hoped that after the changes the staff would be able to spend more time conversing and doing activities with residents in the lounge–kitchen area. Hence, the focus was on creating more visible cues of a 'familiar, engaging, home-like' environment.

Method

Initial visits were made, and meetings held with the management, care managers, buildings manager and manager of the residential home being renovated. During these visits information was collected about: the design and layout of the building; the range of 'behavioural stages of dementia' that staff were accommodating in a limited area; the typical behaviours of each of the residents; the most difficult aspects that staff reported about their work in a particular unit; and the scope for making changes to the layout, décor and daily work routine of the unit (see Box 1.5).

Key staff (manager and team leaders) working on the unit attended the 5-day course 'Communication and Care-giving in Dementia: A Positive Vision', as did the directors of the housing charity, the buildings manager and some of the trustees. (Course content included the information contained in this chapter, as well as practical tips to aid assessment of what a resident could see; the importance of determining a person's visual field and locating information, object and oneself/others in it.) The need for a 'shared vision for both care and change' was seen as the key starting point, so that all concerned would be aware of the rationale for proposed changes, the specific strategies being used to effect such changes and then be able to explain such changes to others concerned (especially family members of the residents, nightshift staff and staff working elsewhere in the residence). A leaflet about the changes to the dementia unit was prepared for staff members and others to help provide everyone with the information about the special adaptations being made to assist the visuoperceptual needs of residents on the dementia unit (see Appendix 1.1).

With the financial resources available, key areas for change were identified and discussed with management. A phased plan for change was drawn up, and is shown in Box 1.6.

Box 1.5 Group summary information and key behavioural observations during initial visits to the dementia unit

Description of population in the dementia unit
Mean age: 84.4 (population SD = 6.24)
Sex ratios: 9 females; 2 males

Diagnoses of dementia received by the residential home at time of residents' admissions
Seven persons had 'presumed AD'; three had a history of strokes and hence presumed vascular dementia; one had Parkinson's disease with dementia or Lewy body dementia and a history of hallucinations

No. persons in each behavioural stage of dementia

Stage 1	0 persons
Transition (T1→2)	2 persons intermittently oriented to place & to time (often critical of residents in stage 2)
Stage 2	9 persons totally lost in time; thinking they are young, with small children &/or at work still
Stage 3	0 persons

Additional health information relevant to providing specialist dementia care

- Two residents were registered blind; one of these was partially sighted & profoundly deaf; one totally blind
- One resident severely permanently stooped forward (very difficult to bring any information into her visual field)
- Four residents were 'prone to falling'; wheelchair use was advised for one, but resident forgot this & kept getting up
- One resident had been multiply diagnosed with Alzheimer's, Parkinson's disease (PD), Lewy body dementia & had reacted adversely to PD medications, anti-psychotics & anti-depressives
- One resident, prone to falling, was found to have been on chlorpromazine for 4 years since admission. (Requested to stop it & reassess her. Two weeks later her overall mood, social skills & mobility were noticeably improved.)
- One resident had a history of hyperthyroidism & was frequently restless & pacing; disturbing to other residents
- One resident had a 'suspected hip or suprapubic fracture' though initial x-rays showed none. She winced with pain on trying to stand and unable to take any steps forward, then collapsing backward or

looking for a handhold. A hip fracture was confirmed several weeks later

Staff reports of residents' behaviours

- Six residents spent much time daily wandering up and down the corridor, several trying to 'find the way out to go home', others got lost in the bedrooms of other residents or started removing/ rearranging objects
- Some residents were urinating in 'inappropriate' places, despite the newly renovated toilets (complete with many new mirrors) near to the lounge

Initial impressions & observations on the first visit to the unit

- Two residents were wandering up and down the corridors trying to get out to 'go home'
- One resident was distressed at having lost a shoe & was looking everywhere to find it
- Three residents who had difficulties walking, required a lot of help from staff to get between the dining room & lounge areas for meals (with only two members of staff present, it meant that remaining residents were alone in the rooms at times, some calling out for help)
- The lighting in the lounge was poor; ceiling & wall-mounted bulb fixtures provided 'patches of light' in only a few areas of the room; residents were noticeably seated in the best-lit parts of the room, avoiding the dark areas
- There was no table in the lounge area (for activities or having refreshments) where residents were for much of the day, though there were some low coffee-type tables & hospital meal tables for individual residents. The tables in the dining room were kept covered with tablecloths for the next meal and not used for activities
- Seating arrangements in the lounge area were not conducive to eye contact needed for social contact between residents, too far apart for them to hear each other easily; social contact between residents was not evident
- There was no visual focus to the lounge, or obvious visual cues suggesting a warm, home-like environment
- There was limited open/visible shelving in the lounge with 'familiar/ meaningful objects' (memorabilia or objects or activities to engage with at will)

Box 1.6 Goals and phased plans to maximize visuoperceptual functioning on dementia unit

Goals	Phased plan
Improve overall ambient lighting in lounge & corridors to reduce shadows & increase overall visibility	Replacing pendant lights to create more even light throughout lounge, & replacing dark carpeting with a lighter floor surface (easy to clean, non-slip, non-reflective wood-effect vinyl floor) so that more light reflects up from the floor, also making it easier for residents to observe foot placement
Remove mirrors & reflective surfaces from locations where there is frequent direct visual confrontation with & potential misinterpretation of them	To minimize visual illusions, startle reactions & residents avoiding the use of the toilet area because of the large mirrors at the entrance to them
Minimize patterned surfaces (walls) with light non-glare surfaces so that important cues can be hung on walls to facilitate a sense of familiarity & orientation	Includes lowering important sign-posting on bedroom & other doors, & painting toilet door a bright yellow, so that they are more readily visible
To provide readily visible, open shelving for key items	Fill shelving with memorabilia & collections of objects appropriate to abilities of persons in stage 2
Renovate the lounge/kitchenette into a combined 'home-like' dining/kitchen/lounge area	Use the old dining room for a quiet lounge & for family visits, or as a separate area if the dementia unit is expanded
Enable staff to work in an environment that maximizes quality contact time with residents, & in which to provide normal ADLs for residents throughout the day	Follow familiar household routines, e.g. setting/clearing/washing the table, bringing dishes to the sink, eating together, so that activities are seen as part of the total care plan, not just the remit of the Activity Worker

Box 1.6 Continued

Goals	Phased plan
Phase 1	
Eliminate the need to **mobilize residents via the long corridor thrice daily from the lounge to the dining room**. This activity seems to disorient residents & takes a lot of staff time. Addition of a 'living room' will hopefully reduce feelings of the 'need to go home'	Renovate the lounge/kitchenette area to create an open plan space into a 'home-like kitchen/living room area'. (The old dining room to be used as a separate visiting lounge or modified when dementia unit increases in numbers)
Replace poor **pendant-type lighting** in lounge; shadows and dark areas in corners of room	Utilize up-lighting on walls, & high luminance non-glare ceiling fixtures
Replace **patterns** on visible surfaces, especially **wallpaper**	Simplify and lighten upper wall areas so that key objects will be more visible
Large **mirrors** located (at eye level) above fireplace in lounge, along corridors & full-length ones at toilet entrance & in bathrooms	Remove mirrors from where they can cause the illusion of persons nearby, watching or following someone
Many **paintings** are vague (poor contrast) & hung above older resident's visual field (as are some **information signs** on doors)	Choose high-resolution, high-contrast artwork (with pleasant emotional themes) & hang them lower than normal, within resident's visual field. Look for interactive, touchable textile work to hang in corridor
Stereo player on opposite side of room from where the CDs and tapes are stored	Sort music, move it to near the new table and stereo
Re-locate the **fireplace**, make it a focal point of the room, visible from the corridor to attract persons walking	Make it a conspicuous 'nice feeling place' where persons & staff can sit & talk & highly visible to residents 'lost' in the long corridor to help

there; enhance visibility of fireplace surround & inside & put familiar/symbolic memorabilia items on top (clock, candlesticks, trophy)

deter wandering. Install a 'mock fire', which looks lit, but disconnect the heating elements. Place a large bouquet of bright yellow silk sunflowers on the floor next to the fireplace to help make the eyes gravitate there.

Add a large **farmhouse-style kitchen table** to lounge area for persons to eat together & do activities at

Also purchase comfortable kitchen-table-type chairs with back support & armrests

Increase the **choice of seating/activity options**

Rearrange seats; a semi-circular cluster in front of the fireplace, a small cluster near the window, a seat near the bird cage, two chairs facing each other with a small coffee table near the window

Make **toilet doors very visible**, so residents can find them without assistance

Paint doors bright yellow colour, with contrasting surrounds & add clear, pictorial signs & eye-level label

Add **memorabilia & extra objects of interest, and objects that can be used for individual activities**

A large bird-cage with two young budgies, non-toxic low-maintenance plants were added along with knick-knacks, hand-crank sewing machine, old typewriter, collections of postcards, embroidery crocheting, calendar photos, easy to see/play games, picture books, costume jewellery, brassware & polishing cloths, etc.

Phase 1 was completed in six weeks, and the responses to the changes reported here are for this stage of completion of the changes made.

The emphasis was on increasing light level, colour contrast of important objects potentially useful for 'reminders of home' and self-orientation purposes. The specific changes made are listed in Box 1.6.

The efficacy of these changes was evaluated by the presence of the care manager, buildings manager and author being present on the first day, after all the building and decorative changes had been made, the day that the kitchen table, budgies, paintings and memorabilia items were located on the unit.

Results

Figure 1.7 shows before and after drawings of the unit and Figures 1.8 and 1.9 show photos of the unit before and after the changes.

The first meal that residents had collectively around the large kitchen table in the newly renovated living room/kitchen area was noteworthy. Several residents were already seated at the table, and it did not take long to encourage the others to sit there for breakfast. One person who needed extra assistance was helped at a small table near the large kitchen table. The meal was relaxed and there was much social interaction. Three hours later, five residents were still sitting at the table, talking with each other (self-initiated) and with staff, having snacks, doing various activities (including arranging biscuits, folding pieces of fabric and playing dominos to self-made rules) and visiting with their family members. During the entire day, not one person wandered the corridors or spoke of wanting to 'go home'.

One gentleman was obviously pleased at the sight of the football trophy on the fireplace, was sure it was one of his own and poured forth with a stream of reminiscences that were new to staff.

At lunchtime, a special 'finger-food' meal, which residents could help themselves to (instead of being pre-served on plates) was served. Staff were surprised that the resident with Parkinson's disease, for the first time ever, was seen to reach out and grab food with difficulty but unassisted, smiling and seemingly pleased to be doing so. This same resident was immediately excited after the installation of the birds and moved to be near them and interacted with them for over an hour. Another resident came to whistle and sing to them thereafter.

Three of four family visits were observed during the day and were obviously positive. One visit seemed to be mixed positive and negative, in that the resident who was in transition from stage 1 to 2 seemed to be agitated by the busy atmosphere of making the changes (extra activity involved in locating memorabilia, placing the birdcage and arranging the shelving), and was more irritated at and critical of other residents and staff than usual. Her family visitor did not find this totally negative though, in that there was much more conversation because there was so much to talk about, including the annoyances with others.

The other three sets of family visitors were pleased that there were new topics of conversation and activities to do with persons. Perhaps the most striking one was where a family group, including a child, came in and sat by the large table to be with their family member to have refreshments together. Usually they left at mealtimes, but on this occasion they remained. It was easy to keep the child occupied. One blind resident who rarely spoke was heard to say to the family visitor, 'There's lots happening here. They're fixing things. It's all a tizz!'

Aerial view of the lounge room before changes

Aerial view of the lounge room after changes

Old lounge (entrance) viewed from corner of room

New lounge (entrance) viewed from corner of room

View of the new lounge/dining room from the entrance to the room. The 'high contrast' fireplace is visible from a great distance down the corridor, as are the large, bright silk sunflowers beside it.

Figure 1.7 Room layout before and after changes.

View of lounge from doorway, no focus, poor light.

Hotel-style dining room at far end of hall.

Meals sometimes eaten in lounge; no table.

Corner of room; one lone chair, pictures too high.

Fireplace, between doorway and kitchen entrance.

Isolated seating, placed alone by fireplace and corner.

Connecting hall to dining room with mirrors.

Mirror at toilet and bathroom entrances and on wall.

Figure 1.8 Dementia unit before changes.

View of room from doorway; increased lighting and visual cues, choice of seating arrangements and familiar objects to select from and engage with, and familiar activities to do. The stereo and music storage has been localized in the far left corner, nearest the table.

The (high-contrast) fireplace is an immediate focal and gravitational point and conversation place that care-givers use well. The heating coils have been disconnected leaving the flickering light effect intact.

The large wooden kitchen table gives a family feel to meals. Note the high-contrast paintings and memorabilia shelves within view.

Objects (dolls, handbags, textiles, etc.) are chosen from the open shelving and brought to the seat of choice.

The large wooden table is a focus for familiar household activities such as mixing up pancake batter.

The birdcage in the corner is another location where persons can choose to sit whilst having a good view of the gardens.

The kitchen table serves for many other simultaneous activities including flower arranging, brass polishing, and bowl sorting tasks.

The fireplace is also a favourite location for an afternoon nap.

Figure 1.9 Dementia unit after changes.

A group of three of the most fragile residents were seated for long portions of the day around the fireplace. They spoke with each other intermittently in somewhat parallel conversations, but undoubtedly in a socially positive way. Each had chosen, and kept with them, an object from the range of items provided on the open shelving: one a doll, another a brass plate and polishing cloth, and another a hat.

The resident's interaction with the hat proved to be the conversation highlight of the day for staff; ironically, it was the best illustrator of the reasons for trying to make accommodations for the poor visuo-cognitive abilities of persons with dementia.

A member of staff had donated a crème-coloured, feather-laden hat to be one of the memorabilia items on the open shelving. It had been selected by the resident, who at first seemed pleased to look at it and have it on her lap. After about 20 min she started stroking the feathers 'the wrong way' to make them stand up rather than lie flat. Staff speculated that perhaps she could feel them better this way, but moments later she started ripping them out and tossing them to the floor. In no time she had de-nuded the hat, like plucking a chicken, just as she had done so often on the farm in her youth. To her, with her poor perception, the hat looked like and 'became' what she was so familiar with. There will always be things that improved lighting and visual aids cannot compensate for.

The key reactions from staff members were that it was easier to be with residents (instead of having to guide each person separately from the dining room to the lounge). They were struck by the observation that not one resident had paced up and down the corridor that day, gone into another resident's bedroom by mistake or tried to leave to 'go home'. The Activity Worker, too, found it easier to engage small groups of persons around the table than in the previous room layout.

Meetings with the manager and staff of the unit two weeks later confirmed that caring for persons in the new environment was easier, and that seating at the table and around the fireplace was well used. The manager and staff both reported that the lady who had been agitated on the first day of the final changes had settled down in the following days as the new routine became established.

Residents seemed to make better use of the toilets with the mirrors removed from the toilet and bathroom areas. Staff were not directly able to evaluate the results of removing mirrors from the hallways and in the old lounge area, but said that residents seemed more 'settled and normal' despite having their dementia and doing unusual things.

Discussion

Staff were pleasantly surprised at the difference in residents' behaviours. They were pleased to have more time to be and speak with residents in lieu of the time they used to spend moving them about between the old lounge and dining room, and looking for them and trying to get them away from the exit door, or out of another resident's room. Staff also commented on how family visits were noticeably longer and easier in the home-like environment (with plenty to look at, do and discuss together), and that staff conversations with family members during visits were 'easier'.

Family members also responded positively; they enjoyed being able to use the different seating arrangements, do things and enjoy refreshments at a table together and even have the option to stay and 'pull up a chair' at meal-times. They were encouraged to choose and use items from the open shelving to do an activity with their family member during their visit.

Special mention needs to be made about the importance of teaching all involved in the changes with such a project. At the mention of using bright colours 'selectively' and providing a special range of objects for persons to chose to interact with at will, two staff were initially resistant. Not fully understanding the visual deficits in AD or rationale for the interventions, they thought it would be age-inappropriate, offending and patronizing to 'turn the unit into a nursery or Disneyland'. It took additional teaching to explain examples of the visual mistakes typical in AD, and also that: all persons, including the elderly and persons with AD, see bright colours the best; the use of colour in environments for the elderly and persons with dementia is not random, but is used deliberately and selectively for items of key importance; and the use of colour and stimulation in babies' rooms and children's nurseries is more ubiquitous, for general stimulation and encouragement of eye fixation points. In the dementia unit, 'dignity' and 'feeling safe' issues were the prime considerations. This included making adaptations so that residents could independently find and use toilet facilities as long as possible; also, making handrails visible, to aid mobility as long as possible, because persons with dementia often cannot remember that they may have mobility aids such as Zimmer frames and walking sticks and often mobilize without them. Adaptations also included creating conditions in which members of staff and objects of interest were visible and accessible. Most important were the attempts to use visual cues to suggest a safe, home-like environment. These concerns on the part of staff are important and need to be addressed seriously or they can lead to hard feelings, misunderstandings and even passive resistance of the implementation of such a plan.

Cleaning and ancillary staff also need to be carefully informed of the reason for the changes. For them, the new seating arrangements made their work more difficult. (It is much easier to clean a room where the chairs are always lined up around the periphery of the room.)

The findings of this initial phase of a pilot scheme are encouraging and point to the need for more formal research in the area of visual adaptations to units for the elderly, but especially persons with dementia.

Implications

To keep visuoperceptual difficulties linked to simultaneous cognitive difficulties in AD, perhaps the notion of 'loss of metaphorical speech in AD' could be extended to include 'loss of metaphorical seeing and thinking'. A key thought for care-giving is that the most important meaning of 'home' is a metaphor for safety, acceptance, familiarity and comfort (aside from any of the factual locations of one's home). The hope is that when people who are 'time-disoriented' say that they '[feel as if] they are at home', and speak as if they are at home (children and perhaps their parents present to them), it is the presence of deliberately placed familiar visual cues and activities that are helping to remind them of this feeling of safety.

Conversely, for a person who is time-disoriented and 'wants to go home', ideal care-giving would include looking for the presence of others, visual aids, activities, cues and reminiscences to make a person 'feel at home' (rather than try futilely to continue to orient them literally as to 'where they are' and that they 'cannot go home').

Summary

The occurrence of visuoperceptual difficulties in AD is undisputed. Because vision is linked to cognition through our ability to attend to, attribute meaning to and remember things, it is more accurate to speak of AD as a visual-perceptual-cognitive disorder than simply a memory or cognitive disorder. Yet, the linkage of these difficulties is largely unknown in the professional care-giving field, or by many diagnosticians and family members of persons with AD, because the link between visual-perceptual impairment and AD was not well understood, and because classic (simple function) vision tests of acuity and visual field cannot detect the earliest known deficits. It is more difficult to explain to persons that tests of contrast sensitivity, visual attention and facial recognition are required (Rosen, 2004), as are specialist and practical visual interventions for minimizing these deficits.

Although the cause and interactions of some types of visual damage reported in AD are not known yet, evidence of the types and range of errors and their consequences on the ability to perform ADLs are abundant. Understanding such visual-cognitive errors can help shed new light on some of the behaviours of persons with AD (some of which could otherwise be thought to be 'strange/crazy/psychotic'); it can help carers and care-givers to realize how 'clever/desperate/normal' many of the attempts of persons with AD are in trying to cope with an ever-changing perceived world.

This chapter has summarized research about visual difficulties in normal aging and AD as well as providing many behavioural examples that occur routinely to persons during the course of an AD illness. These examples have been linked to both the behavioural staging model of AD as well as to the pathological staging of AD. Examples for teaching this material have also been presented. The first phase of changes made to a dementia unit shows that adjusting visual variables can make a significant impact on the daily life of persons with dementia in residential facilities, their family visitors to the unit and the professional care-givers. These are ample reasons to encourage further work in this area.

What will be more difficult to research and prove (in creating safe, perceptible home-like environments for persons with dementia) is that ultimately the concept 'home' is not, in the most important meaning of the word, literally a place but rather a feeling. Where does one feel 'at home', accepted and included regardless of one's limitations, foibles and past history or state of perceptual-cognitive illness?

Acknowledgements

Thanks to the Dorset Trust, UK, for their permission to report on the changes made to the dementia unit described in this chapter, and for the enthusiasm of their entire management, care staff, residents and families of the residents for this project. A special acknowledgement goes to Trevor Jones for his efforts in working quickly and tirelessly to realize and help record this project. The skills of Damian Hartley who produced the 'before and after' line drawings of the lounge are gratefully acknowledged. Thanks also go to Isaac Jones for help in preparing the other figures and to Susan Meese for her proof-reading.

Appendix 1.1

Information for those associated with the modified dementia unit

Recent changes to the dementia unit

Some of you will have noticed that the upstairs lounge, corridors and dining areas have undergone some major changes in the past few weeks.

What has changed?

Most noticeably, the lighting has been made brighter; a very large kitchen table has been added (new chairs have been ordered), the fireplace has been re-located and a 'light-only-effect' fire has been added. Also, seating arrangements have changed to give persons a choice of activities and social seating. Additional 'open' shelving has been added to the unit. It has been filled with memorabilia and baskets of collections of objects. New paintings have been hung in the lounge and corridors (high contrast, fun to look at). The paintings and signs have been hung lower than usual, so that they are noticeable to the residents. Perhaps you have been wondering at the reason for these changes.

The Trust has been working strategically over the past few years to work towards a new vision of providing specialist care for persons with dementia. There are a number of different types of dementing illness, but the majority of persons will have Alzheimer's type dementia and vascular (or multi-infarct) dementia.

New knowledge of visuo-spatial difficulties in dementia

It is now understood that having dementia means far more than having difficulties only with short-term-memory ability. Attention, logical thinking ability, language, spatial awareness, sequencing, time-perception and calculation can also be affected. Also, time-orienting and visual abilities are often very significantly impaired.

Anyone who has worked on or visited a dementia care unit will recall visions of persons wishing to 'go home', 'asking after their long-since deceased parents', 'pacing up corridors fretfully' and other characteristic behaviours of persons who are time-disoriented. They may have seen that persons can have difficulty recognizing and correctly naming objects and family members as a result of such deficits.

Designed specialist care units to accommodate these difficulties

The current understanding of dementia allows us to take such things into account when designing and re-decorating special care units.

The key idea is to make living spaces feel 'home-like' (hence the fireplace and kitchen table), and to make the visual cues salient, in keeping with the knowledge about the ways in which vision is deteriorating.
Changes include:

- improved lighting;
- simplifying the wall and floor surfaces so that only the most important bits of information are visible;
- use of colour and maximum contrast to provide important visual cues;
- use of the normal daily routine at home, to help persons keep track of familiar activities of daily living, and to engage them in familiar tasks wherever possible;
- providing familiar objects within the room to interact with at will, so that persons do not have to search for them.

If you have any questions, please contact the Head of Care at the Trust headquarters.

References

Armstrong, R.A. (1991) Looking at Alzheimer's disease (parts 1 and 2). *Optometry Today*, **3 June**: 10–11; **July**: 14–15.

Armstrong, R.A. and Syed, A.B. (1996) Alzheimer's disease and the eye. *Opthalmic Physiology*, **16**: S2–S8.

Arnold, S.E., Hyman, B., Flory, J., Damasio, A. and van Hoesen, G. (1991) The topographical and neuroanatomical distribution of neurofibrillary tangles and neuritic plaques in the cerebral cortex of patients with Alzheimer's disease. *Cerebral Cortex*, **1**: 103–116.

Balazas, E. and Denlinger, J. (1982) Aging changes in the vitreous. In R. Sekulen, D. Kline and K. Dismukes (Eds), *Aging and Human Visual Function*. New York: Alan R. Liss, pp. 45–57.

Bouras, P., Constantinidis, J. and Morrison, J. (1989) Balint's syndrome in Alzheimer's disease: specific disruption of the occipito-parietal visual pathway. *Brain Research*, **493**: 368–375.

Braak, H. and Braak, E. (1998) Evolution of neuronal changes in the course of Alzheimer's disease. *Journal of Neural Transmission* Supplement, **53**.

Braak, H., de Vos, R.A., Jansen, E.N., Bratzke, H. and Braak, E. (1998) Neuropathological hallmarks of Alzheimer's and Parkinson's diseases. *Progress in Brain Research*, **117**: 801–819.

Breen, N., Caine, D. and Coltheart, M. (2004) Mirrored-self misidentification: two cases of focal onset dementia. *Dementia Review Journal*, **2**: 16–17.

Campbell, S. (2005) *Report: Deteriorating Vision, Falls and Older People: the Links*. Glasgow: Visibility.

Cernin, P.A., Keller, B. and Stoner, J. (2003) Color vision in Alzheimer's patients: can we improve object recognition with color cues? *Aging, Neuropsychology and Cognition*, **10**: 255–267.

Clark, V., Keil, K., Maisog, J.M., Courtney, S.M., Underleider, L. and Haxby, J. (1996) Functional magnetic resonance imaging of human visual cortex during face matching: a comparison with positron emission tomography. *Neuroimage*, **4**: 1–15.

Cormack, F., Tovee, M. and Ballard, C. (2000) Contrast sensitivity and visual acuity in patients with Alzheimer's disease. *International Journal of Geriatric Psychiatry*, **15**: 614–620.

Croisile, B. (2004) Benson's syndrome or posterior cortical atrophy. *Orphanet Encyclopedia*. http://www.orpha.net/data/patho/GB/uk-Benson.pdf.

Cronin-Golomb, A. (2001) Color vision, object recognition and spatial localization in aging and Alzheimer's disease. In P.R. Hof and C.V. Mobbs (Eds), *Functional Neurobiology of Aging*. San Diego: Academic Press, pp. 517–529.

Cronin-Golomb, A. and Gilmore, G.C. (2003) Visual factors in cognitive dysfunction and enhancement in Alzheimer's disease. In S. Soraci Jr. and K. Murata-Soraci (Eds), *Visual Information Processing*. Westport: Praeger, pp. 3–34.

Cronin-Golomb, A. and Hof, P.R. (2004) *Vision in Alzheimer's Disease. Interdisciplinary Topics in Gerontology*. Basel: Karger.

Cronin-Golomb, A., Corkin, S., Rizzo, J., Cohen, J., Growdon, J. and Banks, K.S. (1991) Visual dysfunction in Alzheimer's disease: relation to normal aging. *Annals of Neurology*, **29**: 41–52.

Crow, R.W., Levin, L., LaBree, L., Rubin, R. and Feldon, S. (2003) Sweep visual evoked potential evaluation of contrast sensitivity in Alzheimer's dementia. *Investigative Ophthalmology and Visual Science*, **44**: 875–878.

Dunne, T.E., Neargarder, S.A., Cippolloni, P. and Cronin-Golomb A (2004) Visual contrast enhances food and liquid intake in advanced Alzheimer's disease. *Clinical Nutrition*, **23**: 533–538.

Eperjesi, F. and Akbarali, N. (2003) Rehabilitation in Charles Bonnet Syndrome: a review of treatment options. *Clinical and Experimental Optometry*, **87**: 149–152.

Fujimori, M., Imamura, T., Hirono, N., Ishii, K., Sasaki, M. and Mori, E. (2000) Disturbances of spatial and object vision correlate differently with regional cerebral glucose metabolism in Alzheimer's disease. *Neuropsychologia*, **38**: 1356–1361.

Galton, C., Patterson, K., Xuereb, J., and Hodges, J. (2000) Atypical and typical presentation of Alzheimer's disease: A clinical, neuropsychological, neuroimaging and pathological study of 13 cases. *Brain*, **123**: 484–498.

Gherghel, D. (2003) The eye and the mind; psychiatric encounters in optometric practice. *Optometry Today*, **21 March**: 38–41.

Haegerstrom-Portnoy, G., Schneck, M. and Brabyn, J. (1999) Seeing into old age. *Optometry and Visual Science*, **76**: 141–148.

Haxby, J.V., Grady, C., Horwitz, B., Ungerleider, L., Mishkin, M., Carson. R., Herscovitch, P., Schapiro, M. and Rapoport, S. (1991) Dissociation of object and spatial visual processing pathways in human extrastriate cortex. *Proceedings of the National Academy of Sciences, USA*, **88**: 1621–1652.

Haxby, J., Horwitz, B., Ungerleider, L., Maisog, J., Pietrini, P. and Grady, C. (1994) The functional organization of human extrastriate cortex: a PET – rCBF study of selective attention to faces and locations. *Journal of Neuroscience*, **14**: 1636–1653.

Hinton, D., Sadun, A., Blanks, J. and Miller, C. (1986) Optic nerve degeneration in Alzheimer's disease. *New England Journal of Medicine*, **315**: 485–487.

Hof, P.R., Vogt, B.A., Bouras, C. and Morrison, J.H. (1997) Atypical form of Alzheimer's disease with prominent posterior cortical atrophy: a review of lesion distribution and circuit disconnection in cortical visual pathways. *Vision Research*, **37**; 3609–3622.

Hutton, J.T., Nagel, J. and Loewenson, R.B. (1984) Eye tracking dysfunction in Alzheimer-type dementia. *Neurology*, **34**: 99–102.

Hyvarinen, L. (2005a) *Changes in Vision in Old Age*. http://www.lea-test.fi/en/eyes/old.html.

Hyvarinen, L. (2005b) *Visual Pathways Lecture*. http://www.lea-test.fi/en/assessme/comenius/pathways.html.

Jaffe, G.J., Alvarado, J. and Juster, R. (1986) Age-related changes of the normal response and variation in the normal hill of vision. *Archives of Ophthalmology*, **104**: 65–68.

Jones, G.M.M. (1990) The cholinergic hypothesis of Alzheimer's disease: the effects of lecithin and nicotine on attention and memory. PhD Thesis, Institute of Psychiatry, University of London.

Jones, G.M.M. (1997) A review of Feil's validation method for communicating and caring for dementia sufferers. *Geriatric Psychiatry/Current Opinion in Psychiatry*, **10**: 326–332.

Jones, G.M.M. (2004a) Metaphors for teaching about changing memory and cognition in Alzheimer's disease: bookcases in a library. In G.M.M. Jones and B.M.L. Miesen (Eds) *Care-giving in Dementia*. Hove: Brunner-Routledge, pp. 37–66.

Jones, G.M.M. (2004b) The loss of meaningful attachments and objects in dementia and behavioural stage-specific implications. In G.M.M. Jones and B.M.L. Miesen (Eds), *Care-giving in Dementia*. Hove: Brunner-Routledge, pp. 261–284.

Jones, G.M.M. and Burns, A. (1992) Reminiscing disorientation theory. In G.M.M. Jones and B.M.L. Miesen (Eds), *Care-giving in Dementia*, vol. 1. London: Routledge, pp. 57–76.

Jones, G.M.M., Sahakian, B.J., Levy, R., Warburton, D.M. and Gray, J.A. (1992) Effects of subcutaneous nicotine on attention, information processing and short-term memory in Alzheimer's disease. *Psychopharmacology*, **108**: 485–494.

Klernan, V. (1994) Where there's light there's brass. *New Scientist* **10 Dec.**: 17.

Koch, C. (2004) *The Quest for Consciousness: a Neurobiological Approach*. Englewood, Co: Roberts and Co.

Kuljis, R.O. and Tikoo, R.K. (1997) Discontinuous distribution of lesions in striate cortex hypercolumns in Alzheimer's disease. *Vision Research*, **37**: 3573–3591.

Kurylo, D., Allan, W., Edward Collins, T. and Baron, J. (2003) Spatial relationships in Alzheimer's Disease. *Behavioural Neurology*, **14**: 19–28.

Laatu, S., Revonsuo, A., Jaykka, H., Portin, R. and Rinne, J.O. (2003) Visual object recognition in early alzheimer's disease: deficits in semantic processing. *Acta Neurologica Scandinavica*, **108**: 82–89.

Leigh, R. (1982) The impoverishment of ocular motility in the elderly. In R. Sekulen, D Kline and K. Dismukes (Eds), *Aging and Human Visual Function*. New York: Alan R. Liss, pp. 174–180.

Leuba, G and Saini, K. (1995) Pathology of subcortical visual centres in relation to cortical degeneration in Alzheimer's disease. *Neuropathology and Applied Neurobiology*, **21**: 410–422.

Lewis, T.L. and Maurer, D. (1986) Preferential looking as a measure of visual resolution in infants and toddlers: a comparison of psychophysical methods. *Child Development*, **57**: 1062–1075.

Lindeboom, J., Schmand, B., Tulner, L., Walstra, G. and Jonker, C. (2002) Visual association test to detect early dementia of the Alzheimer type. *Journal of Neurology, Neurosurgery and Psychiatry*, **73**: 126–133.

Lord, S. and Ward, J.A. (1994) Age associated differences in sensori-motor function and balance in community dwelling women. *Age and Ageing*, **23**: 452–460.

Lott, L., Schneck, M., Haegerstrom-Portnoy, G., Brabyn, J., Gildengorin, G. and West, C. (2001) Reading performance in older adults with good acuity. *Optometry and Visual Sciences*, **78**: 316–324.

Marmor, M. (1982) Aging and the retina. In R. Sekulen, D. Kline and K. Dismukes (Eds), *Aging and Human Visual Function*. New York: Alan R. Liss, pp. 59–78.

Mayer, R. and Darby, S. (1991) Does a mirror deter wandering in demented older people? *International Journal of Geriatric Psychiatry*, **6**: 607–609.

Mendez, M., Turner, J., Gilmore, G., Remler, B. and Tomsak, R. (1990) Balint's syndrome in Alzheimer's disease: visuospatial functions. *International Journal of Neuroscience*, **54**: 339–346.

Mendez, M., Cherrier, M. and Meadows, R. (1996) Depth perception in Alzheimer's disease. *Perceptual and Motor Skills*, **83**: 987–995.

Mendez, M., Ghajarania, M. and Perryman, K. (2002) Posterior Cortical atrophy: clinical characteristics and differences compared to Alzheimer's disease. *Dementia and Geriatric Cognitive Disorders*, **14**: 33–40.

Mendola, J.D., Cronin-Golomb, A., Corkin, S. and Drowdon, J.H. (1995) Prevalence of visual deficits in Alzheimer's disease. *Optometry and Visual Science*, **72**: 155–167.

Milner, D.A. and Goodale, M.A. (1995) *The Visual Brain in Action*. Oxford: Oxford University Press.

Nobili, L. and Sannita, W.G. (1997) Cholinergic modulation, visual function and Alzheimer's dementia. *Vision Research*, **37**: 3559–3571.

Oberlink, M. (1997) Keeping an eye on vision: primary care of age-related ocular disease. *Geriatrics*, **52**: 30–37.

Ordy, J., Brizzee, K. and Johnson, H. (1982) Cellular alterations in visual pathways and the limbic system: implications for vision and short-term memory. In

R. Sekulen, D. Kline and K. Dismukes (Eds), *Aging and Human Visual Function.* New York: Alan R. Liss, pp. 15–29.

Pankow, L., Pliskin, N. and Luchins, D. (1996) An optical intervention for visual hallucinations associated with visual impairment and dementia in elderly patients. *Journal of Neuropsychiatry*, **8**: 88–92.

Pastalan, L. (1982) Environmental design and adaptation to the visual environment of the elderly. In R. Sekulen, D. Kline and K. Dismukes (Eds), *Aging and Human Visual Function.* New York: Alan R. Liss, pp. 323–333.

Patel, M. (1994) Ocular side effects of cardiac drugs. *Optometry Today*, **24 Oct.**: 30–34.

Rizzo, M. and Hurtig, R. (1987) Looking but not seeing: attention, perception and eye movements in simultanagnosia. *Neurology*, **37**: 1642–1648.

Rizzo, M. and Vecera, S.P. (2002) Psychoanatomical substrates of Balint's syndrome. *Journal of Neurology, Neurosurgery and Psychiatry*, **72**: 162–178.

Rizzo, M., McGehee, D., Jeffrey, A. and Steve, N. (2001) Simulated car crashes at intersections in drivers with Alzheimers disease. *Alzheimer Disease and Related Disorders*, **15**: 10–20.

Ro, T. (in press). Neural mechanisms for conscious and unconscious vision. In B. Breitmeyer and H. Ogmen (Eds), *The First Half Second.* Cambridge, MA: MIT Press.

Ro, T, Shelton, D., Lee, O.L. and Chang, E. (2004) Extrageniculate mediation of unconscious vision in transcranial magnetic stimulation-induced blindsight. *Proceedings of the National Academy of Services, USA*, **101**: 9933–9935.

Rosen, P. (2004) Vision screening for Alzheimer's disease: prevention from an Opthalmologist's perspective (There is more to vision than meets the eye). *Permanente*, **8**: 9–33.

Rumney, N. (1992) Low vision aids in practice. *Optometry Today*, **21 Sept.**: 23–30.

Sacks, O. (1985) *The Man Who Mistook His Wife for a Hat.* New York: Summit Books.

Sadun, A.A., Borchert, M., DeVita, E., Hinton, D. and Bassi, C. (1987) Assessment of visual impairment in patients with Alzheimer's disease. *American Journal of Opthalmology*, **104**: 113–120.

Sakai, S., Hirayama, K., Lwasaki, S., Fujii, T., Hashimoto, R. and Yamadori, A. (2002) Yellow glasses improve contrast sensitivity of a patient with a visual variant of Alzheimer's disease. *European Neurology*, **48**: 224–225.

Sekuler, R. and Owsley, C. (1982) The spatial vision of older humans. In: R. Sekulen, D. Kline and K. Dismukes (Eds), *Aging and Human Visual Function.* New York: Alan R. Liss, pp. 185–202.

Serby, M. and Almiron, N. (2005) Dementia with Lewy bodies: an overview. *Annals of Long-Term Care*, 13: 20–22.

Spector, A. (1982) The aging of the lens and cataract formation. In R. Sekulen, D. Kline and K. Dismukes (Eds), *Aging and Human Visual Function.* New York: Alan R. Liss, pp. 30–43.

Tetewsky, S.J. and Duffy, C.J. (1999) Visual loss and getting lost in Alzheimer's disease. *Neurology*, **52**: 958–965.

Traub, J.R. and Baucer, R. (1986) Seeing but not recognizing. *Survey of Ophthalmology*, **30**: 328–336.

Ungerleider, L.G. and Mishkin, M. (1982) Two cortical visual systems. In D.G. Ingle,

M.A. Goodale and R.J.Q. Mansfield (Eds), *Analysis of Visual Behavior.* Cambridge, MA: MIT Press, pp. 549–586.

Van Rhijn, S.J., Glosser, G., de Vries, J., Clark, C., Newber, A. and Alavi, A. (2004) Visual processing impairments and decrements in regional brain activity in Alzheimer's disease. *Journal of Clinical and Experimental Neuropsychology,* **26**: 11–23.

Watson, M.E., Welsh-Bohmer, K.A., Hoffman, J., Lowe, V. and Rubin, D.C. (1999) The neural basis of naming impairments in Alzheimer's disease revealed through positron emission tomography. *Archives of Clinical Neuropsychology,* **14**: 347–357.

Weddell, B. (2003) Examining the elderly population: strategies for the optometrist. *Optometry Today,* **7 Feb.**: 31–34.

Whitfield Grundy, J. (1992) A glimmer of light. *Optometry Today,* **21 Sept.**: 18–21.

Williams, M. (1956) Studies of perception in senile dementia; cue-selection as a function of intelligence. *British Journal of Medical Psychology,* **29**: 270–287.

Wong Riley, M., Antuoni, P., Ho, K., Egan, R., Hevner, R., Liebl, W., Huang, Z., Rachel, R. and Jones, J. (1997) Cytochrome oxidase in Alzheimer's disease: biochemical, historical, immuno-histochemical analyses of the visual and other systems. *Vision Research,* **37**: 3593–3607.

Yilmazer-Hanke, D. and Hanke, J. (1999) Progression of Alzheimer-related neuritic plaque pathology in the entorhinal region, perirhinal cortex and hippocampal formation. *Dementia and Geriatric Cognitive Disorders,* **10**: 70–76.

Chapter 2

Visual phenomena in Alzheimer's disease: distinguishing between hallucinations, illusions, misperceptions and misidentifications

Gemma Jones, Jeremy Harding and William van der Eerden-Rebel

Overview

In the literature about visual hallucinations in Alzheimer's disease (AD) one can find a frequency of occurrence of 40%, with a range of 13–73%. These high estimates and range are problematic for clinical practice and care-giving, in that they suggest that hallucinations are frequent occurrences in AD and, implicitly, that they 'should' be present and found by clinicians. Reports that visual hallucinations are an even more frequent feature of Lewy body dementia (LBD) than AD have undoubtedly influenced the 'probable' diagnosis of both illnesses, but what exactly are visual hallucinations (in view of the new understanding of pathology to the visual system in AD) and the resultant perceptual deficits? How many types of 'visual phenomena' are there in AD? Are they sometimes mislabelled? Does such mislabelling have consequences for the care of persons with AD?

With current understanding about the extensive damage to the visual system in AD, we build upon the information in Chapter 1, and again propose that AD needs to be understood as a visuoperceptual disorder as well as a cognitive disorder (visuo-cognitive for short). With this perspective, many separate visual phenomena such as illusions, misperceptions and misidentifications are seen to occur in AD, not just hallucinations. The former are rarely mentioned in the literature and neither is their order of occurrence or relatedness to each other.

Current definitions and understanding of visual phenomena and hallucinations in AD are given and summarized in the context of the visuo-cognitive deficits in AD. Clinical examples of visual phenomena that have mistakenly been reported as visual hallucinations are given, as well as a case history that illustrates the difficulties in determining the presence of genuine visual hallucinations in AD.

Two retrospective case-note studies (a Pilot Study and a Main Study) are presented. They look at GP referrals of persons with dementia with 'presumed hallucinations' to an Old Age Psychiatry Service. In the AD group, 60% of visual events reported as visual hallucinations were recategorizable as 'illusions', 'misperceptions', 'misidentifications' and naming errors. In the Parkinson's disease (PD)/LBD group, 53% of reported visual hallucinations were reclassifiable as other types of visual events. Extracampine (multi-sense, kinesthetic) hallucinations were not present in the AD group but in 'Toxic/Infectious' and 'Rare dementia/Brain tumour' groups. Both studies found 'possible genuine visual hallucinations' in persons with 'probable AD' present in only about 3% of persons with AD. More research is needed to distinguish between both different types of visual phenomena and different types of visual hallucinations in specific types of dementing illness.

The nature and frequency of occurrence of illusions, misperceptions and misidentifications in AD (and PD/LBD) leads us to question their frequent miscategorization under the term 'hallucinations'. Such miscategorization can lead to missed opportunities to assist visuo-cognitive deficits through the use of visual aids, appropriate communication and reassurance and drugs that boost cholinergic functioning.

This chapter concludes with recommendations about the assessment of visual phenomena in AD, and points to the need for education about the range of visuo-cognitive phenomena in AD for healthcare professionals, diagnosticians and carers. It urges caution in the use of neuroleptic medication (especially anticholinergic antipsychotic) in any persons experiencing visual phenomena, AD and LBD being cholinergic deficit illnesses.

Introduction

The term 'visuo-cognitive' has been used to describe the visuoperceptual link to cognitive difficulties in AD, because the distortions that are 'seen' must also be 'neurally reconstructed' and then 'understood'. Attempts to understand visuo-cognitive errors in AD are enabling a new view of behaviour changes in dementia. This involves understanding persons with AD as 'behaving [relatively] normally in a "perceptually abnormal" world' (versus the more common notion of persons with dementia 'behaving abnormally in a normally perceived world').

Medical/psychiatric versus ophthalmic/perceptual research consideration of visual hallucinations

In the UK, where the diagnosis and treatment of AD and other dementia falls primarily under the remit of Mental Health Services, there seems to be a common expectation of 'psychiatric and behavioural disturbances' (PBD: personality change, depression, hallucinations, paranoid ideas, mania, psychosis and delusions). This is reflected in the high rates of antipsychotic medication prescription to this population (30% in our currently-in-progress study of their use in residential homes and specialist dementia homes). With this expectation, it is not surprising that other visual phenomena (illusions, misperceptions and misidentifications, and the various types of visual hallucinations) are easily 'lost' within a smoke-screen of 'PBD thinking'.

In medical/psychiatric research studies about AD, 'visual hallucinations' (and delusions) are usually placed under 'neuro-psychiatric' or 'psychotic symptoms'. Few studies mention baseline visual assessment, let alone the more specialized visual assessment required to detect the visual changes known to occur in AD (see Chapter 1). Even fewer studies describe how hallucinations were defined and assessed, in what stage of the illness persons were in (i.e. including key information such as whether persons were disoriented to time and experiencing language difficulties) and what Staging Model of AD was used. With the exception of acute delirium and urinary tract infections, few studies allude to other possibilities for causes and explanations of what, at first, are thought to be visual hallucinations in dementia.

Ophthalmic/ perceptual research, however, makes a strong link between visual pathology and a range of visual disturbances/phenomena, of which hallucinations are only one. For example, Hyvarinen (2005a) points out that 'illusions caused by retinal lesions vary and should not be confused with hallucinations. Macular and retinal degeneration do not cause all cells to be lost in the scotomatous (blind spot) area. Imperfect functioning of the damaged cells still causes activity in the visual pathways and the brain can interpret this as a visual image ranging from 'glowing lights to pleasant or unpleasant vivid images'. She notes that such illusions can be especially disturbing to persons with dementia and low intelligence because he or she may not comprehend the illusory nature of the phenomena. Pankow et al (1996) present optical interventions for visual hallucinations associated with visual impairment in persons with dementia.

How have visual hallucinations and psychiatric/ behavioural disturbances become associated with Alzheimer's disease?

In 1906, clinical psychiatrist and neuropathologist Alois Alzheimer described a female patient in her fifties who had cognitive deficits: 'delusions and hallucinations'. He observed her personally, followed her illness through the years to her death, and studied her brain post-mortem (Hippius and Neundorfer, 2003). Alzheimer had only the psychiatric vocabulary of his times with which to record the presence of her behavioural phenomena. Though he identified and described the presence of the hallmark 'plaques and tangles' in the disease, now named after him (in both early- and late-onset forms), he was not in a position to know how their presence affected the visual-perceptual difficulties that often (see Chapter 1) accompany Alzheimer's disease (AD), nor the cognitive and behavioural effects of such visual deficits.

Burns (1999) summarized four theories about PBDs in AD: (1) PBDs result from specific biological brain changes; (2) PBDs are inevitable consequences of the illness itself (but understandable, given the cognitive deficits that occur); (3) PBDs result from acute confusional states that are part of the whole dementia illness profile (from superimposed physical illness, such as urinary tract infections); and (4) PBDs are a natural reaction of people with dementia to their environment (and the knowledge that they are losing their abilities). He concludes that a combination of these factors likely accounts for the presence of PBDs in AD.

With regard to the second and fourth explanations, it has only been in the past decades that there has been a focus on obtaining a more accurate understanding of what persons with AD perceive and how they are reacting to these perceptions.

In the past, some became uncomfortable about 'assumptions of craziness/psychosis' behind 'everyday lay-expressions' and 'minimal care-giver education' about AD and dementia. However, with minimal neuropathological information about the illness, it was difficult to counter notions like: (1) 'There's three types: the ones who are happy and away with the fairies in gaga-land, the nasty ones, and the wanderers'; (2) 'If you practise Reality Orientation Methods using a 24 milieu approach, the facts will be re-learnt, the delusions will stop and persons will be able to participate in reality again'; and (3) 'She's just lost her memory and mind, that's all'.

Even references by persons who are 'time-disoriented' to 'long since deceased parents as being alive' (also to 'grown-up children as being young' and 'thinking they are working still') were often considered to be delusions and hallucinations in the past. Questioning this understanding led to Feil's Validation approach (1982) and later to Jones and Burns' (1992) Reminiscing Disorientation Theory and Miesen's development of PoPFID theory (B.M.L. Miesen, 1992, personal communication).

Jones and Burns (1992) described 'disorientation in AD' as a transit difficulty between various normally occurring states of consciousness. 'Reminiscing Disorientation Theory' was postulated to distinguish what was happening to persons with late-onset AD in residential settings from the notion of 'psychosis' in mental illness. They suggested that under certain conditions of visual and cognitive impairments (including disorientation in time), in conjunction with conditions of sensory deprivation, persons with AD reminisce so intensely (self-stimulate) that they superimpose images from eidetic (visual) memory onto a poorly perceived present environment. This was taken to be a process distinct from more classically described hallucinations at that time.

Miesen (1992) showed that persons with AD were often frightened, relentlessly searching for 'deceased parents and family' and 'grown-up children' (attachment figures), and that in the absence of being able to secure 'symbolic attachment figures' (care staff) this search ended by seeking safety in 'memories of connectedness to key attachment figures'. He showed how 'attachment behaviour' developed gradually and was eventually universally present in (behavioural stage 2) time-disorientation. Jones (2004) built on the theme of attachment to include 'attachments' to objects and feelings of safety and comfort (feelings of home).

The use of psychiatric concepts, such as PBDs, to understand AD continues to be questioned, resulting in new attempts to understand the 'perceived (and hence experienced) world' of persons with AD, including their 'awareness context' and coping responses (Clare, 2004a,b).

Despite such questioning, the use of 'psychiatric vocabulary' to describe persons with dementia persists, along with the frequently assumed presence of 'psychosis' when hallucinations (and/or delusions) are considered to be present, much as in other psychotic syndromes such as schizophrenia.

The old assumptions and vocabulary are changing

Though Sweet (2004) pursues the notion of parallels in psychosis between schizophrenia and AD, arguing that they share brain circuitry abnormalities, others consider that there is no neuropathological substrate for such a parallel (Religa et al, 2003). Increasingly, AD is being studied from a more neurological-neuroscientific perspective (in keeping with other progressive degenerative illnesses such as multiple sclerosis). To pursue this trend, a more phenomenologically based vocabulary will be needed to replace the vague notion of 'neuropsychiatric symptoms' in current use for dementia (Martin, 2002).

Neuroscientific advances in understanding the specific visual deficits in AD, in addition to normal age-related visual changes and often concurrent visual pathology, make it possible for clinicians to start asking more explicit questions about the nature of the 'experienced world' for a person with dementia, particularly how to assess it and plan appropriate care interventions. Cronin-Golomb (2004) states that 'lower-level visual deficits can contribute to, or masquerade as, higher-order cognitive impairments . . . and that vision-based interventions may improve patients' lives'.

(Chapter 1 in this volume deals with the nature of these deficits and the design issues in providing specialist dementia care environments to take account of these deficits.)

The 'thought trains' associated with 'psychiatric' versus 'neurological damage' descriptive lenses are illustrated in Box 2.1.

Box 2.1 Thought trains linked to our understandings of visual changes in Alzheimer's disease

Hallucination

⇒ psychosis => mentally ill => unpredictable => unreasonable => crazy => may be dangerous => need to be on guard => may need to distance oneself to stay safe

Drugs of choice

*   The old-style antipsychotics are anticholinergic, which make symptoms of AD worse (AD is a cholinergic deficit illness).
*   Olanzapine & risperidone were recommended against in the UK in 2004 due to evidence of increased risk of stroke.
*   Atypical antipsychotic drugs still prescribable are quetiapine, clozapine & amisulpiride.

Illusion/ misperception/ misidentification/ naming difficulty

⇒ a visual mistake => easy to identify with as we all make mistakes => a fragile person who needs careful observation and listening to => may need visual aids & help to enhance key cues in the environment, and help them to interpret and manage in their environment
(extra lighting, shadow elimination, photos of what is contained behind doors and cupboard doors, frequent help & the proximity of others to compensate for their difficulties and increased fear)

Drugs of choice: those that boost cholinergic functioning (Edwards et al, 2004; Ffytche, 2004; Mosimann and McKeith, 2003)

The range of visual phenomena that can occur in illness/altered states

To start a discussion of visual hallucinations in AD requires mentioning the diverse conditions in which they can be found, as well as other visual phenomena that are sometimes also called hallucinations. Table 2.1 provides an overview listing of the range of visual phenomena and conditions in which they can be found, including AD, LBD, PD, fever, delirium tremens, peducular brain area lesions, bereavement, schizophrenia, epilepsy, migraines, Charles Bonnet syndrome, macular degeneration, diabetic retinopathy, macular degeneration, upon waking or whilst falling asleep (hypnagogic and hypnapagogic hallucinations), induced by medications, as well as other

Table 2.1 Summary of visual phenomena described in humans

A   Sleep **dream** vision (eyes closed)

B   **Hypnapagogic and hypnagogic or (hypnopompic)** vision and sleep deprivation states
     (just falling asleep & starting to awaken – semi-stuporous vision, sometimes classified as hallucinations)

C   **Daydream/ fantasy** vision (**visualizing** whilst conscious with eyes open)

D   **Reminiscing vision** (conscious eyes open or closed, recall of stored visual/ eidetic images) (Jones and Burns, 1992)

E   **Normal retinal vision** (relatively accurate) used in most waking hours to observe and perform life activities

F   **Normal age-related visual changes** (wear and tear without pathology)

G   Vision changes in **altered states & systemic stress**
     Grieving (hallucinations of widowhood)
     Trauma (including post-traumatic stress)
     Sensory deprivation environments
     Dehydration/exhaustion/hypothermia/anoxia

H   Normal vision affected by **reduced or absent sensory input** due to gradations of **pathological damage to the visual system** leading from varying degrees of total sight loss to sensory deprivation from blindness
     Macular degeneration
     Charles Bonnet syndrome
     Retinal detachment
     Blindness

I   Vision alterations affected/caused by **systemic disease & illness**
     Fever
     Insulin excess (diabetes)
     Tumours
     Cataracts
     Migraines
     Epilepsy
     Brain infections; (eg encephaphalitis & post-encephalitic)
     Alzheimer-type dementia
     Lewy body/Parkinson's dementia
     Vascular dementia
     Huntington's chorea

J   Vision affected by prescribed **medication/drugs** (see Appendix 2.1)

K   **Complex constructed hallucinations** known to occur during:
     Toxic, infectious states
     Schizophrenia (visual hallucinations less common than auditory)
     Psychadelic/hallucinogenic drug states
     Acute alcohol withdrawal, and alcohol excess

L   **Less common visual phenomena**
     Hypnotic state visualizations
     Looking at colours or kaleidoscopic images resulting from letting strong light fall on our eyelids
     Ideoretinal light phenomena; the visual field becoming brighter in the absence of real light

conditions. The new reader of the subject of hallucinations will soon see the variety of understandings and definitions of this word and other words to describe visual phenomena (Siegel and West, 1975; Cline et al, 1980; Stedman, 1982; Larousse, 1995).

Where do delusions fit in?

Although delusions are not the focus of this chapter, they need a brief mention because of their frequent association with hallucinations in the literature (Staff et al, 1999; Holtzer et al, 2003; Sultzer et al, 2003; Venneri and Shanks, 2004).

A delusion is usually defined as a false belief based on incorrect 'inference' about external reality that is held despite proof to the contrary. The difficulty in applying this definition to persons with AD is twofold: it may be an incorrect 'perception', not an incorrect inference; and, with damage to logical thinking ability in dementia, any attempts at offering logical proof to correct a person's incorrect understanding may not be fully comprehended or remembered.

For the purpose of this discussion we take delusions in AD to be 'mistaken explanations' for a poorly perceived world that is becoming less predictable and more frightening. Delusions are an early response to poorly remembered thoughts about fragmented, distorted or incorrectly combined pieces of information. They can be seen as a coping response to early visuo-cognitive changes and are inseparable from a person's attempt to understand and control (in behavioural stage 1) what is happening to him/her, though with limited abilities. What a person perceives (or even unknowingly perceives incorrectly) necessitates an attempt to try to find a rational explanation for what is experienced as 'seen' (see Box 2.2). However, 'what we perceive of

---

Box 2.2 Understanding how perceptions are linked to faulty thinking in dementia

Past experience, expectation & motivation → visual expectation → something is poorly/incorrectly seen → it needs to be enhanced (from visual/contextual memory) & assimilated → interpreted (an attempt to understand causation with whatever logical thinking ability one has & linked to one's former experiences & current fears) → acted upon → remembered (as accurately as possible) → explained to others (with waning language ability)

Cognitive difficulties in AD create extra places in this chain for difficulties to occur

---

our world is much more a composition of [by] our brain than an exact image [reconstruction] of the surrounding physical structure' (Hyvarinen, 2005b).

Numerous visual deficits due to Alzheimer's disease pathology; potential for mistakenly labelling illusions as hallucinations in Alzheimer's disease

A variety of types of visual damage have been reported in AD at a number of locations along the visual pathway, including the retina, optic nerve, lateral geniculate nucleus and primary and secondary visual cortices (Hinton et al, 1986; Sadun et al, 1987; Curcio and Drucker, 1993; see also Chapter 1 of this volume).

Most of this damage seems to result from the presence of plaques (Haxby et al, 1991, 1994; Kuljis & Tikoo, 1997) and tangles (Braak and Braak, 1998; Braak et al, 1998) along the primary visual pathway, including the ventral and dorsal pathways, attributed to object recognition and spatial localization and facial recognition areas (Clarke et al, 1996; Haxby et al, 1991, 1994), although other types of cell damage and death have been reported but are as yet unexplained (Mapstone et al, 2001). The Tectal Pathway, now known to be important for less understood automatic visual functioning and eye movement control (Sumner and Mollon, 2001), is also damaged in AD (see Chapter 1).

Beta-amyloid (the main constituent of neurofibrillary plaques in AD) and amyloid precursor protein levels were found to be related to retinal aging and degeneration, although not to tau protein (the 'tangle' component in AD) (Loffler et al, 1995). Plaque and tangle damage to the nucleus basalis causes the limbic system cholinergic deficits in AD. According to Nobili and Sannita (1997), acetylcholine acts as a long-lasting stimulatory/excitatory substance in the visual cortex and hippocampus, which monitors time-based patterns of neural activity. In the somatosensory cortex, acetylcholine enhances responsiveness (sensitivity) by lowering the stimulation threshold, possibly enlarging the receptive field size. By implication, reduced acetylcholine (in the nucleus basalis and limbic system and projections) would decrease responsiveness to stimulation and possibly decrease the receptive field size.

Although the exact mechanism, and combination effects, of such damage to the visual system in AD has not been determined yet, findings to date have shown a range of specific perceptual dysfunctioning, including reports of decreased acuity, poor colour vision (especially the darker and blue colours), poor figure/background contrast sensitivity and eye movement difficulties (both types of saccadic movements). This translates into an inaccurate and ever-changing 'distorted estimate' of what is being perceived by persons with AD. These difficulties affect every aspect of activities of daily living (Arnold et al, 1991; Cronin-Golomb, 2001; Cronin-Golomb and Amick, 2001; van Rhijn et al, 2004). The latter paper promotes the potential of special environmental design to reduce/compensate for these difficulties.

Visual perceptual effects with eyes closed

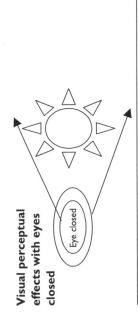

Retinal stimulation by light through closed eyelids produces perception of a range of visual experiences from colour and scintillations through to shapes, and movement, as does pressing one's hands upon one's eyes.

Normal retinal vision of images

Object

Open eye

Intact lens, retina, optic nerve, visual pathways and cortex etc. enable one to see a measurably accurate 'image' or 'percept' of the object that has stimulated the retina...subject to normal illusion effects.

Illusions

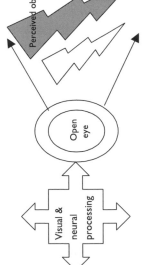

Perceived object

Open eye

Visual & neural processing

Illusions are not a degraded image, but a distortion of reality through the physical properties & characteristics of the image (reflections, shiny or bright surfaces, figure/ background contrast, etc.), or the difficulties inherent in the visual interpretive system that synthesizes visual signals to resolve the image accurately.

4 types of illusions: distortions, ambiguity, paradox, implied, but not a real object.

Illusions are affected by the timing, expectations of, location of the event & the separation & superimposition of visual information. Some can be analysed & corrected, but not usually by persons with dementia or AD.

Misperceptions of Illusions

What is already incorrectly seen, may be further distorted by visual system compromise or damage.

Misperceptions

A 'best guess' at inaccurate, degraded or distorted visual information due to state of consciousness, systemic, visual system damage, or visual and/or cognitive interpretive difficulties. Influenced by motivation, previous experience and expectation.

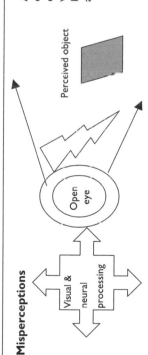

Perceived object

Non-retinal perception of visual images

Non-problematic visual constructions:

An internally generated (or retrieved) visual image can be experienced with eyes closed or open (superimposed in part or full on the outside world), but the person is aware that it is not retinally seen and present in the outside world. The images can be stopped at will.

True hallucination

Internally (currently produced &/or stored visual image) experienced with eyes open (experienced as occupying the full visual field or superimposed in part on the outside world) but one is NOT aware that it is not present in the outside world. The image can/cannot be stopped at will.

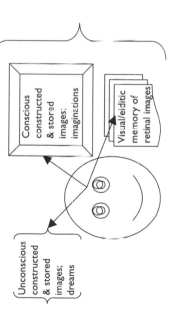

Conscious constructed & stored images; imaginations

Visual/eidetic memory of retinal images

Unconscious constructed & stored images; dreams

Open eye

Visual & neural processing

Figure 2.1 Definitions of various visual phenomena.

Defining visual hallucinations (versus illusions, misperceptions and misidentifications)

The simplest definition of a visual hallucination is 'perceiving something in the absence of sensory (retinal) stimulation for it'. This is distinct from an illusion (an incorrect or distorted perception) or a misperception (a best guess at inaccurate or degraded information of an external sensory stimulus) or a misidentification (incorrect naming or explaining of what is seen). Both illusions and hallucinations are altered forms of perception.

This chapter uses the definition of a visual hallucination to mean those visual phenomena that are non-retinal in origin (neither illusions nor resultant from misperceptions or misidentification errors) and that a person believes to be real. These definitions are elaborated with simple images in Figure 2.1.

Difficulties in using the definition of visual hallucination for dementia in practice

How are hallucinations in Alzheimer's disease normally diagnosed and described?

A person who hallucinates, experiences a perception subjectively yet objectively to others there is nothing to perceive (as opposed to illusions, which are distortions or misperceptions of an object that is perceivable to all). If the visual hallucinated object is obviously unreal or disappears quickly, or if the person can blink or do something to make it stop, the person often reaches insight into having had a hallucination. Sometimes it is others who dismiss such perceptions and confront a person about their hallucinations, to help them realize that they are having a hallucination. In some instances, the person cannot achieve insight into this or believe it, and tries to reason the perception away and hold on tightly to their rationale. [Teunisse et al (1996) found ways of teaching persons with Charles Bonnet syndrome a number of strategies to make their hallucinations go away, including moving towards them, blinking and shouting at them.]

Estimates about the frequency of visual hallucinations, therefore, are based upon reports of someone having (presumably) experienced perceptions that are not confirmed by others. In the case of persons with AD, it is often a family member who reports what they assume to be hallucinations to the GP.

Why hallucinations may be over-reported and poorly described

Hallucinations are not well understood yet and, apart from the literature suggesting that they are a common feature of AD, many professionals have not been taught about them in any detail. To most lay-persons the very mention of 'hallucinations' is immediately suggestive of the presence of a 'serious mental health problem'. There seem to be two other reasons why the presence of hallucinations in AD may be over-reported, one coming from professionals and the other from lay-persons.

Firstly, some of the assessment tools in current use, e.g. the Neuropsychiatric Symptom Inventory, contain only one question (usually asked of the primary carer, not the person with the dementia) to ascertain the presence of hallucinations, namely: 'Does this person have hallucinations?' Because there are no other questions in place to check for other visuoperceptual or language difficulties, illusions, misperceptions or misidentifications, there is a bias towards finding hallucinations.

Secondly, many family members of persons with AD use the word hallucination incorrectly, having learned it from any number of sources. The self-help literature, much of it written by non-healthcare professionals, frequently contains the words 'hallucinations' and 'delusions' (and paranoid and psychotic) incorrectly and liberally, further adding to the expectation of their 'normal' presence in AD. Two such examples taken from Koenig Coste's work (2003) illustrate this. On page 123 she refers to a misidentification as a hallucination: '. . . the stimulus behind Keith's hallucinating and paranoia was the shadow from the neighbour's flag moving across the window shade [not a man walking in front of his window]'. On page 98 she writes: 'shadows may elicit hallucinations'. A more accurate explanation would be: 'shadows are easy to misinterpret, often in a frightening way, when someone has perceptual and cognitive deficits'.

Although the simplest definition of a hallucination seems clear, it is not always easy to apply it to persons with dementia in clinical practice. Box 2.3 summarizes some of the other difficulties involved in assessing for hallucinations or other visual phenomena in AD.

Language deficits in Alzheimer's disease: mistaking incorrect descriptions for hallucinations

Some clinical examples

Naming difficulties

Loss of the ability to find or use nouns correctly is generally referred to as a 'naming difficulty', and is a common early feature of AD. Difficulty using complex tense constructions or word forms is concurrent with this (e.g. a lady could not say 'It was a compulsory operation; I had a hysterectomy for uterine cancer', instead she said 'I can't remember what I had but it was a compulsion, . . . and because of it I couldn't have any more children').

Box 2.3 Difficulties in assessing for hallucinations and visual phenomena in Alzheimer's disease

- The very process of establishing a 'probable diagnosis of AD' (in conjunction with identifying and following behavioural changes occurring during the dementia process) can take considerable time & be problematic (this is shown in the case history later). It is compounded by the presence of hallucinations in several dementing illnesses (Verhey et al, 1993)
- Many types of visual pathology & medications can lead to experiencing visual phenomena, including hallucinations. Visual assessment (& adapted visual assessment for cognitive impairment) is rarely done when investigating these phenomena in persons with dementia (Hyvarinen, 2005a)
- AD visual pathology can cause/compound existing visual difficulties (Cronin-Golomb, 2004)
- The understanding of what a hallucination is, on the part of the carer (reporting the visual event on behalf of the person with dementia) or the doctor, may be limited.
- Some persons have alternating misperceptions and hallucinations (Ffytche, 2004)
- Some types of 'incorrect seeing' apply to real things and hallucinations (Ffytche, 2004)
- Some persons may mistake the visual dream-like images on falling asleep or waking (hypnagogic/hypnopompic) with real events (Sweet, 2002)
- The period of time taken to 'problem solve' that a dream-like state was not real may take longer (or not be possible it all) with cognitive deficits in AD
- Language difficulties can make it difficult to understand what the person is trying to describe. If the person is time-disoriented, 'present tense' is often used to describe the events being thought of now as real, even though they are long past
- 'Fashions' in diagnosis can lead to over-diagnosing them through bias of expectation, e.g. the numerous reports in recent years about the association of visual hallucinations with LBD have led to a 50% over-diagnosis of LBD compared with autopsy findings (Serby and Almiron, 2005)

An example from clinical practice

Mrs S had been diagnosed with AD several years earlier and was walking outside for the first time with her physiotherapist after a hip fracture. At one point in the walk, Mrs S had pointed excitedly to the 'little red people dancing in the tree'.

The physiotherapist looked to where Mrs S was pointing but saw no red people, little, dancing or otherwise, and told her so. Later, she noted on the records that Mrs S was having hallucinations. On reflecting about this later, after learning about noun-finding difficulties and noun-substitutions in dementia, she realized that Mrs S had been pointing to a tree, heavily laden with red apples, which was blowing in the wind. Was the phrase 'little red people dancing' Mrs S's best-attempt to describe the apples moving about in the wind? She did not make any other such mistakes in describing things. Possibly this was not a visual hallucination.

Loss of metaphorical speech

More complex yet is the loss and/or incorrect use of metaphorical speech, which is also an early stage feature of AD (e.g. a gentleman in a care facility repeatedly said that he was being 'slow poisoned, a little every day' and soon there would be nothing left of him. He was thought to be psychotic. During a lengthy discussion, however, he explained that 'it felt as if everything in life was bitter now, very bitter, that he was dying slowly and no-one cared, not family or staff . . . that it felt like he was being slow-poisoned').

Tense errors

A gentleman told his granddaughter, on being shown her overseas honeymoon photos, 'I've been there'. In fact, his own travel plans had been cancelled because of his dementia and he had never left the UK. What he more likely meant was 'I was supposed to have gone (or had been planning on going) there too'.

Time perception errors and tense errors

Mrs W, 72, mother of several children and a former primary school teacher, had been presumed to be hallucinating on the basis of often referring to 'children around'. The assumption was that she was actually seeing children frequently. After more detailed discussions with her husband he recalled that her references to children were usually in the form of queries such as 'Where are the children?', or an assumption that they were sleeping or playing quietly. Sometimes she requested him to 'be quiet so as not to disturb them'. He could not recall a single instance where she had pointed to 'the supposed presence of a child' who was not there, or had been asked whether he also saw a child.

Mrs W was disoriented in time throughout the day. She thought she was teaching still and that her children were still at home. She used present tense to speak about her expectation that the children were present.

Her husband related that her ability to read (well-rehearsed) music, which had persisted longer than her ability to read printed letters, had also deteriorated in recent months. An eye examination subsequently revealed early-stage cataracts.

The doctor who diagnosed dementia told Mr W to keep telling his wife that 'there were no children' and that she 'was seeing things that were not there'. He did this constantly, believing that it would help her to get better and understand that what she thought she was seeing was not really present. Instead, he found that it upset her and the atmosphere between them. He had been very anxious and protective of her, avoiding taking her out socially, not wanting to be seen correcting her in public or having the stigma of mental illness attached to her, and so they were becoming more reclusive.

The husband had no knowledge about 'loss of time perception' in dementia or the possibility of language or visual changes such as illusions and misperceptions. With other possible explanations and new communication options explained to him, he found that he could support her in a new way that was not repeatedly confrontational throughout the day. He also improved the light levels in the house.

Case study illustrating the difficulty of assessing visual hallucinations in dementia

Mr F, 78, was separated, living on his own, with presumed AD. He was admitted to a mental health assessment unit after saying that men in black suits were trying to shoot him and becoming too frightened to care for himself adequately at home. His cognitive status had deteriorated somewhat post-retirement, but noticeably so during the past year according to family and friends.

Those assessing him in the weeks post-admission had conflicting views about whether he was actually seeing the 'men in black suits' outside in the trees. Some thought he was; others thought not but that he was frightened at the 'thought that they were out there' (having mistaken moving shadows or something for such men, and now believing this initially mistaken perception). Another member of staff observed that Mr F never directly acknowledged seeing the 'men in black suits' to him, but only made comments suggesting that they were there, such as: 'They're behind the trees right now, you won't see them. They only come out if they think you're not looking.'

Sometimes Mr F asked staff, 'Look there, out the window, don't you see them? I know what you'll think if you say you don't see them.' So, it seemed as if he really was seeing something, having the insight to acknowledge that 'seeing things that weren't really there was not good news'!

Trials of the atypical antipsychotic olanzapine apparently made no difference and his distress continued, as did his retreats to his room and trying to hide from view when he was near windows. The medication was discontinued.

In week 6, the computed tomography scan results showed a large right-sided occipital infarct that had not been reported. The infarct to the visual area helped to explain why he was not responding to the antipsychotic medication, and ruled out AD as the reason for his recent hallucinations.

His fearful behaviour (including staying in his bedroom, avoiding being near windows and yet looking out of them frequently) continued into week 8, with him saying at one point, 'Doctor, this is the 14th attempt they've made on my life, and you're doing nothing!'

He was not compliant or forthcoming with information during a later attempt to interview him more formally about the questions in Appendix 2.1 of this chapter. He did not reveal anything at this time about his supposed hallucinations. By week 14, mention of 'the men in dark suits' had stopped, as had his distress, and he was transferred to a long-term residential care facility.

[The Ffytche (2004) Palette Theory of visual hallucinations (described later) would suggest, on the basis of his occipital lesion and 'Vision Pathway Palette hallucinations', that if his hallucinations were genuine they would have been expected to have been only brief, though they were perceived by some staff to be of long duration. Note that the very recollections of 'men in suits with guns trying to kill you' would be enough to keep anyone's behaviour abnormal for some duration, even if this 'nothing' subsequently was seen.]

Clinical illustrative examples of stories reported as hallucinations

Box 2.4 gives examples of situations and stories that have been reported as hallucinations in persons with dementia. While some of them are unclear, most are obviously not hallucinations.

Description of hallucinations

Duration of hallucinations

Momentary hallucinations are suggestive of visual system disturbances, posterior cerebral artery infarcts, partial (occipital) seizures and migraine (Ffytche, 2004).

There are various precedents for defining what constitutes a 'persistent' hallucination, ranging from hallucinations for a number of weeks, to a

Box 2.4 Examples of events reported as hallucinations by GPs and nurses

- A gentleman reports that 'little people' are living in his garden shed, though on checking this story only garden tools are found therein. He tells this story to everyone who visits for several weeks. His story stops as suddenly as it started, without any obvious change in circumstances.
- A lady, whose wall is full of photos of prize-winning horses, asks a Community nurse if she can 'see the horses out in the garden'. This is reported as a hallucination. The next healthcare professional who visits this lady at her home notices that the horse photos are reflecting into the small panes of the French doors leading onto her garden . . . indeed it looks just 'as if' the horse photos are appearing in the garden. This person reports the lady having 'misperceptions'.
- A lady mistakenly refers to the four green ruffled edged pillows on her couch as 'cabbages'. Family tell the doctor she is hallucinating when asked if she sees things they don't, and this goes onto her medical record.
- A lady tells a healthcare visitor (without any sign of distress) of seeing thousands of 'wasps' on the floor, which is covered by patches of alternatingly aligned black/yellow finely striped carpet. This is reported as a hallucination. When a subsequent professional does a follow-up visit, and notes how the light coming through the lounge windows makes the lines scintillate, he decides to remove the carpeting, replacing with unpatterned carpeting. The lady never reported seeing wasps again.
- A gentleman takes a photo of his deceased wife for a drive. This is reported as a hallucination, but is challenged by a colleague who says it is a not uncommon, temporary grieving or bereavement behaviour.
- A lady, after many months of playing with a doll in her room and hiding it before visitors come (but acknowledging to care staff that she just enjoys holding a doll because it reminds her of happier times), starts to leave it out more frequently as her memory worsens. She names it, makes a bed for it in her living-room chair and starts to behave and refer to it as a real baby. Her daughters are indignant and confront staff, to find out who gave her the doll. After further investigation and family discussions, it was found that the lady purchased it herself. She named it after her first husband, who died during the war, only weeks after they were married. Her daughters had not previously known about her first ephemeral marriage, or perhaps her desire for a son.

- A social worker had been asked to investigate complaints of anti-social behaviour in an elderly gentleman living in his flat. He explained that his toilet seemed to be endlessly full of 'strangers'. (These turned out to be his own reflection being seen as another person in the mirror above his toilet.) After one incident of endless waiting and shouting for the occupant of his toilet to leave, the desperate man ran from his apartment and urinated over the first floor railing onto people in the mezzanine below, not having seen them. First reports were written up as this gentleman hallucinating, being anti-social, possibly mentally ill.
- A very elderly lady could not find her way out of the bedroom to find the toilet although she has lived in this home for 65 years. She lifted the sash window, sat on the window ledge, and urinated from the first floor, to the great consternation of the neighbours opposite, who reported her as hallucinating and psychotic to Social Services.
- A lady, recently widowed, reported that she sees her husband still sometimes even when she is at the supermarket. The nurse recorded this as a hallucination.
- A lady in a residential care home mistook the caricature-like large shadows on the wall, cast by the sun passing by two large vases with elaborate handles (located on top of a wardrobe), for 'thugs hiding in her room'. Though hallucinations were originally recorded in her file, staff eventually realized what was happening and tried to explain it to her. She could not retain the explanations and kept having 'startle responses' and becoming distressed when she looked at the wall. Staff's eventual solution was to remove the vases each evening at sundown, only to have to return them quickly in the morning, often after the lady had pressed the call button or phoned to report them as being 'stolen' by thieves in the night.

month, to being present on at least two consecutive six-monthly visits (Burns et al, 1990). Jeste and Finkel (2000) point out that care needs to be taken to exclude the possibility that hallucinations and delusions are not limited to episodes of acute delirium or transient medication-induced states, and say that the symptoms must persist for at least several weeks. Ffytche's (2004) work, which is discussed in more detail later, distinguishes between hallucinations that last from seconds to minutes, and from hours to days.

Types of hallucinations

Four types of hallucinations are commonly referred to: positive (seeing something when nothing is there); negative (not seeing the thing that is there but seeing something else); simple (dots, flashes, colours, patterns, lattices); and complex (well-formed images of faces, people, animals, scenes and landscapes that can include moving images). Pseudohallucinations, as defined in the European psychopathological tradition, refer to vivid visual images; in the American psychopathological tradition this term refers to hallucinations that a person has insight into and recognizes as not real (Ffytche, 2004).

Some doubt whether the perceptions in dream states (hypnagogic: just before the onset of sleep; hypnopompic or hypnapagogic: just before waking) should be called hallucinations. For theoretical purposes many researchers do include them, though they are considered to be normal phenomena with most persons recognizing that they are not real (Ohayon, 2000). (It is not yet known whether persons with dementia, at a certain stage of their illness, have extra difficulty in making the 'reality check' necessary to 'shut off' such perceptions, or, to conclude that such hypnagogic or hypnapagogic perceptions are not real.) Ohayon et al (1996) reported that they occur in 37% and 12.5% of the general population, respectively.

Classification of hallucinations

There is a long history behind attempts to try to categorize hallucinations (Siegel and West, 1975; Mavromatis, 1987). Kluver (1966) described three classes of perceptual pathology to fit a range of clinical descriptions: form constants; alterations in number, sizes and shapes of objects; and alterations in spatio-temporal relations (e.g. unduly lengthy persistence of objects, which can be transferred to other objects, or, to the reappearance of objects).

Investigating visual hallucinatory phenomena resulting from different pathologies, but not specifically AD, has led Ffytche and Howard (1999) to describe eight categories of pathological vision (three of their own description). These are: perseveration (objects from the visual field seem to 'follow' or continue to be present in the person's subsequent gaze); illusory visual spread (visual field defects where a missing area is 'filled in' with a surrounding pattern or texture, as happens in normal subjects across the foveal blind spot); polyopia or spatial palinopsia (multiple copies of an object in rows or columns); prosopometamorphosia (perception of distorted faces, often with prominent eyes); micro/macropsia (size illusions; nearer focal point projection leads to smaller object perception, and distant projection leads to larger objects); tessellopsia (repetitive geometric patterns); hyperchromatopsia (hallucinations where colour or colour perception is unusually vivid); and dendropsia (irregular dendroptic patterns of trees, maps and branches). They point out that their patients with Charles Bonnet syndrome (eye pathology alone) reported the same visual phenomena as the patients of Critchley (1951), who all had posterior cerebral lesions. Ffytche and Howard summarize studies to show that identical phenomenological descriptions of visual hallucination have been reported across a variety of conditions and experimental conditions, such as sensory deprivation, cerebral lesion, mescaline or LSD administration and migraine. This has led them to suggest that these hallucinated percepts reflect fundamental visual processes.

Content of hallucinations

In trying to elucidate the final neural pathway for such hallucinatory symptoms, or the visual percept itself, Ffytche and Howard (1999) state that they have deliberately chosen not to make distinctions between hallucinations and illusions nor between perceptual experiences that are recognized as real by the patient and those that are not.

Explanations for hallucinations

Past psychoanalytic explanation

Freudian theories explained hallucinations as projections of unconscious wishes and desires. This view has largely been replaced by biological theories, which see hallucinations as caused by functional deficits of the visual system and/or brain. These two views will have to be reconciled in a new way when our understanding about how thoughts (desires and fears) influence brain chemistry has grown.

Current biological explanations for hallucinations

The visual 'Deprivation Hypothesis' (Rabins, 1994) suggested that the lack of visual input leads to the appearance of spontaneous visual percepts.

Anomalies in the levels and interaction between the neurotransmitters dopamine, acetylcholine and serotonin are most frequently mentioned in the literature about hallucination causation (Perry and Perry, 1995; Kapur, 2003). Hof et al (1997) report a special subset of persons with AD who have prominent posterior cortical damage and in whom visual circuitry is severely disrupted.

Different hallucination syndromes

Some researchers have described several pathways or syndromes for explaining the occurrence of hallucinations that match the different brain areas involved in their production. With what is currently known about visual pathology in AD, it seems likely that these can be overlapped into a larger set of difficulties extending throughout the entire visual system (see Chapter 1).

One theory put forward suggests a central deficit of the visual association areas or primary visual cortex (Mielke et al, 1995; Martinelli et al, 1996; Katz and Rimmer, 1989: all cited in Cormack et al, 2000); another suggests a degeneration of the subcortical pathways linking the retina to the primary visual cortex (Sadun et al, 1987; Katz and Rimmer, 1989; Sadun, 1989).

Manford and Andremann (1998) speak of three possible visual hallucinatory pathways: direct irritative processes acting on cortical centres integrating complex visual information (as in epilepsy, where the association cortex generates and discharges signals that are interpreted as sensory inputs); visual pathway lesions that cause defective visual input (causing faulty cortical stimulation), processing (where input is normal but lesions result in an inappropriate pattern of cortical excitation) or abnormal cortical release phenomenon; and brainstem lesions affecting cholinergic and serotonergic pathways, which are also frequently involved in sleep disturbances (as in Parkinson's disease).

Ffytche (2004) describes hallucinations in terms of two major 'palettes of visual symptoms' or 'hallucination syndromes', and a possible third one being a mixture of the first two. These are shown in Figure 2.2

The 'Visual Pathway Disturbance Palette and/or higher visual area disorders' reflects hallucination features seen in macular degeneration, diabetic retinopathy, glaucoma, Charles Bonnet syndrome, posterior cerebral infarct, occipital seizure and migraine. The second 'Brainstem and/or Cholinergic Disorders Palette' reflects hallucination features seen in Parkinson's disease, narcolepsy, peduncular lesions or iatrogenic causes, (e.g. from tricyclics, oxybutirin, benztropine).

The visual pathway palette (palette VP) is usually characterized by some but not all of the following, for seconds to minutes: simple unformed lines, dots, colours, flashes, grid patterns, lattices, distorted faces, unfamiliar figures in strange costume or extended landscape scenes. These may only be present in part of the visual field.

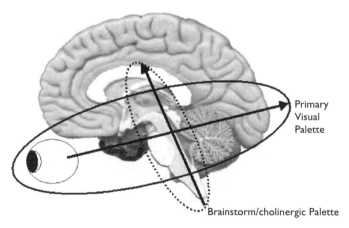

Figure 2.2 Anatomical pathways implicated in visual hallucination palettes (after Ffychte, 2004).

The brainstem/cholinergic palette (palette BC) is characterized by hallucinations ranging from brief intervals through to hours and days: isolated (often familiar) animals and figures through to 'feeling rather than seeing a person is watching you', through to extracampine (multi-sense modality hallucinations; hearing talking, feeling something on one's skin). This may include complex delusional explanations for the experiences.

Ffytche speculates that a third possibility, a 'mixture of both palettes', could arise in persons having conditions for which the pathology is not yet fully known, such as AD, LBD, vascular dementia, schizophrenia, bipolar illness, delirium and bereavement.

He suggests that knowing which palette a person's hallucinatory experiences are from can aid in giving a prognosis and suggesting interventions. Palette VP disorders such as macular disease tend to have a better prognosis, and a range of corrective opthalmological interventions and 'reassurance' are most helpful. Palette BC disorders such as Parkinson's disease are best treated with cholinesterase inhibitors, anticonvulsants or atypical antipsychotics.

Reported frequencies of hallucinations in general and in Alzheimer's disease

Box 2.5 summarizes a number of studies that report hallucination frequency in various groups ranging from the normal elderly to persons with AD and LBD. Our recent studies about the frequency of hallucinations (versus illusions, misperceptions and misidentifications) are presented in Appendices 2.2 and 2.3, and the findings are summarized in Box 2.5. (Note the large variations in estimates for all of the groups.)

Box 2.5 Reported frequencies of visual hallucinations in different groups

Sidgewick et al (1894)	10% of the population hallucinate in some modality
Ohayon (2000)	30% of people in a multi-country survey report hallucinating
	27% of these were non-drug daytime experiences
Ohayon and Schatzberg (2002)	12.5% of the 16.5% of the public who reported depressive symptoms had hallucinations or delusions;
	feelings of worthlessness or guilt were associated with hallucinations in 9.7% of sample (4.5% with delusions)

Box 2.5 continued

Ostling and Skoog (2002)	Hallucinations in 6.9% of non-demented 85-year-olds (delusions in 5.5% of this group)
Ostling et al (2003)	CT scans of above group showed basal ganglia calcification in 64% of hallucinators & in 19% of non-hallucinators
Teunisse et al (1996)	10% of persons with severe visual loss (Charles Bonnet syndrome & macular degeneration), 5% in low-vision clients

Reported frequencies of visual hallucinations in persons with AD & LBD/PD

Pitt (1974)	'Hallucinations are not typical of dementia'
Ronch (1989)	20%
Burns et al (1990)	13%
Paulsen et al (2000)	41%
Deutsch Lezak (1995)	20–73%
Ballard et al (1997)	80% suspected LBD report hallucinations at baseline interview
Ballard et al (2004)	18% of autopsy-confirmed AD sample had persistent hallucinations (31% with delusions); 59% of confirmed LBD; Braak stages V or VI (55% delusions)
Pilot Study (Appendix 2.2)	3% of AD sample referred by GPs had 'possible visual hallucinations'; 50% of all reported visual hallucinations were reclassifiable as illusions, misperceptions & misidentifications
Main Study (Appendix 2.3)	Visual hallucinations occurred in about 3% of this AD sample; 60% of reported visual hallucinations were reclassifiable as illusions, misperceptions and misidentifications in the AD group; 53% of reported visual hallucinations were reclassifiable in the PD/LBD sample; extracampine hallucinations were only found in the Toxic/Rare groups; no auditory hallucinations occurred in the AD sample

The content of hallucinations

Teunisse et al (1996) describe the content of visual hallucinations in Charles Bonnet syndrome, and Ballard et al (1997) provide details of the types of hallucinations in LBD patients. Both sets of descriptions share many similarities with the types of hallucination described in Appendix 2.3, suggesting that there are common mechanisms for the production of some visual events.

However, we have not yet found an explanation for the very bizarre and frightening visual hallucination content of those with dementia who were toxic (infections and alcohol) or had brain tumours or rare types of dementia, suggesting that much remains to be known about the content and causation of the as yet undescribed palletes, or mixture of palettes of hallucinations in other dementias and illnesses.

Concluding discussion

Confusion in clinical practice about visual hallucinations: increased referrals of persons with visual hallucinations and diagnosing Lewy body dementia?

Findings from the Pilot and Main Study show that illusions, misperceptions and misidentifications are frequently mislabelled as hallucinations, not only in persons with AD but also in those with PD/LBD.

Our data suggest that there may be an increasing tendency to expect and find visual hallucinations in persons with dementia. The Main Study data contain (older) GP referrals from the past 8–9 years to an Old Age Psychiatry Service, whereas the data in the Pilot Study are referrals from the last calendar year. The Main Study showed that 12% of persons (91 of 755) were referred for 'hallucinations'. In the more recent Pilot Study this had doubled to 24% (60 of 250).

If this is because of the recent 'trend' to link the presence of 'presumed visual hallucinations' to LBD, it is in line with the findings of Serby and Almiron (2005), who found a 50% over-diagnosis of LBD on the basis of visual hallucinations.

They point out (p. 21) that visual hallucinations are said to occur 45% of the time in PD and 40% of the time in LBD, but if persons are on dopaminergic medications the reported hallucinations go up to 69% in PD and 64% in LBD. Both disorders show an increased sensitivity to neuroleptic medication. Recently, reports about the efficacy of cholinesterase inhibitors for such symptoms are accumulating (Cummings, 2000; Mosimann and McKeith 2003; Ffytche, 2004; Edwards et al, 2004).

Implications of mislabelling other types of visual events as hallucinations

The findings of our studies indicate that the differences between hallucinations and other visual events in dementing illnesses seem to be poorly understood and hence are not differentiated between. This leads to great over-reporting of hallucinations in AD and PD/LBD groups.

The immediate implications of this are that persons experiencing visual events other than hallucinations, with or without known visual pathology, may: miss out on opthalmological treatment and low-vision aids; be inappropriately treated with antipsychotic medication; and miss out on a detailed exploration of their incorrectly perceived, ever-changing world, accurate empathy, frequent reassurance and helpful communication, and appropriately adapted interpersonal interventions (they may instead be argued with, orientated to the facts).

The consequences of potentially mislabelling any visual event as hallucinatory (hence potentially psychotic) and subsequent administration of anticholinergic antipsychotic medication, which can further reduce already impaired cholinergic functioning in AD and PD, range from unhelpful to serious.

The need to describe a separate visual hallucination palette for Alzheimer's disease

Our data support Ffytche's (2004) observation that the nature of the 'presumed visual hallucinations' and other visual events reported in AD do not fit into the two major hallucination palettes, and that a combination of palettes (or separate palette) is required to describe them.

The findings suggest that future studies need to look for evidence of an order of progression of visual symptoms reported in AD to establish if there is a specific order of occurrence of illusions, misperceptions, misidentifications and hallucinations.

Possibly, reports stating that visual hallucinations cease in the 'moderate stage' of AD (Cronin-Golomb, 2004) have either not considered the possibility that other visual difficulties (perhaps also visual hallucinations) continue to occur throughout the AD process, or have not looked for them. Undoubtedly, given the increasing language and orientation difficulties that occur as AD progresses, it will be more difficult to ascertain their presence, and those working/living closest to persons with AD will need to provide accurate descriptions of specific visual behaviours to supplement research measures. This will require them to have knowledge of what they are reporting.

Implications of the literature and the findings of the Pilot and Main studies

Assessment of vision and visual events in dementias

Hyvarinen (2005a), writing for doctors and psychologists, is critical of existing visual testing for the elderly and elderly with cognitive deficits, and points out common testing errors. She says that 'acuity testing' is the starting point of all assessment, and that assessment should be done (or adapted) for the distance that is clearest. Likewise, 'contrast sensitivity testing' needs to establish how 'low' contrast details can be seen for the test distance.

She points out that agnosias are far more common than diagnosed, including facial recognition, expressions, sizes and direction of movement. When testing 'perception of expression' deficits, she notes that the assessor must find out whether loss of contrast sensitivity plays a role in this. She notes that some visual disturbances are not readily reported by the fragile elderly: '*Vascular accidents* in the retina or visual pathways cause patchy, sectorial or half field defects in the visual field. These may not be diagnosed for months or years if visual functions are not decreased so much that it would disturb the daily activities' (Hyvarinen, 2005a).

In addition to such adapted sight testing, those assessing visual events in the elderly with dementia need to be aware of factors such as medication, language ability and orientation level, which can affect the presence of and/or description of the visual event.

Appendix 2.1 offers an overview of information that may help the recording and assessing of such events.

Communication

Labelling a visual experience as a hallucination in someone with AD (when it is an illusion, misperception or misidentification) can have the consequence of inappropriate communication, as was shown earlier in the example of the lady thought to be seeing children but making tense errors in her speech, and also illustrated by examples of visual events reported by medical staff as hallucinations (in Box 2.4).

More research needed about the variety of visual phenomena in dementias

Already in 1986, Corbin and Eastwood raised the issue of the need to study the association between visual and auditory sensory deficits and so-called 'mental disorders' in old age. They emphasized that large sample sizes would be needed to study the relationship between the myriad of variables affecting this fragile population.

Perhaps the samples sizes will not have to be as large as they imagined, because we now have some idea of the variables involved. With the increased knowledge about visual deficits and range of visual phenomena in AD (and PD/ LBD), as well as the differing types of visual hallucination palettes (and increased possibilities for pharmacological and non-pharmacological treatment), additional 'stage-specific, dementia-specific' research would be timely for assisting this fragile population.

Education

If the real nature of the visuo-cognitive difficulties and visual phenomena in AD and other dementias are as varied and problematic as studies suggest, then there is a great need for increased education about them: how to name, assess, monitor and intervene to limit their effects. Diagnosticians need such education, and so do healthcare professionals and family carers involved in the care of those with dementia.

Education also needs to include practical suggestions to minimize illusions and misperceptions: e.g. Sweet (2002) mentions that many family members have hung mirrors backwards, to stop further illusions, which can be disorienting or distressing to persons with AD. (See Chapter 1 in this volume for other ideas.)

Such education needs to emphasize the potential fears and dangers inherent in having a visuo-cognitive illness, which causes the world of a person to be ever changing and inaccurate, despite the attempts of the person to understand it and cope with it 'as normal'.

Ultimately, the presence or absence of fear, in response to whatever is being seen/experienced (hallucination or other type of visual phenomena), is a key determinant of subsequent behaviour. In caring for persons with AD whose visuo-cognitive abilities are diminishing it is important to have some idea about the range of obstacles that persons may face, and hence to know that reassurances will need to be provided frequently, as well as ensuring the provision of a 'visually safe' engaging environment, and that despite such efforts there will be visual-cognitive phenomena that we must continue to try to find new ways to intervene for.

Appendix 2.1

Questionnaire to assess visual hallucinations, illusions, misperceptions and misIdentifications in persons with dementia (adapted from Jolyon West, 1975; Santhouse et al, 2000)

Background health questions

Any conditions/somatic illnesses that can cause visual difficulties?

Diabetes
Migraines/headaches
Epilepsy
Sleep disorders
Elevated blood pressure
Transient ischaemic attacks, strokes
Surgery for vascular disorders

Balance disorders (Menierre's)
Recent bereavement
Alcohol/recreational drug use
Major psychiatric illness?
Depression?
Other?

Is the person on any medications, if so which, how much and how often, and for how long?

The following can cause visual effects:

MISCELLANEOUS

Antimalarials
Cimetidine
Corticosteroids
Decongestants
Hydroxyurea
Khat
Ketamine
Megloquin
Phenylephrine
Phenylpropanolamine
Propmethazine
Pseudoephedrine
Ranitidine
Salbutamol
Sulphasalazine
Toterodine

EYE MEDICATION

Sympathomimetic eyedrops
Anticholinergic eyedrops e.g. atropine, homatropine, scopolamine, cyclopentolate

PSYCHOTROPIC DRUGS

Alcohol
Amphetamines
Benzodiazepines
Carbamazepine
Fluoxetine
Gabapentin
Impipramine
LSD
Maprotiline

Methadone
Midazolam
Nelazodone
Phenalzine
Tricyclics
Sodium valproate
Zolpidem
Zopiclone

CARDIOVASCULAR DRUGS

Beta-blockers
Clomidine
Digoxin
Diltiazem
Procainamide
Streptokinase
Timlol

NON-STEROIDAL ANTI-INFLAMMATORY DRUGS

Buprenorphine
Fenbufen
Indomethacin
Nefopam
Pentazocine
Salicylates
Tramadol

ANTI-INFECTION DRUGS

Amoxycillin
Ciprofloxacin
Gentamicin

ANTI-PARKINSON DRUGS

Amantadine
Anticholinergics
Bromocryptine
Levodopa
Pergolide

Present or past visual pathology?

1   Does the person have any known visual injury or pathology?
Cataracts   Diabetest-related retinal problems
Glaucoma   Last sight test
Macular degeneration   Acuity
Corrected now? What prescription lens?
Any current visual complaint?
2   What can this person *see* accurately? (Door? Furniture in room? Objects around?)
3   What can this person *read* accurately? (Wrist-watch face? Wall clock? Size of newspaper text?)
4   What can this person *describe* accurately?

Possible language difficulties affecting description of what is being seen

Does this person sometimes:

- lose the thread of their story?
- even with help, find it difficult to finish the story?
- sometimes make up an ending to 'save face'?
- use the wrong name for persons?
- have difficulty finding the right noun/ name for other objects?
- seem self-conscious about making mistakes and being forgetful?
- try to cover-up for such mistakes?
- have difficulty using past tense correctly? ('I see it', versus 'I saw it')
- assume that other persons are present and speaking about them in the present tense without actually seeing them?
- have difficulty using metaphors or similes correctly?
  ('Those frilly edged green pillows on the couch look just like cabbages' versus, 'Look at those cabbages')
- have difficulty finishing their sentences?
  (Is this because they speak slowly, have difficulty getting their words out, stutter, appear to be distracted or simply seem to forget what they were saying?)

Current eyesight difficulties and possible illusions

Does this person have difficulty:

- doing tasks in dimly/poorly lit surroundings?
- distinguishing between dark colours/pastel colours?
- mistaking patterned surfaces/carpets/walls/tables for real objects?
- seeing objects on a surface of the same/similar colour?
- mistaking shadows or changing colours/patterns on the flooring for obstacles or height changes in the floor?
- mistaking images/reflections in the mirror/TV/photos for others or real objects ?

Orientation information

Is this person oriented to:

- day, date, year, season?
- their relative age, current season?
- time of day?
- where they are?
- the identities of those around them?
- where they are?
- what is happening around them?
- what household tasks they normally perform?
- normal hygiene and toileting times?

Details of what was seen/experienced

INFORMATION OBTAINED FROM PERSON, CARER, OTHER WITNESS OR HEALTHCARE
PROFESSIONAL?

1   When did the unusual visual event/s occur (date)?
2   When did they start? When was the last one?
     Do you see multiple copies of the image at the same time? (in a row)
     Surfaces filled with objects, patterns or shapes?
     Does an image ever persist even when you look away? Or some time later?
3   What is the duration of such an episode?
     Seconds, minutes, hours, longer?
4   Was it close in time to another distinct event?
     After a recent illness, upsetting event, bereavement, medication change?
5   In what circumstances did/does it happen?
     When alone, with others, or both?
     In the morning, afternoon/evening/night/near meal-times
     Any time during the day
     Only in dimly lit rooms
     Near time of falling asleep near or after awakening
     After exercise or walking? After a nap?
6   Is there an obvious recent or past memory association to explain where such
     images might be coming from?
     Visions that start by motion (being in car, train, other?)
     Past dreams, nightmares, fantasies, reminiscences, traumatic recent events?

Visual pathway palette and brainstem/cholinergic palette descriptors

Flashes
Simple forms/small particles (raindrops, specks, snowflakes)
Colours
Lines/zig-zags
Patterns: geometric (brickwork, netting, honeycomb, lattice)
Patterns: organic (leaves, maps, branches, bushes)
Grids/matrices
Insects
Faces (Ugly, distorted prominent eyes or teeth)
Parts of persons (faces without bodies, bodies without faces)

Human figures in strange dress or costume or hats
Monsters
Landscapes
Person/persons
In costume? Other dress?
Small/normal size/large? . . . (known/unknown)
Deceased persons
Animals (unknown/like former pets)
Complex scenes
Other things: words, letters, musical notes or number?
   Children
   Food
   Furniture
   Machines
   Vehicles

DETAILS OF MORE COMPLEX IMAGES

- Are the images still or moving?
- If image is of persons, are the images doing anything?
- Are they silent, whispering or saying anything ?
- How are they dressed?
- How old/young or small/large do they appear to be?
- Are they familiar or not?
- Are the visions individual objects/figures or whole scenes?
- Do the visions change from one thing into another?
- Where does 'this vision' appear?
  (inside the person or in their body?, nearby externally, distant externally: in an object, room, house, garden?)
- How much of the visual field is taken up by the thing seen? Part or all?
- Is the image in front of you or in the corner of your eye?
- Do you also see the image with your eyes closed?
- Do the visions move if you move your head?

QUALITY OF THE VISUAL EVENT AND OTHER DESCRIPTORS

- How vivid/real/cartoon-like/otherwise, does it appear?
- Could you see through it?
- Was/is it clear or blurred?
- Any associated colour or black/white? Vague/strong?

OTHER SENSORY MODALITIES?

- Were you able to hear, feel, smell, taste or sense anything while you were seeing this?

ARE ANY OTHER UNUSUAL THINGS BEING REPORTED?

- Do you ever hear things while you have the vision?
- Do you ever taste, feel or smell things with the vision?
- Are the visions ever of bugs, small animals, snakes, insects?
- Does the experience frighten/affect you or your judgement?

CAN YOU MAKE THE IMAGE 'GO AWAY'?

- By approaching it, blinking/speaking to it, closing your eyes, clapping?
- Other?

Information to ask of others if not possible from the person

- Were you with the person when this visual event happened?
- If not, how did you hear about it? Reports of other?
- Does this person live alone or with others? What times of the day are they alone?
- Can/does the person point to where the image appears to be to them?
- Can the person describe what happened properly? Or do they struggle?
- Has the person told anyone else, or just you?
- Does the person's description of what was seen remain constant?
- Did they seem to be afraid/embarrassed about telling you?
- Are they afraid of being alone as a result of what they saw/are seeing?
- Did they indicate whether they were worried what people would think of them if they were thought to be hallucinating?
- Did the person say/imply that only they can see 'the thing being seen? (i.e. that the thing disappears when you or others are present, but when they are alone that it happens again?)
- Did you try telling the person that you could not see what they saw?
- If so, what was their reaction to your explanation?
- Does the person have ability to understand other possible explanations for what is/was being seen?
- If you explain that you do not see this, how do they react?
- Do they accept alternative explanations from you?
- What, if any other, idea or emotion is evoked by what is seen? (e.g. does seeing a reflection in a mirror, and interpreting it incorrectly cause the person to think there are others in the house?)
- Does the person acknowledge or deny that this visual experience is unusual, in that you/others cannot see it?
- Does this apply equally to others as well as to the first person they reported it to?
- Did the person acknowledge that maybe they were not 'seeing things correctly' or that their eyes were 'playing tricks' on them? or deny any such suggestion on your/others' part?
- Does the appearance of person/object seen affect the person's behaviours, emotions or immediate actions?

Appendix 2.2

The Pilot Study: frequency of hallucinations in patients with Alzheimer's disease referred to Old Age Psychiatry service by GPs

Background and Method

A computer search for keyword 'hallucinations' was done for all 250 case notes of persons newly diagnosed with dementia, within an old-age psychiatry practice, in a single calendar year (within the last three years). This term 'hallucination' was present in letters of referral from GPs requesting the service for patients. Sixty of the 250 files were found to contain a reference to hallucinations; these were read in detail and were further categorized by diagnosis, and then into visual event categories of illusions, misperceptions, misidentification, misinterpretations and hallucinations (as per the definitions earlier in this chapter).

Findings

Sixty files contained references to hallucinations. Thirty of these could be more accurately reclassified as illusion, misperception and misidentification errors in persons with 'probable AD'. The remaining 30 of these descriptions seemed to refer to genuine hallucinations: 25 were diagnosed with Parkinson's disease or Lewy body dementia; 5 had a 'probable' diagnosis of AD. Therefore, only 5 of the 225 (2.2%) persons initially referred to this service for further investigation for dementia symptoms, with a non-Lewy body or Parkinson-type dementia, were found to be persons with probable AD with apparently genuine hallucinations. Only 5 of the 35 (non-Parkinson Lewy body-type dementia) persons (14.3%) having 'probable AD with hallucinations' and originally documented as having hallucinations were found to have them after recategorization of the description of their visual symptoms. Thirty of the 35 persons (84.2%) who were initially documented as having hallucinations could be more accurately described as having some visual misperceptions or misidentifications.

In this sample, 50% of all GP case-note references to hallucinations could be more accurately described as illusions, misperceptions and misidentifications (see Figure 2.3).

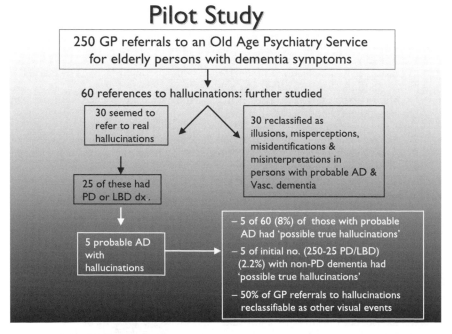

Figure 2.3 Pilot Study summary.

Discussion

These results suggest that once visual, linguistic assessment and contextual information is taken into account, hallucinations in AD occur with less frequency than is generally thought. It confirms that many visual phenomena experienced by persons with AD are placed into the category of hallucinations. It is not known how many of these events were linked to language difficulties because there was insufficient information recorded to determine this.

The findings of this pilot study are lower than the lowest estimates of persistent visual hallucinations in persons with AD in the literature: Ballard et al (2004), 18%; Burns et al (1990), 13%. These findings seem to concur with a recent consensus that visual hallucinations are reported more often for persons with LBD/PD than AD. (This brief study did not examine other visual phenomena in the PD group.)

Appendix 2.3

The Main Study: hallucinations versus misinterpretations, illusions, misperceptions and misidentifications in patients with dementia referred to an Old Age Psychiatry service

Background

In light of the Pilot Study results, a larger retrospective case-note study was conducted to look at the frequency and range of visual phenomena experienced by persons with AD compared to other conditions associated with hallucinations in the cognitively fragile elderly population. This study again looked at how often the word 'hallucination' occurred in GP referral letters and subsequent diagnoses.

Method

The 755 case notes from 8 years of consecutive referrals to an Old Age Psychiatry service in a region with a population of 60,000, in Berkshire, were examined. The case notes were searched for references to the mention of any hallucinations (visual, auditory, tactile or taste) in initial letters of referral by GPs. Ninety-one references to hallucinations at the time of referral were identified. The majority of persons were referred for specialist assessment because of their presumed hallucinations.

Diagnoses were classified under five categories: Toxic; Rare/other causes of disorientation (mostly brain tumours); AD; PD; and Vascular. The Toxic group comprised those with dementia and acute infectious (mostly urinary tract infections); three had infections as well as histories of cognitive impairment and alcohol abuse. The Rare group comprised those with brain tumours or secondary cancer to the brain and previous serious depressive illness history with present cognitive deterioration. The PD group was inclusive of those suspected of Lewy body dementia as well as those with Parkinson's features and cognitive decline (so as to avoid false-positive diagnosis *a priori* by diagnosing all those with suspect visual hallucinations into the Lewy body dementia group).

Hallucinations were defined as visual phenomena that are non-retinal in origin (not illusions or resultant from misperceptions or misidentification errors) and that a person believes to be real. Visual hallucinations were separated from auditory hallucinations and other non-hallucinatory visual events as per the definitions in Figure 2.1. Misinterpretations were considered to be faulty-thinking errors as a result of seeing incorrectly, or combining facts incorrectly with difficulty in recalling what was seen (or perhaps misperceived); we see this to be distinct from delusions, which are false 'beliefs' held despite logical persuasion attempts to the contrary in persons whose logical thinking and memory ability may not be damaged as it is in AD.

Notes of persons with AD were read for information to distinguish between hallucinations, illusions, misperceptions and misidentifications. Details about visual disability in the case notes were recorded and linked with the particular type of diagnosis, age, sex and any other information that seemed relevant.

Findings

OVERALL

On the basis of GP letters of referral to Old Age Psychiatry services, 12% (91 out of 755) of persons with some sort of dementia were thought to be hallucinating. Eighty-eight of the 91 files were read for specific details; 3 were not accessible. Details of a total of 99 visual events, 7 auditory events and 5 extracampine events were reported.

After separating out auditory and extracampine hallucinations and recategorizing all visual events that were non-hallucinatory, only 53% were found to be 'possible visual hallucinations'. Summary information of the sex, age and type of visual/hallucinatory events by diagnostic grouping are shown in Table 2.2.

Twenty-eight percent of the study population were male. The youngest person was 66 and had a pituitary tumour; the oldest person was 101 with probable AD. There were 99 visual events reported and 7 auditory hallucinations. Forty-six percent of all visual events reported by GPs as hallucinations could be more accurately recategorized as misinterpretations (13%), misperceptions (9%), illusions (4%), agnosias (14%) and extracampine (5%; visual and feeling; mixed sensory hallucinations).

In the AD group, 60% of visual events were mislabelled; in the PD group, 53% of events were mislabelled; in the Vascular group, 17%, in the Toxic group, 25%. No visual events were mislabelled in the rare dementia group. Details of the types and contents of the visual/hallucinatory events are given in Table 2.3.

1 Age
The AD group and Toxic groups were on average 5 years older than the Rare, PD and Vascular groups. The AD group was significantly older than the PD group (P <0.0005).

2 Vision
Poor vision was recorded for 8 persons on case notes: The 3 persons with AD (who had poor vision reported in the case notes) had hallucinations of 'people in the house', as did the person who was toxic. In the Rare dementia group, the person with poor vision had auditory hallucinations. In the PD group two of those with poor vision mistook TV images as being present in the room; the other mistook the patterns on floor carpeting as being real objects.

SUMMARY BREAKDOWN BY PHENOMENON

3 Simplest visual hallucination
The simplest and briefest hallucination was of a reported flash of light seen in a remote garden by a 74-year-old male with a confirmed occipital infarct.

Table 2.2 Summary overview of data showing the diagnostic breakdown and ages of all those cognitively frail elderly persons referred by GPs to Old Age Psychiatry service for any type of event referred to as a hallucination

	Toxic[a]	*Rare*[b]	*AD*	*PD*[c]	*Vascular*
No. persons in group	14	6	32	15	21
No. visual events in group (some persons had more than one event)	16	4	38	17	24
Mean age/SD	84.1/8.5	79.2/6.8	84.3/5.9	78.6/6.86	80.4/6.0
Males/females in group	5m/9f	1m/5f	7m/25f	7m/8f	8m/13f
No. cases with obvious visual difficulties recorded	1	1	3	3	0
No. possible real visual hallucinations	10	2	15	8	19
No. misinterpretations and incidents of mistaken thinking (delusions)	1	0	8	3	1
No. illusions	0	0	2	2	0
No. misperceptions	0	0	5	3	1
No. object agnosias	1	0	2	1	1
No. spouse agnosias	1	0	4	0	1
No. toy animal agnosias	1	0	2	0	0
No. auditory hallucinations	2	2	0	1	1
No. extracampine hallucinations (kinaesthetic multisense, i.e. feeling/seeing)	2	2	0	0	1
No./% fear reactions: phoning police, council, sleeping on floor, ordered spouse out of house	1/7%	2/33%	**6/19%**	1/7%	0/0%
No./% mislabelled visual hallucinations per group	4/25%	0/0%	**23/60%**	9/53%	4/17%

[a] Infections, mostly of the urinary tract.
[b] Brain tumours and serious past depressive illness.
[c] Includes possible LBD.

Table 2.3 Summary overview of the content of hallucinations by diagnostic group (some persons had more than one event)

	Toxic	Rare	AD	PD	Vascular
Possible real visual hallucinations about people (also possibly some misperceptions or misinterpretations)					
People in house/flat (non-specific)	5	I	10	3	9
People in room (non-specific)	2	I	2	I	5
'Little people'/'children' in room/house	0	0	2	0	0
People dancing in room	0	0	I	0	0
Dead family/friends seen in house/bed (hallucinations of bereavement?)	0	0	I	2	I bed
People in bed	0	0	I	0	0
Likely visual pathway palette-type hallucinations					
People up a tree/people having sex in a tree	0	0	0	0	2
People (naked) in house	0	0	0	0	I
People on a ship	I	0	0	0	0
Lumberjacks & emus in room	I	0	0	0	0
Light flash in a remote garden	0	0	0	0	I
Total no. visual hallucination events	9	2	17	6	19
Agnosias					
Spouse not recognized (imposter)	0	0	4	I	I
Objects not recognized (TV remote = shaver)	I	0	2	I	I
Toy animals thought to be real	I	0	2	0	0
Total no. agnosia errors	2	0	8	2	2
Misinterpretations/faulty thinking (delusions)					
People on property	0	0	0	2	0
People stealing or behaving suspiciously	0	0	4	I	I
Neighbours are irritating/noisy (parties/kids)	0	0	4	0	0
People physically having harmed/shot them	I	0	0	0	0
Misperceptions/illusions					
Photos/TV images seem real/present in room	0	0	2	2	0
Patterns/watermarks on carpet/walls	0	0	5	3	0
Auditory hallucinations					
Noises (from plug)	I	I	0	I	I
Family members talking from photo	I	0	0	0	0
Voices from own head	0	I	0	0	0
Extracampine/kinaesthetic					
Sees/feels flies/bugs/mites on skin & in mouth	2	2	0	0	I

4 The most commonly reported visual hallucinations
The vast majority of visual hallucinations were non-specific accounts of people in the house or room (89% of the 53 presumed real visual hallucinations).

5 Most complex visual hallucinations
The most complex though short-duration visual hallucinations were by persons in the Toxic/infectious and Rare dementia groups. These included seeing emus and lumberjacks in the room, and people (up trees, in ships and having sex in trees).

6 Hallucinations of bereavement
Four persons reported seeing dead family and friends, one of them in their bed. One person reportedly tried to kick her sister's ghost out of bed.

7 Auditory hallucinations
Seven auditory hallucinations were reported in total: none in the AD group, three in the Toxic group, two in the Rare dementia group, one in PD and one in the Vascular group.

8 Extracampine hallucinations
Five extracampine events were reported: none in the AD and PD groups, one in the Vascular groups, and two each in the Toxic and Rare groups.

9 Agnosias
Fourteen events were incorrect identifications of spouses, objects and stuffed toy animals. None occurred in the Rare dementia group, two each in the Toxic, PD and Vascular groups and eight in the AD group.

10 Misinterpretations (faulty thinking and remembering)
These events included persons thinking that others were stealing from them or behaving suspiciously, neighbours being annoying and noisy and people on the property. One person (in the Toxic group) reported that someone had shot them. Thirteen such supposed incidents were reported in total: none in the Rare dementia group, one in each of the Toxic and Vascular groups, three in the PD group and eight in the AD group.

11 Misperceptions and illusions
These events included misperceiving photos, TV images and reflections as being real persons; also mistaking patterns and watermarks on carpets and walls as being real objects. Twelve such events were found: none in the Toxic, Rare and Vascular dementia groups, five in the PD group and seven in the AD group.

12 Fear reactions
There were ten reports of fear reactions to a range of visual events. One person in the Toxic group was reportedly 'very frightened' of people in the room. Two persons in the Rare group were frightened (one called the council about flies, the other hid their money from supposed people in the flat). In the AD group there were six fear reactions noted (one slept on the floor because of someone thought to be in their bed, one ordered his wife out of the house, one was too frightened to go into the room, one called the police, one was afraid of a supposed bomb somewhere outside and one was afraid of the neighbours). In the PD group, one person called the police about people

in the house. In the Vascular group, one person tried to kick her sister's ghost out of the bed.

13 Toxic group

In this group of 14, half of all persons had 'likely visual hallucinations' of people in the house or room. Two events seemed to fit Ffytche's 'visual pathway palette hallucination description'. They were of implausible scenes of persons on a ship and lumberjacks and emus in the room. One person used a toothbrush as a razor (object agnosia) and one person had complex extracampine hallucinations and reported seeing/feeling worms, and 'hairs from fingers', as well as hearing voices. There was one auditory event reported of 'a person's son talking to them from a photo'.

14 Rare group

In this group of six, two persons had 'likely visual hallucinations' of people in the house or room, two had auditory hallucinations and two had extracampine hallucinations of mite and fly infestations they could see and feel. One called the council about the fly infestation. One of the auditory hallucinations was sensed as voices in the person's own head and the other was of non-specific 'noises'. There were no obvious 'visual pathway palette type hallucinations' in this group.

15 AD group

In this group of 32, 17 persons had 'likely visual hallucinations' of people in the house or room. None had auditory or extracampine hallucinations. Eight had agnosias, eight had misinterpretations and seven had misperceptions and illusions. There were no obvious 'visual pathway palette type hallucinations' in this group.

16 PD group

In this group of 15, six persons had 'likely visual hallucinations' of people in the house or room. One had auditory and none had extracampine hallucinations. Two had agnosias, three had misinterpretations and five had misperceptions and illusions. There were no obvious 'visual pathway palette type hallucinations' in this group.

17 Vascular group

In this group of 21, 15 persons had 'likely visual hallucinations' of people in the house or room. One had auditory and one had extracampine hallucinations. Two had agnosias, one had misinterpretations and none had misperceptions and illusions. There were four possible 'visual pathway palette type hallucinations' in this group (light flash in a garden, people in a tree, people having sex in a tree and naked people in the house).

Discussion

Visual events of all sorts, including what we have called genuine hallucinations, occurred in 13.6% of the total population in this study. This is in keeping with the estimates of Burns et al (1990) for the total number of hallucinations in the AD population, but it does not fit with our estimate of visual hallucinations in the AD group. Our findings of the number of visual hallucinations in the AD group are lower than the literature suggests. (Even if 60% of the total initial population of 755 in this study had 'probable AD' then only 3% of this populations had visual hallucinations. This is close to the findings of the pilot study reported above.) Of the 32 persons with AD reported to have visual events, only 15 of these were found to have 'possible visual hallucinations'.

Of all the events reported by GPs as visual hallucinations (in the total population referred to Old Age Psychiatry services) 46% were not found to be genuine visual hallucinations but were recategorized as other types of visual phenomena; 59% and 60% of visual events (illusions, misperceptions, misidentifications/agnosias and mis-interpretations) were mislabelled as hallucinations by GPs in the Parkinson's and AD groups, respectively. The GP estimates of visual hallucinations in the Rare, Toxic and Vascular groups were reasonably accurate (a range of 0% to a maximum of 25% mislabelled).

Although mislabelling was expected in the AD group on the basis of the pilot study, the degree of mislabelling in the PD group was not anticipated. (With numerous studies having found higher levels of visual hallucinations in PD/Lewy body dementia than AD, it was surprising to find that many of the events reported for this group could also be recategorized as non-hallucinatory visual events. These led us to question how much misunderstanding there is of the visual events in PD-type illnesses and how many persons have been diagnosed with possible Lewy body dementia as a result of incorrectly labelled 'visual hallucinations'. These findings suggest the need for further study of such visual events in persons with PD/Lewy body dementia, especially since neuroleptic medication can be detrimental to their occurrence.

There were qualitative differences between the AD group compared with the Vascular, Rare and Toxic groups, in that no auditory and extracampine events were found in the AD group; neither were there any events typical of 'visual pathway palette' hallucinations. The visual hallucinations of persons who were in the Toxic and Rare groups seem to be, overall, of a more bizarre and fearful nature than the events experienced by persons in other diagnostic groups.

It is likely that the population studied (those referred to special Old Age Psychiatry services by their GPs) is not representative of the overall population of persons with dementia in the community (who were not referred to specialist services). Presumably the population studied was more fragile and had a more complex presentation of symptoms or were widowed or living alone without adequate support. The mean age of the AD group in this study lends support to this. (Anecdotally we know there are older persons with dementia in the community and in care facilities who also experience similar visual phenomena but whose families/care-givers do not see these as problematic.) This study did not examine whether the persons were living on their own or alone for long portions of the day. Presumably those who do not have the distractions or frequent reassurances of others to allay their fears come primarily to the attention of GPs with complaints from neighbours and visiting relatives when circumstances are more likely to be in a crisis state.

References

Arnold, S.E., Hyman, B., Flory, J., Damasio, A. and van Hoesen, G. (1991) The topographical and neuroanatomical distribution of neurofibrillary tangles and neuritic plaques in the cerebral cortex of patients with Alzheimer's disease. *Cerebral Cortex*, 1: 103–116.

Ballard, C., McKeith, I., Harrison, R., O'Brien, J., Thompson, P., Lowery, K., Perry, R. and Ince, P. (1997) A detailed phenomelogical comparison of complex visual hallucinations in dementia with Lewy Bodies and Alzheimer's disease. *International Psychogeriatrics*, **9**: 381–388.

Ballard, C.G., Jacoby, R., Del Ser, T., Khan, N., Munoz, D.G., Holmes, C., et al (2004) Neuropathological substrates of psychiatric symptoms in prospectively studied patients with autopsy-confirmed dementia with Lewy Bodies. *American Journal of Psychiatry*, **161**: 843–849.

Braak, H. and Braak, E. (1998) Evolution of neuronal changes in the course of Alzheimer's disease. *Journal of Neural Transmission Supplement*, **53**.

Braak, H., de Vos, R.A., Jansen, E.N., Bratzke, H. and Braak, E. (1998) Neuropathological hallmarks of Alzheimer's and Parkinson's diseases. *Progress in Brain Research*, **117**: 801–819.

Burns, A. (1999) Fact Sheet 7. Psychiatric and behavioural disturbances in dementia. *Alzheimer's Disease International*, **March**.

Burns, A., Jacoby, R., and Levy, R. (1990) Psychiatric phenomena in Alzheimer's disease. II: Disorders of perception. *British Journal of Psychiatry*, **157**: 76–81.

Clare, L (2004a) The construction of awareness in early-stage Alzheimer's disease: a review of concepts and models. *British Journal of Clinical Psychology*, **43**: 155–175.

Clare, L (2004b) Awareness in early-stage Alzheimer's disease: a review of methods and evidence. *British Journal of Clinical Psychology*, **43**: 177–196.

Clark, V.P., Keil, K., Maisog, J., Courtney, S., Ungerleider, L. and Haxby, J. (1996) Functional magnetic resonance imaging of human visual cortex during face matching: a comparison with positron emission tomography. *Neuroimage*, **4**: 1–15.

Cline, D., Hofstetter, H.W. and Griffin, J.R (1980) *Dictionary of Visual Science* (3rd edn). Kadnor, PA: Chilton Book Co.

Corbin, S.L. and Eastwood, M. R. (1986) Sensory deficits and mental disorders of old age: causal or coincidental associations? *Psychological Medicine*, **16**: 251–256.

Cormack, F., Tovee, M. and Ballard, C. (2000) Contrast sensitivity and visual acuity in patients with Alzheimer's disease. *International Journal of Geriatric Psychiatry*, **15**: 614–620.

Critchley, M. (1951) Types of visual perseveration: 'paliopsia' and 'illusory visual spread'. *Brain*, **74**: 267–299.

Cronin-Golomb, A. (2001) Color vision, object recognition and spatial localization in aging and Alzheimer's disease. In P.R. Hof and C.V. Mobbs (Eds), *Functional Neurobiology of Aging*. San Diego: Academic Press, pp. 517–529.

Cronin-Golomb, A. (2004) *Vision in Alzheimer's Disease*. London: Karger.

Cronin-Golomb, A. and Amick, M. (2001) Spatial abilities in aging, Alzheimer's disease and Parkinson's disease. In F.Boller and S. Cappa (Eds), *Handbook of Neuropsychology* (2nd edn), vol. 6. Amsterdam: Elsevier Science, pp. 119–143.

Cummings, J.L. (2000) Cholinesterase inhibitors: a new class of psychotropic compounds. *American Journal of Psychiatry*, **157**: 4–15.

Curcio, C.A. and Drucker, D.N. (1993) Retinal ganglion cells in Alzheimer's disease and aging. *Annals of Neurology*, **33**: 248–257.

Deutsch Lezak, M. (1995) *Neuropsychological Assessment*. Oxford: Oxford University Press.

Edwards, K., Hershey, L., Wray, L., Bednarczyk, E., Lichter, D., Farlow, M. and Johnson, S. (2004) Efficacy and safety of galantamine in patients with dementia with Lewy bodies: a 12-week interim analysis. *Dementia Geriatrics and Cognitive Disorders*, **17**: 40–48.

Feil, N. (1982) Edward Feil Productions, 4614 Prospect Rd., Cleveland, OH.

Ffytche, D.H. (2004) Visual hallucination and illusion disorders: a clinical guide. *Advances in Clinical Neuroscience and Rehabilitation*, **4**: 16–18.

Ffytche, D.H. and Howard, R.J. (1999) The perceptual consequences of visual loss: 'positive' pathologies of vision. *Brain*, **122**: 1247–1260.

Haxby, J.V., Grady, C.L., Horwitz, B., Ungerleider, L.G., Mishkin, M., Carson, R.E., et al (1991) Dissociation of object and spatial visual processing pathways in human extrastriate cortex. *Procedures of the National Academy of Science*, USA, **88**, 1621–1652.

Haxby, J.V., Horwitz, B., Ungerleider, L.G., Maisog, J.M., Pietrini, P. and Grady, C.L. (1994) The functional organization of human extrastriate cortex: a PET-rCBF study of selective attention to faces and locations. *Journal of Neuroscience*, **14**: 1636–1653.

Hinton, D., Sadun, A., Blanks, J. and Miller, C. (1986) Optic nerve degeneration in Alzheimer's disease. *New England Journal of Medicine*, **315**: 485–487.

Hippius, H. and Neundorfer, G. (2003) The discovery of Alzheimer's disease. *Dialogues of Clinical Neuroscience*, **5**: 101–108.

Hof, P. R., Vogt, B. A., Bouras, C. and Morisson, J. H. (1997) Atypical form of Alzheimer's disease with prominent posterior cortical atrophy: a review of lesion distribution and circuit disconnection in cortical visual pathways. *Vision Research*, **37**: 3609–3622.

Holtzer, R., Tang, J., Devanand, D., Albert, S., Wegesin, D., Marder, K., Bell K., Albert, M., Brandt J. and Stern, Y. (2003) Psychopathological features in Alzheimer's disease: course and relationship with cognitive status. *Journal of the American Geriatrics Society*, **51**: 953–960.

Hyvarinen, L. (2005a) *Changes in Vision in Old Age*. http://www.lea-test.fi/en/eyes/old.html.

Hyvarinen, L. (2005b) *Visual Pathways Lecture*. http://www.lea-test.fi/en/assessme/comenius/pathways.html.

Jeste, D.V. and Finkel, S.I. (2000), Psychosis of Alzheimer's disease and related dementias. Diagnostic criteria for a distinct syndrome. *American Journal of Geriatric Psychiatry*, **8**: 29–34.

Jolyon West, L. (1975) A clinical and theoretical overview of hallucinatory phenomena. In R.K. Siegel and L. Jolyon West (Eds), *Hallucinations*. Chichester: John Wiley, pp. 287–311.

Jones, G.M.M. (2004) The loss of meaningful attachments and objects in dementia behavioural stage-specific implications. In G.M.M. Jones and B.M.L. Miesen (Eds), *Care-giving in Dementia*. Hove: Brunner-Routledge, pp. 261–284.

Jones, G.M.M. and Burns, A. (1992) Reminiscing disorientation theory. In G.M.M. Jones and B.M.L. Miesen (Eds), *Care-giving in Dementia*, vol. 1. London: Routledge, pp. 57–76.

Kapur, S. (2003) Psychosis as a state of aberrant salience: a framework linking biology, phenomenology, and pharmacology in schizophrenia. *American Journal of Psychiatry*, **160**: 13–23.

Katz, B. and Rimmer, S. (1989) Ophthalmologic manifestations of Alzheimer's disease. *Surveys in Ophthalmology*, **34**: 31–43.

Kluver, H. (1966) *Mescal and Mechanisms of Hallucination*. Chicago: University of Chicago Press.

Koenig Coste, J. (2003) *Learning to Speak Alzheimer's*. London: Vermillion.

Kuljis, R. and Tikoo, R. (1997). Discontinuous distribution of senile plaques within striate cortex hyper columns in Alzheimer's disease. *Vision Research*, **37**: 3573–3589.

Larousse (1995) *Dictionary of Science and Technology*. New York: Larousse Publications.

Loffler, K. U., Edward, D. P. and Tso, M. O. M. (1995). Immunoreactivity against tau, amyloid precursor protein, and beta-amyloid in the human retina. *Investigative Ophthalmology and Visual Science*, **36**: 24–31.

Manford, M. and Andermann, F. (1998) Complex visual hallucination; clinical and neurobiological insights. *Brain*, **121**: 1819–1840.

Mapstone, M., Rosler, A., Hays, A., Gitelman, D.R. and Weintraub, S. (2001) Dynamic allocation of attention in aging and Alzheimer disease: uncoupling of the eye and mind. *Archives of Neurology*, **58**: 1443–1447.

Martin, J. (2002) The integration of neurology, psychiatry, and neuroscience in the 21st century. *American Journal of Psychiatry*, **159**: 659–704.

Mavromatis, A. (1987) *Hypnagogia*. London: Routledge & Keagan Paul.

Miesen, B.M.L. (1992) Attachment theory in dementia. In: G.M.M. Jones and B.M.L. Miesen (Eds), *Care-giving in Dementia*, vol. 1. London: Routledge, pp. 38–56.

Mosimann, U. and McKeith, I. (2003) Dementia with Lewy bodies – diagnosis and treatment of cognitive and neuropsychiatric features. *Swiss Medical Weekly*, **133**: 131–142.

Nobili, L. and Sannita, W. (1997) Cholinergic modulation, visual function and Alzheimer's dementia. *Vision Research*, **37**: 3559–3567.

Ohayon, M.M. (2000) Prevalence of hallucinations and their pathological associations in the general population. *Psychiatry Research*, **97**: 153–164.

Ohayon, M.M. and Schatzberg, A.F. (2002) Prevalence of depressive episodes with psychotic features in the general population. *American Journal of Psychiatry*, **159**: 1855–1861.

Ohayon, M.M., Priest, R.G., Caulet, M. and Guilteminault, C. (1996) Hypnagogic and hypnopompic hallucinations: pathological phenomena? *British Journal of Psychiatry*, **169**: 459–467.

Ostling, S. and Skoog, I. (2002) Psychotic symptoms and paranoid ideation in a nondemented population-based sample of the very old. *Archives of General Psychiatry*, **59**: 53–59.

Ostling, S., Adreasson, L.A. and Skoog, I. (2003) Basal ganglia and psychotic symptoms in the very old. *International Journal of Geriatric Psychiatry*, 18: 983–987.

Pankow, L., Pliskin, N. and Luchins, D. (1996) An optical intervention for visual hallucinations associated with visual impairment and dementia in elderly patients. *Journal of Neuropsychiatry*, **8**: 88–92.

Paulsen, J.S., Salmon, D.P., Thal, L.J., Romero, R., Weisstein-Jenkins, C., Galasko, D., et al (2000) Incidence of and risk factors for hallucinations and delusions in patients with probable AD. *Neurology*, **54**: 1965–1971.

Perry, E.K. and Perry, R.H. (1995) Acetylcholine and hallucinations: disease-related compared to drug-induced alterations in human consciousness. *Brain Cognition*, **28**: 240–58.

Pitt, B. (1974) *Psychogeriatrics: an Introduction to the Psychiatry of Old Age*. London: Churchill Livingstone.

Rabins, P.V. (1994). Delirium. *Maryland Medical Journal*, **43**: 145–147.

Religa, D., Laudon, H., Styczynska, M., Winblad, B., Naslund, J. and Haroutunian, V. (2003) Amyloid beta pathology in Alzheimer's disease and schizophrenia. *American Journal of Psychiatry*, **160**: 811–814.

Ronch, S. (1989) *Alzheimer's Disease: a Practical Guide to Those who Help Others*. New York: Continuum Books.

Sadun, A. (1989) The optic neuropathy of Alzheimer's disease. *Pediatric Systems of Ophthalmology*, **12**: 64–68.

Sadun, A., Borchert, M., DeVita, E., Hinton, D. and Bassi, C. (1987). Assessment of visual impairment in patients with Alzheimer's disease. *American Journal of Opthalmology*, **104**: 113–120.

Santhouse, A., Howard, R. and Ffytche, D. (2000) Visual hallucinatory syndromes and the anatomy of the visual brain. *Brain*, **123**: 2055–2064.

Serby, M. and Almiron, N. (2005) Dementia with Lewy bodies: an overview. *Annals of Long-Term Care*, **13**: 20–22.

Sidgewick, H., Johnson, A., Myers, F.W.H., et al (1894) Report on the census of hallucinations. *Proceedings of the Society for Psychical Research*, **34**: 25 39.

Siegel, R. and West, L.J. (1975) *Hallucinations*. New York: John Wiley.

Staff, R., Shanks, M., Macintosh, L., Pestell, S., Gemmell, H. and Venneri, A. (1999) Delusions in Alzheimer's disease: SPECT evidence of right hemispheric dysfunction. *Cortex*, **35**: 549–560.

Stedman, T. L. (1982) *Illustrated Stedman's Medical Dictionary* (24th edn). Cincinnati, OH: Anderson.

Sultzer, D., Brown, C., Madelkern, M., Mahler, M., Mendez, M., Chen, S. and Cummings, J. (2003) Delusional thoughts and regionalfrontal/temporal cortex metabolism in Alzheimer's disease. *American Journal of Psychiatry*, **160**: 341–765.

Sumner, P. and Mollon, J.D. (2001) Exogenous orienting of attention to stimuli visible only to short-wave-sensitive cones: a test of collicular mediation. *Experimental Psychology Society Meeting*, Bristol, 2001 (http://www.eps.ac.uk/meetings/prog0401.html).

Sweet, R. (2002) Taking a new look at psychosis in Alzheimer's disease. *Psychiatric Times*, **19**: 1–7.

Sweet, R. (2004) Web page for the University of Pittsburgh, Department of Psychiatry, Sweet Laboratory: http://www.wpic.pitt.edu/research/sweetlab/postmortem.htm.

Teunisse, R., Cruysberg, J., Hoefnagels, W., Verbeek, A. and Zitman, F. (1996) Charles Bonnet's Syndrome: CBS. *Lancet*, **347**: 794–797.

Van Rhijn, S., Glosser, G., de Vries, J., Clark, C.M., Newberg, A. and Alavi, A. (2004) Visual processing impairments and decrements in regional brain activity in Alzheimer's disease. *Journal of Clinical and Experimental Neuropsychology*, **26**: 11–23.

Venneri, A. and Shanks, M. (2004) Belief and awareness: reflections on a case of persistent anosognosia. *Neuropsychologia*, **42**: 230–238.

Verhey, F.R., Jolles, J., Ponds, R.W., Rozendaal, N., Plugge, L.A., de Vet, R.C., Vreeling, F.W. and van der Lugt, P.J. (1993) Diagnosing dementia: a comparison between a monodisciplinary and a multidisciplinary approach. *Journal of Neuropsychiatry and Clinical Neuroscience*, **5**: 78–85.

Chapter 3

Attachment in dementia
Bound from birth?

Bère Miesen

In memory of Joep Munnichs (1927–2000), teacher and friend

Summary and overview

This chapter starts with a fairly detailed introduction to Bowlby's attachment theory, as a way of moving on to show the usefulness of the 'attachment' concept to understanding behaviour in old age, and in particular to the field of care-giving in dementia (see Box 3.1 for a brief summary of Bowlby's work). The link between these areas has to do with 'attachment history'.

Box 3.1 A summary of Bowlby's attachment theory

Attachment behaviour is any behaviour that aims to achieve or maintain the proximity of an **attachment figure**. Attachment develops on the basis of the different ways in which attachment figures respond to the attachment behaviour of the young child. This attachment can take various forms. These forms of attachment are referred to as **attachment patterns**. The most important patterns that can be distinguished are: secure attachment, anxious/avoidant attachment and anxious/ambivalent attachment. These patterns are internalized by the child and form an integral part of the individual's personality. In other words, these attachment patterns have future effects (prospective). Such 'internal working models' are used to determine the way in which individuals deal not only with themselves and others, but also with the (threatening) loss of people who are (have become) important to them. From the perspective of old age – retrospectively – it can therefore be said that a person's **attachment history** is extremely important to an understanding of the behaviour of older individuals.

In 1986 I interviewed the then 79-year-old John Bowlby at the Tavistock Centre in London. Here are some memorable quotes from that interview:

> 'Attachment' is not a characteristic but a property of the relationship (. . .) There are many reasons why patterns once developed tend to persist. (. . .) But I do want to emphasize, although it does tend to persist in the ordinary course of events, it need not – it is not inevitable. (. . .) I am using attachment to mean a pattern of behaviour, which is care-seeking and care-eliciting from an individual who feels they are less capable of dealing with the world than the person to whom they are seeking care. (. . .) I have a very strong impression that these patterns do continue and that we do meet with them in adult life (. . .) You might say the securely attached, and I think the secure versus insecure versus unattached, is a pattern – it's an organization of the personality which a person tends to take through life. (. . .) Danger activates attachment behaviour and in dangerous conditions people do make relationships of a more intense sort than they would ordinarily do. (. . .) we have good reason to think that healthy personalities – they are not invulnerable to adverse events – but they can manage adverse events better than others. Mentally healthy people are people who have had a history of secure attachment and who are capable of making secure attachments and are likely to be securely attached in the present day.

Bowlby's Attachment Theory

Anyone who has had the chance to study John Bowlby's classic trilogy *Attachment and Loss* (Bowlby, 1969, 1973, 1980) will conclude that much of what Bowlby suggests about attachment actually relates to the (grieving) behaviour of individuals, young or old, when confronted with the (threatened) loss of an emotional link with people who are important to them. The direct consequences of a dementing illness on families, partners and also the persons with dementia themselves results in an often expected but very tough confrontation with a similar (threatening) loss of attachment.

After World War II, John Bowlby, an English child and family psychiatrist with a psychoanalytical background, started to research one of the terrible effects of the war on the millions of orphaned children in Europe. He studied the consequences of the loss of such family connections on their personality development. This research was grounded by his previous experience in studying the psychological consequences of unstable nurturing situations on young children.

van Dijken (1997) proposed in her dissertation that separation problems can be seen as the central theme of Bowlby's work and that experiences from his own childhood must have made him sensitive to these. de Ruiter (1993) wrote a historical review in 'De Psycholoog' ('The Psychologist') of

---

Box 3.2 Ethology as a basis for the attachment theory

Bowlby's theory, inspired by ethologists like Lorenz and Harlow is actually a biology-based development theory, in the same way that Chomsky's theory of inherent language ability relates to dynamic system theory. Ethology studies the behaviour of people and animals from an ontogenetic, evolutionary perspective. It proposes patterns to explain aggressive behaviour and stress reactions and focuses primarily on instinctive behaviour. In other words, behaviour that is not learned but is inherent, and has a marked survival function. The field of ethology stresses that we can only comprehend certain human behaviour patterns in their original context or application. This is specifically the original ethological context in which the behaviour started and reached its conclusion.

---

the origins of Bowlby's attachment theory. She also summarized the research inspired by this theory. In doing so she mentioned Bowlby's most significant assumption, that everyone is equipped from birth with what is referred to as 'attachment behaviour', the behaviour used to achieve the proximity of the nurturer. Box 3.2 makes the link to the ethological basis for this work.

Attachment theory outlines the development of the attachment between young children and their parents. It offers an insight into the possible consequences of the absence of 'secure attachment'. In his books Bowlby also describes the disruptions that occur in the forging of enduring emotional links as a result of a lack of secure attachment in early childhood or its sudden disappearance (separation). According to de Ruiter, Bowlby's attachment theory is an important integrational theory of personality development, not just because the theory itself integrates ethology (see Box 3.2), system theory and psychodynamic insight, but also because the theory places social, emotional and cognitive development in one context.

Attachment behaviour

Any behaviour that aims to secure or retain the proximity of an attachment figure (father, mother or carer) and the associated 'caring behaviour' is described by Bowlby as 'attachment behaviour'. He refers to behaviours such as (occasional) exchanges of looks or words, checking someone by watching or listening (monitoring), going away and coming back, chasing after someone (continually), touching, turning to the attachment figure, smiling and laughing, beckoning, reaching for someone, clinging, crying, calling, screaming, etc. According to him all these forms of attachment behaviour retain their vital function throughout a person's entire life history and extend beyond parent/children contacts. He sees attachment behaviour as an inherent part of human nature, not related to age or a specific phase of life.

You do not learn attachment behaviour, you are born with it. The behaviour is potentially there from the cradle to the grave but becomes manifest or explicit in certain conditions, circumstances or situations. Individuals use attachment behaviour from childhood to forge affective links. This instinctive seeking for an attachment figure, when threatened with danger or loss, is clearest during childhood and old age, according to Bowlby. The caring behaviour that this elicits in the attachment figure does not just occur between child and parent(s) but also mutually between adults, e.g. between partners, and this occurs primarily in situations of diminishing health, stress and in old age. According to Bowlby, the occurrence of intense attachment behaviour in (older) adults does not indicate psychopathology or regression but rather a natural reaction, often coloured by a specific attachment pattern or the attachment history of an individual.

Attachment

Note that there is a difference between the concept of 'attachment behaviour' as described above and the concept of 'attachment'.

Attachment is the emotional link that an individual forges or has with someone. The quality of this link may vary. These variations in attachment are also called 'attachment patterns'. According to Bowlby, attachment is an intrapsychological, interpersonal and relational phenomenon. Attachment may be understood as a basic human quality that comes into being in early life and continues to play a role in the subsequent (personality) development of an individual. According to him, psychopathology is principally due to developmental abnormalities in the forging of affective links, particularly if secure attachments are not developed, for whatever reason. The way in which the parent or carer reacts to the attachment behaviour of the child (i.e. the nurturing style or responsiveness of the parent) determines the quality of the attachment. 'Responsiveness' may be understood as being aware of the emotional needs of the child and responding appropriately to them. The quality of this interaction between young child and parent determines whether or not secure attachment is established with the parent.

Table 3.1 Attachment patterns related to nurturing style

Nurturing style	Attachment pattern
Consistently responsive	Secure attachment
Consistently non-responsive (rejecting)	Anxious/avoidant attachment
Inconsistently responsive	Anxious/ambivalent attachment

Sources: Ainsworth et al (1978); de Ruiter (1993).

The individual must experience security in order to be able to develop the healthy psychological and cognitive competence needed to be able to adapt to changing (need) situations. The quality of this link with the parent is later internalized. Such a basic feeling of security leads, for example, to explorative behaviour in which principally the person's experience of their own effectiveness and their perception of support are tested. Am I successful in what I do? Do I get help when I ask for it? Positive responses to both questions have proved to be important components in personality development but not every individual takes this basic feeling with them in their subsequent development.

Attachment patterns

John Bowlby's attachment theory focuses on observable behaviour and explains this behaviour in terms of its adaptive function with respect to the (social) environment. If the individual, for whatever reason, fails to adapt to changed (life) circumstances, this generates tension or stress. Mary Ainsworth and her colleagues (Ainsworth et al, 1978) observed young children in an experimental but naturally occurring stress situation in which children were separated from their parents. This experiment became well known as the 'strange situation'. They studied the way the young children coped with the separation anxiety that was created when separated from the attachment figure, and concluded that there was a difference in the quality of this attachment. Also based on this experiment, Bowlby concluded that secure and insecure attachment patterns can occur between young children and parents, depending on the way the caring parent responds to certain signals from the young child – referred to above as responsiveness. These attachment patterns are secure attachment, anxious/avoidant attachment and anxious/ambivalent attachment (see Box 3.3). In other words, there are different qualities of parental management of children. The level of responsiveness and nurturing style of the parents may vary and these differences lead to differences in the quality of emotional links between child and parent. These links too are associated with specific behaviour patterns. If, for example, a child is frequently ignored when it cries – crying is attachment behaviour – the child forms (an image of) a link with a rejecting parent. This can lead to the child seeing itself as unloved or worthless. These differences in attachment of children to parents become visible in the different reactions of the children on separation (see Box 3.3).

Consequences of attachment patterns

During the course of their subsequent development, children internalize the way in which their parents dealt with them. They internalize their parents' way of dealing with their separation anxiety. On the basis of their daily interaction with carers, young children form a 'mental image' of these

---

Box 3.3 Attachment patterns in young children

Mary Ainsworth differentiated between three types of attachment in young children. She generally classified the three types as A, B or C.

Type A children are children with anxious/avoidant attachment. They never really seek the proximity of the parent and generally pay little attention to the parent's return. These children seem only to be concerned with their toys or are generally apathetic.

Type B children are children with a secure attachment. They feel secure with a trust-inspiring parent, even when they feel stressed because the parent leaves them alone or with a stranger. They may frequently cry when left alone but are generally soon comforted and quickly go on to explore their surroundings with great confidence. Type B children show no real avoidant or ambivalent behaviour, unlike type C children, who seem to be completely ambivalent when their mothers return after a separation.

The anxious/ambivalent type C children may cling onto their parents on their return or demonstrate panic behaviour, while affectionate behaviour on the part of the parent may be rejected at almost the same time. These children are often much more difficult to comfort and are less likely to explore their surroundings calmly. They seem to protest against the parent who 'left them in the lurch'.

(Verhofstadt-Denève et al, 1998, p. 78)

---

relationships with their carers. Bowlby calls these the children's 'internal working models'. According to Verhofstadt-Denève et al (1998):

> Parents, who can comfort their children effectively in situations of panic, distress or after separation, reinforce in their children the idea that their behaviour and feelings are recognized. Attachment thus develops into a powerful factor within the thoughts and feelings of the children. (. . .) The children operate with certain feelings, images and expectations relating to the behaviour of others and their effectiveness.

This means that these behaviour patterns become an integral part of the personality or the self. Children learn to have confidence in their parents but they also develop a feeling of confidence in themselves. Attachment patterns in turn affect the way in which individuals deal with forging new emotional links and/or the disappearance of these links later in their own lives. In his theory of grief, Bowlby describes at length the consequences of loss, the reaction of the individual to it and the state of tension and pain resulting from loss. According to Bowlby, the first reaction to threatening loss is always protest and anger, acute physiological tension and emotional pain. He then describes all the phases of the grieving process.

According to de Ruiter (1993), later researchers such as van Ijzendoorn (1994), using meta-analyses of, for example, 'cross-cultural research' and research into 'intergenerational transfer', showed that once a person is insecurely attached the likelihood is great (approximately 70%) that this person will remain so throughout life. This confirms Bowlby's conviction that attachment patterns persist to a certain degree: '(. . .) patterns once developed tend to persist. (. . .) But (. . .) it is not inevitable.'

Research has also shown that attachment patterns affect play behaviour, symbolic play, task-solving behaviour, conflict-resolving behaviour, people's belief in their own effectiveness, choice of partner, self-confidence, feeling of competition, anxiety, depression, support-seeking behaviour in stress situations (daring to ask for help), affective regulation, ways of dealing with contemporaries, ideas about themselves and social relationships, people's ability to express emotions, dealing with (emotional) dependence, social and emotional development, cognitive skills, frustration tolerance, self-worth, social competence and acting-in and acting-out behaviour. The conclusion is that attachment patterns do not just influence the way in which people deal with disappointment, illness, loss and stress, but in general can determine the behaviour of people in many difficult situations or in circumstances of experienced separation.

Attachment history

If children have been able to trust their parents in times of need, pain, panic or distress, they also learn to trust themselves. Without this basic trust, children do not develop self-confidence.

However, according to Bowlby, people who were insecurely attached as children may have positive experiences later, e.g. in secure situations during adulthood or as a result of psychotherapy, and these may 'correct' an originally insecure attachment pattern. The way in which the individual deals with new loss experiences during later life makes possible the acquisition of new attachment patterns – and to some extent can change the personality structure.

The 'attachment history' of individuals is crystallized in their reactions to (threatening) loss. Their attachment patterns are manifested in their grieving behaviour. People's make-up – their emotional baggage, how they have developed and what they have become – manifests itself in situations of extreme need. At the end of their lives, the life histories (ontogenesis) of individuals are inseparable from their personalities.

An important question in current research into attachment is the degree to which the attachment history of the individual, in addition to temperament or character, is a determining factor in later life and behaviour in old age. As far as intergenerational transfer is concerned (i.e. the transfer of attachment patterns to other generations), there is another central question, namely whether the parents' own attachment histories (their responsiveness due to their own attachment histories) can be traced down to their own children.

Attachment, old age and dementia

Antecedents of old age

> Old age is not something isolated. Old people are not born old. They have grown old. Old age only attains its unique place and value from the perspective of life as a whole.

The above view by Munnichs and Miesen (1986), over 30 years since it was first voiced, has become more than just a belief. Based on scientific knowledge, it is the obvious starting point for researchers and clinicians studying all kinds of behaviour in old age. This is true not just of problematic behaviour but also of the behaviour of older adults, as well as of children and young adults. All current behaviour should be studied in the perspective of antecedent life history. Personality development and the psychological growth of younger adults can also be best understood from their experiences and events in early childhood and later times. Earlier experiences, attachment experiences and events in a person's life history help to determine the way in which they will deal with old age, and the problems in it.

Old age and stress

Old age is frequently associated with a number of potentially stressful circumstances, such as physical, functional, social or psychological limitations, and confrontations with particular life events (e.g. Brugman and de Groot, 1998). At the same time, in this last phase of life itself, the fact that life is drawing to an end, also the 'imagined' nature of death or anxiety about dementia, can be experienced as extremely stressful. Individual variations about such perceptions in old age are large.

In The Netherlands around 10% of older adults above age 65 are confronted by dementia, most of them in the form of Alzheimer's disease. Dementia has many consequences for partners and children and can therefore rightly be seen as an extremely stressful event in an individual's life. If old age itself represents a stress situation for some people, dementia in old age is the ultimate extremely stressful life event.

Dementia as a psychological trauma

A purely medical/neurobiological perspective of dementia has steadily been supplemented by a more psychosocial perspective (see Jones and Miesen, 1992; Miesen and Jones, 1997). This includes, for example, the perception of the disease and the way in which both people with dementia and those around them cope. Psychosocial interventions have developed, aimed at dealing with spared abilities and the emotions experienced by a person with dementia.

A core idea in this newer perspective is that a considerable part of the behaviour of persons with dementia is a direct consequence of the awareness that persons themselves have of their decline and the emotions that this induces in them. This view supplements our knowledge about how behaviour can be affected by specific tissue changes or brain dysfunction. In other words, persons with dementia seem much more intensely involved in what is happening to them than was thought for a long time and much behaviour in dementia must be seen as a reaction to this. This means that what people with dementia say, think, feel and do is not only influenced by the type of dementia and the stage of dementia (i.e. the level of cognitive functioning or residual cognitive skills) but also by their personality structure and earlier events in their life history, including their 'attachment history'. Coping ability is therefore also determined by a person's experiences and character.

And, in my experience, old pain often resurfaces in dementia. This 'awareness context' means that it is essential to view coping (by persons with dementia and their family members) also as coping with a trauma. It is specifically the 'awareness context' that causes people with dementia to exist in a state of chronic trauma. The illness usually brings about a slowly unfolding catastrophe in the life of the person and in the lives of those around. Dementia is often a permanent 'shocking event' or a 'specific loss experience/separation experience'. The question then is: What do people think, say, feel and do when permanently faced with such an ongoing catastrophe of which the persons themselves have an awareness?

A multi-disciplinary definition of dementia

Bringing together the medical/neurobiological and psychosocial perspectives provides a new and broader definition of dementia. It gives a better understanding of the conditions required for successful intervention in terms of treatment, support and care for persons with dementia. Dementia should be understood as a potentially stressful life event that can result in powerlessness, disruption, upheaval and distress. If you then include the factors involved in coping with disease in general, you can realistically investigate and estimate the suffering of both the persons and their family. What Johan van Oers calls the 'specific gravity' of apparently the same situation is different for everyone. The gravity of the illness situation can be expressed by the person with dementia in a number of ways and can result in different ways of explaining their behaviour. More research into the possible explanations of the behaviour of dementia patients is still required, but attachment theory offers a promising perspective from which to do this.

Behaviour in old age psychiatry considered on the basis of attachment theory

All types of behaviour

In the past decade, a number of authors from various disciplines (Miesen et al, 2003a, 2003b) have reviewed the many types of disturbed behaviour that can occur in old age (see Box 3.4). The explanations usually given for this behaviour relate to dealing with loss in general, brain conditions, disorders resulting directly from cerebral dysfunction, disruption of somatic balance, extreme tension or over-reaction, personality disorders, psychiatric syndromes, sensory deprivation, social isolation, environmental and psychosocial factors and frustration. If this list of explanations is reduced to 'biological/medical' and 'psychological explanations', then about one-third fall under the first category and the rest under the second.

Much behaviour change in dementia relates to a person's 'awareness context', their reaction to their psychological trauma, the threatening losses and therefore also their attachment history.

Background to the behaviour

If we take the attachment theory as a starting point for an explanation of behaviour in dementia, we assume that the person with dementia is confronted with an insecure, threatening 'separation situation' and the anxiety associated with this. Awareness of 'an organic shortcoming' always provokes a direct emotional conflict, leading to a defensive reaction in order to achieve resolution. Attachment theory teaches us that separation anxiety involves (basic) proximity-seeking or attachment behaviour. This behaviour differs in form in the various phases of dementia.

The form in which attachment (proximity-seeking) behaviour manifests itself is dependent on residual cognitive functions. We saw earlier that clinging, chasing after, calling out and screaming can be seen as a form of proximity-seeking behaviour. Confrontation with insecurity in some persons can cause feelings to re-surface that relate to old psychological pain (i.e. previous insecurity). At a different stage of the illness, persons with dementia may once again long for the presence of their parents, think of them more often and come to the point where they believe them to be alive again and close by.

Box 3.4   Disturbed behaviour in old age

- **Affective lability**: a diminished ability to adapt expressions of feeling to the situation, manifested by severe oscillations in expression of feelings
- **Anxiety**
- **Claiming behaviour**: appealing incessantly and sometimes insatiably for someone else's help, attention or support, leading to lack of balance in the relationship with others and causing irritation
- **Disinhibited behaviour**: diminished impulse control, whereby the restraints applied normally by individuals disappear wholly or partially
- **Suspicion**: the strong emotions and defensive behaviour that result from the experience of a threat, or anxiety about pending calamity
- **Aggression**: aggressive expression of thoughts, feelings, actions
- **Depressive behaviour**: mournful moods
- **Inertia**: reduction of tempo in speed, thoughts, actions (and allowing others to act in one's stead)
- **Apathy**: absence of activity and initiative combined with low level of involvement with surroundings
- **Illusions, misperceptions, hallucinations and imagining**: perception of things that apparently or seemingly do not correspond to objective reality
- **Calling out**: making loud, moaning sounds and crying for 'help' or similar attention for no apparent reason
- **Suicide (or attempts at)**
- **Eating and drinking**: changes in desire to eat, in eating patterns, eating habits, in weight or in feelings of hunger and thirst
- **Forgetfulness**: all kinds of changes relating to the processing and recall of information
- **Sleeping**: changes in waking and sleep times, the required amount of sleep or relating to sleep habits
- **Compulsive behaviour**: actions that one feels compelled to do, even against one's will and better judgement; little rituals or sometimes a feeling of being driven by an inner force that is not always within one's control
- **Delirious behaviour**: an acute initial change in consciousness, whereby periods of clarity and confusion alternate
- **Isolation**: the experience of a painful, intense and permanent distance between the desired and achieved level of social contact

On the basis of the attachment theory, we can also ask what the effect is of a secure or insecure attachment pattern.

As we have already said, the emotions arising from insecurity can generate a defensive reaction. In this sense the behaviour of persons with dementia can be seen as 'adaptive'. Persons are trying to cope with the insecurity. According to Verwoerdt (1981), there are generally three types of defence, namely controlling, denial and withdrawal. An example of trying to control is 'overcompensation'. The person tries to rectify the physical and/or psychological failures experienced in an exaggerated way. Denial can be expressed in 'trivialization'. The failures or incapacities are passed off as insignificant, whereas they in fact cause a lot of anger and grief. Withdrawal may be expressed in an exaggerated focus on physical functions, such as going to the toilet, or the tendency to relate everything around solely to themselves, as well as by apathy, energy-saving behaviour and avoidance. It can, however, be assumed that the organic changes in the brain over time will attack such defences, which can be seen as part of the personality. (This probably also applies to the prevailing attachment pattern.) The defence mechanisms against separation anxiety, which an individual used throughout life, slowly lose their effectiveness. The diminishing defensive reaction also means that it is likely that old pain can no longer be suppressed and therefore resurfaces, e.g. war trauma, unfinished grieving, past disappointments, etc.

Finally, the duration of the effect of a response to the attachment behaviour (by those around) also depends on the phase of dementia or the degree of disruption in information processing. The caring behaviour of those around makes less and less of an impression and has less and less of an effect on the patient's feeling of insecurity. Sometimes the effect lasts just as long as the interaction/intervention. 'Out of sight' is literally 'out of mind' at the point where new information cannot be stored as memory.

Behaviour in dementia and attachment

What is the relationship now between the behaviour of people with dementia and their individual attachment patterns or histories? In other words: can the person's attachment patterns explain some of their behaviour? Why does one person withdraw and another cling tightly? Research into this is in its infancy and it could be of enormous help in understanding the support that we need to give to persons with dementia and their carers.

Anxiety and aggression

It is not always possible to specify a direct cause of anxiety in a person with dementia but usually it is a consequence of the feeling of insecurity and uncertainty that the disease involves. Anxiety may occur in conjunction with all kinds of other 'behavioural disorders' but is often linked to a person's personality structure or diminished defensive reaction or coping abilities. Usually anxiety has a long (previous) history, related to a person's life experiences and the way in which the person and those around them reacted to or dealt with them.

Aggressive expressions may be explained on the basis of hereditary factors (nature), learning experiences (type of nurturing), frustration, overload, a restricted environment, the wrong treatment (incorrect management), etc. Anxiety and the resulting aggression are basic emotions that may occur in any person with dementia, regardless of the attachment pattern, in both securely and insecurely attached persons.

Proximity-seeking behaviour

In persons with dementia with a secure attachment pattern, we frequently see that they seek the solution to their emotions in their environment and in other people. They seek out their partner, carer or another persons and try to cling to them, chase after them, scream, call out, look for their parents or assume that they are still alive nearby somewhere. They trust others. Their anxiety finds a response, albeit temporary. When persons are upset, they can be comforted. They are accessible and allow people access to them.

Affective lability and suspicion

People with dementia are no longer able to adapt their feelings appropriately to the situation and therefore show extreme fluctuations in their expression of these feelings. This may be the direct consequence of a brain disorder (such as cerebral infarction or other brain pathology) or 'excessive stress'. The most significant causes of the extreme emotion resulting from perceived threat or anxiety about threatening insecurity (causing suspicion) are sensory deficits and motor impairment. Such deficits bring about isolation and alienation. A person's personality structure and specific life experiences are also considered to be associated causes of such behaviour. But this behaviour could also be typical of persons with anxious/ambivalent attachment patterns. The essence is always ambivalence. They may look and ask for something, but in fact they do not 'trust' what they are given. They continue, as it were, to protest about an unreliable 'response'. They mistrust the help, the panic and anxiety persist, they are inconsolable, remain agitated, cannot find peace and often continue to call out.

Apathy and depression

Lack of activity and initiative in conjunction with little involvement in one's surroundings (apathy) are often seen as 'functional' in the context of dealing with loss, particularly if the behaviour is temporary. It may also be a direct consequence of a brain condition. However, the consequences of dementia also often lead indirectly to a feeling of powerlessness, fear of failure or a feeling of insecurity. People experiencing this repeatedly start to be wary of everything. The cause of mournful moods is usually a combination of psychosocial, biological and personality factors. However, apathy and depression can also characterize persons with 'anxious/avoidant attachment patterns'. They have learned: 'even if I ask, I don't get anything, so I'll be quiet and not do or ask for anything'. There is no activity or exploration, no claiming or calling out.

Claiming behaviour

Persistent and sometimes insatiable calling out for someone else's help, attention or support can relate to all kinds of causes. Such behaviour often leads to a lack of balance in the primary caring relationship and not infrequently causes irritation. The characteristic of claiming behaviour is that it persists and is often unchangeable. It may be the result of incorrect or inadequate treatment, insecure attachment patterns (which by definition do not deliver adequate need fulfilment) or brain disorders (which hinder the perception of even correct treatment). As soon as the current attachment figure disappears from the person's field of vision, the need for attention resurfaces.

Forgetfulness

Forgetfulness in dementia has a clear biological/medical explanation, but if you also add the consequences of 'awareness of this forgetfulness' then there is also to some extent a psychological explanation. Forgetfulness can then appear as a form of amnesia that blocks the painful awareness of 'forgetting' in itself. In the trauma theory, amnesia has the function of denial and avoidance of permanent confrontation with a painful or shocking event. The act of forgetting (or amnesia) is a survival strategy and by extension, once amnesia has taken on permanence, we refer to dissociation.

To summarize, anxiety about a threatening insecure situation, such as normally occurs in dementia, can trigger all kinds of behaviour, including attachment behaviour. This is linked to the pain that every person must process. At the same time the attachment pattern or attachment history continues. The quality and type of attachments determine whether the way dementia is dealt with is positive or not. The quality determines the 'specific gravity' of the pain, and this is different for every person.

Attachment and dementia

The 'awareness context' of the person with dementia can cause different types of behavioural responses whereby persons with dementia try to reduce their feelings of insecurity and discontinuity. Research has also shown that 'assuming that deceased parents are still alive' is a frequent phenomenon in dementia. However, this tendency to think increasingly of one's parents occurs even in mentally healthy elderly people.

These phenomena have been called *parent orientation, parent experience* and *parent fixation* (see Box 3.5 and Chapter 13 in this volume). Such behaviour is usually considered to be a direct consequence of brain disorders related to dementia. Attachment theory provides a way of understanding them.

Attachment theory and parent fixation

In *Gehechtheid en Dementie* (Attachment and Dementia) (Miesen, 1990, 1993) it is shown that, because of progressive difficulties, persons with dementia find it increasingly difficult to maintain familiar, existing security and attachment figures. At the same time, it becomes almost impossible to find new security or attachment figures. The result is that the person with dementia feels left in the lurch and ends up in a separation situation, often feeling very much alone.

In this research, the experimental observation situation that Mary Ainsworth originally developed with young children (known as the 'strange situation') was adapted into a 'standard visiting procedure' for observing attachment behaviour in elderly persons with dementia. The purpose of this experimental procedure was to create a naturally occurring but 'acutely insecure situation' in order to observe behaviour.

This research was not able to consider the attachment history of the

---

Box 3.5 Levels of thinking about parents

- **Parent orientation** is the term used when a person is aware that the parents are deceased but still thinks about them
- **Parent experience** means that a person 'consciously' experiences 'moments', as if their parents are still alive. In such cases, it appears that the person also thinks or feels that they are still there. Persons may still correct themselves if they find themselves speaking of their parents in present tense, or they may accept being corrected by others
- **Parent fixation** means that a person believes that their parents are still alive, although this is not the case. The person is definitely convinced that their parents have not 'yet' died, and will not let others correct them

(Miesen, 1985)

persons with dementia when interpreting the results. It remains to be shown whether the manifestation of parent fixation relates to the degree of dementia (or the level of cognitive function) or to earlier attachment patterns.

Perhaps in situations of increasing insecurity (as dementia advances or the level of cognitive function declines), the craving for parental security is blocked somehow if the relationship with the actual parents was 'insecure' in any way. If parents offered adequate security, such memories of security might operate as an imagined or otherwise safe haven. Parent fixation and other attachment behaviour could then be linked to the 'internal working models' of the individual or with their 'internalized' attachment.

The fact that the phenomenon of 'parent fixation' can be explained by other theories as well as the attachment theory has been shown elsewhere (Miesen, 1992, pp. 46–47).

Coping and attachment

The person with dementia

In addition to coping with a number of practical and emotional problems, having dementia also means having to cope with the separation and management of familiar emotional links. This puts pressure on attachment relationships, or, as Bowlby puts it, 'threatening danger intensifies the attachment relationship'.

People with dementia depend more and more for their feeling of security on the proximity of the partner or carer, but this poses the following problem: how do partners and children react to this? For instance, while shopping or during a family visit, they might deal with the person in a patronizing or in an overanxious way. What happens to the patient if the spouse cannot cope with the situation?

The dementia process is a further complicating factor. People with dementia have fewer and fewer cognitive skills to help them cope, let alone the direct consequences of their illness. It appears, however, that their greatest pain relates to dealing with the emotional consequences of having dementia. It is then primarily a matter of finding a response to the powerlessness, disruption and upheaval, not forgetting that denial and avoidance, experience and level of alertness all take their toll. In short, for the persons with dementia, it often becomes a question of self-trauma management, in which attachment patterns always play a part. Insecure attachment often goes hand in hand with a relentless attempt to remain emotionally independent and avoid asking for help when it is necessary. It is clear that persons with dementia characterized by such an attachment pattern find it even more difficult to deal with their situation.

Byatt and Cheston (1999) recently reported an interesting observation. Using an intervention known as 'simulated presence therapy' (in which the partner's voice recounts memories of their lives and relationship on tape), they demonstrated that the intended calming effect of this intervention is determined by the attachment pattern that persons had with their healthy partners. In the case of persons with an insecure attachment pattern to the partner, the agitation persisted. It seemed that each partner failed to function as a secure attachment figure. Magai and Cohen (1998) and Magai and Passman (1997) also recently made a link between the attachment pattern of patients to their partners and behavioural disorders. Insecurely attached partners seem to show more suspicious, depressive and anxious behaviour than securely attached persons with dementia. Thus the attachment pattern to the spouse before diagnosis of dementia may predict the behaviour of the person with dementia but also the degree of 'subjective burden' experienced by the partner.

de Ruiter (1993) says that future research will have to focus on the link between this internal representation of the attachment pattern and psycho-pathology. This will mean primarily that (longitudinal) research will be needed to examine the link between the attachment history of persons with dementia and the way in which they deal with their dementia. Since individuals' attachment patterns can affect the degree of vulnerability to psychological disorders, a better knowledge of individual attachment patterns would throw new light onto the way in which partners deal with their spouses with dementia. For them too, the internal representation of the attachment pattern, established in early childhood, influences patterns in their relationship(s) with important attachment figures in later life.

The family

Dementia is also a shocking event for the family, for example the spouse. The gradual loss, which remains invisible for a long time, also puts them in a position similar to that of having 'a missing person' in the family. For carers, without evidence of concrete death the loss is never final. As long as the person with dementia is still alive, the loss has no clear expression, no status. This means that family too undergo a sustained confrontation with power-lessness, disruption and upheaval. The partner not only has to manage the pain of the slow loss of life but also the way in which their loved one deals with the consequences of their disease. The partner or the family is always a spectator of the disaster of dementia. From clinical experience, this seems to result in a sort of 'loyalty conflict'. In order to keep their heads above water in such circumstances, to survive, partners have to take and keep a certain emotional distance, whilst the person with dementia often needs and wants greater proximity and shows increasing attachment behaviour.

Ingebretsen and Solem (1997) used case studies to show that the attach-ment pattern between partners is of crucial importance in determining the subjective load of the partner. They came up with four attachment patterns in the relationship of the partner to the patient, specifically characterized by (1) anxious attachment, (2) compulsive care-giving, (3) impulsive self-sufficiency and independence and (4) secure attachment. On this basis, the loss suffered as a result of a partner's dementia takes on a different significance, the means of coping is different and the (purpose of) intervention is also different. Partners who had secure attachments in their relationships appeared less vulnerable than others.

Both Ingebretsen and Solem (1998) referred to the above and stressed that the essential thing is to understand how dementia focuses the existing attachment pattern in order to be able to 'understand' the way in which partners cope. Finding a balance between proximity and distance in respect of the patient is primarily linked to the partner's own attachment history and that of the marital relationship.

My own clinical experience confirms this. In a dementia situation, the primary care-giving relationship crystallizes immediately, whether it is with the partner or a child. This fits in with the general trauma theory. When coping with loss or trauma, the relationship you have with the person or thing you lose plays an important role. This is confirmed with adult children caring for their parents with dementia. The attachment of children to parents influences the way they cope and their subjective burden. These researchers also stress another obvious aspect, namely that dementia disrupts the existing attachment pattern, and this affects the perceived subjective burden. In other words, caring for a person with dementia is primarily a separation experience, whether you are child or partner.

The professionals

It is also interesting to look at how far the attachment theory contributes to an understanding of the way in which professionals cope with persons with dementia and their families. In other words, what is the significance of attachment to the quality of professional care of the person with dementia and his/her family? What role does their self-awareness and understanding of how they themselves relate to the problems of dementia have to their knowledge of attachment?

We have already shown that the condition of dementia triggers attachment behaviour in persons with dementia (which may or may not be 'filtered' by their internalized attachment). Care-givers therefore do not just encounter 'persons with dementia' but 'persons experiencing a disaster'.

The fact that the history of their attachment is just under their 'psychological skin' must make us pause for thought when considering any intervention. It is not a blank situation to start with. As Bowlby said earlier: '(. . .) Danger activates attachment behaviour and in dangerous conditions people do make relationships of a more intense sort than they would ordinarily do.'

Dementia represents a sort of 'crossroads' within a catastrophe. At this crossroads attachment and care patterns meet: those of the person with dementia, family members and also professional carers and care-givers. So dementia is potentially rife with (counter-)transfer processes. Professionals too are 'signified' by a specific attachment pattern and are characterized by a specific complementary care pattern that may have developed to compensate for their own attachment pattern. Whatever intervention we undertake, it is up to us to be aware of what we are doing and why we are doing it.

Care-givers are also vulnerable at crossroads in disaster areas. They run the risk that their own old pain will be reactivated. The 'guardian angel syndrome' is a well-known phenomenon among professional care-givers that sometimes leads to burn-out. The continuing decline of the person with dementia increases the risk of counter-transfer. Without adequate knowledge and experience, confrontation with the resulting powerlessness is not always easy to deal with. In this respect, care-givers working in a long-term situation with patients and families may be more vulnerable than those working in short-term situations. My experience with volunteers (sometimes former family members!) is that the less knowledge they have, the more emotionally involved they become and the greater their risk of counter-transference. If they have inadequate knowledge and self-awareness, they carry an excessively great burden of unconscious motives and motivations. So, persons with dementia and their families sometimes do not get the care they need but rather what the care-giver (unknowingly) needs/wants to offload.

A group of researchers and clinicians led by Marie Mills and Peter Coleman (Mills et al, 1999) at Southampton University is looking at dementia care in homes, specifically on the basis of courses focusing on Bowlby's attachment theory. These are 'effect studies', looking into the quality of the relationship between care-givers and persons with dementia and 'well-being' after a 12-month training programme (18 sessions of 3 h a week with a group of care-givers from two homes). This group was compared with a group from a different home that 'only' had a shorter, conventional education programme. They found the first evaluation extremely positive. Greater self-awareness and personal growth were mentioned. As a result of 'playing out' all kinds of counter-transfer situations and their own old pain, the perceptions and experiences of people with dementia and families were judged to be better and relationships with the first improved considerably. They concluded that the attachment theory did in fact offer a number of interesting explanations for various types of relationship that affected the welfare of persons with dementia. They also found that attachment implies both knowledge and awareness of other people's and one's own life history. According to the Southampton researchers, the theory should form a substantial part of any dementia training. This would allow the development of secure attachment in the care relationship, despite continuing cognitive decline, until the final phase of the dementia process.

In The Netherlands I have repeatedly had the same experience in the last

10 years in various clinical settings. I taught a course about dementia to persons aged 20–98, based on *Dementia: zo gek nog niet* (i.e. the first part of Miesen, 1999). In this course, Bowlby's attachment theory frequently crops up. One of the things it makes clear is that carers will sometimes function as attachment figures for persons with dementia (and in some cases even their families). Depending on the perspective from which the approach/ management is considered, this figure would be described by Verdult as a 'good enough mother' (Verdult, 1993). In the course evaluation, it was notable that the appreciation for the 'common sense nature of the theory and its practical application' increased with the age of the course members.

Aggressive behaviour towards carers may occur as a result of feeling powerlessness or insecure. In order to 'save their skins' carers usually take a step back. The frustrating thing is that carers know they must keep a distance, whereas the persons with dementia actually want proximity (attachment behaviour). The same conflict of loyalty comes into play, as we saw, with partners of persons with dementia. They are at a loss in situations in which they have to maintain a certain emotional distance in order to survive, whereas the person with dementia is demanding proximity from them. This is not easy, particularly when it goes on for too long.

Society

We mentioned earlier that old age is associated with stressful circumstances of all sorts. The approach of death is experienced by some as particularly stressful and the perceived 'risk of dementia' plays an important role in this image. This is why the last few years have seen a steep rise in the number of wills and living wills. One in ten older adults above age 65 are affected by dementia themselves, and the number affected indirectly is far larger. In this context dementia seems to symbolize an extremely undesirable end to life that must be avoided at all times. If death itself is seen as the ultimate trauma in life, the possibility that people might have to experience that trauma in the form of dementia (a situation ultimately associated with loss of control of one's own life) is perhaps even more terrifying.

Can Bowlby's attachment theory help us to understand how society deals with this? Again we start with the view that dementia is in fact a catastrophe or a disaster with which society as a whole is confronted in different ways. This may be personal, as someone directly involved, via the media or through the way in which dementia care is organized.

Many Dutch people are familiar with the help provided for many post-World War II victims by the psychiatrist Bastiaans. The social context of his dissertation *Psychosomatische gevolgen van onderdrukking en verzet* (Psycho-somatic consequences of oppression and resistance), based on individual patient files, is less well known (Bastiaans, 1957). It allows a glimpse of the battles he fought to obtain sickness benefits for his patients. His battle for their financial security is characteristic of a post-war social climate in which there was a predominant lack of understanding, interest, care and support for the many who survived the war with a certain level of physical and/or psychological damage. The pain and suffering of many was silenced with all kinds of arguments, however understandable these might have been.

If we are to learn something from this, it is that denial and avoidance of another person's pain seems to be a natural defence mechanism against too great a confrontation with our own pain, powerlessness and in some instances guilt. This is not just true of individuals but also of society as a whole.

Dementia is not a one-off catastrophe. It is different from talking about 'reliving traumatic experiences', which generally diminish in intensity over time. Dementia is a continuous, progressive catastrophe. It cannot be re-experienced because the experiences themselves are ongoing. This makes the over-reactions – the marked tendency of people with dementia and their families to deny and avoid – all the more understandable, which is a very daunting thought. No wonder that for so long society has tried to pretend that 'the person with dementia has no awareness of the pain or suffering of their situation'. The significance is clear: we prefer not to be confronted with other people's pain, especially if it plunges us into feelings of powerlessness. The physical invisibility of the 'catastrophe of dementia' also contributes to the ease with which others can dismiss and avoid it, resulting in a further isolation of the person with dementia.

Thankfully, the image of dementia has slowly started to change in the media. More attention is being paid to the awareness and experiences of persons with dementia themselves. There is more openness. As a result there is more demand for education and information. People are less afraid to hear 'the worst' and what the pain and suffering will be like. Such change (reflected in increased support and care) is increasingly being felt in places and organizations where persons with dementia, families and friends meet, and is starting to seep through into society. The fact that most clinicians practise openness in diagnosis, the development of Alzheimer Cafés and similar initiatives and the increased interest of the media in such stories are examples of this.

One of Bowlby's propositions was: 'People who do not feel secure do not explore (the world).' The fact that more and more persons with dementia and their families are daring to explore the area of dementia possibly signifies that they feel a little more secure in their situation. Some of this can be credited to the many professional care-givers who are aware of what is going on in this disaster area.

Attachment in practice

Given the view of dementia as a catastrophe or trauma, the most important thing is to get a good diagnosis as quickly as possible and waste as little time as possible denying and avoiding what is going on. After that, it is then possible to access (practical) assistance from expert (multi-disciplinary) support right to the end. This primarily means continuity of support and care. But not just this. Given the fact that the cognitive part of the catastrophe usually shows a constant and phased decline, the secondary focus of this support is on retention of the autonomy, control, confidence, security and independence of the person with dementia.

The person with dementia

The examination room

It is clear that in order to make a good diagnosis (in trauma terms, to establish the nature of the catastrophe), specialist multi-disciplinary/memory clinic assessment and extensive neuropsychological examination are essential at an early stage of the illness. Psychological tests (which are done in safe environments in later stages of the illness, e.g. in day-care centres or nursing home settings) have a different purpose. Such testing can be seen as an experimental variant of the person's everyday situation, wherein the person with dementia is confronted with their powerlessness. It is essential that researchers/psychologists express security in what they do or say and that they function as 'instant attachment figures'. The testing environment also needs to provide a safe feeling (see Miesen, 1992, p. 49). The psychological function of such a room can best be demonstrated by the words of a lady with dementia on entry: 'Oh, how lovely. You've asked me to come to your home.' In fact, the furnishings of the room, which offers up a general image of one of the consequences of the dementia catastrophe situation, links seamlessly to the basic premises of 'warm care', reminiscence, validation and differentiation of patients by lifestyle in psychogeriatric nursing homes. You offer security in painful circumstances.

Investigation focus and report

If we start with the awareness context of people with dementia (and therefore their perception of the situation and themselves), the examination must not just comprise a neuropsychological assessment but also must focus on perception/experience-oriented diagnosis and an interpretation of the degree of coping with dementia or cognitive decline. Measurement of 'thoughts of parents' (by examining parent orientation, parent experience and parent fixation, as discussed earlier) is always part of our examination. These phenomena provide an insight into the actual experience of the person with dementia: how he or she feels. This requires measurement of the awareness context, a description of reactive behaviour at three levels, examination of personality structure, including the attachment pattern, and collecting knowledge of life history, particularly bereavements, traumatic events and loss experiences (see Appendix 3.1).

Measuring attachment patterns is presently based on interpretations of the 'Relationship Scales Questionnaire' (Griffin and Bartholomew, 1994) and Shaver's Relationship Questionnaire (Hazan and Shaver, 1987). The earlier these data are collected in the dementia process the better, because it can be utilized but not collected later. This makes it more possible to antici-pate a person's coping problems and also the behaviour problems that the carers may have to deal with. These can be planned for in management guidelines.

Advice, psychological education and counselling

Much of the behaviour of people with dementia must be seen as normal behaviour in an abnormal situation and that dementia signifies a psy-chotrauma and sometimes (re)activates old pain. Individuals may be inun-dated with all kinds of feelings that make them powerless, defenceless and helpless and that do not always go away. To some extent this can be compared with post-traumatic stress disorder. What is complex about the situation is that the dementia is both the cause (the shocking event itself) and one of the factors, which has a lasting effect on the degree of coping.

Obviously advice is needed but it is complicated. It is generally known that psychological education plays a positive role in dealing with and managing chronic diseases. This requires security and trust but most importantly, espe-cially in the case of dementia, it requires continuity. This means giving advice at as early a stage as possible about the progress of the disease and everything this involves and then offering a secure 'environment' in the context of a support strategy with a guarantee of continuing support. This is different from a short-term, one-off communication and leaving it there.

I find it important to have regular, brief meetings with persons with dementia about their perception of the situation, preferably with their part-ners present. These meetings are recorded on video and given to the family, to be watched together before our next meeting. This focus on 'awareness' and 'personal experience' may also be achieved with Alzheimer couples counselling, individually or in groups. Another option is regular visits to an Alzheimer Café (Threels, 2003). In this way the catastrophe remains explicit, persons with dementia and partners feel less quickly isolated in respect of each other and society and new emotional links (attachments) are formed. Recent research into coping effects after one year of couples counselling in groups showed that it is the person with dementia who benefits particularly. This can be seen from the reduction in or disappearance of their denial and avoidance behaviour. It is striking that the degree of dementia is irrelevant and almost all the persons with dementia were assessed as being 'insecurely attached' (Huybrechtse and Kouwenhoven, 2000; Krouwer, 2001).

The family

For families, or more specifically partners, dementia also signifies a trauma or loss experience that can cause extreme vulnerability. The complexity of their emotional situation is easily underestimated. This complexity can be explained in brief as follows.

The partner's dementia is the 'shocking' event in itself. It means a loss of one's partner. Then there is the invisibility of this loss to people in the outside world. The public nature of widowhood is clearer and perhaps easier. Earlier in this chapter, this was compared with the situation of a loved one who had 'gone missing'. Dementia cannot be marked in time, it never stops. It cannot therefore be 'left behind'. With dementia you slowly lose a mate (and possibly an attachment figure) who supported you in difficult situations. The pain of this loss is naturally determined by the previous attachment pattern with the person with dementia.

There is diversity, even mutual diversity, in attachment patterns between partners. A (mutually) secure attachment pattern usually results in intense suspicion, but in principle signifies healthier management than in the case of an insecure attachment history. Another aspect, as mentioned above, is the coping strategy that the person with dementia uses, with or without a general increase in attachment behaviour in respect of the partner. A last complicating factor is that the person with dementia is in fact a person with an illness (which they have not themselves asked for or been responsible for) for whom you are doing something. Where do partners turn to with their anger, or if overwhelmed with empathy? Not to mention the impact of many other factors that can play a decisive positive or negative role in loss management.

The above issues have the same consequences for the family as for the person with dementia with regard to the needed advice, psychological education, early diagnosis and ongoing counselling. The attachment history of partner and spouse should therefore be recorded at the first meeting. It often adds a dose of realism to the hope of favourable changes in coping strategies if it is clear from the start that there are insecure attachment patterns. The prognosis of counselling and support becomes more realistic and the offer of help is more effective. Practical help can, in certain circumstances, offer more solace than well-intended, time-consuming attempts to influence coping strategies.

The professionals

The first thing that professionals, of whatever discipline, must be aware of is that they are operating in a disaster area and a catastrophe process wherein there are (emotional) separation problems. Essentially their 'care behaviour', however it is expressed, must be complementary to the attachment behaviour (emotional needs) of the person with dementia. Particularly in a long-term process, professionals end up in a sort of adoption process, with potential (counter-)transfer problems and perhaps new attachments with people with dementia. This process is tangential to the separation problems of family members. How professionals deal with this updates their own attachment history and sometimes their own list of instantaneous loss experiences.

Adequate security and trust within management and care teams must be part of the care provision offered. Ongoing training, and debriefing, in order to keep in touch with and give expression to what is happening inside oneself is also needed. With dementia, emotional 'involvement' on the part of the professional is not only natural but essential. However, adequate distance must be ensured to keep going. Unconsciously this (often spontaneous) emotional investment in the person with dementia and his or her family may be so great that burn-out can easily occur, certainly in conjunction with external factors. In 'normal' catastrophe management and victim support, provision for 'rescuer support' is the norm. Consider emergency service providers, whose work is done to a certain level of routine but also is regularly interspersed with crises. They are given opportunities to share their own emotions. Hopefully, this will increasingly be so for those professionals supporting persons with dementia and their families, over time.

Society

The image of dementia in society reflects how insignificant a role 'inadequate, restricted or damaged lives' play in our image of human society. Dementia confronts society with vulnerability and our ultimate inability to control our lives. Daring to enter into this confrontation starts with the courage to dare to contemplate and confront individual suffering. Increasing openness about what dementia involves is a good start to allowing the vulnerability of life into our image of humanity. (Exposure to the Alzheimer Cafés can be a starting point for this.)

Conclusion

Different angles of approach from a number of disciplines are necessary to explain behaviour in dementia. The value of the attachment theory is its ability to explain a range of behaviours and relationship issues, as well as providing clues for offering support and care-giving for those affected. A simple medical 'organic' explanation is not enough. In dementia it is a question of normal behaviour occurring in an abnormal situation. Looked at from the perspective of the attachment theory, a lot of puzzling behaviour takes on quite a different significance. The theory makes a significant contribution to clinical and scientific research in a number of areas of psychology. The perspective that this theory gives to 'abnormal behaviours' in old age is broad, and it provides a guideline for psychologists actively involved in long-term support.

Bowlby's attachment theory provides a framework of concepts that can be used to understand and explain both normal behaviour and psycho-pathology in old age. This also helps to define the necessary intervention options. The focus moves from dementia as a disease to real persons with an illness and their families and carers. Persons with dementia become both the object and subject of their disease. They are part of it and remain involved in it. Interventions based on the psychological trauma model are very appropriate.

In order to study how people with dementia, families and carers cope with the chronic disease of dementia, continuity is a primary requirement in the relationship between clinician/researcher and person/family. Such investigation requires a longitudinal research structure and real partnership in the care-giving relationship.

Appendix 3.1

Conclusion of psychological investigation

- **Cognitive function**

  Level
  ....
  Awareness context
  ....

- **Responsive behaviour**

  Cognitive
  ....
  Affective
  ....
  Other
  ....

- **Personality aspects**
  ....

- **Biographical details**

  Characteristics
  ....
  Traumatic 'events'
  ....

References

Ainsworth, M.D.S., Blehar, M.C., Waters, E. and Wall, S. (1978) *Patterns of Attachment: Assessed in the Strange Situation and at Home*. Hillsdale, NJ: Lawrence Erlbaum.

Bastiaans, J. (1957) *Psychosomatische gevolgen van onderdrukking en verzet*. Amsterdam: Noord-Hollandse Uitgeversmaatschappij.

Bowlby, J. (1969) *Attachment and Loss Volume I. Attachment*. London: Hogarth Press; New York: Basic Books.

Bowlby, J. (1973) *Attachment and Loss Volume II. Separation: Anxiety and Anger*. London: Hogarth Press; New York: Basic Books.

Bowlby, J. (1980) *Attachment and Loss Volume III. Loss: Sadness and Depression*. London: Hogarth Press; New York: Basic Books.

Brugman, G. and de Groot, F. (1998) Coping in levensloopperspectief. Buigen of barsten? In M. Allewijn, F. de Groot, C. Hertogh, B. Miesen and I. Warners (Eds), *Leidraad Psychogeriatrie C1*. Houten: Bohn Stafleu van Loghum, pp. 27–54.

Byatt, S. and Cheston, R. (1999) Taped memories: a source of emotional security. *Journal of Dementia Care*, **March/April**: 22–24.

Dijken, S., van (1997) The first half of John Bowlby's life. A search for the roots of attachment theory. Dissertation, University of Leiden.

Griffin, D. and Bartholomew, K. (1994) The metaphysics of measurement: the case of adult attachment. In K. Bartholomew and D. Perlman (Eds), *Advances in Personal Relationships*, vol. 5. London: Jessica Kingsley Publishers, pp. 17–52.

Hazan, C. and Shaver, P. (1987) Romantic love conceptualized as an attachment process. *Journal of Personality and Social Psychology*, **52/53**: 511–524.

Huybrechtse, P. and Kouwenhoven, C. (2000) Coping met dementie. Een onderzoek naar het effect van echtpaarcounseling bij partner en patient. Dissertation, University of Leiden.

Ijzendoorn, M.H., van (1994) *Gehechtheid van ouders en kinderen. Intergenerationele overdracht van gehechtheid in theorie, (klinisch) onderzoek en gevalsbeschrijving*. Houten: Bohn Stafleu van Loghum.

Ingebretsen, R. and Solem, P.E. (1997) Attachment, loss and coping in caring for a dementing spouse. In B.M.L. Miesen and G.M.M. Jones (Eds), *Care-giving in Dementia: Research and Applications*, vol. 2. London: Routledge, pp. 191–209.

Ingebretsen, R. and Solem, P.E. (1998) Spouses of persons with dementia: attachment, loss and coping. *Norwegian Journal of Epidemiology*, **8**: 149–156.

Jones, G.M.M. and Miesen, B.M.L. (1992) *Care-giving in Dementia: Research and Applications*, vol. 1. London: Routledge.

Krouwer, M. (2001) Gehechtheid en coping met dementie. Een exploratief onderzoek naar de rol van gehechtheid op het effect van echtparen-counseling. Dissertation, University of Leiden.

Magai, C. and Passman, V. (1997) The interpersonal basis of emotional behavior and emotion regulation in adulthood. *Annual Review of Gerontology and Geriatrics*, **17**: 104–137.

Magai, C. and Cohen, C.I. (1998) Attachment style and emotion regulation in dementia patients and their relation to caregiver burden. *Journal of Gerontology*, **53B**: 147–154.

Miesen, B.M.L. (1985) Meaning and function of the remembered parents in normal and abnormal old age. Paper presented at the XIIIth International Congress of Gerontology, New York.

Miesen, B.M.L. (1990) *Gehechtheid en dementie. Ouders in de beleving van dementerende ouderen*. Almere: Versluys.

Miesen, B.M.L. (1992) Attachment theory and dementia. In G.M.M. Jones and B.M.L. Miesen (Eds), *Care-giving in Dementia: Research and Applications*, vol. 1. London: Routledge, pp. 38–56.

Miesen, B.M.L. (1993) Alzheimer's disease, the phenomenon of parent-fixation and Bowlby's attachment theory. *International Journal of Geriatric Psychiatry*, **8**: 147–153.

Miesen, B.M.L. (1999) *Dementia in Close-up. Understanding and Caring for People with Dementia*. London/New York: Routledge.

Miesen, B.M.L., and Jones, G.M.M. (1997) *Care-giving in Dementia: Research and Applications*, vol. 2. London: Routledge.

Miesen, B.M.L., Allewijn, M., Hertogh, C., de Groot, F. and van Wetten, M. (2003a) *Leidraad Psychogeriatrie. Een handboek voor de praktijk Volume 1*. Houten: Bohn Stafleu Van Loghum.

Miesen, B.M.L., Allewijn, M., Hertogh, C., de Groot, F. and van Wetten, M. (2003b) *Leidraad Psychogeriatrie. Een handboek voor de praktijk Volume 2*. Houten: Bohn Stafleu Van Loghum.

Mills, M.A., Coleman, P.G., Jerrome, D., Conroy, M.C., Meade, R. and Miesen B.M.L. (1999) Changing patterns of dementia care: the influence of attachment theory in staff training. In J. Bornat, P. Chamberlay and L. Chant (Eds), *Reminiscence: Practice, Skills and Settings*. London: Open University and University of East London, pp. 15–20.

Munnichs, J. and Miesen, B. (1986) *John Bowlby. Attachment, Life-span and Old Age*. Deventer: Van Loghum Slaterus.

Ruiter, C., de (1993) De gehechtheidstheorie van Bowlby-Ainsworth. *De Psycholoog*, **3 April**: 145–151.

Threels, R. (2003) Het Alzheimer Café. Een onderzoek naar de behoefte aan psycho-educatie en counseling. Dissertation, University of Leiden.

Verdult, R. (1993) *Dement worden: een kindertijd in beeld; belevingsgerichte begeleiding van dementerende ouderen*. Nijkerk: Intro.

Verhofstadt-Denève, L., van Geert, P. and Vyt, A. (1998) *Handboek Ontwikkelingspsychologie. Grondslagen en theorieën*. Houten/Diegem: Bohn Stafleu Van Loghum.

Verwoerdt, A. (1981) Individual psychotherapy in senile dementia. Clinical aspects of alzheimer's disease and senile dementia. *Aging*, **15**: 187–208.

Chapter 4

Awareness and people with early-stage dementia

Linda Clare, Ivana Marková, Barbara Romero, Frans Verhey, Michael Wang, Robert Woods and John Keady

When we talk about awareness and dementia, we might mean one of two things.

We might mean awareness *about* dementia, either at a societal level or at a personal level. Many of us can draw on the experience of a friend or relative who has developed dementia in later life and therefore have a very strong personal awareness about dementia. At the wider public level, society needs to be aware of how many people are affected, what this means and what can be done about it. Alongside this, though, there is another very important aspect of awareness – the awareness that someone who has, or is developing, dementia has about the changes she or he is experiencing and their implications. It is this aspect of awareness, which we could broadly term awareness *of* dementia, that we will be focusing on in this chapter.

Recently, we conducted a project called AWARE (Clare et al, 2004a,b; Verhey et al, 2004) to investigate current knowledge about awareness of dementia. The project aimed to bring together people living with dementia, family carers and people with a professional interest in dementia to explore the issues and outline practical implications and directions for future research. This chapter is based on the work of the AWARE project.

Why is awareness of dementia important?

Awareness is an important issue in dementia care, and has been the focus of a considerable amount of research effort. However, reviews suggest that so far this has produced little clear evidence and little guidance for practitioners (Clare, 2004a,b; Aalten et al, 2005). There is still often an assumption that many people with dementia, even in the early stages, are 'unaware' of what is happening to them. Anyone who really spends time talking with people who have dementia, though, will know that many people with dementia, especially in the early stages, can be very aware. Yet it is also true that people who are developing dementia, or are in the early stages, do seem to differ a lot in how they describe this experience and in how much awareness they have of the changes that are occurring. Differences in awareness of dementia imply that people with early-stage dementia may have very different subjective experiences. This in turn may affect their relationships with family members, friends and the community in general. It can be very frustrating for the care-giver if, for example, the person with dementia does not recognize problem areas and is reluctant to allow the care-giver to provide the support or obtain the help that is needed. This increases feelings of stress and burden for the carer (De Bettignies et al, 1990). Similarly, it can be very frustrating for people with dementia when their views and feelings are ignored by others who assume that they are unaware of what is happening to them.

The extent to which people with dementia are aware of changes also affects access to sources of support, and has implications for how health professionals might help. Awareness is one factor that medical professionals may take into account in reaching a diagnosis, and the level of awareness they perceive or assume the person to have might also affect decisions about whether to disclose a diagnosis (Keady et al, 2004). Following diagnosis, it seems that people who are more aware of having difficulties with their memory tend to get more benefit from rehabilitation interventions and therapeutic help (Koltai et al, 2001; Clare et al, 2004c). Awareness can also have a down-side: people with dementia who have higher levels of awareness may tend to experience more depression and emotional distress. In the context of an increased emphasis on obtaining the perspective of the person with dementia alongside that of family members and paid care-givers, the issue of awareness becomes central to the appraisals made by people with dementia and their care-givers of their situation and quality of life.

For people with early-stage dementia, level of awareness has implications for future planning. Many individuals with early-stage dementia wonder what level of awareness they can expect to have as their dementia progresses; they ask whether there will come a point at which they are no longer aware, or whether they will continue to have awareness despite being unable to express themselves clearly, and what this will imply for their quality of life. In the early stages of dementia, awareness also has very significant implications for immediate decision-making (Woods and Pratt, 2005). The person with dementia may emphasize a preference for continued independence, while family members become particularly concerned with managing risk and maintaining safety. A person who is unaware of cognitive difficulties may, for example, continue driving when this is no longer safe. In contrast a person who has good awareness and is prepared to make, or allow others to make, appropriate adjustments is likely to be able to maintain independent functioning for longer.

As dementia progresses, the question of just how much awareness a person has is often troubling to family members and carers. Apparent fluctuations in levels of awareness, with moments of clarity following periods of confusion, can be hard to understand. Particularly for people with more advanced dementia, assumptions that the person is unaware may be largely or partly unwarranted, yet such assumptions can have major implications for care practices and hence well-being, and may even be used to justify inappropriate or possibly harmful treatment.

We have begun the chapter by explaining why awareness is an important issue. We will next introduce three couples – Iain and Ivy, Heather and Harry and Stuart and Sheila – who are coping with the onset of Alzheimer's disease, and whose experience illustrates the expression and impact of different levels of awareness. We will return to their experience at various points during the chapter as we go on to explore different ways of understanding awareness and unawareness, considering the interplay of neurological changes, psychological factors and social context. Based on this analysis, we will present a biopsychosocial model of awareness in early-stage dementia and then discuss the implications for evaluating level of awareness. Drawing again on our examples of people living with dementia, we will explore the way in which the level of awareness perceived by others relates to subjective experience. Finally, we will draw on the key messages learned from the involvement of people with dementia and family carers in the AWARE project and emphasize the need to move from a focus on deficits to a readiness to look for evidence of awareness among people with dementia.

The experience of developing Alzheimer's disease

Here we introduce the experiences of three couples coping with the onset of Alzheimer's disease in one partner.

Iain and Ivy

Iain was given a diagnosis of early-stage Alzheimer's disease a few years after retiring from his career as a social worker. Both Iain and Ivy had gradually noticed problems with Iain's memory, and eventually agreed these were serious enough to seek medical advice. When the diagnosis was made, Iain was initially reluctant to accept it, but after observing how he was doing in various situations he eventually came to accept that 'dementia' was an accurate description of his condition. He did not, however, accept the term 'Alzheimer's', insisting that this did not apply to him. Ivy, meanwhile, sought out information and tried to find out more, fighting to secure Iain the right to have medication prescribed. Iain and Ivy were able to talk together about much of what was happening, but they had to face some difficult issues such as how they felt about the idea of assisted suicide for Iain. They also had to work out a way of managing some practical situations, such as negotiating how much help Ivy should give Iain when they were out in public. They were able to look at information provided by the Alzheimer's Society, although Iain found this very difficult. Iain liked the idea of receiving some practical help with his memory difficulties and wanted to take responsibility for fighting the effects of dementia as far as he could. He also wanted to do whatever he could to help other people in the same situation. Iain continued to do various kinds of volunteer work in his local community for as long as he could. As his difficulties progressed, he remained adamant that he did not want to become a burden, and wondered about whether he should perhaps move out of the family home into sheltered accommodation. Iain and Ivy got involved in the Alzheimer's Society network, which allowed Iain to make a contribution through expressing his views on service provision and service needs. Through this activity they established a strong friendship with another couple in a similar situation, and the four of them started doing all kinds of things together as a group.

Heather and Harry

Heather had been forced to take early retirement from her job as a lecturer due to increasing difficulties with memory and planning, and had been diagnosed with early-stage Alzheimer's disease. She experienced a number of difficult symptoms including seizures and perceptual anomalies. However, she maintained there was nothing really wrong with her, and while she acknowledged that her memory was not as good as before, she insisted that in this respect she was no different to anyone else of her age. She described using strategies like writing things down to aid her memory, although Harry said that she did not use these strategies efficiently and they did not usually work well. Heather and Harry were not able to talk together about what was happening and Heather often criticized and attacked Harry, usually verbally but occasionally also physically. Although Harry understood this to be a way in which she maintained her own self-esteem, he still found it hurtful. He was often left feeling desperate for support and for a break from caring for Heather. He had been able to join a carer support group, but had to keep this secret from Heather. Harry thought Heather was struggling more and more with everyday situations, and losing confidence, but Heather refused help of any kind, and would not even take medication. Harry felt he could not go out and leave her alone, as she might not be safe, and therefore he gave up most of his own independent activities. As the difficulties progressed, it became necessary for Heather to move into a residential home, where Harry visited her every day. She mostly seemed confused, uncommunicative and unaware of her surroundings, although once in a while she would say something to Harry that indicated she understood with absolute clarity where she was and what was happening. Harry found this in some ways more upsetting than the confusion.

Stuart and Sheila

Stuart, a retired high-ranking military officer, went missing from home and some hours later was travelling south at 75 mph on the northbound carriageway of the motorway when he was stopped by police. Afterwards, he maintained the road signs had been misleading and thus caused him to make a mistake about the direction he should take. His wife Sheila, meantime, was desperately anxious about his safety. When Stuart came to the Memory Clinic, he found it hard to make sense of what he was doing there. He insisted that he had come there to assess the staff, in line with his pre-retirement occupational status, although he proved to be quite willing to complete all the tests and assessments the staff wanted to do. In response to questions, he made it clear he was quite certain there was nothing wrong with him, and he seemed in very good spirits. The staff thought it was likely he had early-stage Alzheimer's disease. When Stuart came back for a follow-up assessment six months later, he seemed to be in a very different frame of mind. He acknowledged that he was having a lot of difficulties with his memory and with everyday skills, and he felt that something was wrong with him. At the same time, he seemed very low in spirits, and was rather tearful. Sheila, on the other hand, was much happier because Stuart had agreed not to drive. They were arguing less, and she felt more reassured about his safety, even though she was still very concerned about him.

Variations in awareness

Clearly Iain, Heather and Stuart are responding in very different ways even though they all have the same diagnosis, and this seems to have something to do with their different levels of awareness. Attempts to understand this variation in awareness might focus on three different aspects: neurological, psychological and social.

Neurological aspects of awareness

One way of trying to understand differences in awareness would be in terms of damage to the brain. This has been the most common approach to date. Disturbances of awareness are evident in many neurological disorders and following some kinds of brain injury, such as head injury or stroke (McGlynn and Schacter, 1989). A useful way of thinking about these disturbances of awareness is by relating them to four different levels of awareness, which build upon one another (Stuss, 1991; Stuss et al, 2001). This is summarized in Figure 4.1, which shows both the levels of awareness and the kinds of disturbances of awareness that might arise at each level.

The most basic level of awareness is being able to take in something of what is going on around us. Obviously we all do this to a different extent

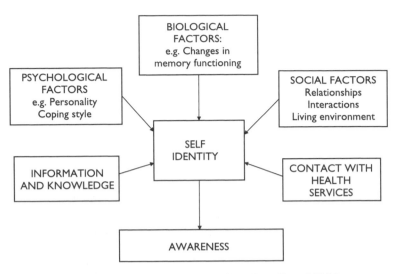

Figure 4.1 A biopsychosocial model of awareness (based on Clare, 2004a).

depending on whether we are asleep or awake. Pervasive disturbances of awareness occurring, for example, in coma and persistent vegetative state reflect impairments at this basic level, although even people who are under anaesthetic, or in a coma, may still have some awareness in this sense. This aspect of awareness is not generally an issue for people with early-stage dementia; Iain, Heather and Stuart were all perfectly aware at this level.

The next level is the ability to register changes in aspects of functioning – for example, memory or concentration. Domain-specific disturbances of awareness involve lack of awareness in a single domain of cognitive functioning. The unilateral neglect that some individuals experience after a stroke, where they appear unaware of things happening to one side, would be an example of this. Most people with early-stage dementia describe being aware of changes in their memory, but some do not acknowledge these changes. Iain and Heather both talked about changes in their memory. Stuart did not acknowledge any changes initially, but gradually became willing to talk about changes he had noticed.

The next level of awareness is the way in which we monitor our actions and use what we know about our current level of functioning to make decisions about how to behave in particular situations. Impairment in the ability to monitor one's own behaviour can result in behaviour that seems disinhibited or inappropriate to others. Both Heather and Stuart were seen as behaving at times in ways that were not appropriate to the situation.

Finally, the highest level of awareness relates to the way in which awareness at all the levels relates to and integrates with the self, i.e. to the experience of self-awareness or sense of identity. A particularly dramatic example of impairments in self-awareness would be the situation where a person believes his loved ones have been replaced by identical-looking impostors who have nothing to do with him. Iain, Heather and Stuart did not show this kind of dramatic change in self-awareness, but they did seem to be struggling with issues about their identity. Iain felt he was losing many things that were important to him and changing as a person. Heather and Stuart seemed to be trying hard not to admit changes in their sense of who they were.

The different ways in which unawareness can be manifested have each been linked to changes in particular brain areas (Prigatano, 1999). Neuropsychologists have tried to develop theoretical accounts of how brain changes affect the way we process information or make judgements in such a way as to produce unawareness (Schacter, 1990; Agnew and Morris, 1998; Morris and Hannesdottir, 2004). For example, problems with memory might mean that knowledge about the self and about one's own abilities is not updated, and the person therefore responds as if his/her abilities are unchanged. Alternatively, problems with the ability to make judgements and comparisons might mean that the person cannot compare current performance with stored information about what should be expected, and therefore cannot detect that a mistake has been made, with the consequence that she or he remains untroubled by a situation that should normally trigger concerns.

Given that dementia involves changes in the brain, which affect cognitive functioning, it is reasonable to suppose that variations in awareness might result from such changes and the resulting impact on how information can be processed in the brain. Thinking about our earlier examples, one obvious difference between Iain and Heather is that Heather experienced seizures, while Iain did not. This suggests a somewhat different profile of changes in the brain, so there might be differences at a neurological level that could account for Heather's apparent unawareness. Heather seemed to see herself as someone who used strategies such as writing herself reminders in order to improve her memory, even though these strategies apparently did not work successfully. Heather is not seeing her functioning as it currently seems to others. This might be explained by the idea that, because of cognitive changes, she is not able to update her knowledge about herself and her abilities. Instead, she is describing herself as she had previously been – an efficient, well-organized professional woman – and as a result she seems to others to be unaware of her current situation and abilities.

Developing awareness can be seen as a dynamic process, in which preexisting beliefs and knowledge about the self interact with the awareness of current functioning that develops in a given situation or task, resulting in a gradual re-shaping of self-knowledge (Toglia and Kirk, 2000). Impairments in memory and other cognitive functions are likely to interfere with this process of restructuring self-knowledge. Heather also sometimes behaved in ways that were difficult for Harry. He described how, when they went to an important social occasion, Heather dressed quite inappropriately. This caused Harry a good deal of embarrassment, but Heather did not seem to notice that she was dressed very differently to the other guests. This may have been because it was hard for her to make judgements and comparisons, and therefore to monitor her own behaviour and its effects. Knowledge of having a difficulty (intellectual awareness) is not enough in this context (Crosson et al, 1989); it is also important to be able to recognize a problem when it occurs (emergent awareness) and identify where problems might be expected to arise in the future (anticipatory awareness).

Stuart differed from both Iain and Heather in that, while their levels of awareness remained much the same, he moved over a period of six months from seeming unaware that anything was wrong to acknowledging that he was having many difficulties. If awareness is straightforwardly the result of neurological damage, it is hard to see how this kind of shift to increased awareness could occur. It is possible that for some people unawareness may have more to do with psychological processes.

Psychological aspects of awareness

All of us, when confronted with difficult or challenging situations, adopt psychological strategies in an attempt to cope. These could be conscious, as when we actively decide to avoid a situation or person in order to reduce our level of stress or distress, or minimize the seriousness of an event to make ourselves feel better about it. Alternatively, psychological defences might operate at a pre-conscious level, with denial serving to ward off intolerably difficult or painful feelings and prevent them reaching into conscious awareness. The development of a serious illness or disability such as dementia is threatening to the integrity and indeed continued existence of the individual and thus likely to elicit psychological responses, whether pre-conscious denial or more consciously accessible strategies such as avoidance or minimization (Weinstein et al, 1955, 1994; Weinstein, 1991; Seiffer et al, 2005). Individuals differ in the psychological resources and coping styles that they bring to such situations, as a result of their personal characteristics and experience – for example, they will have particular attachment patterns and personality traits. Weinstein suggests that people who have always been very conscientious, disciplined and hard on themselves, very work-oriented and reluctant to express their emotions, may be more prone to denial than others.

Going back to our examples, Heather seemed to fit this description and she herself described how she had always viewed signs of illness as a form of weakness, and avoided doctors and hospitals as far as possible. She continued to resist any contact with medical services, disliked any kind of assessment and rejected the offer of medication. This could have been evidence of denial, but the fact that she actively tried to normalize her situation and minimize her difficulties suggests that perhaps her awareness of difficulties was not solely pre-conscious but also consciously available.

Stuart also came from a background where discipline was important and signs of weakness or vulnerability were discouraged. At the clinic, what he said was incongruent with his behaviour – he believed he was there to assess the staff, but in practice he was quite willing to allow the staff to assess him. This inconsistency did not seem evident to him, which suggests that pre-conscious rather than conscious processes were influencing his reactions. He could have been showing evidence of denial, which resolved over time as he was gradually able to begin to accept what was happening to him. Most awareness research to date has considered only the awareness that is explicitly expressed in what a person says, without asking whether the person is behaving in a way that shows implicit awareness. Implicit awareness can be thought of as hidden, or unconscious, knowledge that influences behaviour. While a person with dementia may explicitly deny any problems relating to the condition, he or she may behave in a way that suggests some awareness; for example, the person may avoid going to social gatherings, suggesting a fear of being embarrassed, or may avoid going shopping, suggesting a fear of getting lost. We need to take into account not only the explicit awareness that is expressed in what a person says, but also the implicit awareness that is shown through what a person does.

Beliefs and knowledge about dementia

At the psychological level, individuals also differ in the working models, or representations, they hold. People who have developed an illness or disability such as dementia, and those who support them, will differ specifically in terms of the beliefs they hold about what the condition is, what causes it, what the prognosis is and what can be done to help. These beliefs relate to the representations held in wider society, which individuals take in and use, and which influence individual behaviour and reactions. Just as in society as a whole, aging is often associated with progressive memory difficulties, so people with early-stage dementia may regard their problems as an inevitable result of aging. Relatively few, it seems, will adopt explanations such as 'dementia' or 'Alzheimer's disease' (Pearce et al, 2002; Clare, 2003). Of course, many people may not be told their diagnosis, or may be given euphemistic explanations such as 'accelerated aging'. Additionally, where people are able to draw on experiences of family members or friends with dementia, their representations are often associated with the later stages of the disease and they may not believe that the problems of early-stage dementia are part of the same illness. In some cases, therefore, people could be labelled as unaware when in fact it is a matter of lacking access to information or knowledge. Langer and Padrone (1992) distinguish between the 'informational' element of awareness on the one hand, and the neurological (implicational) and psychological (integrational) aspects on the other. Level of knowledge is likely to interact with other pre-existing beliefs and preferences to affect an individual's response. Knowing a lot about dementia might mean that one is very alert to changes in memory and inclined to seek help early on, but alternatively it might lead one to avoid thinking about such a difficult issue.

Social aspects of awareness

This brings us to the third element we need to consider: the social context in which individual awareness arises and is expressed. The way in which individuals perceive dementia relates to the way in which society perceives and responds to dementia. Society's model, currently, is focused on the later stages and on frightening images of confused, distressed individuals in uncongenial and often unpleasant residential care settings. We still lack strong representations relating to living with dementia in the earlier stages, or to the possibility of higher levels of well-being in the later stages.

The awareness context

These perceptions and representations that pervade society at a social and cultural level are likely to influence the way in which families and social networks respond when individuals develop cognitive difficulties. For many individuals developing dementia, the social context is exemplified particularly in contact with family members, who may support or hinder the process of developing awareness of changes and difficulties. The concept of the 'awareness context' is helpful here. This idea originated in work with people who were terminally ill, which identified the importance of the context in determining whether issues could be acknowledged and openly discussed (Glaser and Strauss, 1965), and has also been applied to thinking about dementia care (Miesen, 1997).

From our previous examples, Iain and Ivy described how they both gradually began to notice changes in Iain. For a time they joked about the problems, laughing about Iain's 'Alzheimer's' when he forgot something, but as time went on things got more serious. It was when Iain got into the car and sat bemused because he could not remember what the various controls were for that they both agreed they needed to seek help. For them, it was a continual process of negotiation and evaluation, building on their long-standing relationship in which they had always discussed difficult issues, including issues connected with preferences about care in later life. Heather and Harry had a much more strained relationship where raising concerns or problems was seen as quite attacking and threatening, and they were not able to talk about the changes. Harry had to find a way to persuade Heather to retire from her job that did not result in loss of face for her. As a couple, they did manage to reach an agreement about this and negotiate the transition, albeit with some difficulty. In this context, it was harder for awareness to be expressed than was the case for Iain and Ivy. Contextual information can, of course, be used in different ways. Heather's friends, with the best of intentions, assured her that they too had memory problems and that her memory difficulties were nothing to worry about, and simply a sign of growing older. This experience is not uncommon, and indeed Iain had also experienced this reaction from others. However, Iain felt angry at what he felt was a lack of understanding, while Heather seized on it as evidence that there was nothing really wrong. Again, feedback from others is likely to interact with pre-existing beliefs and preferences to influence individual responses. Family and friends telling one that one's memory is not working well might convince one that there is something wrong, or it might mean one becomes more determined than ever to insist they are mistaken. People who live alone, or are rather isolated, may be less likely to get this kind of feedback, with different kinds of implications for access to help and support.

Family members differ in the way they deal with the problems they experience in interaction with the person with dementia. Some of them are more successful in adapting and responding to the needs of the person with dementia than others. A recent study found three types of care management strategies: nurturing, supporting and non-adapting strategies (de Vugt et al, 2004). Care-givers using a nurturing strategy try to manage the person with dementia by 'taking them by the hand' and taking over most of the daily chores. They tend to focus on personal care tasks and try to protect the person with dementia. A supporting strategy is characterized by efforts to adapt to the person's level of functioning and by stimulating his or her existing abilities. These care-givers only support or assist the person with dementia when needed. They also tend to be calm and patient with their relative. In contrast, a non-adapting strategy is characterized by a lack of understanding or acceptance of the situation. These care-givers tend to approach the person with dementia with impatience or anger. They try to deal with behavioural or memory problems by confronting or ignoring their relative.

These different care-giver approaches to perceiving and managing the situation may have important implications for the person with dementia. In particular, a non-adapting approach may be very frustrating for a person who is aware of cognitive and other difficulties, because their problems are not understood by their relatives and they are confronted with their difficulties and mistakes. This can create a very unsafe environment for the person with dementia and affect their well-being. In contrast, supporting care-givers create a safer environment by adjusting to the needs of the person with dementia and supporting their preferred level of functioning. In this context perceived changes and difficulties can be discussed more easily.

The environmental context

The environmental context is also important. If one realizes that one's concentration is not as good as it used to be, the implications will differ depending on whether one lives in an urban area with good public transport or an isolated rural area where there is no option but to depend on the car to get around. In the former case the person may be more ready to acknowledge the difficulties and give up driving, whereas in the latter it would be understandable if the person tended to minimize the problems in order to hold on to the possibility of driving.

Interactions with health services

When memory problems become serious enough to seek help, the resulting interactions with health services provide another important element in the social context, and can interact with the person's beliefs and expectations to influence the expression of awareness. If consulting the doctor about memory problems elicits the view that these are just a sign of aging, some people will allow themselves to be reassured, whereas others will feel that the doctor has not listened properly and seek out other information. Heather, who had always disliked hospitals and medical treatment, was unhappy about the experience of attending the memory clinic and being assessed because she felt that the process was designed to show her limitations and make her fail at things. The whole situation, she said, made her feel she 'couldn't do it', whereas in different circumstances she would have been able to function better. This reaction meant that she was even less likely to feel inclined to acknowledge any difficulties. Iain, on the other hand, felt that he had a good rapport with the psychologist who assessed him, and this seemed to have facilitated the process of evaluating his own difficulties and coming to accept the diagnosis.

Another memory clinic attender, Martin, asked his GP for a referral because he was worried about his memory and concerned he might be developing dementia. After his assessment, he received his diagnosis in a rather blunt letter from a junior doctor. This seemed to be just too much for him to bear. He immediately shifted into a stance of insisting that his difficulties were no more than just the result of aging, and refused to try any anti-dementia medication. He backed this up by insisting that he had had a second letter from the clinic correcting the first and saying that he did not have Alzheimer's disease or dementia, although as far as could be determined no second letter had ever been sent to him. The awareness that people show in a clinical context will be influenced by the beliefs and expectations they have in that context. If a person believes, as many older people currently do, that society's attitude to dementia involves 'putting people away' in long-stay hospitals or residential care, that person may be very concerned to make sure that she/he puts on a good show for the doctor and convinces the doctor that she/he is managing well.

A biopsychosocial model of awareness

In trying to understand variations in awareness, we cannot just assume that where people do not seem aware this is due to brain damage. Certainly changes in the brain will play a part for some people in the early stages, and eventually perhaps for all. But if we talk with people who have dementia we can see that the situation is much more complex (Clare, 2002). We need to take account of the person's coping style and social relationships. We need to think about the information and knowledge that the person has, and the impact that any contact with health or other care services may have had. We need to remember that awareness is expressed in a particular situation at a particular time, and so we cannot assume that it is a stable trait. Most studies of awareness have taken a 'snapshot' at one point in time but, as Stuart's experience shows, expressed awareness can change over time so it is also important to consider changes over both short and longer periods of time. All of this means that we need to work from a comprehensive biopsychosocial model of awareness. An example of such a model is shown in Figure 4.2.

All of the factors shown in Figure 4.2 may have an influence on a person's apparent level of awareness. The next challenge relates to how we determine what that apparent level of awareness might be.

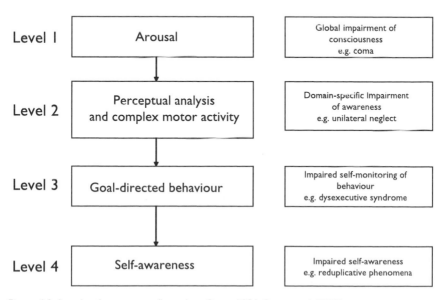

Figure 4.2 Levels of awareness (based on Stuss 1991; Stuss et al, 2001).

Evaluating awareness

As we have already seen, awareness itself is a complex concept and has many different facets (Marková et al, 2005). Similarly, attempting to evaluate the awareness that another person has is not at all straightforward (Clare et al, 2005). Quite a lot of research has focused on trying to establish which other factors are associated with impaired awareness by exploring the relationship between level of awareness and other features, such as years of education, mood or psychiatric symptoms. So far this research has not produced many clear or definitive findings (Clare 2004b; Aalten et al, 2005), and this is partly because studies have looked at different aspects of awareness and attempted to measure awareness in differing ways. In addition, being aware implies being aware of something – this has been called the 'object' of awareness (Marková and Berrios, 2001) – and studies have chosen different 'objects' of awareness to investigate. Examples of objects of awareness for a person with dementia might be, for example, having a memory difficulty, needing more help with daily activities or having dementia and what this implies. Each of these aspects is quite different and it is not possible to compare them directly. A person who is very aware in relation to one 'object' may be much less aware in relation to another. Typically, studies have focused on awareness of memory problems. However, other aspects may be more important or practically-relevant. All of this tells us that the phenomenon of awareness that can be evaluated may be just one aspect of the overall picture, and furthermore it can only be evaluated in relation to a specific object.

Assessing awareness

A number of different methods have been used to evaluate awareness in people with early-stage dementia (Clare 2004b; Clare et al, 2005). One widely used method is the clinician global rating. An example of a clinician rating approach is the Global Rating of Awareness in Dementia (GRAD; Verhey et al, 1993), in which ratings of awareness level are made on the basis of a brief structured interview. Another widely used method is the discrepancy score approach. An example of a discrepancy measure is the Memory Insight Questionnaire (Marková et al, 2004). The person with dementia and the family carer complete parallel versions of a questionnaire about the person's functioning, and discrepancies between the two sets of ratings are calculated. Small discrepancies are seen as indicating that the person with dementia has good levels of awareness, whereas if the person with dementia rates his/her functioning much more positively than does the carer, this is taken to indicate limited awareness. A further approach is to look at discrepancies between self-ratings of functioning and actual task performance. Another recently developed measure, the Memory Awareness Rating Scale (MARS; Clare et al, 2002), evaluates two sets of discrepancies: firstly those between the ratings made by the person with dementia and the carer, and secondly those between the ratings made by the person with dementia and his/her scores on a set of objective everyday memory tasks. This measure also potentially allows an evaluation of the carer's awareness of his/her memory functioning. The MARS was validated against detailed interviews with people who have dementia, which aimed to explore subjective experience and understand this in relation to awareness (Clare, 2003).

The phenomenology of awareness

This phenomenological approach (Clare, 2003) identified a continuum of coping styles among people living with the onset of dementia. Different individuals fall at different points along the continuum, and this has links with their level of expressed awareness. At one end of the continuum of coping was the 'self-adjusting' coping style. This reflected a readiness to adjust the self-concept in response to the changes that were taking place. Iain is an example of someone who coped using a predominantly self-adjusting style. He was adjusting his sense of who he was to take account of the fact that he had been given a diagnosis of dementia. He had gradually realized that what was happening to him meant something was wrong, and had come to accept the diagnosis as a result of his experience. This was frightening for him, and he sometimes had a sense of disintegration. He had spent time in the depths of a very distressing and bleak emotional experience. However, he came to feel that he could start to fight back and as a result he looked for ways to make a contribution. Iain clearly was very aware of the changes he was undergoing.

Heather is an example of someone who coped using a predominantly self-maintaining style. She tried to keep everything the same, and did not want to acknowledge any changes in herself or her abilities. She made light of her memory difficulties, insisting they were no different to those of her friends. Heather continued to hold on to her past sense of identity and did not admit to any changes. Heather might be considered someone who was 'unaware'. It does seem that neurological factors played more of a part for her than for Iain. However, describing Heather as unaware is not a fully satisfactory explanation. She did, at some level, realize things were not right, but she seemed to cope by trying to avoid this knowledge, deflecting situations where her difficulties might be apparent, putting the blame on external factors, and criticizing Harry to deflect attention from her difficulties.

Stuart, initially, did not acknowledge that anything was wrong. He too was described as unaware. However, it would also be possible to see this as an example of self-maintaining coping, and a few months later he was acknowledging the problems and moving towards a more self-adjusting style. The continuum of coping styles provides a framework for understanding individual responses and how they differ, which in turn can contribute to an overall picture of a person's level of awareness. No one coping style is intrinsically better or worse than another, but the assumption is that an individual will adopt the coping style that is most adaptive and most achievable for him/her at a given time. As we noted before, this will have implications for how we support the person and for the choice of interventions. Where the person's coping style results in difficulties, there may be value in addressing the relevant psychological and social or contextual factors in order to allow the person more flexibility in the selection of coping styles. This needs to be approached within the biopsychosocial framework, acknowledging the constraints imposed by neurological impairments.

Conclusions: looking for evidence of awareness

Involving people with early-stage dementia and family carers was a key aim of the AWARE project, which provided the stimulus for this chapter. One of the key messages resulting from that involvement was the call for an emphasis on looking for evidence of awareness, rather than evidence of unawareness. Awareness research should move away from focusing just on deficits and impairments. This means that we need to go beyond the immediately obvious and try to really understand what is behind a person's response. We need to think about the context the person is in and the effect this might have. In early-stage dementia, some aspects of awareness will be determined by neurological changes, but not all. It is important to accept that there are different ways of coping with developing dementia, and at times some of these may look like a kind of unawareness but actually reflect psychological processes or reactions to the social context. It can be more helpful to view these as coping styles that indicate what the person finds best for him or her at that time. If we can understand where each person is at in terms of awareness, and why that might be so, this is a good starting point for finding ways of being helpful for that person and his/her family.

Acknowledgements

The AWARE (Awareness in early-stage dementia: understanding, assessment and implications for early intervention) project was supported by the European Commission, contract number QLK6-CT-2002–30491. The project team were Linda Clare (coordinator), Geraldine Kenny, Ivana Marková, Frans Verhey, Mike Wang, Bob Woods and Orazio Zanetti. The project was conceived and developed by members of the INTERDEM network, which is coordinated by Esme Moniz-Cook (e.d.moniz-cook@hull.ac.uk). We would like to thank everyone who took part in the project meetings and contributed to the work of the project. In preparing this chapter we drew on presentations forming part of a symposium about the work of the project given at the Alzheimer Europe Conference held in Prague in May 2004.

References

Aalten, P., van Valen, E., Clare, L., Kenny, G. and Verhey, F. (2005) Awareness in dementia: a review of clinical correlates. *Aging and Mental Health*, **9**: 414–422.

Agnew, S. K. and Morris, R. G. (1998) The heterogeneity of anosognosia for memory impairment in Alzheimer's disease: a review of the literature and a proposed model. *Aging and Mental Health*, **2**: 7–19.

Clare, L. (2002) Developing awareness about awareness in early-stage dementia. *Dementia*, **1**: 295–312.

Clare, L. (2003) Managing threats to self: awareness in early-stage Alzheimer's disease. *Social Science and Medicine*, **57**: 1017–1029.

Clare, L. (2004a) The construction of awareness in early-stage Alzheimer's disease: a review of concepts and models. *British Journal of Clinical Psychology*, **43**: 155–175.

Clare, L. (2004b) Awareness in early-stage Alzheimer's disease: a review of methods and evidence. *British Journal of Clinical Psychology*, **43**: 177–196.

Clare, L., Wilson, B.A., Carter, G., Roth, I. and Hodges, J.R. (2002) Assessing awareness in early-stage Alzheimer's disease: development and piloting of the Memory Awareness Rating Scale. *Neuropsychological Rehabilitation*, **12**: 341–362.

Clare, L., Canning, R., Driver, B., Kenny, G. and Litherland, R. (2004a) AWARE: exploring awareness in early-stage dementia. *Journal of Dementia Care*, **March/April**: 35–37.

Clare, L., Romero, B. and Wenz, M. (2004b) Krankheitseinsicht bei Kranken mit beginnender Demenz: Bericht über ein europäisches Projekt. *Zeitschrift für Gerontopsychologie und – psychiatrie*, **17**: 135–138.

Clare, L., Wilson, B.A., Carter, G., Roth, I. and Hodges, J.R. (2004c) Awareness in early-stage Alzheimer's disease: relationship to outcome of cognitive rehabilitation. *Journal of Clinical and Experimental Neuropsychology*, **26**: 215–226.

Clare, L., Marková, I.S., Verhey, F. and Kenny, G. (2005) Awareness in dementia: a review of assessment methods and measures. *Aging and Mental Health*, **9**: 394–413.

Crosson, B. C., Barco, P. P., Velozo, C. A., Bolseta, M. M., Werts, D. and Brobeck, T. (1989) Awareness and compensation in post-acute head injury rehabilitation. *Journal of Head Trauma Rehabilitation*, **4**: 46–54.

De Bettignies, B. H., Mahurin, R. K. and Pirozzolo, F. J. (1990) Insight for impairment in independent living skills in Alzheimer's disease and multi-infarct dementia. *Journal of Clinical and Experimental Neuropsychology*, **12**: 355–363.

Glaser, B.G. and Strauss, A.L. (1965) *Awareness of Dying*. Chicago: Aldine.

Keady, J., Woods, B., Hahn, S. and Hill, J. (2004) Community mental health nursing and early intervention in dementia: developing practice through a single case history. *International Journal of Older People Nursing*, **13**: 57–67.

Koltai, D.C., Welsh-Bohmer, K.A. and Schmechel, D.E. (2001) Influence of anosognosia on treatment outcome among dementia patients. *Neuropsychological Rehabilitation*, **11**: 455–475.

Langer, K. G. and Padrone, F. J. (1992) Psychotherapeutic treatment of awareness in acute rehabilitation of traumatic brain injury. *Neuropsychological Rehabilitation*, **2**: 59–70.

Marková, I. S. and Berrios, G. E. (2001) The 'object' of insight assessment: Relationship to insight 'structure'. *Psychopathology*, **34**: 245–252.

Marková, I.S., Berrios, G.E. and Hodges, J.R. (2004) Insight into memory function. *Neurology, Psychiatry and Brain Research*, **11**: 115–126.

Marková, I.S., Clare, L., Wang, M., Romero, B. and Kenny, G. (2005) Awareness in dementia; conceptual issues. *Aging and Mental Health*, **9**; 386–393.

McGlynn, S. M. and Schacter, D. L. (1989) Unawareness of deficits in neuropsychological syndromes. *Journal of Clinical Experimental Neuropsychology*, **11**: 143–205.

Miesen, B.M.M. (1997) Awareness in dementia patients and family grieving: a practical perspective. In B.M.M. Miesen and G.M.M. Jones (Eds), *Caregiving in Dementia: Research and Applications*. London: Routledge, pp. 67–69.

Morris R. G. and Hannesdottir, K. (2004) Loss of 'awareness' in Alzheimer's disease. In R. G. Morris and J. T. Becker (Eds), *The Cognitive Neuropsychology of Alzheimer's Disease*. Oxford: Oxford University Press, pp. 275–296.

Pearce, A., Clare, L. and Pistrang, N. (2002) Managing sense of self: coping in the early stages of Alzheimer's disease. *Dementia*, **1**: 173–192.

Prigatano, G. P. (1999) *Principles of Neuropsychological Rehabilitation*. New York: Oxford University Press.

Schacter, D. L. (1990) Toward a cognitive neuropsychology of awareness: implicit knowledge and anosognosia. *Clinical and Experimental Neuropsychology*, **12**: 155–178.

Seiffer, A., Clare, L. and Harvey, R. (2005) The role of personality and coping in relation to awareness of current functioning in early-stage dementia. *Aging and Mental Health*, **9**: 535–541.

Stuss, D. T. (1991) Disturbance of self-awareness after frontal system damage. In G. P. Prigatano and D. L. Schacter (Eds), *Awareness of Deficit after Brain Injury: Clinical and Theoretical Issues*. New York: Oxford University Press, pp. 63–83.

Stuss, D. T., Picton, T. W. and Alexander, M. P. (2001) Consciousness, self-awareness and the frontal lobes. In S. Salloway, P. Malloy and J. Duffy (Eds), *The Frontal Lobes and Neuropsychiatric Illness*. Washington, DC: American Psychiatric Press, pp. 101–109.

Toglia, J. and Kirk, U. (2000) Understanding awareness deficits following brain injury. *NeuroRehabilitation*, **15**: 57–70.

Verhey, F.R.J., Rozendaal, N., Ponds, R.W.H.M. and Jolles, J. (1993) Dementia, awareness and depression. *International Journal of Geriatric Psychiatry*, **8**: 851–856.

Verhey, F.R.J., Aalten, P., Wortmann, M., Clare, L., Canning, R., Driver, B., Kenny, G. and Litherland, R. (2004) AWARE: een onderzoek naar ziektebesef bij vroege stadia van dementie. Een verslag van een internationale bijeenkomst over ziektebesef. *Tijdschrift voor Gerontologie en Geriatrie*, **35**: 33–35.

Vugt, M.E. de, Stevens, F., Aalten. P., Lousberg, R., Jaspers, N., Winkens, I., Jolles, J. and Verhey, F.R.J. (2004) Do caregiver management strategies influence patient behaviour in dementia? *International Journal of Geriatric Psychiatry*, **19**: 85–92.

Weinstein, E. A. (1991) Anosognosia and denial of illness. In G. P. Prigatano and D. L. Schacter (Eds), *Awareness of Deficit after Brain Injury: Clinical and Theoretical Issues*. New York: Oxford University Press, pp. 240–257.

Weinstein, E. A. and Kahn, R. L. (1955). *Denial of Illness: Symbolic and Physiological Aspects*. Springfield, IL: Charles C. Thomas.

Weinstein, E. A., Friedland, R. P. and Wagner, E. E. (1994) Denial/unawareness of impairment and symbolic behaviour in Alzheimer's disease. *Neuropsychiatry, Neuropsychology and Behavioural Neurology*, **3**: 176–184.

Woods, R.T. and Pratt, R. (2005) Understanding awareness: ethical and legal issues in relation to people with dementia. *Aging and Mental Health*, **9**: 423–429.

Part II

Interventions in care facilities

Chapter 5

The role of humour in dementia

Will Blake, Marie Mills and Peter Coleman

Humour produces psychological and physiological effects on our body that are similar to the health benefits of aerobic exercise . . . These benefits are some of the best kept secrets from those persons who probably have the most to gain from that information – older adults

(Berk, 2001)

Humour is one of the soul's weapons in the fight for self preservation

(Frankl, 1984)

Laughter is the shortest distance between two people

(Victor Borge)

Introduction

This chapter will explore definitions and theories of humour and suggest that humour has an important role to play in dementia care. We examine the positive and negative aspects of humour in the care of people with dementia, arguing that informal and expert professional carers can employ humour and laughter to capitalize on the beneficial effects of humour. However, humour is a powerful tool that can be used to both encourage and/or discourage others. We find that negative use of humour, often associated with victimization, can be linked to the old culture of dementia care, whereas the more gentle interactions of the new culture of dementia care lend themselves to the positive use of humour in care practices. Our arguments will be underpinned by case studies gathered through many years of formal practical and professional experience.

Although we have frequently seen the enjoyable and therapeutic use of humour by family carers, we will tend to focus on less familial relationships, and the importance of the skilled, self-aware practitioner who recognizes the personhood of the person with dementia. We regard this practice as a marriage of knowledgeable professionalism and altruistic care, a view typically echoed in the literature and prominent in practical approaches advocated by Kitwood and Miesen, among others. However, this type of individual is often described as possessing professional knowledge and skills that are so well developed as to be almost second nature (Coleman, 1994; Mills, 1995). The integral nature of these skills frequently makes it difficult for carers to recognize the value of these skills and to communicate them to other less experienced staff (Benner, 1984). The value of humour in their work is also likely to be under-recognized.

The origins of humour

Simply put, humour is an emotional response to an internal or external event. Emotion theorists argue that emotions are psychoevolutionary and adaptive, ensuring social bonding and communication between infant and care-giver (Izard, 1991). Izard reminds us that emotions define our humanness, they link feeling and thought. Affective-cognitive structures can, of course, be both simple and complex. In the case of joy, this can be a result of another's smile or the triumph of hard-won achievement. Izard also suggests that there is a genetic element to the appreciation of joy in that some individuals have a greater potential to experience joy than others.

Humour, at its best, is most closely associated with the emotion of joy. When it is at the expense of others it is driven by anger, contempt and perhaps guilt. These emotions are regarded as fundamental; other fundamental emotions are interest, surprise, sadness, disgust, fear and shame (Izard, 1991). Humour, therefore, is an emotional experience, that can be both publicly and privately expressed, i.e. performed before an 'audience' of several or enjoyed with another or alone. The literature strongly indicates that emotion and dementia have a close association (Mills and Coleman, 1994; Kitwood, 1997; Mills, 1998, 2000). Further, joy is known to influence physiological change, such as heart rate and skin temperature (Ekman et al, 1983). The absence of joy is, of course, most obvious in depression.

Most of us have no doubt that humour can be beneficial to us throughout the lifespan. It can '. . . detach us from our world of good and evil, of loss and gain, and enable us to see it in proper perspective. It frees us from vanity on the one hand and from pessimism on the other by keeping us larger than what we do and greater than what can happen to us' (Kline, 1907). Chapman and Sheehy (1987) suggest that society now places a high value on humour. It benefits individuals and society as a whole, for example through its ability to preserve order, maintain or change group norms and the quality of our relationships.

Berk (2001), in a synthesis of 30 years of research, gathers an impressive amount of data to support his assertion on the restorative properties of humour and laughter (see Table 5.1). Thus, it is possible to suggest that the influence of positive humour in dementia may help to mitigate the effects of an illness that is overwhelming in its totality and diminishes the individual. Any interactions across the lifespan that produce smiles, laughter or other

Table 5.1 Physiological benefits of laughter

Benefits	Examples
Improves mental functioning	Increases interpersonal responses, alertness and memory
Exercises and relaxes muscles	Exercises facial, chest, abdominal and skeletal muscles, improves muscle tone, decreases muscle tension and relieves discomfort from neuralgia and rheumatism
Improves respiration	Exercises the lungs and improves breathing and blood oxygen levels, relieves chronic respiratory conditions and reduces chances of bronchial infection and pneumonia
Stimulates circulation	Exercises the heart like aerobic exercise, followed by decreases in heart rate and blood pressure
Decreases stress hormones	Reduces stress
Increases immune system's defences	Fights viral and bacterial infections
Increases production of endorphins	Decreases pain and produces a euphoric state without liquor, drugs or aerobic exercise
Kills common viruses and bacteria	Psoriasis, gangrene, gingivitis, anthrax and malaria

overt signs of humour will certainly have a physiologically beneficial effect. This continues into later life and in older people with dementia (Mills, 1998). In addition, some humorous interactions can provide 'deep communion', where there is 'a deep human contact beyond words . . . sharing in another's experience . . . moments of unique togetherness' (Norberg, 1999, pp. 164–165). Possibly for precious minutes, humour can enable the person with dementia and the formal or informal care-giver to co-exist in a space where the illness ceases to exist.

This implies a more equal relationship in which humanistic principles guide the professional care-giver in helping the individual to regain a sense of 'wholeness' (Miell and Croughan, 1996; Mills, 2000). However, this relationship is not equal due to the dependency of the individual and the power of the 'expert' care-giver. Nonetheless, interactions that take place in this relationship are capable of being equal, intersubjective experiences. They are diametrically opposed to those interactions with people with dementia based on unequal power relationships (see Foucault, 1979, 1980). In these unequal exchanges, people with dementia tend to be public objects of humour, a stance more frequently associated with old style dementia care and 'custodial' task-based regimes. Here humour is used to objectify the individual and to 'perform' or entertain the staff audience.

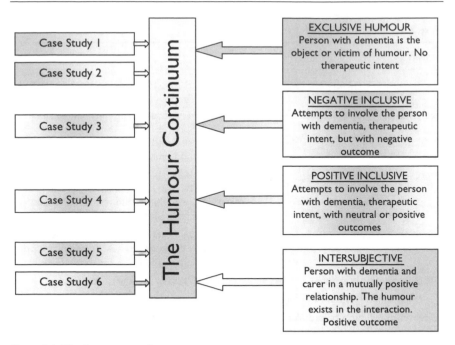

Figure 5.1 The humour continuum.

We believe that interactions with people with dementia that involve the use of humour operate on a continuum (see Figure 5.1). At the negative extreme the interaction excludes and objectifies the person with dementia. At the other extreme, the humorous interactions are intersubjective. The protagonists are equal partners in moments of unique togetherness. There are certain important landmarks along this continuum and these are described in the boxes on the right in Figure 5.1. The position of the case studies on the continuum that we will use to illustrate this theory are shown on the left in Figure 5.1.

It is perhaps difficult for us to understand how the victimization of the vulnerable individual with dementia can be a source of humour, but an examination of humour theories and their association with care provision indicates how the use of humour can, paradoxically, encourage both equal and unequal relationships (Chapman and Sheehy, 1987).

Definition and theories of humour

The word 'humour' is derived from the Latin 'humoreum' meaning moisture. It relates to the four ancient Hypocratean humours: phlegm, blood, choler and black bile. An imbalance of these humours was believed to determine the 'temper of mind and body'. A just balance made a good compound called 'good humour' (Brewer, 1993). Dictionary definitions include that from the Collins Gem English Dictionary (1985), which describes the word as a noun for the 'faculty of saying or perceiving what excites amusement'.

Humour is the inducement of amusement (Ziegler, 1998). Robinson (1991) suggests that laughter is the indicator and humour is the cause, with smiling and other changes in facial expression being alternative responses. It needs to be acknowledged that laughter is not always an indicator of joy. Cardoso (2003) believes that only 10–20% of laughter is a response to humour. She suggests that laughter is also involved in events such as the release of fear, and that laughter is a primitive reflex that can be observed in many animals, including primates such as chimps and gorillas, and even rats. R.D. Lawrence (1986, 1997) has spent over 30 years observing wolves and howling behaviour. His descriptions of the many social contexts in which howling takes place, particularly how they sometimes seem to howl just 'for the fun of it', suggests that howling may, in some circumstances, be the laughter of wolves.

Ziegler (1998) views humour as any communication 'written, verbal, drawn or otherwise displayed, including teasing, jokes, witticisms, satire, sarcasm, cartoons, puns, clowning which induces (or is intended to induce) amusement, with or without laughing or smiling'. Ziegler's definition is important for a number of reasons. Firstly it acknowledges that humour, with all the psychological and physical benefits, can be transmitted and received using a range of communication channels. This is particularly important if the benefits of humour are to be experienced by people with dementia. As Norberg (1999) asserts, there is loss of language and communication abilities associated with the progress of Alzheimer's disease and this can potentially preclude some individuals from the benefits of verbal and written humour. However, options still remain, such as the use of mime, clowning, the use of sound and music, pictures and video.

Ziegler's definition also acknowledges that humour can be used to victimize individuals through teasing and sarcasm. That humour can be 'exclusive' or 'inclusive' has particular relevance in the healthcare arena and this will be discussed later in the case studies. It echoes early humour theories relating to superiority.

Superiority and incongruity theories form the basis of many early attempts to account for humour. According to Moreall (1987, pp. 14–16), Aristotle thought that the ludicrous was to be found in the defects of others, whereas Hobbes (1651) believed humour to result from the 'sudden glory arising from some conception of some eminency in ourselves, by comparison with the infirmity of others, or with our own formerly'. It could be argued that this theory is at the heart of 'exclusive' forms of humour such as racist and sexist jokes.

Humour and incongruity

Other early writers thought that humour was more closely connected to incongruity. For example. Beattie (1776) held that laughter resulted from the unification of two ill-suited ideas. Kant (1790) held more elaborated views that remain, however, faithful to the notion that incongruity is a vital component of humour. Kant calls humour the 'whimsical manner', which he describes as 'the talent enabling us to put ourselves at will into a certain mental disposition, in which everything is judged in a way quite different from the usual one (even vice versa) . . .'. Humour in these examples is seen as a personal characteristic that enables an individual to interpret the world in an idiosyncratic manner and, as Marmysz (2001) suggests, 'is able to find pleasure where others find only pain and displeasure'.

What also emerges from examining literature on the subject of humour is its subjectivity. What one individual finds humorous, another individual will not. Davis (1996) cites two examples. The first is by George Bernard Shaw, the playwright, who felt that in the 1890s the farces on the London stage, although extremely popular, were akin to:

> Join*(ing)* in the laughter of a crowd of peasants at the village idiot . . . laughing at a farcical comedy, which is at the bottom the same thing: namely, the deliberate indulgence of that horrible, derisive joy in the humiliation and suffering which is the beastliest element in human nature.
>
> (Shaw, 1958)

The second is a view recorded by Muller, who reported a friend's opinion of his preoccupation with jests and jokes:

> In psychology I learned that jokes are the expression of an inborn sense of fear, insecurity, and aggression. Jokes ridicule the poor, the naïve, and the helpless. They are always cruel to someone. It hurts me, therefore, to see you enjoy jokes so much.
>
> (Muller, 1980)

Davis (1996) has attempted to summarize what she feels are the main schools of thought and how these relate to comic forms in the theatre. These are presented in Table 5.2.

Despite all of these attempts to categorize laughter and comedy, an all-embracing theory of humour seems elusive. Authors such as Bergson suggest that the reason for this is that laughter and comedy are a reflection of the cultural and historical context in which they are created.

To understand laughter we must put it back into its natural environment,

Table 5.2 Theories of humour and examples found in the theatre

Theory	Examples
Superiority	Ridicule, mockery, social correction, wiser than dupes
Taboo-violation and celebration of the life force	Forbidden subject matter, 'good life' characters, indulgence plots
Mechanical and nonsensical	Inflexibility in characters and in plot devices, exaggeration and repetition, inversion, illogic, naivety, incongruity in predictability and surprise

Source: Davis (1996).

which is society, and above all we must determine the utility of its function, which is a social one.

(Bergson, 1987)

Watts asserts that laughter, comedy and humour are potential agents of social change:

Whether during the Puritan Interregnum in England, at the formation of the French Constitutional Assembly in 1789 or in the turbulent Berlin in the Nineteenth Century, the inherent dichotomy of humour manifests itself and calls upon society to respond. Depending on the context laughter may be liberating, subversive, conservative or coercive, or more probably a combination of all these at once.

(Watts, 2000)

Watts also cites Bremmer, who suggests:

Enjoying humour and boisterous laughter is eminently opposed to striving to keep all life under control, which can be observed among the Pythagoreans, the Spartans and, to a much more marked degree, the ascetic Christians . . . To enjoy humour and laughter freely is the mark of a relaxed, open community, not of an ascetic ideology.

(Bremmer, 1997)

Negative uses of humour

The above definitions cited by Davis (1996) also note the negative side of humour that may be associated with the dark ages of custodial care. Humour can be used to victimize individuals with social and cultural differences, including disability, through mockery, teasing and sarcasm, producing feelings of ascendancy in the instigator. It can be used also to marginalize others. Contemporary disposition theory (Zilman, 1983) suggests that humour disparagement of the other depends on the balance between affective dispositions between the disparaged and non-disparaged parties. Humour appreciation is strong when someone has a negative affect towards the disparaged individual or group, and more so when the person providing the disparaging humour is viewed in a positive light (Chapman and Sheehy, 1987); they suggest that it is especially useful in explaining humour directed at less able minority groups.

As noted above, there are several longstanding theories that speak of the sense of superiority as a well-spring for humour. According to Moreall (1987), Aristotle thought that the ludicrous was to be found in the defects of others, whereas Hobbes (1651) believed humour to result from the comparison of infirmity with non-infirmity. These early theories support the notion that humour frequently targets and creates victims.

The possibility for carers to mock older people with dementia has been recognized by Kitwood (1997), among others, and cited as a 'personal detractor' in an interaction that robs individuals of their essential personhood. He offers some support for our continuum of humour model, where humour may be exclusive, inclusive or intersubjective, in recognizing the joyful interaction in intersubjectivity as:

> Celebration – the ambience here is expansive and convivial. It is not simply a matter of special occasions, but of any moment at which life is experienced as intrinsically joyful. . . . Celebration is the form of interaction in which the division between caregiver and cared-for comes nearest to vanishing completely.
>
> (Kitwood, 1997, pp. 90–91)

Mackinley (2001, p. 191) also asks 'is there a spiritual component in humour?', arguing that humour allows people to transcend life's difficulties.

However, in sharp contrast, the negative use of humour can encourage a malignant social psychology imposed on the neurologically impaired individual that can damage the fragile self-esteem and personhood of the older person, as the following case study, which is at the 'negative exclusive' extreme of our humour continuum, indicates.

Case study I

'Teasing' Joan: an example of exclusive humour

The following case study from the 1970s offers an example of both superiority and incongruity. It is set against the backdrop of the old culture of dementia care in the United Kingdom. The case in question was set in a typical red-brick Victorian building. The floors were bare and the paint-chipped furniture consisted of orange vinyl armchairs and Formica-topped tables. There were long dormitory-style bedrooms with no curtains around the beds. It was a depressing environment for both staff and patients.

There was one large sitting room where patients sat with their backs to the walls with little opportunity to communicate with each other. If they did so, they restricted their ability to gain eye contact with the staff. The staff varied in age and experience. Some had been there for many years. Others were very inexperienced, with little understanding of the behaviour of older people with dementia. One young male member of staff could not understand why one particular patient, whom we will call Joan, called him 'Dad'. She called all the male staff 'Dad' except for the older ones, who she called 'Granddad', which caused them some amusement.

The ward was home for Joan. It held 25 older women who had a medical diagnosis of dementia or long-term functional illness. To a greater or lesser extent all were dependent on the care staff for their well-being and essential care. There was no open visiting and relatives were not encouraged to complain. It was very much a closed institution.

Joan, herself, was 76 years old. The staff saw her as a 'bit of a character', because she had a sharp tongue and they felt she could bring some much needed humour to the task-based environment. Staff would tease Joan and this teasing could often be coarse. It would not be tolerated today. One senior male member of the care team would frequently invite Joan to give him one of her verbal set downs by jokingly asking her if she would be willing to sleep with him. Joan would instantly retort: 'I wouldn't have anything to do with you if your arse was studded with diamonds'.

Staff found these remarks very amusing, especially as Joan presented as a small sweet white-haired and gentle lady. Unlike us, they did not see her as a 'victim' and as an 'object of humour'. Neither were they aware that her lack of inhibition was probably due to early dementia, encouraged by the environment. Today such exchanges and lack of awareness would result in severe disciplinary measures.

However, even though they colluded with the teasing, not all the care staff were uncaring or cruel. Several genuinely well-meaning members of staff felt that the teasing was, in some way, good for Joan. They felt that this type of interaction showed that she still existed as a person and that they were encouraging individuality and her ability to withstand the influence of the illness. They saw 'the teasing' and her ability to make waspish retorts as somehow strengthening her sense of self. Unfortunately they did not use her communication skills as a way of entering into her world, rather the teasing became a means in itself where certain staff with low self-esteem and awareness were able to maintain a sense of power and superiority.

Humour as a defence mechanism

How can this use of exclusive humour develop in groups charged with the care of others? One possible explanation for the use of humour in an environment such as this, which results in distancing the self from people with dementia, is an inability to confront suffering. This type of humour may provide a method of emotional self-preservation. Although initial exposure to individual people with dementia might evoke a strong response of sympathy and compassion in care staff, ongoing exposure to large groups over time, particularly in the very poor overcrowded conditions in old-style wards, will modify or nullify the response. Morse et al (1992), in a discussion of caring for those who suffer, argue: 'The experience of shared suffering must be controlled by the nurse: (a) so that the nurse may leave the distressed patient and move on and care for other patients and (b) so that the nurse can limit his or her involvement in the patients suffering and avoid becoming emotionally drained and exhausted.' In this instance humour becomes a defence mechanism. Freud (1960) suggests that people use humour to protect themselves from being overwhelmed by the situation . . . 'and overrides with a jest the possibility of . . . an emotional display'. He perceives humour as allowing objectivity and an emotional 'standing back' from the distress.

Where older institutional environments were the norm, helplessness and distress were both part of the lives of people with dementia and of those who cared for them. In this light it is perhaps understandable, although not acceptable, why some used any means to gain a sense of superiority and control over their frequently under-recognized and under-valued role. However, once again the formal carer may find that the source of humour for the person with dementia may challenge their own values. The following case study illustrates this point.

Case study 2

The dark side of humour: exclusive humour

Wendy was in her late 70s and had reached a stage where dementia had robbed her of most of her abilities. She was virtually mute, only able to manage very basic sounds in response to questions. She was reliant on formal care staff for all of her personal care and was unable to stand and walk unaided. She spent most of her time during the day sitting in an armchair in the continuing care unit that had become her home. Her inability to instigate any communication, together with her apparent lack of response when spoken to, had led the staff to believe that she was fairly oblivious to her surroundings. Day after day she sat quietly, cut off from the world, surrounded by impregnable barriers. One busy morning a nurse was attending to the needs of one of Wendy's fellow residents. Out of the corner of her eye she saw a frail lady trip and stumble. The resident tried to regain her balance but fell and hit the floor at Wendy's feet, letting out an anguished cry as she did so. The nurse ran to assist, and as she bent down to comfort the lady who had fallen she heard laughter behind her. Turning round she saw Wendy shaking with mirth looking down at the lady who had fallen at her feet. The nurse was conscious of feeling shocked by Wendy's response. Reflecting on the incident later she described how she felt that the sudden expression of mirth from Wendy was as important as it was unexpected. It demonstrated that people severely affected by dementia can still appreciate humour. She felt that it might be possible to reach out to Wendy through the use of humour but that the fact that her laughter was prompted by another person's discomfort and pain made her uncomfortable and unable to act upon this belief.

As previously noted, some theories of humour are connected to incongruity (Beattie, 1776; Kant, 1790). In the following case study, incongruity theory can be seen as generating a base for the humour. This story also serves to illustrate the 'negative inclusive' category of the humour continuum, where care staff attempt to use humour without fully considering the communication difficulties. Although there is a genuine consideration for the feelings of the person with dementia, his or her perception is that their intentions are harmful and this elicits a negative response.

Case study 3

Bernard's story: an example of negative inclusive humour

Bernard was an older client who was an inpatient on a continuing care ward, again some years ago. He was permanently suspicious and angry. Any interaction had to be undertaken with extreme care due to his tendency to misconstrue the most beneficent input from care staff as an assault. He would frequently resort to physical violence. Further, his poor short-term memory had seriously impaired his ability to understand verbal communication.

Bernard was in his early 60s, physically fit and strong. This posed a considerable risk to staff if he did erupt and lose his temper. There was a general agreement that staff would only physically intercede in difficult situations as a last resort in order to reduce his levels of distress and risk to themselves.

One afternoon he was roaming through the female dormitory, which was laid out as two rows of beds facing one another in the traditional Victorian style. He was rummaging through residents' wardrobes and belongings as he went. This did not usually cause a problem because in those days access to sleeping areas was restricted, and all the residents spent their day in another part of the ward in what was known as the 'Day Room'. Normally staff would wait until the end of the shift and put everything back in place before their respective owners returned and noticed that things were not as they should be. This particular day was slightly different. It was normal practice to check on him every quarter of an hour to make sure he did not require nursing input.

During one of these checks a male nurse walked into the dormitory and saw Bernard at one end of the dormitory where domestic staff had begun to raise beds for cleaning. Bernard was standing behind one of the raised beds and thus was only visible from the waist up and all looked well. He was wearing a very conservative olive green knitted cardigan, checked shirt and tie. He saw the male nurse and moved to greet him. As he emerged from behind the bed it was apparent that Bernard had not only been investigating the contents of the women's wardrobes but had also decided to dress himself in their clothing. He had removed his trousers and in their place was wearing a somewhat tight fitting short tweed skirt, which amply displayed his masculine white hairy legs, brown socks and brogues.

The incongruity between knowing this man to be a serious aggressive threat yet seeing him standing perfectly at ease in his strange garb caused the nurse to be overcome by uncontrollable mirth. In order to compose himself, the nurse took himself away from the situation to re-think. He knew he was going to have to try to coax Bernard into his own clothes because his family were due to visit any moment. This was important because his family were having great difficulty in coming to terms with the drastic change in his behaviour over the last 6 months. The nurse felt that seeing him dressed in this manner would be devastating for them.

Together with a colleague he approached Bernard with a pair of trousers. The humour and the incongruity of the situation made it very difficult for them to know what to say. Both were struggling not to laugh. There was a general atmosphere of suppressed laughter. One nurse tried to make light of the situation and said 'Do you think that these might suit you better than what you've got on?'

Both nurses could feel Bernard's body tensing as they tried to get him to put the trousers on. They knew that he was going to explode and the danger seemed to add to the humour of the situation. The whole interaction then spiralled out of control. As Bernard exploded, they burst into gales of laughter and headed for a neutral corner of the room to re-think their tactics while Bernard calmed down. Eventually they managed to persuade him to allow them to dress him more appropriately. The somewhat negative aspects of this story were due to Bernard being unable to appreciate the effects of his appearance on the staff, and the staff's relative inability to use humour effectively as a method of diversion or in defusing the situation.

The following example indicates how humour can be used positively to promote good care and represents an example of the positive inclusive use of humour.

Case study 4

Mary, using positive inclusive humour

Mary was 72 years old and had a diagnosis of dementia. She had deteriorated to the extent that she had been admitted to a long-term psychogeriatric care home in the late 1990s. The building was, again, far from purpose built but did have the provision of individual bedrooms. Staff were keen to support her abilities and not demean her by assisting in her personal care, but Mary found it difficult to manage and staff were sensitive to her recognition of her failing abilities. Nonetheless, she was always encouraged to try to dress herself. In order to promote her independence with dressing, staff would ask her what she would like to wear from her wardrobe. The clothes were laid out on her bed in order and she was left to dress herself. However, she did make mistakes and these needed tactful handling from staff to avoid Mary experiencing overwhelming frustration. One particular day a member of the team saw her emerge from her bedroom with her bra on top of her blouse. Without haste the nurse approached and greeted her, exuding 'good humour'. Mary smiled in return. The nurse exchanged general pleasantries and then, when she felt that Mary was fully engaged, said 'Oh look Mary, it looks like you got dressed in the dark this morning' and pointed at the way she had dressed. Mary smiled but looked puzzled. Her ability to understand language was restricted by the effects of the dementia (Norberg, 1999) but she seemed to be swept along by the nurse's warm good humour, kindly smile, tone of voice and non-verbal communication. The conversation continued as the nurse gently steered a smiling Mary back to her room, thus ensuring that her self-esteem was still intact.

Although this account is similar to the previous example, the application of humour and the outcomes were very different. In this account there is a positive outcome, with the client's sense of dignity and well-being maintained. This interaction is more akin to Kitwood's (1997) example of 'celebration' and can be seen to be part of the 'positive inclusive' humour continuum. However, it still lacks the true intersubjectivity found at the extreme of the humour continuum. It can be suggested that the use of language to communicate the humour was not fully appropriate. It was the facial expression and non-verbal elements in the exchange that projected the good humour.

All too often dementia is seen as an illness that attacks cognitive function and erodes the quality of life. There are a few accounts of older people with dementia who demonstrate a joyful capacity for life and who deliberately set out to amuse. Such accounts are liberating and deserving of a wider audience because they lift the spirits of dementia care workers and the individuals themselves.

Case study 5

Movement to music: a positive inclusive example

Mrs Winstanly was 80 years old and lived in a small friendly residential home with a high resident/staff ratio. She had a mild dementia that was slowly deepening but did not as yet seem to have impaired a quiet sense of fun. By this time she was rather frail and walked slowly with the help of a member of staff. She was encouraged to retain her independence and the home provided a weekly exercise class. Occasionally Mrs Winstanley would agree to attend. In spite of her age she remained an attractive woman, always well dressed, with a ready smile and a deep husky voice. She was a favourite with the male residents who would vie to sit next to her.

Mavis, an earnest and trained person running the class, would welcome the group and invite members of staff to hand out various pieces of equipment to the residents, such as small batons, scarves or soft balls. They would then begin to exercise to the music. Mavis would call out clear instructions and staff would help less able residents. Mrs Winstanley began to look mischievous and instructions to pat one's knee with a stick or ball were taken to mean patting her male neighbour's knee with these items. There were never any complaints, except from Mavis who always felt that Mrs Winstanley had somehow misunderstood. Mavis's voice began to rise: 'No Mrs Winstanley, your knee not Mr Brinkley's!' This would often continue throughout the session. Scarves meant to be waved in the air found themselves around Mr Brinkley's neck, tapping one's own knee to the music became patting his knee and foot exercises became playing 'footsie'. By this time Mavis's voice sounded like a distraught nursery school teacher, Mrs Winstanley continued to 'play up' and the staff convulsed with laughter, often to the point of having tears in their eyes. Mrs Winstanley was aware of their amusement and would smile quietly to herself. It was a great performance that gave joy to the onlookers, thwarted authority and allowed her to feel autonomous. 'Well really!' Mavis would say, 'You could almost think she did all that on purpose!' Perhaps it was fortunate that Mrs Winstanley did not attend her class every week.

Norberg (1999) has described the importance of the potential therapeutic interactions that can exist between people with dementia and their carers. Jimmy's story in the next case study is one example of how non-verbal communication can be utilized when there is a deep understanding between client and carer (Mills, 2000). The experience is mutually inclusive and although humour was utilized it existed solely in the interaction between the staff member and Jimmy himself. It was private and there was no intent to play to an audience. An uninformed observer would find little meaning in the performance; it is also likely that they would not find it particularly amusing.

Moreover, this type of intervention requires awareness of the needs of the individual and an environment that permits a flexible but united approach.

Case study 6

Jimmy's story: an example of the intersubjective use of humour

In 2000, Jimmy was a potentially explosive character. He was 75 years old and an inpatient in a psychogeriatric assessment unit for people with dementia. He was short tempered and easily provoked. His behaviour patterns were very repetitive and he would march purposefully up and down the corridors of the unit, often pushing an empty wheelchair. He would stop if he spotted a face that seemed familiar and liked to chat. His conversation was impossible to follow as far as content was concerned, but staff would note his tone and nod and smile appropriately, and occasionally interject.

The unit was on two floors with doors at either ends of the stairs. Often Jimmy would repeatedly open and shut the door at the top of the stairs. His behaviour was very predictable. Each time he opened the door he would close it with a bang and then rattle the handle as if checking to see if it was locked. He would then open it slightly again. This cycle was repeated constantly, driving staff and clients to distraction. In the past, attempts to intercede and divert his attention had resulted in violent incidents. Jimmy seemed to think that this was important work that should not be interrupted and he should be left to continue. Staff pondered this problem and eventually developed a type of clowning 'mime' that they felt might safely overcome potential problems.

A staff member would approach and engage Jimmy in conversation or establish eye contact. The door key would then be produced with flourish, like a sword from its scabbard, and held for Jimmy to see. He would recognize the key and smile or laugh, often saying 'That's it'. The staff member would lock the door again with vastly exaggerated body language, ensuring that Jimmy was watching. The key was then returned to the staff member's pocket again, still using exaggerated body language. They would then rattle the door handle with theatrical gusto. Jimmy tended to follow suit, and would seem happy and relieved that the door would not open. He would frequently repeat 'That's it', smiling and patting the nurse on the shoulder. He seemed to be reassured, comforted, contained and entertained.

Using humour as a therapeutic tool

In formal care settings where professional care is provided, there is not the same depth and richness of shared understanding and knowledge as that between the person with dementia and a partner or family member. When coupled with the communication problems associated with dementia, the use of humour is made more difficult. However, the benefits that we have highlighted above, both in terms of the physiological effects of laughter and the support of the individual's 'personhood' through 'celebration', encourage the exploration of opportunities for its use. We suggest that the elements that facilitate the use of humour in these relationships are: firstly a deep knowledge of the 'humour preferences' of the person with dementia prior to the onset of the illness; and secondly an understanding of how the illness process may have affected the person's abilites to appreciate humour, particularly how the individual's perception and understanding of language are affected.

Firstly, if we consider the gathering of knowledge and information on the individual's humorous responses and tastes, these could come from various sources and methods. Observation and interaction would enable professional carers to discover what promotes amusement and 'celebration' in individuals within the context of the care setting. Using reminiscence to elicit any 'celebratory' and amusing memories from the person with dementia is also recommended. The literature strongly suggests that this is pleasurable both for the person with dementia and the carer, particularly if this could be undertaken with members of the family.

Relatives and friends could assist in the recall of specific examples of humorous episodes from the person's past. Specific information such as favourite comedians, comic films or music would be useful. Anecdotes, family catchphrases, nicknames and running jokes would also be very helpful. Less specific information, such as the favourite flavour of humour (albeit Benny Hill or Woody Allen), might also provide valuable information and insight, furthering enabling them to be seen as 'whole' people. Professional carers could utilize this information in many ways. It would be invaluable for further reminiscence work and as a validation tool. It would also be useful in situations such as with 'Jimmy', where carers need to find a way into the world of the other. Most important would be its strengthening of the individual's 'personhood' in the eyes of those who care in formal situations.

The need for self-awareness in those who work within mental health services has been recognized for many years. Practitioners are encouraged to recognize and understand their own beliefs, motivation, prejudices, aspirations and limitations, and how these colour therapeutic relationships. If formal carers are to utilize humour, this self-awareness is essential to avoid judging the person with dementia's own humour preferences. As we have seen, humour can be dark and threatening. It can victimize and exclude. Formal carers may need to accept that a person with dementia may find great humour in situations that they themselves might find offensive or even shocking, as in the situation illustrated in Wendy's case study. Their humour heritage may be considerably less politically correct times when jokes and humour were overtly racist and sexist. This raises considerably complex ethical issues for the formal carer. There needs to be careful consideration and balance of the use of humour as a therapeutic tool with the person with dementia and the need to challenge all forms of discrimination. It may be useful to consider the view of Watts (2000), who asserts that: 'Depending on the context, laughter may be liberating, subversive, conservative or coercive, or more probably a combination of all these at once.'

In examining the abilities of people with dementia to appreciate humour, and how these might change over time, some of the 'stage' models of dementia may give an indication of what should be considered. The aim will be to find the most effective and appropriate communication channels and media for humour.

There are many assessment tools based on describing the stages of the dementia process. In her work on the use of music therapy, Ruth Bright (1992) utilizes the Reisberg Descriptive Scale (Reisberg et al, 1982). In the same volume Feil describes four discrete behavioural stages (Feil, 1992), and there are many others, including the Clinical Dementia Rating Scale (CDR; Hughes et al, 1982) and Folstein's widely used Mini Mental State Examination (MME; Folstein et al, 1975). As Bright and others suggest, the validity of some of these scales is open to debate and some researchers and clinicans question their use. There can be little doubt, with or without the use of formal assessment, that the abilities of people with dementia do change over time and this is often reflected in their ability to use language (Norberg, 1999). If language skills are impeded by the progress of dementia, then more visual forms of transmission may be appropriate.

Video and DVD may have an important role here due to the availability of vintage comedy. Silent, slapstick films where the plot is less important and the humour is obvious and instantaneous may prove effective. Wendy's case study may indicate that some of the recent programmes based on the use of home video footage portraying members of the public coming to grief in a range of situations may be effective. Crucial to the success of using these form of media are the visual acuity of the individual and the practitioner's ability to engage and hold their attention. As illustrated in the case study with Jimmy, clowning and exaggerated comic 'mime', particularly in one-to-one situations, can succeed where other forms of communication fail.

We believe that the use of humour in therapeutic relationships with people with dementia can be demonstrated to have huge benefits, including physical and emotional well-being. People like 'Jimmy' show how some people with dementia have their personhood recognized and their individuality enhanced through the use of intersubjective communication, but again this is not unproblematic. Formal and familial carers may feel challenged if the content of the humorous interaction with a person with dementia clashes with their own belief and value system, and this raises considerable ethical considerations around discriminatory attitudes.

In conclusion, perhaps it is fitting that the last word should be left to Victor Borge, regarded as 'the funniest man in the world' by the *New York Times*. He said: 'Laughter is the shortest distance between two people.' Humour in dementia bridges the distance and allows us to reach out empathically to the other, to share in the moment and, together, make that moment more meaningful.

References

Beattie, J. (1776) *Essays*. Edinburgh: William Creech.

Benner, P. (1984) *From Novice to Expert: Excellence and Power in Clinical Nursing Practice*. Menlo Park, CA: Addison-Wesley.

Bergson, H. (1987). In J. Moreall, (Ed.), *The Philosophy of Laughter and Humour*. New York: State University of New York Press, pp. 117–126.

Berk, R.A. (2001) The active ingedients in humor: physiological benefits and risks for older adults. *Educational Gerontology*, **27**: 323–329.

Bremmer, J. (1997) Jokes, jokers and joke books in ancient Greek culture. In J. Bremmer and H. Roodenburg (Eds), *A Cultural History of Humour*. Cambridge: Polity Press, pp. 11–28.

Brewer, E. (1993) *The Dictionary of Phrase and Fable*. Ware, Hertfordshire: Wordsworth Reference.

Bright, R. (1992) Music therapy in the management of dementia. In G. Jones and B. Miesen (Eds), *Care-giving in Dementia: Research and Aplications*. London: Routlege, pp. 162–180.

Cardoso, S. (2003) *It's No Laughing Matter*. http://www.newscientist.com/opinion/opinterview.jsp?id=ns23436 (accessed Jan 2003).

Chapman, A.C. and Sheehy, P.C. (1987) Humour. In R.L. Gregory (Ed.), *The Oxford Companion to the Mind*. Oxford: Oxford University Press.

Coleman, P.G. (1994) Reminiscence within the study of ageing. In J. Bornat (Ed.), *Reminiscence Reviewed: Perspectives, Evaluations, Achievements*. Buckingham, PA: Open University Press, pp. 8–20.

Davis, J.M. (1996) Taking humour and laughter seriously. *Australian Journal of Comedy*, **2**(1). http://www.ozcomedy.com/journal/21milner.htm (accessed June 2001).

Ekman, P., Levenson, R.W. and Friesen, W.V. (1983) Autonomic nervous system activity distinguishes amongst emotions. *Science*, **221**: 1208–1210.

Feil, N. (1992) Validation therapy with late-onset dementia populations. In G. Jones and B. Miesen (Eds), *Care-giving in Dementia: Research and Applications*. London: Routledge, pp. 199–218.

Folstein, M.F., Folstein, S.E. and McHugh, P.R. (1975) Mini-Mental State. a practical method of grading the cognitive state of patients for clinicians. *Journal of Psychiatric Research*, **12**: 189–198.

Foucault, M. (1979) *The History of Sexuality*. London: Allen Lane.

Foucault, M. (1980) Truth and power. In C. Gordon (Ed.), *Power Knowledge: Selected Interviews and Other Writings 1972–1977*. Brighton: Harvester, pp. 109–133.

Frankl, V. (1984) *Man's Search for Meaning: An Introduction To Logotherapy*. New York: Simon & Schuster.

Freud, S. (1960) *Jokes and Their Relation to the Unconscious* (Trans. J. Strachey). London: Routledge and Kegan Paul.

Hobbes, T. (1651/1969) *Leviathan*. London: Collins (original work published in 1651).

Hughes, C.P., Berg, L., Donziger, W.L., et al (1982) New clinical scale for the staging of dementia. *British Journal of Psychiatry*, **140**: 556–572.

Izard, C. (1991) *The Psychology of Emotions*. New York: Plenum Press.

Kant, I. (1790) *Kritik der Urteilskraft* (Trans. 1987). Berlin: Lagarde.

Kitwood, T. (1997) *Dementia Reconsidered: the Person Comes First*. Buckingham, PA: Open University Press.

Kline, L. W. (1907) The psychology of humor. *American Journal of Psychology*, **18**: 421–441.

Lawrence, R.D. (1986) *In Praise of Wolves*. New York: Henry Holt & Co.

Lawrence, R.D. (1997) *The Trail of the Wolf*. Buffalow: Firefly Books.

Mackinley, E. (2001) *The Spiritual Dimension of Ageing*, London: JKP.

Marmysz, J. (2001) *Humor, Sublimity and Incongruity*. http://users.aol.com/geinster/Sub.html.

Miell, D. and Croghan, R. (1996) Examining the wider context of social relationships. In D. Miell and R. Dallos (Eds), *Social Interaction and Personal Relationships*. Milton Keynes: Open University Press/Sage, pp. 267–318.

Mills, M.A. (1995) Narrative identity and dementia: narrative and emotion in older people with dementia, volume 2. PhD thesis, University of Southampton.

Mills, M.A. (1998) *Narrative Identity and Dementia: a Study of Autobiographical Memories and Emotions*. Aldershot: Ashgate Publishing.

Mills, M.A. (2000) The gift of her friendship. In S. Benson (Ed.), *Person-centred Care: Creative Approaches to Individualised Care for People with Dementia*, Journal of Dementia Care Person-Centred Care Series. London: Hawker Publications.

Mills, M.A. and Coleman, P.G. (1994) Nostalgic memories in dementia: a case study. *International Journal of Aging and Human Development*, **8**: 203–219.

Moreall, J. (1987) *The Philosophy of Laughter and Humour*. New York: State University Of New York Press.

Morse, J.M., Bottroff, J., Anderson, G., O'Brien, B. and Solberg, S. (1992) Beyond empathy: expanding expressions of caring. *Journal of Advanced Nursing*, **17**: 809–821.

Muller, R. (1980) *Most of All, They Taught Me Happiness*. New York: Double-day.

Norberg, A. (1999) Communication with people suffering from severe dementia. In M. Clinton and S. Nelson (Eds), *Advanced Practice in Mental Health Nursing*. Oxford: Blackwell Science, p. 158.

Reisberg, B., Ferris, S.H., de Leon, M.J. and Crook, T. (1982) The Global Deterioration Scale for assessment of primary degenerative dementia. *American Journal of Psychiatry*, **139**: 1136–1139.

Robinson, V. (1991) *Humour and the Health Professions* (2nd edn). New Jersey: Charles B. Slack.

Shaw, G.B. (1958) Our theatre in the nineties. In E.J. West (Ed.), *Shaw on Theatre*, vol. 2. New York: Hill & Wang, pp. 118–119.

Watts, V. (2000) *Humour: a Sketch*. http://www.dance.ohio-state.edu/people/gradpage%20/vickiwatts/humour.html (accessed July 2001).

Ziegler, J.B. (1998) Use of humour in medical training. *Medical Teacher*, **20**: 341.
Zilman, D. (1983) Disparagement humor. In P. McGhee and J. Goldstein (Eds), *Handbook of Humor Research*, vol. 1. New York: Springer-Verlag, pp. 85–108.

Chapter 6

Occupational therapy use of sensory stimulation techniques to enhance engagement in later stage dementia care

Lesley Ann Wareing

Summary

It is hoped that the reader will take away the following from reading this chapter: knowledge about the origins of sensory stimulation (SS) work; the development of this work with persons with dementia; and two occupational therapy (OT) frameworks about sensory techniques as they apply to dementia. Research is showing that, even in the later stages of the illness, persons with dementia can be reached through adapted occupational and communication techniques. A new Compensating Balance Framework has been developed for pilot research based around SS sessions facilitated by care-giving staff for persons with dementia in Behavioural Stages 3 and 4. So far, four discrete phenomena within communication interactions have been identified: conscious waiting; non-verbal turn taking; a pivotal moment where the communication imbalance begins to normalize; and an increased momentum for engagement. The role of the occupational therapist has a special place in the care for persons in the later stages of dementia. Suggestions are made for future directions within OT.

Introduction

The author is a Clinical Occupational Therapist with 30 years of experience and a special interest in occupation for older people with Alzheimer's disease (AD) and other dementing illnesses, especially in the later stages when verbal communication skills are limited or not available. Frustration at the lack of activities and interpersonal interventions for people in the later stages of the dementia illness led to an exploration of any available SS techniques, especially non-verbal sensory ones that would be appropriate to those who could not engage in more conventional methods and activity approaches. After utilizing and comparing a number of sensory environment milieu approaches, the author was involved in a pilot research trial of Snoezelen® techniques using audiovisual and tactile SS. Further research was conducted to determine which of these approaches best suited individuals in different stages of dementia. The most successful interaction engagements were with persons in Behavioural Stages 3 and 4 (Jones, 2004, p. 261). These engagements are now the subject of more detailed qualitative component analysis.

Background

Multi-sensory rooms

The history of sensory research will be reviewed, how sensory environments changed, through to more specific studies and techniques and finally a detailed analysis of what is happening during sensory interactions will be given. Multi-sensory environments were first pioneered in The Netherlands for children with severe learning disabilities (Kewin, 1994). In the UK the use of this technique for persons with dementia dates to the early 1990s.

Initial research was carried out in a purpose-built multi-sensory room. The room was white, with cream-coloured curtains to exclude natural daylight, and had a cream carpet to provide tactile stimulation to the feet (shoes were removed). A number of objects were also located here: a beanbag; several floor cushions, one of which vibrated when hugged or pushed; two deep-seat chairs; a projector; 'panoramic rotator' (for projecting moving images around the room); and a 'mirror ball and spotlight combination' that enabled changing coloured spots to be projected onto the walls and floor or as stationary changing colours. The focal point for the room was a 'bubble tube' placed in front of a mirrored corner opposite the door that slowly changed colour. A 'fibre-optic spray' projected from the wall with easy access to touch, stroke, twist or simply watch. An 'aroma diffuser' provided a pleasant scent and a cassette recorder 'played New Age' music. A large mobile of a seagull (with a pull cord to make its wings flap) hung in another corner.

Some persons with dementia who spent time in the room appeared to become relaxed. This subsequently had an impact on the atmosphere in the ward environment, which became calmer. Moffat's evaluation (Moffat et al, 1993) showed an overall increase in happiness and interest, decrease in fear and sadness, improved engagement and relationships with care-givers and significantly reduced stress levels of family carers; it was multi-sensory but the effect was not always lasting and it varied with each individual. Similar observations were being made in The Netherlands where colleagues were using a similar approach (Achterberg et al, 1997). The aim of their study was to determine whether the experience in the room was pleasurable at the time, and whether there were any lasting benefits for persons, staff and carers. Although not every person responded favourably, the results indicated that most became calmer. They also found that the effect was variable between persons and not always lasting.

Methods to find out through which sense/s a person is most 'reachable' are required, alongside gathering as much life history information as possible when attempting to provide meaningful activity (occupation) for individuals. Larger studies and randomized controlled trials using predominantly quantitative methodology have been conducted but have not been able to pick up the subtleties of the individual interactions (Baker et al, 2001).

Other sensory stimulation methods

Sensory stimulation may be defined as the use of stimulation to maximize each of the six sensory modalities:

1   Vision, e.g. through changing unpatterned projected images.
2   Olfactory, e.g. stimulation through aromas.
3   Auditory, e.g. through music that can be varied.
4   Tactile, e.g. through handling of objects.
5   Taste, e.g. through detection by tongue and mouth, usually inducing pleasure.
6   Kinaesthetic, e.g. through movement and rhythm.

Because sensory objects or 'triggers' often activate more than one sense (e.g. vision and touch when holding a piece of fabric), the multi-sensory approach uses methods that try to target a combination of sensory modalities. These can often be adapted to meet individual needs and preferences. The use of SS as an occupation for people with dementia has been explored in a variety of ways and settings. Norberg et al (1986) published an exploratory study into reaction to music, touch and object presentation in late dementia. Music (auditory stimulation) is being used increasingly to create a calming atmosphere (Bright, 1992; Broersen and Van Nieuwenhuizen, 2004), especially in residential care home settings (Ragneskog et al, 1996). The Sonas approach uses a sensory approach to all of the senses (Hamill and Connors, 2004, p. 119).

Diminishing cognitive and communication abilities present clinicians and carers with particular difficulties when striving to enable the person with dementia to continue to live a fulfilling life. Providing meaningful activity seems to elude many care providers despite knowing that people with dementia do retain skills (e.g. long-term memories, humour, some social skills and the ability to respond to the senses). The ever-changing nature of the dementia process makes providing meaningful activities an ever-changing problem.

As unique human beings we all respond differently to a similar stimulus, however there are some approaches that have a commonality that can be shared. Sensory stimulation falls into this category and can also be viewed as a tool to facilitate and optimize communication and contact. It is becoming apparent that the care-giver, rather than the equipment, is the significant feature in this approach and therefore requires some basic foundation training. Wareing (1999) has documented a training course detailing the components of good SS practice.

Communication and relationships

Professional care-givers often have huge unrealized opportunities to communicate with people with dementia. Jones (1992) found very little verbal communication between staff and persons with dementia in a long-term care facility (an average of only two statements made to each person by staff in a 2-h block of 'prime communication time'). Others have found that as little as 7% of all communication is verbal, 93% coming from tone of voice and body language.

Empirical work conducted by Hoffman et al (2000) demonstrated that: people with advanced dementia are responsive to the emotional undertones of 'outbursts' in the environment; 'positive affective non-verbal communication' elicits positive verbal and non-verbal responses; and 'negative non-verbal communication' elicits withdrawal and apparent discomfort. Hoffman et al suggested that cognitive losses may actually serve to sharpen non-verbal communication abilities in a similar way to a blind person developing greater hearing sensitivity, although Jones (2004) has linked this to 'emotional memory centres' remaining intact in the AD process longer than other cognitive abilities.

An 'Enabling, Person-led, Failure-free Approach' (EPFA) to SS seems essential to successful outcome when communicating with people with dementia. It provides an opportunity to participate in the environment and gain a feeling of self-esteem and well-being, which in turn is reflected in a person's emotional responses, mood and behaviour. Sensory stimulation can provide meaningful engagement and interaction through activity, which enhances communication opportunities and sometimes skills, and can enrich the relationships of care-givers and persons with dementia. Although time spent on one-to-one activity for people with dementia has been criticized as a luxury (Woodrow, 1998), the benefits of 30 min of quality interaction or engagement in purposeful activity are discussed later in the chapter.

Sensory deprivation

We take our senses for granted, and also the emotional responses and well-being that the stimulation of our senses can bring. Well-being is fundamental to our happiness and to our relationships with others. It is through our senses that we experience and communicate with the world. Sensory cues capture our attention and provide us with an awareness of what is happening around us, keeping us in touch with our environment.

Sensory deprivation can result from the absence of, disuse or malfunction of our sensory receptors. The effects of sensory deprivation have been extensively documented. Research has shown that 'prolonged or frequent restriction of appropriate and understandable stimulation can lead to negative psychological outcomes for individuals' (Zuckerman, 1964). Although the amount of stimulation that one can access is important, sufficient variation in stimulation is as important (stimulation that is unchanging and monotonous can be as detrimental as no stimulation at all). People with dementia are highly vulnerable to the effects of sensory deprivation. They have a primary need for stimulation, which their disease can prevent them from fulfilling. Whilst verbal skills may decrease in dementia, the need to communicate and relate to others may not change. The need to sustain personal human relationships to the extent possible remains a key aim in optimal care.

The impact of sensory deprivation and loss on well-being

The impact of sensory deprivation on people with dementia can lead to negative outcomes on mood, e.g. anxiety, stress, depression, withdrawal, reduced motivation and agitation and disturbed behaviour (Wareing et al, 1998). During normal care-giving routines people may experience sensory deprivation through poor communication skills, e.g. lack of both words and eye contact. Inappropriate stimulation can also be damaging (during a Snoezelen session, a lady interpreted the flashing red lights of the 'fibre-optic light sprays' as hot coals, and was frightened by them). An awareness of a person's 'sensory range' is necessary to promote well-being, from sensory deprivation through to appropriate SS and sensory overload.

Sensory functioning and loss

Sensory changes with age and different pathologies are often subtle, numerous and complex (Nusbaum, 1999); occupational therapists need to be familiar with these changes. There is also increasing evidence of specific types of sensory damage in specific types of dementing illness, which is key to understanding how to optimize sensory functioning, particularly vision and perception in AD (see Chapters 1 and 2 of this volume).

Sensory overload

Over-stimulation of persons with dementia is also undesirable because it can prevent the processing of any, rather than limited amounts, of the information present in the environment.

'The impact of an environment that continually forces someone to be alert, to be on the defensive against meaningless stimuli, may be a greater threat to his or her identity than dementia itself' (Warners, 1997). An example of a not uncommon, detrimental situation in residential care homes is that the television or radio may be continually turned on at high volume, even though no-one is paying any attention to it. This may result in residents and staff raising voices to try to compete with the purposeless background noise. Without the opportunity (or even physical ability) to escape such noisy, threatening environments, frustration, anxiety, loss of control and reduced 'information-processing ability' may occur.

Some persons 'cope' with this sensory overload by withdrawing from social contact and interaction, a psychological 'flight' of isolating themselves and retreating into their own world. This may lead to decreased motivation and activity, even apathy (Wareing, 1999). People with dementia are often unable to explore or change the environment in order to obtain the SS they require, particularly in the later, often immobile, stages of the illness. It is easy for staff to misinterpret persons with dementia, who have difficulties in expressing their responses to unpleasant, undesired or abrupt changes in the environment (Hoffman et al, 2000).

The link to occupational therapy: why consider sensory stimulation as an 'occupation'?

Those who pioneered SS at Kings Park Community Hospital in Bournemouth, Dorset, UK wanted to use sensory deprivation as a base for promoting further sensory research work with persons with dementia. Sensory deprivation studies had demonstrated fairly conclusively that even when 'cognitively able' people were subjected to sensory deprivation the resulting change in behaviour was significant and frightening, with many persons even experiencing visual and auditory hallucinations (Solomon et al, 1961). Liederman et al (1958) suggested that the environments for persons with dementia were actually promoting sensory deprivation. Bower (1967) indicated the need for SS in the treatment of 'senile dementia', as it was then called, but there is a dearth of information about the extent to which this was accepted in practice.

Anecdotally, staff said that they found the SS approach helpful, particularly with those people in the later stages of dementia; however, a combination of subjective judgement and 'trial and error' attempts was being employed to ensure a successful outcome. There had to be a way to understand the successful elements to interaction in more detail so that they could be described, taught and assessed; there had to be a way to get beyond the uncertainties expressed by staff.

The concept of 'balancing' used in the study described hereafter was an attractive one to use as a starting point for many reasons. The background to this thinking is linked to the work of others involved in SS for persons with dementia in the following paragraphs.

Cognitively able people have to balance their stimulation levels all the time because they are constantly stimulated; each individual learns to discriminate automatically between helpful and unhelpful SS. This developmental process begins before birth. In everyday life we are all bombarded with sensory information and messages from our environment (Soper and Thornley, 1996), which our nervous systems generally respond to and filter appropriately. We usually receive sensory information that we do not need to respond to (e.g. if the touch of clothing on our skin is comfortable we automatically disregard the sensation), but sometimes we need to (e.g. if the clothing is uncomfortable, tight or scratches then we become very aware of the sensation and respond by adjusting the clothing). As such, some types of sensory input are calming and others cause us concern or alert us. Our brain matches our level of arousal to the demands of the environment and we automatically use different strategies to do this (e.g. fidget to concentrate, rock to comfort and calm ourselves). Sensory integration happens unconsciously and is about sensory feeling rather than thinking; perceiving rather than knowing. Our environment is therefore very important and the need for both relaxing and stimulating environments has now been recognized as a requirement for hospitals and residential care homes.

Persons with dementia cannot do this stimulation-balancing themselves, and helping to provide them with such balance is difficult for many reasons: with memory loss, confusion or communication difficulties they are often unable to express preferences or change their environment to provide the appropriate stimulation to meet their needs at any given time; and they are often unable to sort and organize stimuli or take control of their environment in order to initiate their own calming or alerting strategies and are therefore often unable to affect their own well-being.

Consider all the positive stimuli in the following example and contrast it with someone with dementia in a residential setting: Mr Ray enjoys a regular afternoon walk. He takes comfort in feeling the warm sun on his back and in the chance to catch sight of the local village cricket match. The sound of the ball on the bat and the enthusiastic clapping of hands bring back fond memories of his younger days when he was team captain. The familiar smell of his wife's baking welcomes him as he returns home to the security of his relaxing armchair where he listens to his favourite music collection and enjoys a slice of warm, freshly baked fruitcake.

Sensory stimulation has been adopted by some as a tool for enhancing effective communication for people with dementia (Maguire and Gosling, 2003). Historical approaches and techniques, which have been used and developed to encourage positive stimulation and communication, are many and varied; an overview is provided in Table 6.1.

Even things such as sensory gardens provide an opportunity for the person with dementia and their carer to make use of SS; to enjoy fresh air, 'a walk with a purpose' and the chance to enhance well-being coming from the sight, the smells, sensations and the memories they have of certain plants and trees. More recently, aromatherapy trials for persons with dementia also continue

Table 6.1 Interpersonal methods and activities utilizing stimulation and communication

Primarily verbal	Primarily non-verbal
Reality Orientation (Folson, 1968)	Sensory Stimulation Groups (Maguire and
Remotivation (Barns et al, 1973)	Gosling, 2003)
Reminiscence (Butler, 1963)	Music (Bright, 1992)
Life Review (Butler, 1963)	Snoezelen (Baker et al, 1997)
Resocialization Therapy (Dröes, 1997)	BCA (Anderson et al, Chapter 7 of this
Psychotherapy (Butler, 1963)	volume)
Psychomotor Therapy (Dröes, 1997)	Sonas (Hamill and Connors, 2004)
The Validation Method (Feil, 2002)	Sensory Stimulation (Baker et al, 2001)
	Contact Clown Therapy (Meulmeester, 2003)

in this vein. The first studies have demonstrated positive effects, especially with lavender oil, which was found to be helpful in reducing agitation in some persons (Holmes et al, 2002).

History of occupational therapists' involvement with dementia

The next few paragraphs will discuss the aims of OT interventions, giving examples from two models currently being used. The purpose of OT with people with dementia is to engage in meaningful activity and communication to promote well-being. Occupational therapists use their core assessment and activity analysis skills to encourage engagement in activities of daily living (ADLs), including leisure activities and sustaining social and community contacts. The aims are to prevent or reduce sensory deprivation and changes in sensory functioning, to prevent isolation (Miesen, 1992) and to maintain substitution attachments 'to routines, objects and people' whether in the verbal Behavioural Stages 1 and 2 or the less-verbal Stages 3 and 4 (Jones, 2004). Thus, the theoretical underpinnings for OT work with persons with dementia come from several sources and include sensory deprivation theory (described earlier), attachment theory (Miesen, 1992, 1993) and the biology of the aging senses.

Well-being through 'occupation'

The philosophy and perspective of an occupational therapist in using activity as a treatment medium and rehabilitation process assumes a holistic view of the person. From an occupational therapist's perspective, therefore, activity is requisite to the emotional, physical and spiritual well-being of the person. Wilcock et al (1998, p. 80) defined well-being as 'an individual perception of a state of happiness, self-esteem, physical and mental health which can be associated with satisfactory relationships, occupations, spirituality and material security'.

For the person with dementia, well-being is difficult to attain due to their declining skills and cognitive and sensory deficits. Care-givers often describe deteriorating relationships, lack of interest, low self-esteem and reduced confidence with a sense of insecurity as the illness progresses. A lack of understanding by care-givers can exacerbate the problem and lead to the person being described as 'difficult' or 'withdrawn'.

At a local day centre in Dorset formal care-givers were complaining about difficulty in 'coping with people with dementia'. They were unaware of the differing needs of the group (Maguire and Gosling, 2003) and were basing their expectations on a higher (cognitive) functioning group. When the occupational therapist explained the OT approach and modified activities appropriate to the individual needs, the care-givers' attitudes rapidly changed (see Box 6.1).

The importance of 'occupational roles' within one's life can have an impact on the sense of well-being. 'Roles comprise a combination of attitudes and

---

Box 6.1 Attitude change requires understanding

Eight people with a dementia-type illness attended a local day centre in Dorset. They mixed with cognitively able clients and were expected to take part in the general activities within the centre.

Care-givers expressed dissatisfaction with the fact that persons with dementia wandered, were 'disruptive' within the activities and could be 'aggressive'. The care-givers felt that they spent most of their time trying to 'contain the situation', to the detriment of the more able clients.

Advice and education was provided by the occupational therapist on the illness, the skills and deficits of the people and on the environment. The introduction of assessment and appropriate activities brought about a change in attitude. A dedicated team of care-givers working with the dementia clients in an appropriate environment as well as the introduction of a special programme of activities (largely sensory based) brought an immediate change.

Care-givers reported a reduction in 'disruptive' behaviour, more confidence in dealing with anything that arises and an increase in engagement, participation and expression from the clients.

Care-givers commented 'I can't believe the change in Lizzie when she is given the bead box; she sits down, looks at them and wants to tell us about them too'. Family care-givers have also reported their satisfaction and have valued the advice given by the occupational therapist on how to use sensory activity at home.

strategies that are used to maintain an individual's status and self-esteem throughout his life cycle. They are modified and balanced according to their developmental stage and associated roles' (Johnson, 1996, p. 104). As people's skills and abilities to maintain these roles (and status and self-esteem) deteriorate, it is important to help them to modify and balance their roles when they have difficulty achieving this themselves. For example, whilst a lady with early-onset dementia may no longer be able to hold down her job as a florist, she may still enjoy the smell and texture of flowers and can achieve satisfaction and self-esteem by helping to create table decorations.

Occupational therapy models linked to dementia care interventions

Hasselkus (1997) and Perrin and May (2000) proffer two OT models that are linked to occupation, well-being and the importance of using sensory approaches to engage the person with dementia

Occupational Process Model (OPM)

This model proposed by Hasselkus (1997) describes three phases: the 'meeting of the minds', 'engagement in occupation' and 'well-being' (Coppola, 1998). The first phase, 'meeting of the minds' (Box 6.2), is vital to enable people to engage and is an area where use of SS plays an important part. To gain a person's attention the care-giver needs to interact with that person at their level; this could simply be by getting into their field of vision before gentle touch to attract their attention.

Hasselkus (1997) and Coppola (1998) focus on 'occupational space' and

---

Box 6.2 'Meeting of the minds' in the Occupational Process Model

Reg has Parkinson's disease and dementia; he is wheelchair bound and appears to be uncommunicative. He frequently sits with his eyes shut, tapping and picking at his clothes or the table. At mealtimes he sits with his hands under the table waiting to be fed. Staff expect little of him, assuming he is unable to participate or speak. If he appears to be asleep they leave him alone.

When approached, with the use of careful touch and kneeling in front of him (so that he can see who is there), he responds. Over time, interaction gradually increased. Using his eyes and limited facial expression, he now signifies that he would like contact. He will now respond with 'yes' and 'no' and sometimes other words to express his likes/dislikes and feelings.

suggest that staff need to pay attention to both the physical and human elements in order to enable the other two phases of the OPM model to take place.

The influence of the environment is also a crucial consideration. Golledge (1998) states 'the influence of the environmental context is immense for successful completion of occupations and is crucial when applying occupations therapeutically'. By being aware of the environment the occupational therapist has an excellent opportunity to utilize SS techniques to enhance and enrich the environment (Merrill, 1990). The second phase of the OPM, 'engagement in occupation' is distinguished by the many levels of engagement that can be experienced by people with dementia. A wide range of items and objects can be used and some examples are given in Box 6.3.

Skilled occupational therapists use SS at the appropriate level for the recipient, being aware of their likes and dislikes, their strengths and deficits and their 'preferred sense' to help them achieve a sense of well-being. This is the third phase of the OPM 'engagement in occupation' (see Box 6.4).

Perrin and May's occupational model

Perrin and May (2000) propose a model of dementia care that assesses for the cognitive changes taking place and the ability of an individual to participate in activity. They describe four phases of ability that run in parallel to the Behavioural Staging Model (Jones, 2004): the reflective phase, the symbolic phase, the sensorimotor phase and then the reflex phase.

Box 6.3 Appropriate education and objects for 'engagement in occupation'

A range of objects, e.g. soft toys, beads, bags with items inside, scarves, inflatable beach balls and large inflatable tools that make a squeak when tapped against a surface, have been slowly introduced at a local day centre after much discussion about the appropriateness of the items. (Some staff, without knowledge of sensory changes in dementia and the need for SS, thought some things to be 'age inappropriate'.)

Following the rest period after lunch, and as a way of overcoming the 'postprandial dip', items are placed around the room for people to explore. Ladies tend to choose cuddly toys, handbags, and activity aprons (Jones, 2004, p. 278), whilst men tend to choose tools and balls. The items usually provoke discussion and often people will begin impromptu games with a ball. Some of the gentlemen will use the inflatable hammers to 'tap' each other if they appear to be 'dozing' for too long. After people have had time to explore and are alert and engaged, a more structured activity will be introduced.

Box 6.4 'Engagement in occupation'

Maureen is 58 with the early-onset form of AD. She often looks lost and troubled when left alone. She converses in incoherent sentences and conveys her meaning by intonation. She also has some difficulty in comprehending instructions, needing to have clear and concise directions along with a demonstration.

She often sits rolling up her clothes and smoothing them, or fiddles with her handbag and its contents, worrying about lack of money in her purse. Care-givers had difficulty engaging her and attempted to remove the handbag, but discovered that this only served to increase her agitation.

The occupational therapist knew that Maureen had done a lot of sewing and embroidery in the past and liked 'pretty' things. She also found out that Maureen's husband had been a train driver, was an enthusiast at a steam railway and often took Maureen with him on the train. Maureen was offered a soft toy train to hold, as a substitute for her handbag, in the hope that it would be a happy reminiscence object of a large part of her life. It was made of a fabric of differing textures and colours.

She began by exploring the colours and textures, discovered that it squeaked and rustled and then sat with it on her lap, stroking the velvet and satin. She proceeded to communicate with the therapist about the train, showing her the different surfaces and noises it could make. Care-givers at the day centre reported that Maureen spent every subsequent session holding the train, attempting to tell others about it. They said Maureen was less agitated, was attempting to interact with other group members and also showed an interest in what others were doing at the time. The occupational therapist noted that there was increased eye contact, smiles, verbal interaction and more attention paid to the structured activity later.

In the 'reflective' phase the person is aware of others, has equality in relationships and can adapt to the environment. They are flexible in thought, can cope with a wide variety of stimuli and have facility with language. They are able to engage in structured goal-oriented activity.

People in the 'symbolic' phase become increasingly limited and dependent in their relationships. Their thoughts become more concrete and the number of stimuli that can be processed is reduced. Language can be impaired, as is the ability to learn new things. Activity now needs to centre on the symbolic, i.e. those activities that have the power to evoke emotions and permit freedom of expression.

In the 'sensorimotor' phase the person experiences the world through their senses. They have little language or evidence of directed thought. Their ability to participate in activity is limited and needs to be of a rhythmic repetitive form, e.g. folding, rummaging, cooking, gardening, toys, etc. In the last phase, the 'reflex' phase, the person experiences the world in the context of reflexes to stimuli. There is little evidence of directed thought, language is lost, movement is limited and the person is totally dependent on others for maintaining multi-sensory communication.

Sensory elements and stimulation become increasingly important. The approach of the therapist, their knowledge of the person and the therapist's ability to engage with the person at their functional level are vital. Smiling, singing, responding with similar noises and tones, encouraging the person to feed themselves, encouraging movement, stroking, cuddling and rocking have been shown to be successful.

Different phases and individual preferences

The reality of care provision sometimes necessitates that people in different stages of the illness are brought together. Even within groups of people at a similar stage they can still be functioning on different levels and find others frustrating to cope with. The skill of the occupational therapist in this instance lies in their ability to analyse and choose activities that can work on several levels at the same time. With knowledge of the phase that each member of the group is in, potential conflicts can be avoided and each person can engage in a meaningful way for their own well-being. Sensory activities often lend themselves to this way of working, e.g. music can be enjoyed on many levels (see Box 6.5) as can activities to do with taste, smell and touch. This is true of Sonas sessions (Hamill and Connors, 2004) or the type of art projects discussed by Anderson et al in Chapter 7 of this volume.

Box 6.5 An example of the different levels that music works at

A popular musical activity at an Outreach Group is a version of 'Hit or Miss'.

A selection of music is chosen, approximately 10 tracks, including the known preferences of group members. Some pieces may also be from their 'era' as well as something completely new. A sample of each track is played and members are encouraged to express their likes/dislikes.

People who are functioning at a higher level may give reasons for their like/dislike, whilst people who are less able may need to be encouraged to give a non-verbal signal, e.g. thumbs up, nods, shakes or facial expression. The tracks with the most votes are played in full at the end.

By engaging on an emotional level, people at different phases of their illness can participate. Mr Enock will close his eyes and listen intently, then reminisce about listening to music with his late wife and the memories this has brought back. Betty, who is often restless and paces up and down, will tend to sit opposite a member of staff so that she can maintain eye contact and pick up cues and sway in time to the music, sometimes singing the words. Reg, who tends to sleep if not directly stimulated, will remain awake, tapping his hands and feet in time to the music. Active participation by clapping and singing is very much encouraged, to promote physical activity.

Non-verbal and novelty activity

Rusted et al (1997) suggest that 'non-verbal cues' can be an aid to retrieval for cues. Persons with dementia may have more potential for remembering through emotional memory ability (Jones, 2004) than previously thought. The comments, memories and interest generated by a session making a Christmas pudding attest to this. People functioning at a higher cognitive level may be involved in actual preparation, yet when the citrus peel, juice and spices are added everyone begins to take notice. When conducting a sensory session with a group of persons in mixed phases, the use of many sensory cues helps everyone to participate (see Box 6.6).

The importance of introducing an element of novelty is discussed by Dickerson (1995), who looked at 'action identification' and its implications for OT with the promotion of self-esteem and well-being. It is recognized that routine and familiar tasks are important for persons with dementia, making people feel comfortable. However, if someone's self-esteem is to be enhanced, an activity that incorporates elements of challenge and novelty whilst giving supportive feedback and encouragement, with helpfulness of 'unpredictability', should also be considered. Simple crafts, cooking, gardening and the use of 'activity boxes' and 'activity aprons' all have scope for novelty and the opportunity for interaction and feedback.

Expensive equipment versus everyday activities

It is easy to think primarily of equipment and the sensory room as vital resources and to assume that without these sensory work is not possible. Many community care providers do not have the finances to have a variety of specialist equipment and they have become adept at improvising. Caregivers can be encouraged to use a variety of SS techniques and aids within the home environment following a period of assessment by an occupational therapist. Less expensive alternatives can be found. The local day centre does not have the space available to have its own multi-sensory room but it

---

Box 6.6 Fruit tasting as an example of a multi-sensory event for mixed phases

---

At the day centre 'fruit tasting' is very popular. Fruits are chosen according to the season and include a wide variety of familiar and exotic items. The whole fruits are placed on a table for all to see.

People are encouraged to look, handle and smell the fruit whilst attempting to identify it. The fruit is then washed and prepared in front of the group, allowing the aroma of each to be enjoyed. People are invited to choose something to eat and to comment on the taste, textures, likes and dislikes. These sessions stimulate discussion, reminiscences (both positive and negative), a sense of camaraderie (e.g. who is brave enough to try the more exotic) and pleasure in discovering something new.

The first time Reg attended a session he sat with his hands under the table and his mouth open expecting to be fed. He was encouraged to feed himself and respond about likes and dislikes. After three attempts at getting the therapist to feed him he began to raise his hand to choose and then took time to inspect and smell the fruit before eating. He remained awake throughout and when the session was over and the remaining fruit was being tidied away he maintained eye contact alternately with the therapist and the bowl of melon. When asked if he would like to finish the remaining melon he said 'yes'. The look of pleasure and enjoyment on his face as he finished the fruit was satisfying. His wife said he had never eaten melon before.

---

has invested in a few items following discussion with the occupational therapist: horsetail fibre-optic light, restful music, a UFO lamp, some children's bubble mixture and an aromatherapy diffuser. Sensory sessions are often used as a way of encouraging relaxation between lunch and a treatment session.

Benefits for relatives

McNamara and Kempenaar (1998) highlight the importance of tailoring sensory stimulation to the person, using their 'preferred sense'. The benefits to family carers of transferring SS activity to the home setting, following a thorough assessment in a day hospital unit, are valued. Carers reported that the person with dementia appeared to benefit, and that they too noticed this benefit. The importance of involving the relatives and friends alongside professional care-givers when considering appropriate activities has been clearly described by Conroy (1992), an occupational therapist who initiated work and research in this field. Carers greatly valued activities that they could enjoy with their relative. Enjoyment is often lacking as a person's abilities and understanding deteriorates. Carers reported that their relationship with the person changed greatly, and that it was difficult to feel that they were spending quality time together. The person can seem so 'detached' that family carers welcome suggestions for practical interventions that work (see Box 6.7).

Which components of communication are affected by sensory techniques?

The 'Compensating Balance' Framework

The body of literature about the positive effects of SS is growing but has not yet focused on the later stages of dementia. For example, Baker et al (2001) published a randomised stimulation for people with dementia, which concluded that when the use of a sensory room was compared with another social activity, e.g. dominoes, both appeared to be helpful activities. However, their research sample included persons in several stages, including earlier ones. They suggested that an activity may only be appropriate when a person can understand simple instructions. Their results found no longer term (post-activity) benefits of activity and that behaviour declined sharply when sessions were withdrawn. Such conclusions do not shed light on what specific aspects of communication and activity bring positive benefits to persons with dementia.

Box 6.7 Simple things often make a big impact

A gentleman in his early 80s had very poor short-term memory. He loves to reminisce about his years as a postman in London's East End and football, which he used to play on a regular basis. He enjoys being in charge and helping people. At the day centre he discovered the inflatable beach ball and began to move it around as if he were playing football. When asked if he would like a game, he kicked the ball to the occupational therapist and then began to encourage other gentlemen to participate.

People sitting down kicked the ball and some of the ladies joined in too. One quiet lady even got up out of her chair to kick the ball. Reg, who was often sleepy at this time of day, made attempts to kick the ball and was encouraged and praised for doing so. Everyone was laughing and enjoying themselves. People were able to talk about the games they enjoyed when they were younger.

An important assumption in the OT field is that an activity becomes an 'occupation' when it is meaningful to the individual. How does one study the process by which this happens in the last two stages of a dementing illness? Figure 6.1 shows the conceptual framework developed by the author to study specific components of interaction around providing and sharing meaningful activity with persons in the late stages of dementia.

The remainder of this chapter describes current research that is trying to identify and further understand the components of communication during those sensory activities that are most helpful in reaching persons in Behavioural Stages 3 and 4. This current work follows on from earlier and multi-centre randomised control trials (Moffat et al, 1993; Baker et al, 1997; Wareing et al, 1998; Baker et al, 2001).

New pilot research: initial findings

The exploration of communication exchange during sensory stimulation activity

Background to the study

A review of quantitative research studies (and also critiques of larger studies) illustrated that larger studies provide less insight into specific components of communication than smaller qualitative and case studies (Wareing, 2001). Even case studies using the quantitative approach still did not explore details of fundamental issues about communication interactions that need to be understood. Therefore, alternative methods of research were explored, leading to a choice of qualitative naturalistic research methods that have proven to be a valuable research strategy in healthcare, especially for studying specific behaviour with small samples. This approach was used to answer the research question, 'What contributes to successful engagement and activity during a sensory encounter?' and to explore further those components found to be positive in most interactive sessions.

Materials and methodology

In 'case study ethnography' the researcher aims to delve beneath the surface and observes responses by individuals to particular interactions. The behaviour and experience become the focus of the research. The individuals become the subjects and not the objects of research. The emphasis is on experience and subjectivity, and because the researcher becomes the tool they need to be acutely aware of what is influencing them and identify the influence of that bias.

The focus of this study was on 'positive results only'. Communication interactions were studies using videotaped recordings of routine sensory sessions

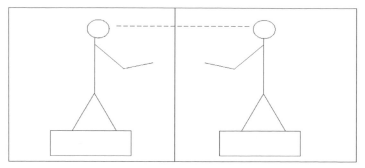

1 A balanced, healthy relationship occurs when two people share a common interest and/or activity. The competencies which each bring to the relationship (in physical, cognitive and emotional abilities) are unique but complementary and provide a balance in the relationship through positive interaction (engagement) allowing both to experience their own well-being.

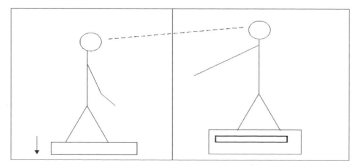

2 An imbalance is created when the competencies of a person with dementia diminish. The 'well' person develops new abilities to compensate for these. This 'increase in abilities' versus 'increasing disability' affects the balance of relationship. The person with dementia becomes increasingly devalued and disengaged, often resulting in apathy, withdrawal and loss of self-esteem.

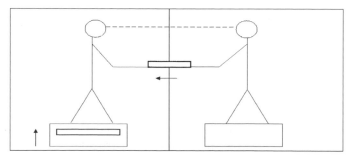

3 The balance is restored when the well person is able to meet the needs of (engage with) the person with dementia so that they can again share in an activity which promotes a balanced healthy relationship. The well person has to reach out to (engage with) the person with dementia who has withdrawn from the relationship (become disengaged). The well person has to adapt their new abilities in a way that allows the person with dementia to absorb, access or make use of aspects of these 'new' abilities for themselves.

Figure 6.1 Developing relationship through activity: the 'Compensating Balance' Framework for studying occupational therapy activity interventions.

of staff with six persons in late-stage dementia. The sessions were followed by semi-structured interviews conducted by the researcher with the member of staff immediately after the sensory session. The aim of the interviews was to capture the thoughts and feelings about the session, especially in relation to engagement and particularly interaction on 'successful' engagement.

Inclusion criteria

All persons selected were in Behavioural Stages 3 and 4 and were being cared for by staff in the Dorset Health Care NHS Trust. (By other staging methods, they had a diagnosis of 'severe dementia' with a score of 18+ on the Behavioural Rating Scale of CAPE; Pattie and Gilliard, 1997.) All had previously participated in routine SS sessions. Persons fitting these criteria were invited to participate in the study.

Occupational therapists and their assistants, who knew the persons well and had experience of using sensory activities with these persons, facilitated the sessions. Ethical approval for the study was obtained from The East Dorset Local Research Ethics Committee.

Comparison of interpretations

Sensory sessions were videotaped and each videotaped session was shown to the staff member for interpretation. Any differences in the interpretation were discussed and recorded. The discussion and the content of the interview led to modification of the design in the subsequent session.

The 'Compensating Balance' Framework already discussed was used to identify the main features, dimensions, factors and variables of each case study. In the current initial study, six cases were analysed using interpretation and explanation together, so that hypotheses were constantly challenged.

Data collection

Data were collected using video recordings (as opposed to creating interruptions to record events on paper), to avoid compromising the development of the relationship that occurred during the sensory session. Sensory sessions were video-recorded in the sensory room where they were normally held. The video recordings were analysed later. The member of staff was interviewed immediately after the session, to gain most insight into what they thought was happening during the sessions.

Initial indications

In the analysis to date, four types of interaction phenomena have been found to occur during SS sessions:

1 'Conscious waiting' for a response from the person with dementia on the part of the care-giver.
2 Non-verbal 'turn taking'.
3 A 'pivotal moment' where the care-giver first notices the balance starting to be restored.
4 'Increased momentum' when the person becomes more confident, interactive and expectant.

Conscious waiting is linked to the care-giver having the expectation of a response from the person with dementia. It is an acquired skill and the caregiver notices increased responses when they allow the person more time than if they do not. 'Turn taking' appears to be happening during interactions, though not in words (i.e. in non-verbal communication). There also appears to be a moment during each session that is pivotal and significant to the caregiver. This is where the care-giver is able to detect something positive or unusual coming from the person with dementia: a new level of interest in the communication or the stimuli used during the sensory SS, an escalation of positive emotion or a novel or especially appropriate response. It is usually the result of the person with dementia responding to, initiating a response or taking a 'turn' during the sensory encounter. This may be occurring because the care-giver has learned how to wait and is prepared to do so. Care-givers reported that they could identify this moment clearly, as could those evaluating the videotape. The quality of all subsequent interaction sometimes changed from this point onwards.

Discussion of findings

In this study the care-givers conducting the SS knew each person with dementia well, as individuals, and had already developed verbal or nonverbal relationships and engagement through SS activity. The research suggests, however, that SS could be used as an effective tool to initially open up channels of interaction and engagement.

The effect on care-givers of seeing a restoration of communication balance starting with the one pivotal moment was considerable. It was positive for both care-giver morale and for the care-giver's image of the person with dementia. It appears to increase the respect for the sense of the person with dementia still being present, in an active way, though with limited abilities.

The hope is that, in time, all care-givers will have access to formal education in acute observational and listening skills so that 'interactive communication' can be continued into the later stages of the illness. Having identified some of the components of non-verbal interactions, and being able to describe them, may encourage others to pursue continuous, strong and prolonged reciprocal relationships through the course of a dementing illness.

Implications of findings for dementia care interventions by occupational therapists

Occupational therapists use ADLs, which encompass not only routine activities but also any activity a person may wish to do, in order to reach their optimal potential as their treatment medium. Anderson et al (Chapter 7 of this volume) suggest that this engagement process may not be fully understood by care-givers (just as when a word has many meanings, but someone is only familiar with one of them). Occupational therapists therefore, as a professional group, have a responsibility to define clearly the unique contribution that they can make to dementia care, extending through to the end of the illness, not just half-way while speech and mobility are present.

An activity becomes an occupation when it is meaningful to the individual. One person may participate in an activity and enjoy it for what it is; another person may take part in the same activity and it may have a profound and meaningful impact on them. Occupational therapists are facilitators of meaningful activity; they are enablers rather than merely providers of occupation. Whereas specialist therapists focus primarily on one sense, e.g. music, occupational therapists are in a unique position with the focus of treatment on the whole person, through access to a huge range of activities to enable the individual to be optimally stimulated, engaged in meaningful activity and relating to others at any given time in this illness.

Occupational therapists need to continue researching and educating students about dementia and stage-specific work in this area; there is still a great shortage of specialist occupational therapists. Those who increasingly choose to work with persons in Behavioural Stages 3 and 4 (precisely those people that other healthcare professionals have disengaged from) have found it to be a rewarding experience. With greater understanding of the variety of sensory needs and SS techniques and the subtleties of verbal and non-verbal communication skills, occupational therapists will be well placed to deliver valuable treatment and care to this vulnerable group of people.

Acknowledgements

The author wishes to thank very sincerely Senior Occupational Therapists Lisa Brook, Sue Southam and Claire Taylor, and PhD Supervisors Peter Coleman and Caroline Ellis-Hill for their assistance with this chapter. Snoezelen is a registered trademark of Rompa.

References

Achterberg, I., Kok, W. and Salentijn, C. (1997) Snoezelen, a new way of communicating with the severely demented elderly. In B.M.L. Miesen and G.M.M. Jones (Eds), *Care-giving in Dementia*, vol. 2. London: Routledge, pp. 119–126.

Baker, R., Dowling, Z., Wareing, L.A., Dawson, J. and Assey, J.A. (1997) Snoezelen: Its long-term and short-term effects on older people with dementia. *British Journal of Occupational Therapy* **60**: 213–218.

Baker, R., Bell, S., Baker, E., Gibson, S., Holloway, J., Pearce, R., Dowling, Z., Thomas, P., Assey, J.A. and Wareing, L.A. (2001) A Randomised Controlled Trial of the effects of multiSS (MSS) for people with dementia. *British Journal of Clinical Psychology*, **40**: 81–96.

Barns, E. K., Sack, A. and Shore, H. (1973) Guidelines to treatment approaches. *Gerontologist*, **Winter**: 513–527.

Bower, H. (1967) SS and the treatment of senile dementia. *Medical Journal of Australia*, **22**: 1113–1119.

Bright, R. (1992) Music therapy in management of dementia. In G.M.M. Jones and B.M.L. Miesen (Eds), *Care-giving in Dementia*, vol. 1. London: Routledge, pp. 162–180.

Broersen, M. and Van Nieuwenhuijzen, N. (2004) Music therapy for persons with dementia. In G.M.M. Jones and B.M.L. Miesen (Eds), *Care-giving in Dementia*, vol. 3. Hove: Brunner-Routledge, pp. 155–181.

Butler, R.N. (1963) The life review: an interpretation of reminiscence in the aged. *Psychiatry*, **26**: 65–76.

Conroy, C. (1992) An evaluation of an OT service for persons with dementia. In G.M.M. Jones and B.M.L. Miesen (Eds), *Care-giving in Dementia*, vol. 1. London: Routledge, pp. 219–238.

Coppola, S. (1998) Clinical interpretation of occupation and wellbeing in dementia: the experience of day care staff. *American Journal of Occupational Therapy*, **52**: 435–438.

Dickerson, A.E. (1995) Action identification may explain why the doing of activities in OT effects positive changes in clients. *British Journal of Occupational Therapy*, **58**: 461–464.

Dröes, R.M. (1997) Psychosocial treatment for demented person with dementias: overview of methods and effects. *Care Giving in dementia*, **2**: 127–141.

Feil, N. (2002) Simple techniques for communicating with people with Alzheimer's type dementia. *The Validation Breakthrough* (2nd edn). Baltimore, MD: Health Professions Press.

Folson, J.C. (1968) Reality orientation for the elderly mental person with dementia. *Journal of Geriatric Psychiatry*, **1**: 291–307.

Golledge, J. (1998) Distinguishing between occupation, purposeful activity and Activity: Part 1: Review and explanation. *British Journal of Occupational Therapy*, **61**: 100–105.

Hamill, R. and Connors, T. (2004) Sonas aPc: activating the potential for communication through SS. In G.M.M. Jones and B.M.L. Miesen (Eds), *Care-giving in Dementia*, vol. 3. Hove: Brunner-Routledge, pp. 119–138.

Hasselkus, B.R. (1997) Occupation and wellbeing in dementia: the experience of day care staff. *American Journal of Occupational Therapy*, 52: 423–434.

Hoffman, S., Platt, C., Barry, K. and Hammill, L. (2000) When language fails: non verbal communication abilities of the demented. In T. Perrin and H. May (Eds), *Wellbeing in Dementia: an Occupational Approach*. London: Churchill Livingstone, p. 89.

Holmes, C., Hopkins, V., Hensford, C., Maclaughlin, V., Wilkinson, D. and

Rosenvinge, H. (2002) Lavender oil as a treatment for agitated behaviour in severe dementia: a placebo controlled study. *International Journal of Geriatric Psychiatry*, **17**: 305–308.

Johnson, S.E. (1996) Activity analysis. In A. Turner, M. Foster and S.E. Johnson (Eds), *Occupational Therapy and physical dysfunction*, vol. 4. Edinburgh: Churchill Livingstone, p. 104.

Jones, G.M.M. (1992) A communication model for dementia care giving in dementia. In G.M.M. Jones and B.M.L. Miesen (Eds), *Care-giving in Dementia*, vol. 1. London: Routledge, pp. 78–86.

Jones, G.M.M. (2004) The loss of meaningful attachments in dementia and behavioural stage-specific implications. In G.M.M. Jones and B.M.L. Miesen (Eds), *Care-giving in Dementia*, vol. 3. Hove: Brunner-Routledge, pp 261–283.

Kewin, J. (1994) Snoezelen – the reasons and the method. In R. Hutchinson and J. Kewin (Eds), *Sensations and Disability – Sensory Environments for Leisure. Snoezelen, Education and Therapy*. Chesterfield: Rompa, pp. 6–17.

Liederman, P.H., Mendelson, J., Wexler, D. and Solomon, P. (1958) Sensory deprivation: clinical aspects. *Achives of Internal Medicine*, **101**: 389.

McNamara, C. and Kempenaar, L. (1998) The benefits of specific SS. *Journal of Dementia Care*, **6**: 14–15.

Maguire, S. and Gosling, A.-L. (2003) Social and stimulation groups: do the benefits last? *Journal of Dementia Care*, **11**: 20–22.

Merrill, S. (1990) *Environment: Implications for OT Practice – A Sensory Integrative Approach*. American Occupational Therapy Association.

Meulmeester, F. (2003) *Care and Humour Journal [Denkbeeld Zorg en humor]*, **Feb.**

Miesen, B. (1992) Attachment theory and dementia. In G.M.M. Jones and B.M.L. Miesen (Eds), *Care-giving in Dementia*, vol. 1. London: Routledge, pp. 38–54.

Miesen, B. (1993) Alzheimer's Disease, the phenomenon of parent fixation and Bowlby's attachment theory. *International Journal of Geriatric Psychiatry*, **8**: 147–153.

Moffat, N., Barker, P., Pinkney, L., Garside, M. and Freeman, C. (1993) *Snoezelen: an Experience for People with Dementia*. Chesterfield: Rompa.

Norberg, A., Melin, E. and Asplund, K. (1986) Reaction to music, touch and object presentation in the final stages of dementia. An exploratory study. *International Journal of Nursing Studies*, **23**: 315–323.

Nusbaum, N. (1999) Aging and sensory senescence. *Southern Medical Journal*, **92**: 267–275.

Pattie, A.H. and Gilliard, C.J. (1997) *Clifton Assessment Procedures for the Elderly (CAPE)*. Kent: Hodder and Stoughton.

Perrin, T. and May, H. (2000) *Wellbeing in Dementia: an Occupational Approach*. London: Churchill Livingstone.

Ragneskog, H., Kitilgren, M., Karlsson, I. and Norberg, A. (1996) Dinner music for person with dementias. *Clinical Nursing Research*, **5**: 3.

Rusted, J. M., Marsh, R., Bledski, L. and Sheppard, L. (1997) Alzheimer person with dementias' use of auditory and olfactory cue to aid verbal memory. *Ageing and Mental Health*, **1**: 364–371.

Solomon, P., Kubzonsky, P., Liederman, P., Mendelson, J., Trumbull, R. and Wexler, D. (1961) *Sensory Deprivation: a Synopsis*. Cambridge, MA: Harvard University.

Soper, G. and Thornley, C.R. (1996) An evaluation of the effectiveness of an OT programme based on sensory integration theory for adults with severe learning disabilities. *British Journal of Occupational Therapy*, **59**: 475–482.

Wareing, L.A. (1999) *It Makes Sense. Sensory Enhancement. Handbook for Carers of People with Dementia*. Gibsonia, PA: TFH.

Wareing, L.A., (2001) SS for people with dementia. What do the studies indicate? *Proceedings of the British Society of Gerontology 30th Annual Conference*, pp. 190–194 (ISBN 1–85769–146–6).

Wareing, L.A., Coleman, P.G., and Baker, R. (1998) Multi-sensory environments and older people with dementia. *British Journal of Therapy and Rehabilitation*, **5**: 624–629.

Warners, I. (1997) Ethical issues in the care of the demented elderly, In B.M.L. Miesen and G.M.M. Jones (Eds), *Care-giving in Dementia*, vol. 2. London: Routledge, pp. 316–336.

Wilcock A. A., van de Arend, H., Darling, K, Soholtz, J., Siddall, R., Snigg, C. and Stephens, J. (1998) An exploratory study of people's perceptions and experiences of well-being. *British Journal of Occupational Therapy*, **61**: 75–78.

Woodrow, P. (1998) Interventions for confusion and dementia. 4: Alternative approaches. *British Journal of Nursing*, 7: 1247–1249.

Zuckerman, M. (1964) Perceptual isolation as a stress situation. *Archives of General Psychiatry*, **11**: 255–276.

Chapter 7

Building Community through Arts (BCA)

Cooperative inquiry using arts media with people with dementia

Jill Anderson, Kitty Lloyd-Lawrence and Hilda Flint

Introduction

This chapter describes the Building Community through Arts' (BCA's) innovative use of John Heron's *Cooperative Inquiry* method (a cycle of 'idea, action and review') with people with dementia (Heron, 1996). Basic communication skills and simple arts activities were introduced, with care staff, clients, school and business volunteers sharing in the inclusive training. Care staff, whose focus has often been limited to physical care, were helped to realize a more creative attitude to their day-to-day routines; clients benefited from the new inclusive attitudes towards 'activities'; the BCA team and community volunteers, including those recruited from business and schools, gained insights, skills and satisfaction from knowing that they helped to make a difference to clients with dementia.

Over the last few decades there has been a profound change of attitude towards people with dementia: no longer 'imbeciles', implying a loss of identity and lack of respect (Farrer, 1962), rather, the work of many, particularly Kitwood (1997), is bringing about a change in the culture of care – 'personhood', individual care plans and activities designed to restore a sense of meaning to the lives of people with dementia.

The provision of activities has involved two main strands: direct intervention by professionals, and staff training to develop skills and awareness that any activity beyond basic physical care can be 'beneficial'.

Direct intervention

Trained facilitators work to produce an end product – often a performance including a great variety of creative activities. Stimulating, fun and providing great enjoyment, the programmes rely on the trained facilitation of the providers (Age Exchange).

Staff training

There are many short courses offering ideas and insights into dementia and appropriate activities but it is not clear how far learning can be sustained on the trainees' return to their institutions. Writing on the effects of a research project using the 'Snoezelen' room (an individual programme of multi-sensory stimulation), Colin MacDonald commented that it was very dependent on the interest of the staff using it; after the project ended there was a 'loss of interest and disillusionment after the staff realised that multi-sensory stimulation was no miracle cure' (MacDonald, 2002).

Sustainability of person-centred staff attitudes to care

Well- and ill-being profiles were used in one home to assess the effect of a careful introduction of person-centred care (Hosking, 2002). As staff became more aware of the value of person-centred care plans, tailored to previous life experiences and present needs, the general well-being scores improved. Hosking commented that a year later staff attitudes were still changing, and that 'what was once considered an unpopular job is now increasingly about enabling people to get the best out of their remaining days'.

Value of shared activity establishing trust

Gottlieb-Tanaka et al (2003) reported on the development of creative activities for people with dementia. They recognized the value of developing friendly relationships between facilitators and the group with whom they were working – sharing their experiences to establish trust and equality in the group (in contrast to traditional training, which discourages sharing feelings or experience). However, it appears that although the day-to-day staff were impressed with the importance of creative activities they were not being trained to carry on with their provision.

Building Community through Arts (BCA)

During this time (1993–2002), the BCA developed a series of workshop programmes focusing on a collaborative style of working and using simple arts media to break down barriers between people who would not normally relate easily to each other, particularly those with disabilities or dementia who are often marginalized or excluded from our community life.

Education and creative activity in homes and hospitals

In his early research, Dr Sidney Jones, social psychologist, observed the effects of introducing activities to homes and hospitals, including music, art, poetry writing, poetry and play reading, French conversation, music and movement (Jones, 1983). The improvements noted were physical, social and psychological – greater self-esteem, physical control, moods and social interaction.

The second author (founder and coordinator of the BCA) followed up Jones' work by developing workshops for enhancing interaction between staff and residents in the care of the Central and Cecil Housing Trust, using simple arts media.

'New' interactive arts sessions

A key value was learned that influenced all further work of the BCA. When asked why she preferred the 'new arts sessions' put on in the home, one resident replied that the other sessions were just for a wet Wednesday – she challenged us to be original. In the other sessions staff went off for a cup of tea. It felt like pouring water into sand when they were not there to take advantage of the process and positive outcomes (taken from a BCA article reprinted from *Disability Times*, February 1994). However, staff were interested and wanted to be included in the new art sessions. After some negotiation, this was achieved.

The BCA's aim has been to enable carers (staff, relatives or community volunteers) to maximize day-to-day opportunities to develop deeper levels of relationship. As far as possible, programmes are designed 'with' rather than 'for' those in their care, enhancing their quality of life and promoting greater interest in their work for the carers.

The BCA team

The BCA team, as well as the two facilitators and consultant, included a widely diverse group of volunteers. They were given an introductory workshop and stayed to participate in the training. From time to time many different people from surrounding communities were included, e.g. relatives, the local minister, school children or business volunteers.

Method: introduction of cooperative inquiry (idea stage)

The third author, a facilitation trainer, helped the BCA to develop a collaborative training style based on John Heron's *Cooperative Inquiry* process (BCA Leaflet *A Way of Working Together*, based on the work of Heron, 1996). This is an action learning approach where participants consciously use a cycle of idea / action / review, working as equal inquirers across several layers of an organization, including clients, sharing together as peers in a learning partnership.

Shift from culture of blame to learning culture in cooperative inquiry

Before entering into a contract for a cooperative inquiry, the BCA and management need to agree their overall goal – to work together collaboratively towards a learning culture. This contrasts with the hierarchical culture of blame that tends to dominate institutional life. Often 'Whose fault?' is the question when something goes wrong, rather than 'Why did that happen, and what have we learned to prevent it happening again?' This is not easy where there has been an authoritarian management style. Failure to achieve this understanding may undermine the whole programme.

Anchoring a cooperative inquiry

An 'initiating group' is set up to anchor a cooperative inquiry. As far as possible this represented all levels of the host community, including relatives and the BCA team of consultant, facilitators and volunteers. The task of this group is described by Heron as three-stranded:

1   To understand and accept the methodology being introduced, so that 'they can make it their own'.
2   To develop 'participative decision-making and authentic collaboration so that the inquiry becomes truly cooperative'.
3   To 'create a climate in which emotional states can be identified, so that distress and tension aroused by the inquiry can be openly accepted and processed, and joy and delight in it and with each other can be freely expressed' (Heron, 1996).

Agreement on evaluation methodology

The initiating group agrees the methodology for the monitoring and evaluation of the project at the beginning of the project. It will meet at the very least three times: at the beginning of the project to define the starting profile of the organization; at mid-point to monitor progress or if necessary adjust the project goals; and at the end of the project to assess progress.

The Weaver's Triangle

Staff training (the action stage)

Programmes comprised training workshops, arts workshops, review time and individual consultations. Supporting materials, explanatory leaflets and learning tools were provided, with final workbooks for staff developed from their own learning experience during the projects. The concept of a fully

cooperative process is unfamiliar to usual management structures or participating staff. Each person is equally important by having a unique view of the
community and can contribute to a more complete picture of how things are
and how they could be – more than any one layer, e.g. management alone,
can achieve. Members could bring their peers' views to the initiating group,
and 'cascade' – share the thinking, information and practice of the initiating
group – with their colleagues.

The Weaver's Triangle

The BCA uses the Charities Evaluation Services' Weaver's Triangle (see
Figure 7.1) as a way of identifying the overall aim and resulting goals of an
organization or programme of work. These aims, objectives and activities in
turn can be tested against the organization's expressed values. This also
enables others, such as trustees, relatives, peer professionals or volunteers, to
understand the work being undertaken.

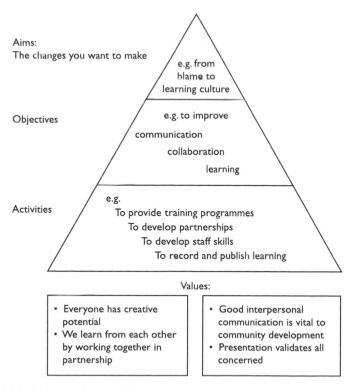

Figure 7.1 The Weaver's Triangle: from blame to learning from experiences.

Cooperative monitoring

The Weaver's Triangle includes markers for success that can be reviewed cooperatively and used as benchmarks for future development (CAF Weaver's Triangle evaluation sheets). One of the three key stages is *review*: looking back to become more consciously aware of the process, accepting successes and shortcomings, planning the next stage and avoiding unproductive 'blame games'.

The Charities Evaluation Services provide further pages to identify the indicators to monitor and test these aims, objectives, activities and values.

Implementing the Weaver's Triangle (action stage of cooperative inquiry)

On working with the Weaver's Triangle in the home for people with dementia, the initiating group identified several overall aims – to achieve more together in building their community, the principal issues being addressed to achieve their aim (communication, collaboration, confidence and care of residents) and the activities planned to achieve these objectives.

Individual goal-setting

Individuals set their own goals, giving added meaning to their day-to-day routine. Private and confidential learning logs helped to clarify learning points, which could be shared in the peer learning groups identified at the start of the programme. These groups were kept together within and, more importantly, outside the workshops. There were also opportunities to consult with the BCA facilitators and the house manager.

Group goal-setting

In the final workshops the staff planned and implemented an activity that could include residents. In one home a tea dance was arranged, in another an Easter bonnet parade and tea party. Responsibility was shifted from a 'management'-led activity to group discussion and shared planning.

Communication skills

The programmes introduced or revisited basic communication skills – listening, body language, use of language, the management of emotions and self and peer assessment. These were practised in the workshops and in small-group work. In many cases we were making explicit and thus validating what staff already practised, yet on one occasion our facilitator was interrupted and told 'I've already done listening'! However, these are lifelong learning skills, achieved by continuing practice and through self and peer assessment, learning more about their own reactions and feelings.

Language

Language is always particular to a group or culture. In one programme we explored different interpretations of words used, such as facilitation, disseminate and even activities. 'Facilitation' was variously interpreted as 'teaching', 'showing how to' or 'training'. For the BCA it means more 'enabling others to develop or release their hidden potential'. For some it was a new idea that 'activities' could refer to any day-to-day routine rather than identified sessions.

Cascade

We encouraged participants to pass their learning on to others not on the programme. This was also relevant for relatives or friends in the community.

Monitoring progress

Pre- and post-programme questionnaires covered personal, group and organizational issues, goals and outcomes. Interpreting results was undertaken internally; not as judgements but as learning points.

Arts intervention (action stage of cooperative inquiry)

The experiential method

We had noted the liberating effect on both residents (with or without dementia) and care staff of experiencing simple creative arts activities together at a level where particular expertise was not required. Arts provide a bridge for building a sense of community, value and purpose, to express feelings and moods. In art there is no 'right' or 'wrong'; we can value differences and enjoy finding commonly held feelings. We can experience working on the right side of the brain – spontaneous, intuitive, open to the unexpected – rather than the left side – logical, methodical, orderly. The arts are particularly appropriate when the cognitive faculties are minimal, as with dementia.

Inclusive training sessions

The process offers a combination of direct intervention and staff training. It included practical sessions that involved clients joining in at an early stage. This helped to set a pattern of inclusive working, adapting to the needs of clients from the start. Even if they could not be actively involved in the proceedings, simply to be present offered stimulation and a feeling of being part of the community.

A typical arts workshop plan

Although the BCA team proposed the outline plan for each workshop, it was open for discussion. Reviews were shared with all participants, recorded to a flipchart and circulated. Timings can be adapted to the clientele, medium used, etc. The aims were to interest and stimulate participants, encourage interpersonal communication and develop facilitation skills. An example is given in Table 7.1

Use of simple arts media

We introduced simple arts media: words; painting with black ink, using unusual tools such as string, sponges or pieces of card, fat or thin brushes, mapping pens; colour, using paint or wax crayons; clay or plasticine; and everyday or old-fashioned objects to stimulate the senses (smell, taste, touch, sound or sight), which provoked reminiscence and often animated conversation and comparisons with modern equivalents. Adapting activities to accommodate individual reactions but not to preclude the experiential elements offered valuable learning experiences.

Setting aside expectations of being able to learn anything new, the present moment and immediate experience of safety, caring and mutual interest is paramount. In one project the home manager had commented that, even if there was no subsequent conscious memory of the experience, a series of 10-min good experiences helped to build confidence for people with dementia.

Results: review stage of cooperative inquiry

In the final review workshop in the home for people with dementia a general feeling of achievement was expressed, summarized by comments such as: 'My confidence grew watching staff develop as I sat back' (house manager); 'There is now more appreciation and respect for each other' (a care team leader); and, crucially, one care assistant said 'At first it was a bit of a challenge. I could not relate the study to the work that I do day to day' but at the end she said 'Having taken guidance from the facilitators I was encouraged to treat it as a normal working day. From then on it was plain sailing' (taken from the Abbeyfield final review). This echoed our experience in earlier projects.

Table 7.1 Sample plan with timings

Time	Activity	Comment
Preparation	Facilitators and volunteers clarify workshop programme	Identify materials and timetable
00.00	Gather	Up to 12 participants
00.05	Introductions (general information) Round: all respond to a question, e.g. 'How am I today?' or 'What colour/animal could I be today? and why'	facing in a circle; clip boards, pens and paper; depending on time and numbers, one-word replies, one sentence or
00.15		1 min . . .
IDEA 00.30	Short description of medium	
ACTION 00.35	Explain working in groups of three, with 'doer', 'helper', 'observer' roles; opportunity for demonstration by facilitator with a volunteer	Groups with mix of people can demonstrate helpful and unhelpful facilitation, with participants commenting as observers
00.50	Working in groups of three for 10 min, taking turns to be doer, helper and observer	Facilitator warns 2 min before each change over
01.20–1.30	Still in small groups, individually give a title or one-liner to the work, drawing out the doer's ideas – not imposing the helper's	
1.30–1.40	Each group shares results with whole group	Copied to a flipchart or blue-tack for a display
REVIEW 1.40–1.50	Group review of workshop: What happened? Did we achieve what we set out to do? What have we learned? How can we take this forward? What might we change next time?	If short of time, can be one word or choice of smiley / angry 'faces' – especially helpful when working with children
1.50–2.00	Closing round (personal): How do I feel? Did I enjoy the workshop? Have I changed?	
Post workshop review	Facilitators and volunteers review with commissioning group	Take note of pluses and minuses for future amendment

Staff training

Participation of management staff

Participation of management personnel in workshops gave the programmes necessary recognition. For a resident, care staff and a member of management to spend time together on a common activity confirmed their common interest in the life of the institution. It helped to develop feelings of safety and a good relationship. When asked what part of the programme she had enjoyed most, a resident had replied 'Sitting down together like this with the staff'.

Individual goals – consultations with management and/or the BCA

Personal goals were discussed, agreed with and validated by the house manager. This raised staff morale, giving them the confidence to pursue their own learning, in contrast to the more usual appraisal or assessment interviews where a junior feels 'examined' by her line manager, with consequent anxiety and stress. Participants were encouraged to monitor their own progress in their private files and by discussion in learning groups. For some, developing a greater awareness of their own learning was unfamiliar: 'It felt very abstract' and 'Too rich a mixture'. Personal consultations helped to clarify the process, reassuring participants that the programme was relevant to their everyday work. Consultations were not always taken up, some preferring to work in their peer groups, reviewing together, with or without the BCA facilitators.

Group goals

Group activities encouraged staff to work together. The tea dance included residents, relatives and other staff. Posters, invitations and suggestions from all involved were incorporated into the programme. The final event was qualitatively different: 'enjoyable; challenging; different'. The house manager particularly appreciated the high level of cooperation and responsibility taken by the staff.

Involvement in 'activities'

By the end, more care staff saw activities as an integral part of their work, regarding each other as resources, more prepared to get involved both in the activities room and in their day-to-day routine. One care worker reported 'At first I was shy, scared, confused, I gradually learned and grew in confidence'. Another said 'Being reinforced around activity gave more confidence to work with residents and in the team'.

Working with community volunteers

Working with this wider group meant that more individual attention, careful listening and sensitive support could be given to clients. Staff contributed their own expertise, winning the respect of the visitors and the BCA team. Business executive volunteers were welcomed in two of the programmes, bringing new insights and energy. Their contribution was affected by shifting priorities outside their control. Ironically, this was parallel to difficulties experienced in the homes themselves, creating a common bond. Nevertheless, one care worker declared 'Thank you for showing us we can be more. I promise you we will be more'.

Social interaction

The registration officer for the borough in which we worked kept in close touch with the BCA. Her verdict was 'BCA were filling a gap by attending to social interaction. This social core training with spontaneous and continuous work on creativity fills a great need in training provision. It's brilliant'.

Effects of arts intervention on staff and residents

Not surprisingly 'playing' evoked making a mess, threatening a loss of control that aroused anxiety for some residents – it was not what they had learned. We needed to be flexible to respond to individual feelings and the response to the workshop activities.

Repeatedly the introduction of simple arts activities aroused a surprised reaction from care staff: 'I didn't know so much could come from so little' said one after a conversation triggered by an old-fashioned sweet. 'I've never heard her talk so much' was another comment.

Presentation

The presentation of finished artworks – notelets, laminated bookmarks or posters, a group poem, the making of cards – was gratifying. This is an extract from a group poem, compiled from responses to an abstract black ink painting on this occasion done as an example by a BCA team member in front of the whole group – clients, care staff, BCA team member and relatives:

> A dark forest
> A tropical forest
> An anteater eating ants
> An overnight train journey
> A lakeside with reeds

A fern reflecting in water
Crashing waves
A windy tree
Birds fighting . . .

Evaluation

While this section gives an overview from the final reviews of the process, at all stages the cycle of 'idea'/'action'/'review' is integral to continuous monitoring. Based on the cooperative work of the initiating group, the process is not felt to be threatening – not like having to respond to external inspection by a registration officer.

Interpreting statistics

Statistics require close interpretation and discussion with the participating group. Where small numbers are converted into percentages (e.g. in a group of ten, one person represents 10%), an 'off-day' or absence can give a very misleading percentage reading. We wondered in one home whether there had been some distortion in the pre-programme questionnaires, which showed remarkably positive scores. Were there anxieties about being too honest and revealing difficulties before trust had been established? In the final post-programme reviews the goals had largely been met, although some scores had shown a deterioration in quality of relationships – were these perhaps more honest in admitting difficulties not yet resolved?

Overall comments made in final reviews ranged from one-word thoughts (Happy, Exciting, Pleased, Challenging, Astonished, Enjoyable, Surprised, Different, Energy, Confident, Rewarding, Connected, Achievement, Teamwork, Delighted, Thank you) to deeper comments taken from the post-programme questionnaires distributed to the staff: 'I learned to let go and enjoy instead of control' (a manager), 'At meetings I used to tell – now I use more open questions' (a manager), 'We learned to listen to one another as a group, more appreciation and respect for each other' (care staff), 'Being reinforced around creativity gave more confidence to work with residents and team' (care staff), 'There's a more relaxed atmosphere, lot more stability; people not so guarded to say what they feel. The organization's culture is getting happier – loosening up, getting more relaxed' (a manager).

Increase in confidence and localized activities

Localized activity initiated by the regular care staff increased. They had developed greater personal confidence and in organizing activities, even small arts workshops with residents, with concomitant stimulation, interest and involvement of the clients. Activities staff became more supportive, providing a resource rather than being sole providers of 'activity'. The idea that day-to-day activities could be used as opportunities for 'building community' developed in a number of cases. A typical comment came from a care worker who summed up her experience: 'At the end of the course I really feel I have achieved something – more relaxed and confident to talk to people'.

One care worker who came to a programme illiterate decided to take up literacy classes. Another realized that instead of bingo she could facilitate a small workshop for residents; later she moved to another home, where she was asked to train other staff.

Process development versus traditional 'training'

Process development through experiential enquiries can result in a sense of some unmet expectations of having 'solutions' handed down by an expert. However, overall results reported in internal reviews, Social Services evaluation sheets and BCA questionnaires showed increased confidence and positive learning by the majority of participants. The post-programme questionnaires indicated that the concept of working cooperatively had met with considerable success. This was also evident in the high level of individual staff commitment to the programmes over a period of several months, and the many hours spent in shared planning, review and learning. The element of 'playing together' was valuable in breaking across barriers of status and between staff, residents and volunteers.

Effects on residents

Observation of mood changes

It is not always practicable to elicit review comments from residents with dementia, however it was possible to assess some level of mood, especially where these revealed changes. 'Smiley faces' drawn large and placed on the floor round the room proved a useful, simple review tool; all participants were invited to choose the expression (miserable, unhappy, OK, pleased, excited) that best matched their mood at the end of a session.

More explicit feedback came from Dr M, a retired GP, who appeared to have had his own past experience of training others and sat comfortably through a training session. At the end he stood to address the reviewing group, encouraging them with his opinion that the session had been 'very good'. Whereas in the morning he had been noticed for his depressed mood, the house manager reported that later that day after the workshop he was in high spirits and cheerful.

Another resident surprised a care worker by commenting on the training session he had enjoyed the previous day, which the staff member had assumed he would have forgotten. We learned never to make assumptions about how much was being understood, and to pay close attention to the sometimes confused or apparently unrelated responses of residents in these arts sessions.

Framing and presenting selected pieces of artwork was important, recognizing the 'psycho-social benefits of presentation', as observed by social psychologist Dr Sidney Jones. Books of poems and artwork were kept and displayed in each of the homes. An open-ended loose leaf 'ABC of Activities' was gathered, ready for additions by staff, and a workbook with instructions on presentation using computers and photocopiers was compiled for the use of the team; in one home a copy was left with an interested member of staff.

A case history: recovery of meaning through art – Elizabeth's story

The story of Elizabeth illustrates the main stages by which the BCA process developed – adapting Heron's cycle of Idea, Action and Review, within a cooperative framework. Names have been changed to preserve confidentiality.

Elizabeth had interfarct dementia. Her story illustrates the various stages by which she came to produce a meaningful image and caption that helped her to relate back into her own life and with her family.

Cooperation   Elizabeth was introduced to the activity in a small group, which included an artist volunteer. She was not left to flounder on her own.

Experimentation   The medium used in the group was black ink and unusual tools – twigs, sponges, card, string as well as brushes – at first simply to play with the ink to make experimental marks. There was no 'right' or 'wrong' – marks could not be rubbed out, but a fresh piece of paper could always be provided for more experimentation.

Random drawing from life   When accustomed to playing with the tools and the ink, a selection of random natural objects were presented to offer inspiration for further working with the ink. Stones, leaves, familiar vegetables, flowers – but *not*, for instance, in a vase with symmetrical sides. It was pointed out that the frustration of failing to get the image 'right' could sidetrack the whole experience. Elizabeth chose to focus on the mushrooms, and covered her paper with a variety of images relating to these.

Selection of images   With the help of the artist volunteer, two or three images were selected and isolated for photocopying. They could be enlarged, reduced, placed together in a group, given some significance.

Listening   While this was going on a volunteer was asking Elizabeth about the mushrooms, and listening intently to her responses. It was then that she made the remark that revealed her underlying feelings: 'Mushrooms, how Tom loved them. Now he's gone'.

Presentation   Together her images and the caption were presented as the cover for a notelet, enlarged as an A4 picture for display in her room, and included in a book of similarly gathered images. An unrelated visitor was so impressed he asked to be allowed to have a copy of this example of art, enabling meaning to emerge from the circumscribed life of someone with dementia.

Sharing   The day came when her key worker showed the picture to her grandchildren. For the first time they were able to understand that Elizabeth had realized that her son, their father Tom, had died – was 'gone'. Together they were able to share their grief with her for the first time. By comforting one another a strand of reality was woven into their relationship, a degree of meaningful interaction, significant to Elizabeth, her grandchildren and also illuminating for her carers. Her key worker's comment was 'This afternoon a lot of healing took place. It is the kind of afternoon that makes my job worthwhile'.

Significance of presentation, display and publicity

In the home where an Easter bonnet competition was arranged it provided valuable publicity material. Combined with an Easter tea, the parade was celebrated with families and friends and significant VIPs from the community. A photographic collage was gathered and kept on display for some time afterwards. The event was reported in a house newsletter, and served to evoke interest among relatives and friends unable to be directly involved.

To have a record in the form of a selected piece of work, carefully produced and presented, is significant. It can bypass the loss of memory and preserve the moment for both the client and others, as with Elizabeth's grandchildren. Indeed, on that occasion it opened up an avenue of understanding to a complete stranger whose assumptions about dementia may have been very negative.

Effect on team members and volunteers

Releasing creative energies in the BCA team

Individual team members demonstrated a variety of new developments after the programmes closed. A visually impaired volunteer enrolled on a drama therapy course. An Indian architect is now working on a paper on the architectural aspects of providing a home for people with dementia. A young girl with cerebral palsy, a wheelchair user, stayed with the BCA team from her introduction at the age of 13 through to graduation from university. Trained in facilitation skills with the team, she puts them to good use working with young children in a local school. She and the drama graduate facilitated a Millennium arts programme introducing children with learning disabilities to a local guide company using a variety of arts activities, culminating in a celebration to which the Mayoress, parents and friends were invited.

Community volunteers

One business volunteer offered the home's management a paper on volunteering that he had written; he was later invited to become a trustee of the home in which he had been involved. A college student who joined in an early project when still at school reported that even 5 years later she recalled it as a life-changing experience.

Case history of a business volunteer's change of attitude: Mathew's story

Mathew worked as a counter clerk for the high street bank sponsoring a programme. He had joined the bank straight from school and was now wanting something to test his abilities. The manager invited Mathew to represent the bank on the project.

Mathew was given a short introductory workshop initiating him in the activity he was later going to use with the older people in the home. Using black ink and unfamiliar tools, Mathew found the process quite threatening. His abstract shape looked to him like a dollar sign!

He wrote afterwards:

On playing with ink

It's hard to let go
I was just experimenting to see
How you could use the brush
Or even the twig
And then I suddenly found
I had drawn a dollar sign
Oh!

I'm still at work I thought
I mustn't do that
And I tried to hide it
I didn't want everyone
Thinking I was still at work

I wasn't sure
If the dollar sign

> Was for myself
> Or for other people

> I wanted to break out of this

Later, reflecting on the workshop where he had been the facilitator for a very confused older lady, he commented 'I enjoyed doing the workshop myself and found it revealing . . .'. Mathew returned to work with renewed enthusiasm and several new ideas. One customer commented 'I know who did that training – he treats us like real people in the queue; no-one, however confused they may seem, is made to feel a nuisance'.

His manager saw the value of the experience to the bank as a form of staff training that had a positive impact on communication between staff and customers. Mathew was later promoted and transferred to a bigger branch.

Mathew's comment at the end was 'You haven't just changed how I see my work; you've changed how I see my life'. This was a theme echoed by other volunteer and team members. Memorably a resident confided that she had wanted to end her life, but as a result of participating in the workshops she had found something worth living for.

Discussion

Staff training

Heron's *Cooperative Inquiry* method was combined with non-judgemental arts activity to enable profound changes in people's lives. The absolute commitment of management and staff to this style of working is essential. It is a challenging shift in view, especially where a blame culture is being replaced by a commitment to learning. The releasing of people's creativity, as shown by Mathew's and Elizabeth's stories, was inspiring and impressive in the variety of ways people expressed themselves. Individual attention, play, collaborative working and letting go of negative attitudes towards themselves set free a remarkable flow of creative inspiration in staff, clients and the BCA team itself.

Financial viability

The BCA training programmes employing two facilitators and a consultant are beyond the budget of most social welfare organizations. We aimed to create working partnerships between a social welfare organization, a charitable trust and a business. However small, it was important that the host organization committed some part of their training budget to the project and that a sponsoring business released a staff member (or team) to participate in the project. Because this was innovatory work not fully understood as being different from the employment of an artist for 'wet Wednesday' afternoon sessions, it was not easy to obtain grants. In our pilot work the role of the charitable trust was taken on by substantial voluntary contributions from our consultant and facilitators.

Business partnerships

Business partnerships were invaluable, and offered not only a useful public relations benefit to organizations with lively community awareness pro-grammes themselves, but also valuable personal development opportunities for those volunteers given leave to participate.

Need for cover for staff in training workshops

Cover is essential to free up staff for the programmes. At times this proved difficult with shift work, agency staffing and routine holidays or staff changes. To be called away in a training session to deal with telephone calls or unexpected visitors is unacceptable. Frequently more time than was originally envisaged was put into a programme by all parties, particularly by the very committed house managers, with some participants voluntarily taking time to attend workshops on their days off or during holidays. It was also difficult for learning groups to liaise effectively. Arrangements may need to be made to accommodate staff making their own plans to overcome these problems (e.g. exchanging shifts with colleagues).

Arts intervention

It was not difficult to enthuse care staff but the availability of an art-trained facilitator was essential both at and outside the training sessions, to respond to unexpected and imaginative initiatives and to develop new ideas.

Use of printing technologies

Selecting interesting typefaces, arranging material, enlarging or reducing, photocopying and laminating is in itself an absorbing and satisfying contri-bution that can be taught to care staff in a home or to a computer-happy volunteer supporting the home.

Future directions

Financial viability

Financial support from partners ready to support a social welfare institution is essential. Developing a relationship with a local firm or business, or local branch of a national organization, is one obvious route whereby substantial financial support can be asked for in return for favourable public relations as a local community involvement and valuable personal development training for seconded volunteers.

Publicity

When the Mayor or other local VIPs are invited to a final exhibition of work, the local press may be attracted and draw attention to a centre that may have felt neglected and unknown. Participation by local business interests or their national training departments serves to raise the profile of the work, encourages participants and raises staff morale.

Residential homes

At the end of each programme the participants were invited to look ahead to the future. Suggestions included improving and building on the work, involving relatives in the activities programme, improving communications and internalizing 'learning culture' and designing/developing volunteer programmes.

Whether such aspirations are carried out depends on an organization's willingness to re-visit their issues after a period of six months or a year. The BCA did not find this easy to implement because 'life moves on' – organizations change, staff change, new goals are pursued and there is a reluctance to look back.

Although the team has now disbanded, by recording our work the BCA hopes to make our experience and learning available for others to use in the same field of 'building community through arts'.

References

Farrer, A. (1962) *Love Almighty and Ills Unlimited*. Fontana, CA: The Fontana Library, p.189.

Gottlieb-Tanaka, D., Small, J. and Yassi, A. (2003) A programme of creative expression activities for seniors with dementia, *Dementia*, vol. 2. London: Sage Publications, pp. 7–18.

Heron, J. (1996) *Cooperative Inquiry: Research into the Human Condition*. London: Sage Publications.

Hosking, C. (2002) Looking after well-being: a tool for clinical audit. *Dementia Care Journal*, **March/April**: 18–20.

Jones, S. (1983) Learning and meta-learning with special reference to education for the elders. PhD Thesis, University of London Library.

Kitwood, T. (1997) *Dementia Reconsidered: The Person Comes First*. Buckingham, PA: Open University Press, 1997.

MacDonald, C. (2002) Back to the sensory world our 'care' has taken away. *Journal of Dementia Care*, **Jan/Feb**: 34.

Chapter 8

Medical care for chronically ill elderly people: nursing home medicine as *functional geriatrics*

Cees Hertogh

Introduction

This chapter looks at nursing home medicine in The Netherlands, internationally a relatively unique medical specialism. What sets it apart is not so much its specialist content – it is a specialist area encompassing elements of geriatrics, rehabilitation medicine and general practice medicine – but primarily the place of nursing home medicine and nursing homes within the organization of healthcare in The Netherlands. Nursing homes here represent an important link between the hospital, the care facility and general practice, and as well as having a residential function also play an important role in the post-acute treatment and rehabilitation of elderly people with functional impairment and chronic conditions. The nursing home physician is both the GP and geriatrician for elderly people living in the nursing home. Because the nursing home physician is employed on a permanent basis by the nursing home, many elderly people requiring care in the nursing home can receive medical treatment for which they would have to be admitted to hospital in other countries (Hoek et al, 2003). The nursing home physician is also involved in the capacity of practitioner or consultant with vulnerable elderly people living at home or in care facilities. This chapter looks at the basic concepts of nursing home medicine against the background of their historical development and at the same time examines their relationship with geriatric practice in the UK.

Nursing homes and nursing home medicine

The first of three academic courses for training nursing home physicians was set up at the Vrije Universiteit Amsterdam in 1989. Official recognition was achieved the following year when the register of certified nursing home physicians was started. The specialism of nursing home medicine was established. This recognition was an important milestone for the professional group involved. One of the primary objectives of the Dutch Association for Nursing Home Physicians (NVVA) set up in 1972 had thereby been achieved.

This recognition was the result of a great deal of hard work, as the development of nursing homes in The Netherlands and the position that this healthcare provision was able to establish in the overall system are largely due to the dedication of the physicians associated with these institutions. They had the unique opportunity – internationally speaking as well – to build up expertise in the provision of care for a clearly defined category of patient, frequently referred to for conciseness as 'nursing home patients'. From a historical point of view, the development can be traced back to the opening of the first hospital for the chronically or long-term ill in 1929: the Zonnehuis in Beekbergen (Oostvogel, 1989). As hospitals increasingly became institutions for short-term specialist diagnosis and treatment and as morbidity patterns moved in the direction of chronic diseases and their accumulation in advanced age, the institution-oriented concept of the 'nursing home patient' became increasingly clear-cut. Nursing homes were increasingly in demand by chronically ill elderly people with multiple health and care problems combined with an inadequate support network of informal care. In short, apart from a minority of younger chronically ill people, the majority of nursing home patients proved to be on the 'geriatric care route' as it were. This led to a premature 'geriatrification' of nursing home care, well before recognition of the first geriatric medical specialism in The Netherlands in the form of 'clinical' geriatrics in 1983.

In the 1970s, nursing home care became a provision of the General Act on Exceptional Medical Expenses (AWBZ) introduced at the time: social insurance for the 'uninsurable' risks of chronic disease and resulting care-dependency. The importance of reducing care-dependency where possible, so that people would not have to claim the AWBZ for a long time, was also recognized. Development of the therapeutic function of the nursing home was addressed according to the Nursing Homes Recommendation by the Central Health Care Advisory Board (Centrale Raad voor de Volksgezondheid, *Derde advies verpleeghuizen*, The Hague, 1972). Dutch nursing home physicians made contact with UK geriatricians and introduced the multi-disciplinary long-term care model. Work started on developing the 'reactivation' or rehabilitation function. Treatment teams were set up associating paramedic and psychosocial disciplines as well as physicians with the nursing home, and the term 'CLSM' care (Continuous, Long-term, Systematic, Multi-disciplinary care) gained acceptance as a means of emphasizing the particular nature of nursing home care.

The assignment of specific professional training and the introduction of the register of certified nursing home physicians can be seen as the completion of this development phase. It is almost ironic that this institutionalization of nursing home medicine as a new medical specialism roughly coincides with the emergence of a new policy trend that increasingly undermines the foundations of the 'nursing home' as an institution. At the beginning of 1987, recognition of the consultation function of the nursing home for the first time broke with the tradition prevailing until then that the provision of 'nursing home care' was limited to care within the walls of the nursing home. A year later in July 1988 the National Health Insurance Council passed the 'Subsidy Order for Substitute Nursing Home Care', enabling nursing home employees to provide care outside the nursing home for insured parties with indications for admission to a nursing home. The nursing home population 'floated' along with the beds. There was an almost explosive growth in all forms of nursing home care in care facilities, referred to as multiple care or substitution projects, with collaboration with primary care-givers operating with varying degrees of success. Nursing home physicians organized 'supplementary' nursing home care for elderly people living at home or in the care facility and in many cases the nursing home sacrificed beds for this. In parallel with this, the burden of care for elderly people in nursing homes and care facilities continued to increase.

Compared with 10–15 years ago, patients now admitted to nursing homes for long-term care are older, have more complex care requirements and more frequently have a psychogeriatric diagnosis combined with somatic and functional problems. Patients admitted with a dementia syndrome now relatively more frequently have serious or advanced forms of dementia and their average stay after admission is therefore shorter. Also the number of short-term admission patients – and therefore the discharge rate – has risen significantly due to a greatly improved treatment function. A corresponding trend can be seen in care facilities. Compared with 20 years ago there are more elderly people in care facilities today with a mild form of dementia, while the 'somatic nursing home patients' from those days are more often admitted or kept in this environment, for example because of the availability of supplementary nursing home care there. It is then also clear that the 'target group' of nursing home medicine has expanded significantly and is now no longer exclusively in the nursing home. More and more elderly people receive the traditional care provision referred to as 'nursing home care' in other places, even in hospitals. This 'nursing home care in hospitals' primarily developed as a response to the bed-blocking problem. Analysis of this showed that elderly patients in particular often remain in hospital longer as a result of an extended recovery period after treatment and the development of or increase in function loss due to the lack of adequate after-care. 'Transition care' was developed as a response to this, with hospitals setting up special departments in collaboration with nursing homes and nursing home physicians for prompt rehabilitation and post-acute care.

In view of these developments it can be concluded that institution-oriented concepts such as 'nursing home care', 'nursing home (indicated) patient' and 'nursing home medicine' are due for evaluation and reassessment. They no longer seem appropriate in a function-based and increasingly transmural healthcare system. Essentially they provide an inadequate and, at the very least, one-sided reflection of the type of care in question, the categories of patient for whom the care is intended and what nursing home medicine expertise comprises. A second, at least equally important, reason for such a reassessment is that the situation described above does not only relate to local conditions in The Netherlands. Almost all Western countries are faced with an aging population and the consequences of this for care provision for the elderly. Even in countries where healthcare is organized in a completely different manner, e.g. the USA, similar trends can be seen and these are increasingly expressed for example in new terms of reference for traditional 'long-term care facilities'.

The explanation of the basic concepts of nursing home care and nursing home medicine given in this chapter is consistent with these trends in that a non-institution-oriented approach is sought, indeed as a continuation of developments from the past, and hence the title of the chapter. Given the nature and content of this type of care provision, it deals with the theory and method of medicine for chronically ill elderly people, but it is a fact that the nursing home has been the environment in which such care has been able to develop its particular character. Without such an institution, medical care for the elderly could never have assumed the form it now has in The Netherlands.

Negative definitions of nursing home care and nursing home medicine

One of the first definitions of nursing home care comes from Oostvogel and dates back to the beginning of the 1960s. According to this definition, nursing homes are intended to provide care for patients who can no longer be nursed or treated at home and who no longer qualify for specialist hospital treatment (Oostvogel, 1961). The emphasis is therefore on 'nursing' and 'non-specialist treatment' and it is evident that in this definition the nursing home care concept is based on the *negative*: when nothing more is possible, people go into nursing homes as a 'last resort'. The positive aspect of nursing home care is ignored and the function of the institutions in question here is largely seen as a care safety net for society.

Twenty years later, in 1980, the first professor of nursing home medicine, Professor Michels, still sees it much the same way (Michels, 1980). He describes the task of the nursing home as looking after patients needing nursing care. All those requiring nursing assistance are eligible for such care. This too is a predominantly negative approach, where the single function of 'nursing' is given the most emphasis. Michels really means that, as well as providing nursing care, nursing homes must endeavour to eliminate the need for nursing. He refers to this endeavour as 'reactivation' and we will return to this later in the chapter. A secondary task of the nursing home in his view is to provide general medical assistance and offer social care. In this context he describes nursing home medicine as 'care' medicine, mainly focusing on the welfare and quality of life of the patient. Again this seems to be a negative definition. 'Care' medicine is indicated for the category of patient for whom 'cure' medicine has not had any effect.

We encounter a related vision in the 'geriatric network' model by the Dutch Geriatrics Society (Nederlandse Vereniging voor Geriatrie, 1989). Here too the division of labour between the various medical disciplines operating in the field of care for the elderly is described in terms of 'cure' and 'care'. The clinical geriatrician is thereby defined as a 'cure' specialist, an expert in the field of diagnosis and curative care, whereas the nursing home physician is defined as a 'care' specialist, primarily responsible for the welfare and well-being of care-dependent elderly people. But words are not the same as concepts and we must take care not to confuse widely used slogans with scientific and practical concepts. This certainly applies to 'cure' and 'care'. These terms lack clear conceptual definition, so a division based on these in the terms of reference of medical disciplines has little more than rhetorical value (Hertogh, 1997).

One definition of nursing home medicine not based on negative characterization, which is also more function-based than institution-based, is provided by Ribbe, who stresses the mode of operation (Ribbe, 1991). The emphasis here is on a cyclical care process that is problem-oriented and organized on the basis of multi-disciplinary teams. A very critical reader may not, however, immediately consider this to be specific to nursing home medicine and nursing home care. Physicians with very different specialisms operate increasingly in this fashion in hospitals, rehabilitation clinics and institutions providing care for people with disabilities. What this definition lacks is a description of the medical expertise of the nursing home physician. There are a number of reasons why this is not mentioned. The most important is ideological rather than substantive. 'Clinical geriatrics' was recognized as a medical specialism some years before nursing home medicine and in the first years of their existence the two areas primarily wanted to emphasize the specific nature of their own fields. So the aspects that set them apart and distinguished them were given more attention than those that linked them. Ribbe therefore dismisses the substantive characterization of nursing home medicine based on the geriatric care concept as being 'simply confusing'. On the other hand, however, the provision of 'geriatric care' can be difficult to understand as an expertise reserved for a specific medical discipline.

Considered on the basis of the subject matter itself, it is very much a question of whether the specific nature of nursing home medicine and therefore also the significance of its problem-based mode of operation can be clarified without the theoretical framework of geriatrics. It has already been mentioned that geriatric thinking has been a significant influence on the development of nursing home care and anyone looking at the curriculum for training as a nursing home physician will see that its content and orientation are largely geriatric. How can it be otherwise given the characteristics of the category of patients requiring the provision of 'nursing home care'? In the professional profile produced by the NVVA in 2000, nursing home medicine is described as integral medical care for vulnerable elderly people in respect of their care system. The last words are important because in the medical care of elderly people it is always important to take into account the setting in which the elderly people live as well as their (formal and informal) care-givers and carers (NVVA, 2000).

Four geriatric principles

In 1881, the French physician Charcot pointed out the importance of a special study into 'diseases of old age'. In the 19th century in many European countries there were two types of hospital: clinics to which patients were admitted for medical tests and treatment; and a sort of receiving house referred to as a 'house of God', hospice or poor house. The latter were large institutions accommodating the poor, unemployed, people with physical and mental health disabilities as well as the elderly. Conditions in these institutions were often so primitive that they were frequently referred to as 'the gate to hell'. It was in one of these that Charcot argued for special medicine for the elderly, the foundations for which were laid several decades later on the other side of the Channel by the British physician Marjory Warren in the 'Poor Law Infirmary'. Since then a body of medical knowledge has been daeveloped based on four 'geriatric principles':

1   From a medical perspective these are elderly people with multiple vulnerability due to the combined occurrence of conditions often with a synergistic effect (multipathology), a number of which can be characterized as more or less . . .

2   . . . Specific age-related diseases, such as dementia, arthrosis deformans, osteoporosis, etc.

3   In many instances there is an atypical presentation of disease, expressed primarily as a reduced ability to live independently, with the result that problems are raised by carers (volunteer carers) rather than by the patients themselves. These are also often elderly people – and this could be seen as the ethical perspective – who are starting to lose control over their existence or have already lost it. They are vulnerable in this respect too.

4   The primary objective of medical intervention with this category of patient ultimately is not the elimination or curing of disease but an attempt to restore functionality and the ability to live independently and the promotion of an optimum quality of life (Anderson, 1991).

On the basis of these four principles, geriatrics can be described as the branch of general medicine dealing with clinical, preventive and rehabilitation aspects of disease in elderly patients.

As mentioned above, the organization of geriatric care in The Netherlands – in contrast to most other countries – has resulted in a division of labour whereby the field of geriatrics is covered by two medical specialisms rather than one: clinical geriatrics and nursing home medicine. The first specialism has around 120 representatives, all associated with hospitals, the majority of them currently connected to a specialist geriatric department. Around 1200 physicians are currently working in nursing home medicine, most of them registered nursing home physicians associated with the 326 nursing homes in The Netherlands. Although both areas overlap to a significant degree, there is also a division of labour between the two. Hospital-based clinical geriatrics is primarily based on diagnosis and short-term treatment. Clinical geriatricians usually focus on assisting and advising general practitioners. Patients may be referred to them if there are diagnostic and/or therapeutic questions that can only be answered with specialist procedures and in consultation with organ specialists. These are often elderly people with an unexplained acute or sub-acute deterioration combined with already existing chronic conditions. One important task of clinical geriatrics is also to co-treat and advise on the treatment of elderly patients admitted for other specialisms.

Geriatric rehabilitation and (the organization and coordination of) supportive care for chronically ill elderly people are primarily the domain of nursing home medicine. Compared with clinical geriatrics, this discipline focuses more on diagnosis and treatment at the level of the consequences of disease. According to the fourth geriatric principle listed above, the key objectives of intervention are: to restore functional autonomy (the therapeutic aspect) and/or to prevent (further) function loss (the preventive aspect). Based on this specific approach and orientation, nursing home medicine can be characterized as a form of functional geriatrics compared with clinical geriatrics. This designation may be pleonastic to a certain degree but it clearly expresses the mutual relationship between the two specialisms and their complementary nature.

New developments

As well as clinical geriatrics and nursing home medicine, it is essential for the sake of completeness to refer here to social geriatrics as well. This developed from (outpatient) mental healthcare in departments for the care of elderly people. Social geriatricians focus primarily on elderly people with social or mental health problems living at home or in care facilities, for whom such problems threaten their ability to live independent lives. They thereby fulfil a bridging function between primary and inpatient provision. In practice they deal mainly with the diagnosis, treatment and support of patients with behavioural deficits as a result of psychogeriatric conditions and their carers. Technically there is a close relationship with nursing home medicine (NVVA, 2003). The growing number of duties of nursing home physicians outside the institution means that both areas have grown together to such a degree that in 2005 they were merged to form one discipline.

Another recent development is the growth of specific areas for elderly people within established specialisms such as psychiatry and internal medicine. There has been a marked increase in super-specialism and sub-specialism in the last-mentioned area (hepatology, cardiology, endocrinology, etc.) in recent years, at the expense of 'general' internal medicine, which has tended increasingly to concentrate on inpatient treatment of elderly patients. This gave rise to the specific area of geriatric medicine. In the meantime there are advanced plans for a merger between clinical geriatrics and this sub-area of internal medicine. Such a grouping and combining of medical specialisms is also – rightly – promoted by the government, to counter any fragmentation of geriatric expertise.

Focus on functionality

What is meant exactly by 'functional autonomy' and 'functional status'? The word 'function' literally means the performance of a task or the carrying out of an action. In 1959, the World Health Organization (WHO) stated that the health status of elderly people can be better expressed in terms of function and that the 'functional status' is a more effective measure of the need for care than the nature and scope of any existing diseases. By functional status we mean the degree to which a person is able to perform the necessary activities for their welfare and to adapt to their (material and social) environment. If they are able to look after themselves completely independently, we refer to functional autonomy, a term that can be understood as the operationalization of 'health' in the area of care for the elderly. Research shows that the term 'function' as described correlates positively to the perception of health by elderly people and that the degree of functional autonomy interprets a significant dimension of their experienced quality of life (George and Bearon, 1980; Proot, 2001).

Functional status is a function of the association and interaction between different areas of human existence: the somatic, the social, the psychological and the communicative areas. More simply (according to Becker and Cohen) the relationship can be expressed using the following (pseudo)mathematical formula (Becker and Cohen, 1984):

$$FS = S \times Soc \times P \times C$$

where FS stands for functional status and the letters S, Soc, P and C respectively stand for the somatic, the social, the psychological and the communicative areas. The multiplication signs symbolize their mutual relationship but also express the fact that for individual patients with the same functional status the relative proportion of each of the areas mentioned can vary.

Potential or real function loss can thus be compensated for by the mobilization of 'reserve capacities' from one or a number of areas. For example, a hemiparesis as a result of a cerebrovascular accident (CVA) results in function loss, which can be compensated for by improving the physical condition (somatic area), teaching new skills (psychological area), successful assimilation of the disease (psychological area), domestic adjustments (social area) and support by a healthy partner (social area). However, a particular feature of aging is a gradual decrease in these 'reserve capacities'. With advancing years the physiological reserve capacity of organs and organ systems diminishes, on the one hand as part of the aging process itself and on the other as a consequence of the manifestation of various – not necessarily age-related – conditions. Changes also occur in other areas, that have implications for the 'functional reserve': experiences of loss, such as the departure of trusted people, role changes, a deterioration in sensory functions, loss of social roles and the changing social regard of elderly people and old age, age-related changes in cognitive skills, etc. The result is a gradual reduction in the arsenal or reserve of compensatory options, as expressed by Becker and Cohen in their 'homeostatic cylinder' model (Figure 8.1).

Ultimately a situation can occur that is referred to by Sipsma – based on another theoretical context – as that of the 'unstable equilibrium', whereby a more or less radical disease incident or even an apparently minor stressor in the psychosocial area exceeds adaptation capacity and results in disruption of the ability to live independently with significant function loss (Sipsma, 1986).

Naturally the homeostatic cylinder model is a metaphor, as is the 'unstable equilibrium' concept, but they are metaphors that are good to use because they show that functional problems can be present subclinically, as it were, for a long time but often only result in a request for help when the function loss exceeds a defined threshold value due to the loss of compensation options. This function loss is therefore the 'final common pathway' of mutually engaging and mutually reinforcing equilibrium problems in different areas. It is also an important secondary symptom of many (chronic) somatogeriatric and psychogeriatric conditions and is frequently more significant than the specific complaints that are referred to in the textbooks as being the characteristic manifestations of various diseases.

Although functional deterioration, or the threat of it, certainly is not the only pretext for action based on nursing home medicine, functional orientation is increasingly the characterizing geriatric approach thereto. Its significance is expressed concisely by Mary Tinetti, according to whom: 'concentrating on diagnosing the disease for which often little can be done, can lead to ignoring or underplaying symptoms or disabilities for which often much can be done' (Tinetti, 1986). While looking at a long list of chronic diseases and impairments produces feelings of frustration and therapeutic impotence, functional thinking can offer an answer. Functional geriatrics therefore requires displacement of the pretext for geriatric intervention as

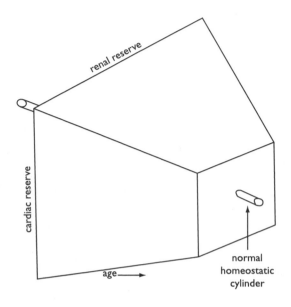

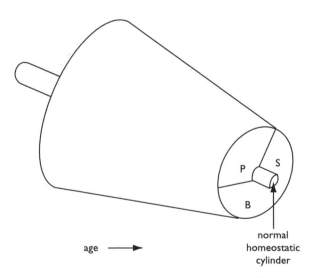

Figure 8.1 **Functional aging.** (*Upper*) The Fries and Crago model, showing the reduction in physiological reserve capacity as a consequence of organ aging. A stressor that exceeds the reserve capacity results in decompensation. (*Lower*) A generalized model, expressing the diminishing physiological reserve capacity as a consequence of a decline in biopsychosocial (letters B, P and S) functioning. Decompensation and therefore also functional dependence occur when a stressor exceeds the compensatory functional reserves (see Becker and Cohen, 1984).

argued by Becker and Cohen: 'a shift towards rehabilitative efforts and social support services and away from medications and invasive procedures' (Becker and Cohen, 1984). This is not care medicine, as referred to earlier, nor is it cure medicine. In fact such dichotomies as *cure* versus *care* and *curative* versus *palliative* no longer hold true here. They refer to the traditional medical paradigm, according to which physicians first and foremost have to know the cause of the patient's symptoms in order to be able to start rational treatment (Wulff et al, 1988). This paradigm has been responsible for the medical successes of the first half of this century – successes that, on the one hand, caused the number of deaths to drop and helped people to live longer but, on the other hand, also paved the way for the different morbidity of chronic disease and a displacement of the disease burden from society to those of more advanced years. It is therefore not surprising that people were first confronted with the limitations of this paradigm and forced to consider its theoretical bases and therapeutic objectives in the field of medical care for the elderly.

The orientation of nursing home medicine towards functional consequences of disease therefore implies that the effectiveness of its intervention cannot be measured using traditional measures of results such as survival time and number of deaths (Hertogh, 1997). Its objectives primarily involve attempts to restore, improve and maintain the best achievable level of functional autonomy or, as Schreuder expressed it, 'it is not a question of preserving biological life but the most independent lifestyle possible' (Schreuder, 1968). This objective involves more than just attempting to achieve the ability to live independently in activities of daily living (ADL) and mobility, because the functional area also has a significantly psychological and social dimension. Being able to live as far as possible according to a concept of existence with which it is possible to identify and being able to carry out the social roles that are appropriate for this are equally part of it. By combining problem-based rehabilitation and supportive care – aspects that are always related in the care context but with a different emphasis for each patient – an attempt is made to fulfil or maintain conditions as far as possible. In this context reference should also be made to the importance of autonomy as an orienting value in care, as expressed by George Agich, i.e. not as a state of independence and self-sufficiency but as a permanent process of development and adaptation and identification with changing life circumstances (Agich, 2003).

Diagnosis of consequences

A diagnosis of diseases such as CVA, dementia, Parkinson's disease, multiple sclerosis, osteoporosis or arthrosis deformans generally says little about the consequences of the disease as experienced by the patient. It directs medical attention primarily to the substrate and – ideally – to the cause of the disease, thereby sometimes providing suggestions for a causal medical treatment or scientific tests. For most chronic diseases there is no such treatment and no prospect of it. Medical care for patients with such diseases then focuses primarily on slowing down and where possible mitigating the progress of the disease, treating the consequences of the disease and preventing complications. A pathology-based diagnosis alone offers too few clues for an intervention based on these objectives.

As a theoretical background to the *International Classification of Impairments, Disabilities and Handicaps* (ICIDH) in 1981, Wood and Badley introduced a model showing the consequences of disease (Wood and Badley, 1981). A deliberate distinction is made here between three levels of the consequences of disease: impairments, disabilities and handicaps. This distinction has also proved to be useful in nursing home medicine. It offers the possibility of a better differentiated diagnosis and intervention and is consistent with the functional geriatric approach. On the basis of this extension of the medical model, in recent years a better understanding has been achieved of the relationship between functional problems and the care needs of elderly people, as well as their prognostic significance. But its use as an analysis model for geriatric problems is restricted for a number of reasons examined in more detail below.

Carrying out a consequence diagnosis according to the ICIDH model for a patient with a simple condition, such as a fractured hip or pulmonary emphysema, generally produces no insurmountable problems; the cause is known and the impairments, disabilities and handicaps can then be derived simply from the cause. The reverse diagnostic route, i.e. using a given functional disability to answer the question of how a patient ended up in this situation, is less easy to follow. In other words, the diagnostic route more or less assumed in the consequence model is the one from a known disease diagnosis to the consequences of it. This is understandable, because this model primarily has to serve as the conceptual justification for a classification system and was therefore not primarily developed for the purposes of clinical practice. In practice, however, the disease → impairments → disabilities → handicaps route has to be followed in the reverse direction, because patients do not present with cut-and-dried diagnoses but with complaints and symptoms. In the case of geriatric patients these often have a specific character, as mentioned above, and function loss is regularly a primary feature but cannot be converted by means of an unambiguous association to a simple pathological primary diagnosis (Fried et al, 1991a). Comorbid conditions frequently occur, which can have a difficult to unravel synergistic effect on the nature and seriousness of the disabilities experienced, whereas the relationship between the disease and the consequences of the disease is strongly influenced by factors such as personality, state of mind, acceptance and assimilation, social support and cultural value patterns. Finally, there is the known downward spiral in which function loss leads to further functional disabilities and in some cases to chronic conditions (for example decubitus) as a result of negative association (consider the relationship between 'disease' and 'disuse') (Guralnik, 1994).

In practice the physician is confronted with the result of all these influences, in geriatric parlance referred to as a 'complex' need for care or help. To analyse this, it is not sufficient to have a model that simply distinguishes *direct* consequences, which can be assigned via a simple cause–effect relationship to an aetiologically or pathophysiologically defined disease substrate. On the one hand the relationships cannot always be established so explicitly and a mobility restriction can, for example, be the common consequence of a coxarthrosis, Parkinson's disease or arterial disease; on the other hand, other influencing factors operate in relation to all these relationships, which the Wood and Badley model fails to take into account adequately. These can be summarized in the term *indirect* consequences of disease, which specifically relate to all the psychosocial factors referred to: how a person deals with their impairments and disabilities, how they manage to keep going, what importance they attach to themselves and how this degree of importance affects their self-image, their experienced quality of life and their need for help. These factors also have to be assessed systematically when analysing a complex request for help. The importance of this is referred to in The Netherlands by Van der Wulp and Dröes for example. The former looks at how the perception and assimilation of disease and admission to a nursing home can result in differences in the need for care and the necessity for care in the case of somatic nursing home patients (Van der Wulp, 1986).

Van der Wulp and Dröes' research is based on the view that behavioural problems in Alzheimer patients should not simply be seen as a consequence of brain degeneration but should also be seen as problematic attempts by the patient to adjust to the consequences of their disease (Dröes, 1991). In this context we refer to *indirect* consequences because there is no one-to-one relationship with specific causes of disease; we are touching here on the psychological and social dimension of (chronic) human illness. From the point of view of providing care, however, they should be seen as the *consequences* of disease because they occur in conjunction with the disease as 'strategies' by the patient to adjust – not always successfully – to their situation and to maintain or restore a certain degree of well-being. On the basis of modern coping theories, we refer increasingly in this context to 'adaptive tasks' (Lazarus and Folkmann, 1984). The importance of this for the provision of care is also referred to based on a neurological and neuropsychological tradition by Oliver Sacks, who writes at the start of *The Man Who Mistook His Wife For a Hat*: 'It must be said from the outset that a disease is never a mere loss or excess – that there is always a reaction, on the part of the affected organism or individual, to restore, to compensate for and to preserve its identity, however strange the means may be: and to study or influence this means . . . is an essential part of our role as physicians' (Sacks, 1986).

If the patient adapts successfully, they recover or maintain their well-being and emotional equilibrium; if they fail to adjust, this can result in all kinds of adjustment problems, such as dependent or other problem behaviour, disrupted social relationships and even depression. It is therefore important to understand why one person but not another is able to cope adequately with a chronic disease, why one complains and adopts a dependent attitude whereas the other retains control of their life. The nature of the indirect consequences also regularly determines why one person but not another with similar functional disabilities is admitted to an institution. Before a problem-based intervention is made it is therefore just as essential to record these indirect consequences as it is to assess the direct consequences of disease. On this basis it can be asked to what extent and how this complex of direct and indirect consequences can be influenced, what the priorities are and which objectives can be set.

Geriatric rehabilitation and supportive care

Not so long ago an expression such as 'geriatric rehabilitation' would have been seen as a contradiction in terms. There are a number of reasons for this.

First of all the principal focus of rehabilitation medicine for younger people is based on a number of historical factors. The large number of service people disabled as a result of the two World Wars provided a first important incentive for the development of rehabilitation services. Initially they were aimed primarily at making 'disabled' adults fit for work again, requiring intensive collaboration with labour experts as well as medical and paramedical treatment. The effect of the polio epidemics was also to broaden the rehabilitation concept, because most of the victims of these were children, and children with other disabilities, such as spasticity, sensory and mental health disabilities, were also included in the target group. This meant that the rehabilitation team now also had to include education and learning experts. Finally, the increase in the number of chronic diseases with disabling consequences, such as cerebrovascular conditions and rheumatoid arthritis, meant that these too form a specific area for rehabilitation provided that the potential rehabilitee is able to comply with the often intensive and challenging treatment programmes and is motivated to do so. In practice this means that the patients are also relatively young(er). As a result of these developments, the concept of rehabilitation has acquired an increasingly broad but also more general content. The WHO defines it as 'the coordinated use of measures in the medical, social, labour-related and education areas, which have to help a person with a disability achieve the best place in society for them' (World Health Organization, 1969). Social (re)integration is another equivalent description of this objective of the rehabilitation process.

A second reason why rehabilitation is not so readily associated with elderly people is that the relationship between being old and having a disability is not immediately obvious. The elderly and people with disabilities represent separate groups in our society. This can be seen, for example, from the fact that care for people with disabilities and care for the elderly are organized in a more or less separate fashion and are represented differently at policy level. It is also expressed in the different social profiles of the elderly and people with disabilities. The image of someone with a disability is increasingly determined by the striving for emancipation, specifically by young people and adults who feel linked to each other because they look different from the norm and have had enough of always having to do their best to appear normal. They want to 'stand on their own wheels' and work hard for a social integration, which requires adjustment not just by people with disabilities but also by society (Spaink, 1996). This striving reflects a completely different world of experience from that of elderly people in our society.

This brings us to the third reason why it is so unusual to refer to rehabilitation for the elderly: the social image of aging and being old, whereby it is important to note that in our society elderly people do not in any way form a homogeneous group. A typical demographic and sociological development in the previous century was the growth of the 'third age': the emergence of a generation of vital people, aged 60, 70 and over, wanting active social participation and preferring to consider themselves as senior rather than elderly or old (Laslett, 1989). This does not of course mean that the proverbial ailments of old age are remedied along with such emancipation of the elderly. Rather, they are displaced to an older age group that we now refer to as the 'fourth age' and they manifest themselves in those who grow old with existing long-term conditions such as Parkinson's disease or (late-onset) diabetes. These are elderly people covered by the area of geriatrics, and anyone mentioning geriatric rehabilitation with regard to such people regularly encounters scepticism: is rehabilitation not rather too much effort for this patient group? There is also an ethically motivated criticism: should we burden elderly people, who feel the weight of the years on their shoulders and are bending under the load, with rehabilitation measures? Of course treatment programmes must be available for those who want them, but should we not leave in peace those who are less articulate and have been brought to the notice of the support system by those around them rather than making an active and considered choice for themselves, for whatever reason? This sort of question is put regularly to nursing home physicians and geriatricians, not just by the families of patients but also by other care-givers, who fear that elderly patients are being overchallenged, overtaxed and overtreated.

This sort of question and consideration also partly reflects the social norm that advanced age now goes hand in hand with dependence. It was the British pioneers in the field of geriatrics in the first half of the last century who first debated this norm. They warned of the dangers of bed rest, inactivity and deprivation, and with their concept of 'active treatment' they laid the foundation for geriatric rehabilitation. Because the literal interpretation of this concept gave rise to an unfortunate term ('active treatment' suggests that there should also be something known as 'passive treatment'), active treatment was referred to as 'reactivation' in The Netherlands (Schreuder, 1966, 1968; Van Proosdij, 1977). Initially it indicated that the nursing of elderly people required a different approach. Bed-based care acquired a bad reputation ('a medical error on four legs' according to Schreuder), social contacts within the department were stimulated and an activation-based attitude took centre stage. However, the term was soon primarily used for the rehabilitation of elderly people and reactivation became a separate function of the nursing home. This function was not referred to as rehabilitation, not just for substantive reasons but also for policy reasons. The term reactivation was intended to emphasize the distinction in content and objective between the rehabilitation function of the nursing home and that of the rehabilitation institution, in order to define the terms of reference and the area of operation of both services.

Schreuder justified the use of the term 'reactivation' by relating it to the term disability. People were able or disabled with respect to various groups of actions. A first group is that of actions relating to the person's own body, a second those relating to household management and a third important group involves actions relating to exercising a profession. Reactivation should be distinguished from rehabilitation in that it only deals with disability in relation to the first two groups of actions. The objective is more limited; a transition to a more independent form of living is preferable but not an essential indicator of a successful reactivation process. There are also a number of substantive differences. The tempo of reactivation is slower due to the limited burden that can be put on elderly patients. Movement therapy is an important part of the rehabilitation process for both the young and the elderly but whereas young people primarily benefit from maximum load over short periods, this must be avoided for the elderly. They can only tolerate a smaller load and require more frequent rest periods due to a reduction in their physiological reserve capacity and to the often-present combination of inactivity atrophy and age atrophy of the muscular system. (Also patients who find it difficult to stand make less efficient use of the (energy saving) force of gravity when walking, requiring relatively more muscle work and resulting in the earlier occurrence of fatigue.) It is also essential to take into account changes in reaction time and the capacity to perceive and learn and of course the nature of existing conditions – generally more than one or two in the case of elderly people.

Finally, reactivation always requires careful and circumspect attention to the motivation of the patient and their associated mental perception. This is also an important distinction from 'regular' rehabilitation, where a positive attitude on the part of the rehabilitee is often more or less assumed in respect of the effort required for the rehabilitation process. With many elderly people, particularly the very old, the opposite generally applies. In practice this leads to complex considerations involving the ethical question of the degree to which an absence of motivation should be respected or whether attempts should be made to convert this to a positive willingness to put apparently real possibilities of improvement to the test.

Rehabilitation within the nursing home is still frequently referred to as reactivation but this term has only achieved a following in The Netherlands. In Anglo-Saxon language areas, what started as 'active treatment' has evolved to 'geriatric rehabilitation'. This term better satisfies the concern of international coordination and standardization of concepts than the term 'reactivation'. Also, the word 'reactivation' is closely associated with the view that in the case of the elderly rehabilitation should (must) be limited to the elimination of the need for help in the area of personal care and domestic activities. It may be the norm in our society that elderly people are no longer involved in the labour process and generally also no longer have any educational or learning tasks to carry out, but this does not mean that their rehabilitation should not, if necessary, aim to achieve objectives that go further than those mentioned. Essentially this 'limited' view of reactivation reflects the social norm that an inward-looking lifestyle is appropriate in old age.

Based on the objectives and pretexts for rehabilitation intervention within the concept of 'geriatric rehabilitation', a general distinction can be made between three forms: special rehabilitation, preventive rehabilitation and maintenance rehabilitation. *Special rehabilitation* includes the rehabilitation programmes developed for patients with functional impairment and disabilities as a result of an acute incident, such as a CVA or a trauma, subsequent rehabilitation treatment being carried out further to a specialist medical intervention, such as total hip arthroplasty, and the rehabilitation of elderly people with functional disabilities as a result of chronic disease(s). *Preventive rehabilitation* was initially aimed only at the 'preliminary' treatment of elderly patients requiring invasive medical treatment with a subsequent period of immobilization and bed rest. Studies of the occurrence and (natural) progress of functional disabilities in elderly people have resulted in the gradual development of a different and more substantial indication area.

People in our society reaching the age of 65 years then have a mean life expectancy of around 14 years (for men) to 18 years (for women). Many elderly people have to struggle for around half of this period with problems relating to their ability to cope alone and their independence. These are often temporary by nature but around a third of all elderly people experience more or less permanently limited activity levels as a result of health problems. The most common causes of disease in this context are cardiovascular, neurological, psychiatric and orthopaedic, whereas less specific problems such as difficulty in walking, balance problems and falling appear to be predictors for the development of impairment and dependence (Fried and Guralnik, 1997). Although rehabilitation measures are generally only taken when impairment has actually been manifested, research shows that this phase of manifest disabilities in a significant group of elderly people with the conditions and impairment referred to was preceded by a period in which 'subclinical disabilities' existed (Fried et al, 2000, 2001). This term refers to a state in which functional autonomy is threatened but the person in question is able to hold their own by means of compensatory measures (Fried et al, 1991b). Such compensation may, for example, involve the avoidance as far as possible of actions and behaviour that the person in question finds difficult, using a stick or umbrella when walking or using a shopping trolley as a walking aid when shopping, using furniture for support when standing, sitting or walking or even using another person's extended hand or arm for support. These are all forms of 'task modification'. By reducing the frequency with which a task has to be carried out to the minimum necessary and by making changes to the way in which it is done, the person involved is able to maintain their functional autonomy (Petrella and Cress, 2004). People who, when asked, say that they are totally or almost totally independent and able to cope alone but nevertheless use this sort of task modification are in a situation of disability concealed by compensation. Their moderate performance in mobility tests (such as the 'stand up and go' test and the Tinetti test) can reveal these functional problems and research shows that elderly people with such preclinical disabilities are significantly more likely to develop more or less serious disabilities in the area of personal care and mobility within 1–4 years (Fried et al, 1991b; Verbrugge and Jette, 1994; Gill et al, 1995; Fried and Guralnik, 1997).

As stated above, the accepted practice is to delay rehabilitation measures until manifest (clinical) disabilities have occurred. However research shows that, with this group of elderly people with subclinical disabilities, benefits can be achieved with earlier intervention in the form of functional geriatric tests and a programme of rehabilitation and supportive measures based on these (Fried and Guralnik, 1997; Binder et al, 2002). It is clear that this preventive rehabilitation requires a different and less-delaying attitude on the part of care-givers.

The third area of application of geriatric rehabilitation, as mentioned above, is *maintenance rehabilitation*. The purpose of this is to maintain and reinforce a functional result that has been achieved or initiated. Maintenance rehabilitation is aimed at patients with a more or less stationary functional level for whom periodic evaluation is indicated with a view to complications of function loss and its progression. For example, in the case of wheelchair patients it is necessary to guard against the occurrence of decubitus, contractures, deformities and loss of transfer skills (such as bed to chair and toilet transfers), which further undermine independence (Portnow, 1989). Maintenance rehabilitation is also expedient as a follow-up for CVA patients for some time after the end of clinical rehabilitation, as experience shows that many skills restored or newly acquired during this process disappear again after discharge and/or are no longer used, with the result that the patient experiences functional decline. Short-term maintenance rehabilitation, in which these skills are re-taught, can be expedient to prevent or reverse such function loss.

Special rehabilitation, preventive rehabilitation and maintenance rehabilitation are three areas of emphasis within the continuum of geriatric rehabilitation. Rehabilitation measures therefore play a role at different levels of medical care for the elderly, always with the aim of achieving or maintaining the optimum level of functional autonomy for the patient. This aim corresponds closely to the general WHO definition of rehabilitation. Although geriatrics and rehabilitation have developed along different paths, in a certain sense they seem to have the same starting point. Both assume an attitude on the part of care-givers based on activation (and keeping active). Of course this does not mean that there is no room for supportive care. On the contrary, geriatric rehabilitation includes supportive care. A treatment plan will always comprise these two cohesive components: rehabilitation treatment where improvement, maintenance or prevention appear possible and indicated; and support in those functions and activities where this is no longer possible. By support in this context we mean not just psychosocial counselling, nursing and care but also the provision of aids and implementation of measures in the domestic environment of the patient. For a number of chronically ill elderly people this support can only be provided in a nursing home, particularly when intensive care is required continuously (24 hours a day). Such nursing home care can be temporary but it regularly becomes permanent. The achievement of an optimum level of functional autonomy is an important care objective even at this stage. The proportion of both aspects (rehabilitation and support) has to be regularly evaluated and where necessary adjusted in the care and treatment plan. In the case of people with advanced dementia and somatic patients requiring intensive nursing, the emphasis will of course be primarily on supportive care. This does not mean that the principles of geriatric rehabilitation do not continue to retain a certain significance even for these patient categories, or that active efforts should not always be made to ensure the values expressed by terms such as functional autonomy and social participation for the individual patient.

References

Agich, G. (2003) *Dependence and Autonomy in Old Age*. Cambridge: Cambridge University Press.

Anderson, F. (1991) An historical overview of geriatric medicine. In M.S.J. Pathy (Ed.), *Principles and Practice of Geriatric Medicine*. London: John Wiley, pp. 1435–1442.

Becker, P.M. and Cohen, H.J. (1984) The functional approach to the care of the elderly: a conceptual framework. *Journal of the American Geriatric Society*, **32**: 923–929.

Binder, E.F., Schechtman, K.B., Ehsani, A.A., Steges–May, K., et al (2002) Effects of exercise training on frailty in community-dwelling older adults: results of a randomized, controlled trial. *Journal of the American Geriatric Society*, **50**: 1921–1928.

Dröes, R.M. (1991) Over psychosociale hulpverlening aan demente ouderen. Academic Dissertation, Vrije Universiteit, Amsterdam.

Fried, L.P. and Guralnik, J.M. (1997) Disability in older adults: evidence regarding significance, etiology and risk. *Journal of the American Geriatric Society*, **45**: 92–100.

Fried, L.P., Storer, D.J., King, D.E. and Lodder, F. (1991a) Diagnosis of disease presentation in the elderly. *Journal of the American Geriatric Society*, **39**: 117–123.

Fried, L.P., Herdmann, S.J., Kuhn, K.E., et al (1991b) Preclinical disability: hypotheses about the bottom of the iceberg. *Journal of Aging and Health*, **3**: 285–300.

Fried, L.P., Bandeen-Roche, K., Chaves, P.H. and Johnson, B.A. (2000) Preclinical mobility disability predicts incident mobility disability in older women. *Journal of Gerontology, Part A*, **55**: M43–52.

Fried, L.P., Young, Y., Rubin, G., Bandeen-Roche, K. and WASH II Collaborative Research Group (2001) Self-reported preclinical disability identifies older woman with early declines in performance and early disease. *Journal of Clinical Epidemiology*, **54**: 889–901.

George, L.K. and Bearon, L.B. (1980) *Quality of Life in Older Persons: Meaning and Measurement*. New York: Human Sciences Press.

Gill, T.M., Williams, C.S. and Tinetti, M.E. (1995) Assessing risk for the onset of functional dependence among older adults: the role of physical performance. *Journal of the American Geriatric Society*, **43**: 603–609.

Guralnik, J.M. (1994) Understanding the relationship between disease and disability. *Journal of the American Geriatric Society*, **42**: 1128–1129.

Hertogh, C.M.P.M. (1997) Voorbij *cure* and *care*: het 'geriatrische' van de verpleeghuisgeneeskunde. *Tijdschrift voor Gerontologie and Geriatrie*, **28**: 3–4.

Hoek, J.F., Ribbe, M.W., Hertogh, C.M.P.M. and van Vleuten, C.P.M. (2003) The role of the specialist physician in nursing homes: the Netherlands' experience. *International Journal of Geriatric Psychiatry*, **18**: 244–249.

Laslett, P. (1989) *A Fresh Map of Life. The Emergence of the Third Age*. London: Weidenfeld & Nicholson.

Lazarus, R.S. and Folkmann, S. (1984) *Stress. Appraisal and Coping*. New York: Springer.

Michels, J.J.M. (1980) *Verpleeghuisgeneeskunde. Inaugurele rede*. Nijmegen: Dekker & Van der Vegt.

Nederlandse Vereniging voor Geriatrie (1989) Nota kerntaken and raakvlakken in de geriatrie. *Medisch Contact*, **44**: 713–714.

NVVA (Nederlandse Vereniging van Verpleeghuisartsen) (2000) *Beroepsprofiel Verpleeghuisarts*. Utrecht: NVVA.

NVVA (2003) *Nota Takenpakket Verpleeghuisartsarts/Sociaal Geriater*. Utrecht: NVVA.

Oostvogel, F.J.G. (1961) Medische aspecten van het verpleegtehuis. *Ons ziekenhuis*, **23**: 1.

Oostvogel, F.J.G. (1989) De historische ontwikkeling van het verpleeghuis. In

J. Trommel, M.W. Ribbe and J.A. Stoop (Eds), *Capita Selecta van de Verpleeghuis-geneeskunde*. Utrecht: Scheltema & Holkema, pp. 3–22.

Petrella, J.K. and Cress, M.E. (2004) Daily ambulation activity and task performance in community-dwelling older adults aged 63–71 years with preclinical disability. *Journal of Gerontology, Part A*, **59**: 264–267.

Portnow, J.M. (1989) Rehabilitation and management of the physically impaired. In P.R. Katz and E. Calkins (Eds), *Principles and Practice of Nursing Home Care*. New York: Springer, pp. 113–126.

Proot, I. (2001) Changing autonomy. Academic Dissertation, Universiteit Maastricht, Maastricht.

Ribbe, M.W. (1991) Wegen in de verpleeghuisgeneeskunde. Inaugural lecture, Vrije Universiteit, Amsterdam.

Sacks, O. (1986) *The Man who Mistook his Wife for a Hat*. London: Picador.

Schreuder, J.T.R. (1966) De geriatrische patiënt. *Nederlands Tijdschrift voor Geneeskund*, **110**: 1825–1828.

Schreuder, J.T.R. (1968) Rehabilitation and geriatrie in het algemene ziekenhuis. *Nederlands Tijdschrift voor Geneeskdunde*, **112**: 1787–1790.

Sipsma, D.H. (1986) *Sociale Geriatrie in Theorie and Praktijk*. Almere: Promedia.

Spaink, K. (1996) Op eigen wielen. Over ziekte, zorg and zelfstandigheid. In A. van, Wijnen, Y. Koster and A. Oderwald (Eds), *Trots and Treurnis. Gehandicapt in Nederland*. Amsterdam: Babylon-De Geus/Gehandicaptenraad, pp. 64–76.

Tinetti, M.E. (1986) Performance-oriented assessment of mobility problems in elderly patients. *Journal of the American Geriatric Society*, **34**: 119–126.

Van der Wulp, J.C. (1986) *Verstoring and Verwerking in Verpleeghuizen*. Nijkerk: Intro.

Van Proosdij, C. (1977) Klinische geriatrie – 'un peu d'histoire'. *Ned Tijdschr Geneeskd*; 121: 152–156.

Verbrugge, L.M. and Jette, A.M. (1994) The disablement process. *Social Science and Medicine*, **38**: 1–14.

Wood, P.N. and Badley, E.M. (1981) *People with Disabilities*, Monograph 12. Geneva: WHO.

World Health Organization (1959) *The Public Health Aspects of Aging in the Population*. Copenhagen: WHO.

World Health Organization (1969) *Report on Rehabilitation*. Geneva: WHO.

Wulff, H.R., Andur Pedersen, S. and Rosenberg, R. (1988) *Filosofie van de Geneeskunde. Een Verkenning*. Amsterdam: Meulenhof, Bunge.

Chapter 9

Dementia and spiritual care

Peter Speck

Introduction

> Are your wonders known in the darkness and your saving help in the
> land of forgetfulness.
> Psalm 88 v.12 Holy Bible, New Revised Standard Version (NRSV)

This verse from the psalms of the Judeo-Christian tradition seems to echo
something of the confusion, fear, darkness and sense of abandonment and
isolation that can be experienced by the person who is severely cognitively
impaired by dementia or other mental deterioration. The syndrome we
usually refer to as dementia is often described in very negative terms and as
something to be dreaded as people become more aware of the aging process
within their own bodies. For many elderly people today memories still exist of
the days when 'dementia' meant no hope, no cure and being admitted into
long-stay care where one was 'warehoused' (Miller and Gwynne, 1972) and
received basic care until the end of life. Because of communication problems
many people were seen as problems, were over-medicated or subjected to
inappropriate behaviour modification or strict reality orientation.

In the mid 1960s I undertook some research into factors affecting the
visiting patterns of relatives to patients admitted to a psycho-geriatric ward
of a large psychiatric hospital (Speck, 1970). Communication problems fea-
tured large in the relationship between visitors and both the patient and staff
members. On the 'back wards' of the hospital were many patients who had
no visitors at all and I became aware of both the enormous difficulty of
relating to many of these patients, but also the tendency to infantalize
them or write them off. In 1967 the report *Sans Everything – a Case to
Answer* was published (Robb, 1967). This report had investigated complaints
about the care and management of people on the 'back wards' of several
UK hospitals. It was a damning indictment of bad practice, abuse, de-
personalizing care of people abandoned by their relatives and cared for by
staff who also felt abandoned by society in their care of these people. The
problem was not new and Goffman (1968) and Barton (1966) had already

described the de-personalizing effect of much institutionalized care within the UK and elsewhere. Things needed to change and there had to be an opening up of these closed-off areas within institutions and society, together with a reversal of the attitude that these were patients for whom 'nothing could be done'.

When Kitwood (1990) produced his critical reappraisal of our understanding of dementia he included a description of the damaging effect of certain care environments, which reflected a cultural inheritance that was 'malignant', although the care-givers themselves worked kindly and with good intent. In this paper he lists ten elements of malignant social psychology from his original work. In 1997 he then added a further seven: *ignoring, imposition, withholding, accusation, disruption, mockery, disparagement* (Kitwood, 1997). In view of *Sans Everything – a Case to Answer* it is painful to read Kitwood's list almost 30 years later. However, his work and that of others since has been very formative in putting the person back in the centre as the focus of care and care planning, together with the development of the concept of personhood. It is this approach that provides a new framework for our understanding of spiritual care for people who have dementia because personhood is intimately linked with identity, meaning, continuity and the experience of loving kindness or 'saving help in the land of forgetfulness' (Psalm 88, Holy Bible, 1995).

What is personhood?

Our understanding of the concept of personhood is important because of its ability to shape approaches to the assessment and provision of spiritual care to people with dementia. Descriptions and definitions vary as the following three definitions show:

1   Personhood is the capacity for feeling conceived as a 'potential' out of which all psychological modes and states of development emerge throughout life (Heron, 1992).
2   A sense of personal distinctiveness, of personal continuity and of personal autonomy (Harre, 1998).
3   A standing or status that is bestowed upon one human being, by others, in the context of relationship and social being (Kitwood, 1997).

It is clear from these and other descriptions (Flint, 2004) that a person needs other people to confirm, or re-affirm, personhood or self-identity, as well as to support and nurture it. There are parallels with the definition of spirituality in the Oxford English Dictionary, which places emphasis on interpersonal relationships and bonding, as discussed later in this chapter. Kitwood and Bredin (1992) make it clear that personhood does not rely on cognitive ability, but it does require social relations in order to sustain the capacity to feel and to experience feelings about people and places. They also state that:

> ... the core of our position is that personhood should be viewed as essentially social: it refers to the human being in relation to others. But also, it carries essentially ethical connotations: to be a person is to have a certain status, to be worthy of respect. (p. 275)

Because older people with dementia lose their capacity to maintain their own personhood it does not follow that they also lose the capacity to have it maintained or promoted by others, and to be treated respectfully by others. Hence there is a reliance on others to reinforce the sense of identity and maintain a sense of continuity of the past in any consideration of the present and future. This continuity may be expressed through words, photographs and images, smell, feelings that evoke past events or objects that have great significance for the individual owner – if not for others (Jones, 2004). Sensitivity is required of care-givers to explore the meaning of significant objects to the owner, who may come from a different culture or faith tradition from the care-giver.

A sharing of the memories associated with objects and maybe different faith traditions can lead to a greater understanding of the life experiences and spiritual needs of older people, with or without dementia, as the following vignette demonstrates:

> An elderly Eastern European Jewish lady, a refugee who did not speak English, was admitted to a busy London hospital ward. She clutched her handbag to her tightly. It contained very little except a small lump of old lard wrapped up in some paper. This was perceived as 'rubbish' by the staff who, for hygienic reasons, wanted to dispose of it. The patient became very agitated and distressed when they tried to gently take it from her, becoming so distressed that an interpreter was called to the ward. It transpired that the woman had been passed from country to country and the only thing she had to represent continuity in her life was this small piece of kosher rendered fat. This had been with her through all of her experiences. It was a symbol of her faith and linked her to her lost family and community. Acting as a transitional object it continued to provide her with a sense of identity in the face of overwhelming loss. This explanation led to the understanding of the many meanings attributed to this object and of the older person herself, including her spiritual needs.

Relating this story to the experience of someone with dementia is not difficult and does indicate the need to be open to other explanations and approaches. Meeting spiritual needs in dementia may also require 'translators' and educators as well as a broad understanding of the term *spiritual*.

What is spirituality?

If you undertake a literature search using the terms 'spiritual' or 'spirituality' you will soon find yourself submerged in a wide variety of literature, ranging from orthodox religion to the very broad and at times bizarre. One also becomes aware of the number of new books and articles entitled 'Spirituality and . . .' or 'Spirituality in . . .'. All of this indicates the enormous growth in interest in spirituality and spiritual care, which still remains for many an awkward topic to explore for themselves and a very intrusive area to explore with others. As Cobb (2001, p. 13) comments:

> Spiritual . . . may suffer from being used in such a generic form that it has become too malleable and therefore lost its distinguishing features. This points to a further aspect of the conundrum: the ambiguity of spirituality and the elusiveness of clarification. Spirituality therefore becomes a self-fulfilling prophecy, respectfully ring-fenced and considered out of bounds to examination, research and exposition.

There has also been a shift in our understanding of the term by differentiating and widening its identification with religion (Speck, 1988). However, this has sometimes led to the accusation that the concept of spirituality is now nebulous and only of relevance to those philosophically minded or in need of a crutch to help them cope with life. The differentiation of spiritual from religious has, for some, led to a complete split of one from the other rather than a varying degree of inter-relatedness. Respect for religious and spiritual belief has, for example, become an important part of the Nursing Midwifery Council (NMC, formerly the UKCC) code for nursing and in other professional codes of practice. But the diffidence felt by many in engaging with this aspect of care has led to much 'lip service' or a narrow focusing on religion and culture with a consequent lack of perception of people's wider needs in the presence of illness or death.

Implications for assessment of need

One of the problems in addressing spiritual care with patients is that many of those attempting to make an assessment are themselves unclear about their own personal beliefs. This can lead staff to feel ill equipped to deal with any of the existential issues that the patient may wish to explore. It can be difficult to go confidently to places you have not been to yourself. In an unpublished Bachelor of Nursing thesis, Dukes (1999) found that nurses who had a strong belief system that was religious were very effective at discerning religious needs for patients and ensured that they accessed chaplaincy or were able to attend chapel worship. However, in the absence of religious requests she found that the staff were less able to discern any wider spiritual need. Nurses with a strong spiritual, but non-religious, belief were best at recognizing and responding to the wider spiritual agenda but often missed the religious unless the patient specifically requested help. Those who had a low strength of belief (whatever its nature) rarely assessed the religious or spiritual needs of patients. There were parallels between these findings and those of Ross (1994), who described some of the barriers to the assessment of spiritual need, of which the nurses' own belief system was a powerful filter.

Recent research by Koenig et al (1998a,b) and colleagues within the USA shows that there is a positive correlation between religion and health, especially mental health, in terms of outcome, protectiveness and sense of well-being. In the UK studies are beginning to show that, in the absence of religion, belief (especially if it is spiritual) is important to a large proportion of people entering healthcare (King et al, 1994, 1999). In the UK a recent report on the spiritual needs of older people in residential care (Regan and Smith, 1997) and a reader on spirituality and aging (Jewell, 1999) have both given attention to dementia while noting the problems of the lack of a shared definition of spirituality. However, if over 70% of newly admitted patients have a belief system that is important to them (King et al, 1994, 1999) it should be taken into account when writing a care plan or preparing a care pathway. Because many of the 70% may not practise a religion any more, the challenge is that much greater. There is a growing evidence base for the importance of belief and it is, therefore, increasingly important to recognize and respond if we are to provide a truly person-centred approach.

In a study day conducted by the author at a large UK teaching hospital, a wide cross-section of staff were invited to identify the key components of spiritual care. The group included a range of healthcare occupations, age, gender and belief. Central in much of their thinking was an understanding that spirituality is about:

- affirming the humanity of the other person, especially when that person is not capable of doing so for themselves;
- relatedness;
- hope;
- the ability to transcend or rise above the current situation;
- finding some sense of meaning and purpose in life, especially as it relates to who and what we are (i.e. an existential dimension).

None of this necessarily requires a religious belief, although most of the major world faiths would address these points within their teachings and religious writings. However, someone who followed a humanistic philosophy would also be able to affirm these core aspects, albeit outside of a religious framework.

The search for meaning

Spirituality is often described in terms of the search for meaning, as reflected so clearly in *Man's Search for Meaning* (Frankl, 1987). Against the background of the holocaust, he describes how people survived such experiences by finding some form of meaning that could interpret the experience to them and enable them to continue to function and retain a sense of personal identity. This was especially important given the de-personalizing experiences many were undergoing. There are perhaps parallels with the effect of cognitive impairment in later life and the potential for undermining personhood. Many authors have linked spirituality to meaning and this is helpful. However, I believe that what we are talking about is actually *existential* meaning. Does the fact that you and I exist have any meaning and purpose at all? If so, what is that meaning, how do I discover it and does it change over time? If I am not able to articulate or express this easily, who will try to discern and meet my unexpressed needs? These are issues rarely reflected in the creation of 'Advanced Directives' or 'Living Wills', yet these ultimate questions can challenge us in a variety of different ways and may only be addressed at key moments in our life when perhaps our very existence is being threatened, or we are undergoing some significant life change that touches on our identity – as illustrated by Goldsmith (1999, p. 128)

> . . . although the (physical) illness may conquer their body, it does not conquer their spirit. But this is not the case with dementia. People cope with loss in different ways; it may affect their personality, but it does not necessarily do so. But with dementia the very person seems to change. This raises basic questions, which have a spiritual dimension, such as 'Who am I?' and 'Which is the real me?'

Many people seek this existential understanding with reference to the existence of a power other than themselves that may not be defined too precisely. If we are concerned with finding existential meaning within any particular life experience, and if this is usually linked to an understanding of a relationship to some power other than oneself, can that power be influential when coping with normal life events and transitions as well as illness? In particular, can that power enable us to transcend the difficulties of the 'here and now' experience and foster hope for a future, especially if our power to communicate is limited?

In studies undertaken by King et al (1999, 2001) not everyone wished to describe this power as a deity or God and were usually much more general in their understanding (e.g. a 'higher power', 'a power in the universe' or a 'force for good or evil', etc.). However, out of the large number of patients interviewed in these studies within a UK acute healthcare setting, and in the external healthy population interviewed, approximately 79% claimed to have a spiritual belief system that was very important to them, even though many of them were not religious (King et al, 1999, 2001).

Spirituality and relationship

The Oxford English Dictionary has defined spiritual as:

> A vital life principle that integrates other aspects of the person and is an essential ingredient in inter-personal relationships and bonding.

There are several key words in this definition: *Vital* and *integrating* imply that we are multi-faceted as people and it is this vital life principle that holds it all together and enables us to become whole people; *relationship* and *bonding* refer to the way in which we can discern that this vital life force is present by the extent and quality of the relationships we have. We all develop affectional bonds with people, animals, places or objects in the course of our life. Events that threaten to separate or damage those bonds, therefore, have the potential to threaten our spiritual health and well-being. Illness and admission to hospital can have this potential effect because hospitalization may lead to an experience of loss of freedom, independence, bodily function or body part with the consequent impact that such loss has on body image and self-worth (Speck, 1978). At times when that bonding is threatened, or actually severed, we may feel the event at a very deep level. Psychologically we may experience a period of mourning and grief (Parkes, 1975). In addition we may feel as if our very existence as a person is under threat. This is especially relevant for those who have lost, or are in the process of losing, their identity as a result of dementia, Alzheimer's disease, stroke or experiencing social isolation. In this context it is important that others affirm our personhood, especially when we are unable to do so, as one aspect of offering spiritual care and of responding to us as a whole person when we may feel fragmented. By 'personhood' I am thinking of that status bestowed upon one human being by others within the context of relationship and social being. In this understanding of the term personhood there is an implied recognition, respect and trust between care-giver and cared-for, which can be affected by degenerative changes consequent to mental or physical illness. A process of alienation can commence, which can be experienced internally as well as externally and socially. It is a sense of disconnectedness from oneself that can have a marked effect on our sense of a continuing identity. This can be exacerbated if people fail to interpret or value our expression of feeling at such times.

Miesen (1992) hypothesizes that the vulnerability associated with feelings of loss and fearfulness in dementia will awaken earlier attachment experiences, leading to nurture-seeking behaviours. Within the uncertainty of dementia develops a need for certainty within the other (the carer, family member, etc). It is the positive, trustworthy, nature of relationships within dementia that can make the condition bearable. If this leads to an experience of being truly accepted and loved then a very profound spiritual encounter can ensue (Mills, 1997). In order for pastoral and spiritual care to be effective it must find ways of addressing and 'healing' this disconnectedness and reassuring that in Christian terms God does not abandon people, even if they feel abandoned. Within the Christian scriptures this is expressed very clearly in the New Testament letter to the Romans '. . . there is nothing in life, nor death, nor all creation that can separate us from the love of God in Christ Jesus our Lord' (Romans 8 v. 38. The Holy Bible, NRSV). Other faiths also have belief statements that express similar sentiments.

Spiritual and religious are not necessarily the same

Distinguishing spiritual care from religious ministry is important and there are many people who would claim to have a deep spirituality but choose not to give expression to it in a religious way (Speck, 1998; Coleman et al, 2001). The absence of a religious expression or activity in a person's life should not be taken as indicative of a lack of spirituality because the needs associated with this aspect of the person may continue to exist but in a less recognizable or accessible form.

Spiritual may be described as the vital essence of human life, often enabling us to transcend life circumstances and foster hope. We may not be conscious of its presence or perceive it as an area of need at all times. The outward expression of this vital force or principle will be shaped and influenced by life experience, culture and other personal factors. Spirituality is a dynamic and will therefore be unique for each individual.

Spiritual:
A search for *existential* meaning within a life experience, usually with reference to a power other than the self, which may not necessarily be called 'God'. It is the sense of a relationship or connection with this power or force in the universe that can enable us to transcend the present context of reality. It is more than a search for meaning or a sense of unity with others.

Religion may be understood as a system of faith and worship that expresses an underlying spirituality. This faith is frequently interpreted in terms of particular rules, regulations, customs and practices, as well as the belief content of the named religion. There is a clear acknowledgment of a power other than self, usually described as 'God', although some faith groups may not have a specific deity but a higher state of being that they will seek to achieve, as in Buddhism. In some religious understandings this power is seen as an external controlling influence. In others the control is more from within the believer, guiding and shaping behaviour. The importance of either an external or internal 'locus of control' within a faith context has been the subject of much research, especially in the USA, where a Religious Orientation Scale has been developed, although the scale is really only of relevance in religious populations (Allport and Ross, 1967; Kirkpatrick and Hood, 1990).

When talking about religion one would not usually separate religion from spirituality. Neither should one use these terms interchangeably or assume that people who deny any religious affiliation have no spiritual needs, because you can be spiritual without being religious.

Religion:
A particular system of faith and worship expressive of an underlying spirituality and interpretive of what the named religion understands of 'God' and the individual's response to the deity.

Some people, therefore, would choose to express their *spiritual* belief within a *religious* framework that might bring with it a measure of social integration. On this basis all religious believers would be spiritual but not all spiritual believers would be religious. This distinction is important when thinking about needs assessment and provision of services.

Sometimes people adopt a set of religious practices without any underlying spiritual belief system. This can sometimes lead to forms of superstitious practice whereby the ritual must be performed or bad luck will follow. At its extreme it is displayed as part of the 'religious' behaviour and obsessive rituals in psychotic illness. There can, therefore, almost be a sliding scale from healthy religion (with a developed underpinning spirituality) to a potentially unhealthy 'religion' (without a deeper spirituality). This latter can lead to restrictive, if not crippling, practices and rituals that can be associated with poor mental health for the individual.

Philosophical belief system

In differentiating between religious and spiritual it is recognized that some people will have developed what may broadly be described as a 'philosophy of life'. This philosophical view may not be formalized and structured but, for some, they will embrace a clear school of thinking that may reject the existence of any external power that can be influential. The belief system may be variously described as existentialism, humanism, agnosticism or 'free thinking'. Atheism, which is the denial of the existence of God, should be distinguished from agnosticism, which allows for a degree of uncertainty as to whether or not a deity exists. Some philosophical people would claim to be spiritual and to have an appreciation of aesthetic experiences and, in particular, to be able to transcend their present situation, especially through achieving connectedness with themselves, others and the world around them. They would, however, usually exclude any reference to a power other than themselves that might be influential unless generated in an interpersonal group dynamic sense.

Philosophical:
Where the search for existential meaning excludes any reference to a power other than themselves. Life events and the destiny of the individual being seen as manifestations of the individual's own personality as expressed individually and corporately.

A wider understanding of the word spiritual, as related to the search for existential meaning within any given life experience, allows us to consider spiritual needs and issues in the absence of any clear practice of a religion or faith but this does not mean that they are to be seen as totally separated from each other (Speck, 1988).

Many recent publications are beginning to refer to this differentiation and to the need for a wider approach from that sometimes offered within pastoral care. For example, MacKinlay (2001, p. 245) states that 'Sacraments are certainly important to a proportion of older adults, but there is also a critical move to a greater sense of interiority in older age. The clergy need to minister to the individual at his or her point of need'. Shamy (2003) offers a very sensitive text that is rooted very much within the Christian pastoral tradition. It provides excellent practical advice to clergy and others offering pastoral care to people with various forms of dementia, but it does not really address the needs of people with existential concerns outside of this tradition. A similar trend can be seen in a valuable collection of papers edited by McFadden et al (2003) in the USA. In this text there is a wide range of papers focusing on well-being for older adults and the relevance of spirituality and religion. While distinguishing between these two factors, many of the articles do focus on the relevance of a spirituality expressed within a faith community and the importance of religious coping.

Relevance for assessment of need

The differentiation between spirituality and religion becomes important when trying to assess 'spiritual' need because people may, incorrectly, deduce that those who decline anything religious have no spiritual needs. Frequently, however, the questions that have been asked only relate to religious practice and need, and so little attempt has been made to explore the spiritual dimension. In planning for the provision of services in hospitals or residential care this distinction becomes important because it recognizes the need for 'spiritual care providers' to be broad, interactive and flexible in their approach. It is especially so if it is necessary to gather information from families and friends concerning the spiritual beliefs and expression of those by patients during their life prior to the onset of dementia.

The assessment of spiritual need often relates to trying to assess the extent to which the person feels disconnected from those people or powers that enable the person to retain some sense of existential meaning and purpose in their life under more normal circumstances. Spiritual well-being may be a valuable resource to support people as they come to terms with terminal illness and try to retain this sense of identity in the face of illness and treatments that may threaten to fragment it. Failure to identify and sustain this resource may contribute to the experience of spiritual pain or distress.

Spiritual pain is often linked to many of the factors that might lead to a brokenness in our relationship with others, with God or an external power, or with ourselves: a sense of hopelessness; focus on suffering rather than pain; feelings of guilt and/or shame; unresolved anger; inability to trust; lack of inner peace; and sense of disconnectedness or fragmentation.

Spiritual pain, or distress, is often identified in people whose physical/emotional pain fails to respond adequately to recognized approaches to symptom relief. It is often linked to issues relating to a sense of hopelessness or meaninglessness, and a desire to 'end it all'. It may be expressed as suffering (rather than 'pain'), indicating that there seems to be no meaning or purpose to the pain and the experience is all-encompassing rather than localized or specific. Feelings of guilt or shame may be expressed and an inability to trust other people, oneself or 'God'. This can lead to breaking away from a previous religious or belief position, or from other people, which can result in greater *dis*-ease or lack of inner peace. Although some of these things can be tackled from a psychosocial perspective, when they assume an ultimate or existential significance the intervention needs to be of a spiritual nature. In the case of people who experience cognitive impairment and who may not be able to respond easily or appropriately to the usual forms of communication, responding to the needs that have been identified may seem quite daunting. Faith leaders and others responsible for spiritual care may need to be imaginative and flexible in the ways in which they offer spiritual support and comfort.

Responding to perceived need

Touch in a safe context is a not insignificant factor in helping to reconnect the disconnected and restore a greater sense of wholeness. Within Christian pastoral care the use of oil for anointing can be very calming and therapeutic, especially for those unable to receive the bread and wine of Holy Communion. Similarly the 'laying on of hands' is a religious ritual associated with healing that can be of benefit in some instances. So too is the simple holding of the person's hand or the stroking of the forehead.

One early morning I was taking Communion to an elderly lady who had been a very active Church-goer but was now very demented and in long-term care. She was in bed with cot sides up. She had looked at me with a fixed gaze during the prayers without a word. As I leant over to place the fragment of wafer (intincted with the wine) into her mouth she suddenly said 'Give us a kiss'. I kissed her forehead and she beamed and opened her mouth to receive the sacrament. The kiss of peace was never more significant.

Reminiscence (written and spoken) and guided imagery are also important aspects of care that may help to ease spiritual pain in terms of allowing some healing or reconciliation of the person with their past. Most patients wish to engage in activities that, they believe, address them more clearly as a person or nourish the non-material aspects of their life. It is difficult for staff always to find the time to sit with a person and try to explore areas of their life that might evoke a reaction. The bedside locker or historical photographs of the locality on the walls of a ward or corridor can sometimes act as prompts. Music can also be a powerful way of evoking feeling and memory. Lowis and Hughes (1997) report the use of sacred and secular music with elderly people to evoke feelings. They found a significant and positive correlation between the spirituality scores of the listeners and the ratings of both kinds of music for reverence or spirituality. Most participants found the selections restful and stimulated memories and thoughtfulness. Lowis and Hughes (1997) feel that spiritual or sacred music may be a useful accompaniment to relaxation therapy and life review techniques. The feelings evoked in this and other ways can be very important for engendering the spiritual and reconnecting the person with an earlier part of their life context.

Other examples of the importance of touch and non-verbal communication are given by Flint (2004).

For those who have had an active religious faith in the past, the imagery, symbols, words and rituals may all evoke happy memories. However, care-givers should beware of assumptions based on information from other people because the previously religious person may in fact have painful memories about Church and faith leaders that we might re-awaken unwittingly. It must not be forgotten that there are also many patients who may not wish to participate in activities but who still value having an aesthetically good setting. For such patients touch, smell, views through a window and beauty can become very important. In this situation it is especially important to focus on the art of *being with* rather than always wanting to be active and *to do*. Spiritual care is as much about the ethos of the place, and the attitudes and quality of care from the care-givers, as it is about the performance of specific rituals and actions.

Spirituality is everyone's concern – or is it?

While in many cases spiritual care will be the specific remit of properly appointed faith leaders, anyone willing to listen to the patient's story and stay alongside can provide spiritual care in its general sense. However, the questions that arise may become quite challenging to the listener, who may then find the faith leader/chaplain a useful resource to help them know how best to respond. Assessment can be a source of difficulty but three simple questions can open the door to an understanding of where the person is spiritually, whether asked of the person direct or through family members. Clearly these questions may be more possible to explore with the person earlier on in the onset of dementia:

1   Do you have a way of making sense of the things that happen to you in life?
2   What helps you cope when life is difficult?
3   Would you like to talk to someone about the way the disease is affecting you and your family?

The answers to these three questions may not be in terms of belief or faith, but in terms of family support, strength of character, etc. However, the questions can also help to identify spiritual strength and health and lead to discussion of whether the patient might wish to maintain contact with these resources while in hospital or other care setting. It is important that the responses are recorded and appropriate action taken through incorporation into the care plan, and regularly reviewed. Faith leaders may themselves require training and help in meeting the religious (let alone the wider spiritual) needs of people with dementia. A partnership needs to develop between the care-givers within care homes/institutions and faith representatives in order to explore together the most appropriate ways of responding to and meeting the needs of people with dementia.

Where the need is for a non-Christian spiritual resource, those appointed to provide spiritual care should establish links with the various faith communities and try to obtain the services of people who can confidently offer supportive care and spiritual support to people with dementia. There may be a steep learning curve for many faith leaders and work is needed to identify their training needs. For some faith communities pastoral care may not be understood in the same way as interpreted in Christianity. For example, in Judaism and Islam the faith leader (Rabbi or Imam) would primarily be a teacher who would instruct what to read, what to eat or not eat and what rituals to follow around the time of death. It would be the family or other designated community members who would visit to offer support. In the case of Judaism many of these visitors, however, would studiously avoid talking about death, if it was imminent, and direct the individual to thoughts of the goodness of God and blessings of this life. Interpreting the approaches of another culture and faith is fraught with difficulty and we need always to remember that each of us speaks from an ethnocentric context, however well informed we may be. In all cases the patient (as far as possible) and/or family should be our guide in terms of need and of who should meet them. Care may need to be exercised, however, because family carers may wish their relative to receive a religious ministry to satisfy *their* personal agenda and not that of the patient. As a healthcare chaplain it was not unknown for me to be asked to perform a religious ritual for a patient 'once the patient is unconscious and won't be frightened by your presence or words'. Relationships are not always positive and loving and having a relative very dependent and weak can sometimes initiate manipulative behaviour in the carers.

In many cases, however, the carers will be the main people who offer the spiritual care. If a family have worshipped together, prayed together or discussed spiritual matters at various times in their life it will be quite natural for them to be aware of and respond to the spiritual needs of the person with dementia. The needs of carers can become hidden or ignored in many aspects of living with a relative who is affected by dementia, and their own spiritual life is no exception. The role of faith leaders and the faith community may be as much to support the carer as to provide any other form of care.

Spiritual care will often be provided by the very staff who have assessed it because the patient has developed a relationship of trust with that individual or group. This can be especially important where the individual has expressed a clear wish for no religious contact. The role of the official pastoral caregivers may then be to support the staff as they follow through with the patient rather than taking over. Where very specific rituals are required then the faith leader and staff could also work together and complement each other's role at such times.

To know who you are and what you believe in is an essential prerequisite to the development of that spirit of openness that allows you to genuinely 'be there' for the other person, whatever their beliefs. It also guards against personal agendas getting in the way of responding to the patient's expressed need and can become truly reflective of a holism that is a hallmark of person-centred dementia care.

References

Allport, G.W. and Ross, J.M. (1967) Personal religious orientation and prejudice. *Journal of Personality and Social Psychology*, 5: 432–443.

Barton, R. (1966) *Institutional Neurosis*. Bristol: John Wright.

Cobb, M. (2001) *The Dying Soul: Spiritual Care at the End of Life*. Buckingham, PA: Open University Press.

Coleman, P.G., McKiernan, F., Mills, M. and Speck, P. (2001) Spiritual beliefs and existential meaning in later life: the experience of older bereaved spouses.

Unpublished paper presented at Stirling University, British Society of Gerontology Conference, October 2001.

Dukes, C. (1999) Nurses assessment of spiritual need. Unpublished Bachelor of Nursing thesis, University of Southampton, UK.

Flint, H. (2004) All God's children: the spiritual needs of people with dementia. In G.M.M. Jones and B.M.L. Miesen (Eds), *Care-giving in Dementia*, vol. 3. Hove: Brunner-Routledge, pp. 22–36.

Frankl, V. (1987) *Man's Search for Meaning*. London: Hodder & Stoughton.

Goffman, E. (1968) *Asylums*. Harmondsworth: Penguin.

Goldsmith, M. (1999) Dementia: a challenge to Christian theology and pastoral care. In A. Jewell (Ed.), *Spirituality and Ageing*. London: Jessica Kingsley, p. 128.

Harre, R. (1998) *The Singular Self: an Introduction to Psychology of Personhood*. London: Sage.

Heron, J. (1992) *Feeling and Personhood*. London: Sage.

Holy Bible (1995) *New Revised Standard Version: Anglicized Edition*. Oxford: Oxford University Press.

Jewell, A. (1999) *Spirituality and Ageing*. London: Jessica Kingsley.

Jones, G.M.M. (2004) The loss of meaningful attachments in dementia and stage-specific implications. In G.M.M. Jones and B.M.L. Miesen (Eds) *Care-giving in Dementia*, vol. 3. Hove: Brunner-Routledge, pp. 261–284.

King, M., Speck, P. and Thomas, A. (1994) Spiritual and religious beliefs in acute illness – is this a feasible area for study? *Social Science and Medicine*, **38**: 631–636.

King, M., Speck, P. and Thomas A. (1999) Spiritual belief and outcome from illness *Social Science and Medicine*, **48**: 1291–1299.

King, M., Speck, P. and Thomas, A. (2001) The Royal Free Interview for Spiritual and Religious Beliefs: development and validation of a self-report version. *Psychological Medicine*, **31**: 1015–1023.

Kirkpatrick, L.A. and Hood Jr, R.W. (1990) Intrinsic–extrinsic religious orientation: the boon or bane of contemporary psychology of religion. *Journal for the Scientific Study of Religion*, **29**: 442–462.

Kitwood, T. (1990) The dialectics of dementia: with particular reference to Alzheimer's disease. *Ageing and Society*, **9**: 1–15.

Kitwood, T. (1997) *Dementia Reconsidered: the Person comes First*. Buckingham, PA: Open University Press.

Kitwood, T. and Bredin, K. (1992) Towards a theory of dementia care: personhood and well-being. *Ageing and Society*, **12**: 269–287.

Koenig, H.G., George, L.K. and Peterson, B.L. (1998a) Religiosity and remission from depression in medically ill older patients. *American Journal of Psychiatry*, **155**: 536–542.

Koenig, H.G., Pargament, K. and Nielsen, J. (1998b) Religious coping and health status in medically ill hospitalized older adults. *Journal of Nervous and Mental Disease*, **186**: 513–521.

Lowis, M.J. and Hughes, J. (1997) A comparison of the effects of sacred and secular music on elderly people. *Journal of Psychology*, **131**: 45–55.

MacKinlay, E. (2001) *The Spiritual Dimension of Ageing*. London: Jessica Kingsley.

McFadden, S.H., Brennan, M. and Patrick, J.H. (2003) *New Directions in the Study of Later Life: Religiousness and Spirituality*. New York: Haworth Press.

Miesen, B.L.M. (1992) Attachment theory in dementia. In G.M.M. Jones and B.L.M Miesen (Eds), *Care-giving in Dementia*, vol. 1. London: Routledge, pp. 38–56.

Miller, E.J. and Gwynne, G. (1972) *A Life Apart*. London: Tavistock Publications.

Mills, M.A. (1997) The gift of her friendship, Person-centred Care Series 12. *Journal of Dementia Care*, **5**: 24–25.

Parkes, C.M. (1975) Psycho-social transitions: comparison between reactions to loss of a limb and loss of a spouse. *British Journal of Psychiatry*, **127**: 204–210.

Regan, D. and Smith, J. (1997) The fullness of time: how homes for older people can respond to their residents' needs for wholeness and a spiritual dimension to care. London: Counsel & Care, p. 8.

Robb, B. (1967) *Sans Everything: a Case to Answer*. London: Nelson.

Ross, L. (1994) Spiritual aspects of nursing. *Journal of Advanced Nursing*, **19**: 439–447.

Shamy, E. (2003) *A Guide to the Spiritual Dimension of Care for People with Alzheimer's Disease and Related Dementia*. London: Jessica Kingsley.

Speck, P.W. (1970) Visiting in a female psycho-geriatric ward. *British Journal of Psychiatry*, **117**: 93–94.

Speck, P.W. (1978) *Loss and Grief in Medicine*. London: Baillière-Tindall.

Speck, P.W. (1988) *Being There: Pastoral Care in Time of Illness*. London: SPCK.

Speck, P.W. (1998) Spiritual issues in palliative care. In D. Doyle, G. Hanks and M. MacDonald (Eds), *Oxford Textbook of Palliative Medicine* (2nd edn). Oxford: Oxford University Press, pp. 805–817.

Part III

Topics related to care-giving issues

Psychotherapeutic groups for people with dementia: the Dementia Voice group psychotherapy project

Rik Cheston, Kerry Jones and Jane Gilliard

Introduction

I've pushed a lot of boats out in my time, it is upsetting to think that I am never going to achieve anything again.

(Bob, aged 69)

Over the last 15 years a wide range of individual psychotherapeutic work with people with dementia has been described, including psychodynamic (e.g. Sinason, 1992), cognitive–behavioural (e.g. Teri and Gallagher-Thomson, 1991) and humanistic (e.g. Stokes and Goudie, 1990), with probably the most frequently reported form of psychotherapy being group work (e.g. Yale, 1995). However, while the clinical growth of psychotherapeutic and counselling work with people with dementia is welcome, it has not yet been matched by an equivalent growth in the evaluation of the impact of such work.

The Dementia Voice group psychotherapy project

This project involved the creation of six psychotherapy groups across Southern England for people who had been diagnosed as having Alzheimer's disease or another form of dementia. Each group met for ten weeks, with each session lasting for approximately an hour and a quarter. Groups were facilitated by the first author (R.C.) in collaboration with either one or two locally based co-facilitators. Five of the six groups consisted of between six and eight people, with the sixth group having ten participants.

The design of this study utilized baseline and follow-up measures. The second author (K.J.), acting independently of the clinical process, collected a variety of data including participants' levels of anxiety and depression at four time points. This enabled three separate phases to be established within the project: a baseline period of between five and ten weeks; an intervention period of ten sessions during which the groups took place; and a ten-week follow-up period. Although the design did not involve a randomly allocated control group, a comparison of data between the intervention and the baseline and follow-up phases enabled meaningful conclusions to be reached about the significance of those changes that occurred during the baseline period (Cheston et al, 2003).

Forty-two participants entered the project at different points, of whom 19 completed the baseline, intervention and follow-up phases of the project. Analysis of the data using a repeated-measure ANOVA provided significant evidence for a statistically significant reduction in the level of depression during the intervention that was maintained at follow-up and a similar borderline-significant trend towards a reduction in anxiety.

Addressing difficult feelings: shame

The central element of group work with people with dementia is to offer participants time and space to think about themselves in the context of other people who are both similar and dissimilar to them. The process of meeting others in a similar position brings both hope and threat: hope, because to experience others in a similar position is to have a sense of not being on one's own; threat, because differences within the group may make losses and change more apparent. An important task for group facilitators, therefore, is to manage the tensions within the group as participants confront the differences and similarities between themselves. In doing so, the group alternates between approaching and avoiding the factor that binds them together – their memory problems and cognitive losses.

In order to illustrate this point we will turn, now, to consider how a group may respond to a central emotion – that of shame. The neurological impairments that are defined as, say, Alzheimer's disease or vascular dementia cause many behaviours or behavioural deficits that would, in other circumstances, be construed as breaching socially agreed norms. People with dementia may not be able to find the words to speak coherently, they may lack the competence to manage their own affairs and they may sometimes even lose control of their bladders. However much these behaviours are attributed either directly to the neurological impairment or to a deficit in their care environment, the experience of the individual remains that of potential shame – it is *their* incoherence, *their* incompetence or *their* incontinence. The experience of a person with dementia, then, may provide many opportunities for shame-filled episodes and consequently a key function for the group will be to enable participants to talk about this.

Shame is associated with three behavioural strategies:

1   *Avoidance.* The social stigma of receiving a diagnosis of dementia has been identified as a key issue in people's experience of the early stages of dementia. Consequently, individuals will attempt to avoid being positioned within a shameful identity and to conceal or to cover up

behaviours that might be taken as confirming the possible validity of that position. Thus, feelings of shame can act within a group to avoid discussion of subjects where the potential for shame is strong. This avoidance may act as a taboo – the group becomes unable to address aspects of their shared experiences that are too shame-filled unless the wish to avoid certain subjects can itself be addressed.

2   *Concealment.* One pervasive feature of the diagnostic process is the variety of accounts that individuals who have been the subject of a memory assessment generate in an attempt to position themselves as having less personal responsibility for a poor test result. Saunders (1998), for instance, argued that memory clinic patients produced up to five separate accounts in an attempt to create an identity for themselves as competent and credible people. She concluded, 'dementia patients manage and protect their own self-image just like any other person' (p. 85). These attempts to manage one's own identity – to position oneself within roles that reflect competence rather than incompetence, and to claim attributes that are consistent with previously established story lines – may be seen by others as attempts to 'cover up' for a shameful attribute or role. In these circumstances others within the group may collude with this concealment. Thus, within the context of group therapy the group may agree collectively that their memory problems are the product of old age, or that, while trivial matters are forgotten, important facts can be remembered if only they try hard enough. These dominant voices asserting the continuity of an unblemished, undamaged identity must be heard and allowed, but at the same time other voices within the group that relate to change and uncertainty also need to be assimilated. The group may well be in two minds about change, reflecting both continuity and discontinuity at different points.

3   *Denial.* Insight and denial are key areas of concern for dementia care research. Within the disease model of dementia, people with dementia tend to be viewed as either having or not having insight into their condition. Such insight is often represented as a fixed entity, an all-or-nothing state that is similar to the neurological syndrome of agnosognosia. In this chapter we will put forward a different account of insight, i.e. a psychological model of awareness in which dementia is viewed as a problematic experience that, within the context of group psychotherapy, can be gradually assimilated into existing concepts about the self, and are thus allowed into awareness. We will illustrate this process of 'coming to terms' with dementia through the use of two contrasting case studies in which participants in groups run as part of the Dementia Voice group psychotherapy project moved from a position of warding off any notion of being ill or having a significant memory problem (effectively being 'in denial') to a position of being able to acknowledge either the diagnosis of Alzheimer's disease and/or their fears for the future.

Dementia as a 'problematic experience'

A diagnosis of Alzheimer's disease, or other forms of dementia, has significant implications for psychological well-being. The person who has been diagnosed as having this illness not only has to accept the permanent nature of those losses that have brought the diagnosis, but also has to adjust to the certainty of future deterioration. At the same time, the direct and indirect effects of the illness on the person's social support network may mean that the emotional adjustment to the diagnosis may well take place without those supports that he or she has been accustomed to using. Finally, adjustment must occur within the context of a failing memory and a reduced capacity to use words to make sense of the world.

The assimilation model of psychotherapeutic change (e.g. Stiles et al, 1992, 1995) is a trans-theoretical model of the process of change involved in psychotherapy. It has been used extensively as a means of understanding how the meanings of events and experiences change for clients during psychotherapy (e.g. Stiles et al, 1999).

The core position underlying the assimilation model is that during the developmental process involved in ordinary learning the experiences are assimilated into existing beliefs, which in turn are altered to accommodate the new material. Problematic experiences are those that, if they were assimilated in this way, would be too psychologically painful. Instead, these experiences are pushed away, out of conscious awareness, although knowledge of their presence may leak back in the form of symptoms of psychological distress, such as outbursts of anger, panic attacks or depression.

The process by which problematic experiences are assimilated (e.g. in successful psychotherapy) involves clients moving through a series of stages or levels as they assimilate their psychological problems into their sense of self. As problematic material is gradually assimilated into existing schema, so the client experiences a sequence of emotional reactions, from being oblivious or feeling only vaguely disturbed to experiencing the content as painful and then as problematic but less distressing. In the later stages of this process, as the problem is understood and new solutions tried out, confidence grows and the client may gain some satisfaction or positive affect from the new way of living (Newman and Beail, 2002).

The assimilation model thus provides a way of understanding how people move from avoiding awareness of the problematic material, through a process of exploration and problem identification, to eventual understanding and insight that permits a wider problem-solving approach and final mastery of the problematic experience. This movement through a series of stages is operationalized through the Assimilation of Problematic Experiences Scale shown in Table 10.1. In the remainder of this chapter we will argue that the process by which people adjust to, or 'come to terms with', a diagnosis of dementia can be construed in terms of the assimilation of a problematic experience.

Table 10.1 Assimilation of Problematic Experiences Scale (APES)

APES level	Content	Affect
0. Warded off	Uninformed, unaware, avoidance	Minimal affect, reflecting successful avoidance
1. Unwanted thoughts	Emergence of thoughts associated with discomfort	Unfocused strong emotions (e.g. anxiety, fear, sadness) that are more salient than content
2. Vague awareness	Problematic experience is acknowledged and uncomfortable; associated thoughts are described	Affect focused on acute psychological pain or panic
3. Problem statement or clarification	Clear problem statement	Negative but manageable affect
4. Understanding/insight	Problem is formulated within a schema including clear connective links	Curiosity of affect, with mixed pleasant and unpleasant recognitions
5. Application/working through	Working on current problem with reference to specific problem-solving efforts	Business-like positive/ negative affect linked to outcomes
6. Problem solution	Success with a specific problem	Positive satisfaction linked to accomplishments
7. Mastery	Generalization through habitual use of problem solution in new situations	Neutral (i.e. this is no longer something to get excited about)

Source: Newman and Beail (2002).

Group psychotherapy and the assimilation of problematic experiences

Anyone entering a psychotherapy group, regardless of their disability, is likely to be anxious. For someone with dementia, these uncertainties will almost certainly be magnified. After all, attending such a group will require participants to engage in a number of tasks: to remember that they cannot always remember, to find words to describe their inarticulacy and to competently represent their incompetence. In many ways the challenge of the group is to witness the dementia that is present in the group, and this consequently will mean participants attending precisely to those things that their dementia limits and restricts.

In order to diminish anxiety the participants will seek to build some sense of unity – to find others within the group who are like them in some way. Yet there will inevitably be differences and similarities within the group – some participants will want to think about their position, other group members will feel more comfortable articulating a wish to forget, some will be happier looking at what remains and others may voice a sense of loss. Whilst different group members may embody these different positions, we can take it that they reflect aspects of relating to dementia that everyone within the group will share, even if some find alternative positions uncomfortable.

Yet, in order for the group to form, participants need to temporarily forget their differences in order to achieve some common agreement. Too early an exploration of these issues risks the group being experienced as unsafe, and consequently disintegrating. If the group is to maintain this exploration of their experiences, then this is only possible if the group is experienced as being a safe place (see Chapter 11 in this volume). Aspects of the group's experiences are alternately approached and then moved away from, as the group struggles to make sense of dementia without being over-whelmed by it.

In the two case studies that we will now describe this group process of approaching and retreating from different aspects of the experiences of dementia accomplished by two participants in different ways: Robert was able to challenge his group directly, asserting 'I don't think that anyone here has Alzheimer's disease', whereas for Martin the process of exploration was both direct and indirect, drawing on stories having a thematic continuity with his emotional experiences within the group.

Robert: being in two minds about dementia

Watkins et al (2006) analysed transcripts made from audiotapes recorded during the ten sessions of one of the six groups in this project. They focused on the changes in awareness shown by one group participant, Robert. During the first session Robert defined his problem as a selective loss of short-term memory that did not affect other areas of his life. He referred to other people he knew at a club that he attended saying, 'half of them have got Alzheimer's or something near'. Watkins et al suggest that during this session he was in a position of warding off awareness of both his diagnostic status and the implications of this.

Without doubt the pivotal session for Robert individually, and perhaps collectively for the group as a whole, was the fourth session. In this session, a series of participants in the group respond to Robert's challenge ('I don't think that anyone here has Alzheimer's disease') by asserting not only that they did have Alzheimer's disease but also that they felt frightened, guilty and ashamed at the knowledge. Watkins et al argued that until the fourth session Robert's inability to confront his feelings of shame and fear prevented him from addressing other emotions, such as anger and loss. The key therapeutic factor, arguably, was that the group managed to convey to Robert that shame and fear were experiences shared by the group as a whole.

Once the ability of the other group members to articulate their feelings of shame and fear had allowed Robert to confront his own avoidance, he was able to move through the psychotherapeutic process of assimilation. Both before and during this fourth session Robert had not acknowledged that he had Alzheimer's disease, but after it he referred to himself as having a memory problem. In session seven, for instance, Robert joked about having had the results from a CT scan fed back to him:

ROBERT: I got the results back yesterday and it said that my brain had shrunk very, very slightly in the cavity, which is fairly symptomatic of the onset of Alzheimer's. And so I asked, 'if it's the *onset*, what happens when you're there' [group laughs], . . . and he said 'very little more' [laughter] I mean if you get to the point where you couldn't remember anything at all then the brain wouldn't have got any smaller but it's this shrinkage that brings about this symptom of short-term memory loss, which is quite intriguing. So I'm not particularly bothered by it, but it was interesting to go through it

Similarly, in the ninth session Robert reflected upon how he had changed over the course of the group:

ROBERT: . . . I don't see the problem now the way, the problem of declining memory, the way I did before. . . .
JANET: You didn't accept it then before?
ROBERT: Well I did accept it but it frightened me. But I thought, well, I'm going mad, I'm going crazy. I thought what am I going to be like in another five years?

Arguably a group achieves much of its therapeutic potency through a sense of universality, to use Yalom's term (Yalom, 1970) – that the shared nature of this condition means that to have Alzheimer's disease is transformed from a shameful property to one of normality.

Martin: exploring threat through narrative

In another of the six groups in the Dementia Voice project, two separate descriptions of change ran in parallel (Cheston et al, 2004). At times members of the group explicitly talked about change within their lives, for instance by speaking about the problems of growing older: at other times participants, and especially one participant, Martin, told stories, recounted dreams or drew on proverbs. Within the metaphorical or indirect exploration that the group engaged in, the themes that emerged frequently related to aspects of change, such as loss or threat. Sometimes participants explicitly related these narratives to their present lives, while at other times they made no specific connections. Both the explicit and metaphorical accounts altered over the course of the group, reflecting a therapeutic process in which Martin moved from originally warding off or pushing away awareness of his problems, to a position where he was able to define the problem and to show that he was aware of the threat of continued deterioration.

During the first session, Martin insisted that the changes that he had experienced were temporary and that his skills and those of other group members would return if the group could talk about them. He angrily attacked another group member who not only found it difficult to talk about the problem but, when he did talk, insisted that his speech would not come back. Whereas the first session had involved considerable discussion of memory problems and other changes, the second session contained a larger number of narratives. In the early stages of therapy, narratives may serve as a distraction – in effect a defensive manoeuvre to avoid the anxiety associated with the problematic material. This seems to have happened within this session – rather than talk about the present, Martin instead recounted stories from his childhood, e.g. describing how as a boy on holiday he had helped clear a makeshift runway on a beach and been rewarded with a trip up in an aeroplane.

During the fourth session, Martin's narratives also began to concern different elements of threat. One story concerned a tidal wave threatening the cruise liner in which he and his family were passengers: at first there was uncertainty over whether the tidal wave that Martin alone sees is real; then, when the true nature of the threat became apparent, the story developed to consider whether the wave could be survived; finally, when the tidal wave has come and gone, it becomes apparent on reflection that, although support has been there for Martin's ship, other vessels had not been so fortunate.

Problematic material that is moving towards emergence is sometimes expressed in therapy sessions in the form of a narrative that symbolizes the client's experiences. The symbolic expression of the problematic material both allows it to be explored but also provides some distance from that material, thereby limiting the amount of psychological pain that would be experienced (Stiles et al, 1999). In this case the main elements of the cruise liner narrative concerned threat, and an exploration of the nature of that threat. Yet the story concluded with the tidal wave having been survived and this, we argued, could be understood as a defensive strategy that allowed one of the most fundamental aspects of the problematic experience (that the progressive decline is inevitable) to be avoided. Thus by introducing the possibility of survival into the story, the experience of threat becomes less painful and more bearable.

During session five, the problems that Martin experienced began to be defined more explicitly. He spoke of how forgetting was like 'a steel door coming down on me' and apologized to the group for the weakness in his bladder that meant that he had to go out to the toilet during the group. This fifth session represented an important therapeutic step forward for Martin. In previous sessions, although other participants had spoken of having Alzheimer's disease, or had discussed their memory difficulties, Martin had restricted himself to speaking vaguely of changes in his life without detailing them. In this session, however, he had been able to speak more coherently of a problem with his memory. At the same time, the nature of the problem is unresolved and Martin said that he was still hopeful that his problem would be resolved.

In the eighth session, for the first time, Martin was able to acknowledge both that the cause of his difficulties had been a stroke and also that he was worried about the future. Not only was the nature of the problem defined, but for the first time Martin was able to present some understanding about why the problem existed, and an awareness of what the problem might mean for his future. Many of Martin's stories still continued to explore issues of threat, for instance in one story he recounted how he used to keep a wonderful flock of chickens that had been attacked and killed first by a fox and then by storms. Unlike the story of the cruise liner, however, these narratives do not conclude with the threat being survived.

The stories that Martin told in the last session were especially moving: he spoke of the value of friendship, of how men could care for each other and of the importance of truth and honesty. At the same time, he openly described his own sadness for how his life had changed, and how these changes were irreversible. Towards the end of the session, Martin recounted a story about his father's experiences during the first world war: 'One day I asked my father about how his commanding officer died, because I was curious. He told me that he died in his arms. That he had been out there in no-man's land and he was badly injured. There were shells exploding all around. You get that sort of man sometimes, who even though he was so badly injured he put his arms around another man and protected him with his own life . . . It takes a war to bring these people out. And they're people that will always talk about the truth, no matter what. They will tell you to your face about what is happening'. Within the context of the group it was hard to escape the conclusion that this story in some way referred to some aspects of being in the group, surrounded by loss and still talking of the truth.

Psychotherapy and people with dementia

Psychotherapeutic work with people with dementia is still very much in its infancy. While it is encouraging to see the field developing, it is important to acknowledge the limitations of the work to date. First of all we need to recognize that group psychotherapy is not something that all people with dementia would either wish to enter into or to be able to benefit from. The groups in this project required a capacity both to engage with other people and to think about one's memory problems. For some participants, this proved to be too much. One woman who had been unable to attend the first two sessions of a group withdrew after attending the third and fourth sessions, while a male participant attended only half of the first session of a group, leaving because he felt that it was not the right environment for him. Nevertheless, the overall drop-out rate of two people from six groups is roughly comparable with that from groups aimed at people with other forms of mental health problems.

Similarly, the majority of participants in this research still had relatively intact verbal and cognitive skills. All had a Mini Mental State Examination (MMSE) score of 18 or above (Folstein et al, 1975), while roughly two-thirds were rated as having a 'mild' level of cognitive impairment. Thus although some group participants undoubtedly had substantial problems in articulating their needs, this work arguably tells us relatively little about work with people with a lower level of cognitive and verbal fluency.

The second main limitation is that while this study showed that participants' levels of depression tended to drop during the intervention compared to a baseline and follow-up period, much more clinical and research work needs to be done before we can conclude with confidence that this form of intervention can be effective even with selected groups of participants. In particular, we do not know whether people with dementia (including Robert and Martin) were able to hold onto any changes in awareness outside the groups.

Nevertheless, the group psychotherapy as presented in this project provides an important place for participants to reflect upon the emotional significance of their experiences of dementia. As such, this approach differs markedly from other therapeutic forms of work with people with dementia, such as validation therapy, life-review therapy (e.g. Garland, 1994), reminiscence therapy (e.g. Bender, 1994) and reality orientation (e.g. Holden and Woods, 1988).

As Mills and Bartlett have described in Chapter 11 of this book, the capacity of a group to allow participants to explore different, sometimes potentially shameful, aspects of them is related to the extent that participants experienced the group as a safe place. While Robert was able directly to challenge the diagnosis of Alzheimer's disease, other participants in other groups could only find an indirect way to voice their fears. These groups provided a setting in which people can gain a sense that they have not been forgotten, that they will be remembered and that what has happened has been important. As one group member said:

Just because I've got a failing memory, doesn't mean that I'm a failure.

Acknowledgements

We would like to thank all those people who took part in the groups and the research, their care-givers, friends and relatives who supported our work. We would also like to thank Elizabeth Bartlett, Jane House and Sandy Preen, Kirsty Thorne and Jennifer Peak, Pat Lysaght and Liz Young, Suzanne Davis and Anna Littlechild for all their hard work in facilitating the groups. Finally, we would also like to thank David Newman and Nigel Beail for giving us permission to use their table.

References

Bender, M. (1994) An interesting confusion: what can we do with reminiscence groupwork? In J. Bornat (Ed.), *Reminiscence Reviewed: Perspectives, Evaluations, Achievements.* Buckingham, PA: Open University Press, pp. 32–45.

Cheston, R., Jones, K. and Gilliard, J. (2003) Group psychotherapy and people with dementia. *Aging and Mental Health,* 7: 452–461.

Cheston, R., Jones, K. and Gilliard, J. (2004) Falling into a hole: narrative and emotional change in a psychotherapy group for people with dementia. *Dementia: the International Journal of Social Research and Policy,* 3: 95–103.

Folstein, M.F., Folstein, S. and McHugh, P.R. (1975) Mini-Mental State: a practical method for grading the cognitive state of patients for the clinician. *Journal of Psychiatric Research,* 12: 89–198.

Garland, J. (1994) What splendour, it all coheres: life-review therapy with older people. In J. Bornat (Ed.), *Reminiscence Reviewed: Perspectives, Evaluations, Achievements.* Buckingham, PA: Open University Press, pp. 21–31.

Holden, U.P. and Woods, R.T. (1988) *Reality Orientation: Psychological Approaches to the 'Confused' Elderly.* Edinburgh: Churchill Livingstone.

Newman, D. and Beail, N. (2002) Monitoring change in psychotherapy with people with intellectual disabilities: the application of the Assimilation of Problematic Experiences Scale. *Journal of Applied Research in Intellectual Disabilities,* 15: 48–60.

Saunders, P.A. (1998) 'My brain's on strike': the construction of identity through memory accounts by dementia patients. *Research on Aging,* 20: 65–90.

Sinason, V. (1992) *Mental Handicap and the Human Condition.* London: Free Association.

Stiles, W., Meshot, C., Anderson, T. and Sloan, W. (1992) Assimilation of problematic experiences: the case of John Jones. *Psychotherapy Research,* 2: 81–101.

Stiles, W., Shapiro, D., Harper, H. and Morrison, L. (1995) Therapist contributions to psychotherapeutic assimilation: an alternative to the drug metaphor. *British Journal of Medical Psychology,* 68: 1–13.

Stiles, W., Honos-Webb, L. and Lani, J. (1999) Some functions of narrative in the assimilation of problematic experiences. *Journal of Clinical Psychology,* 55: 1213–1226.

Stokes, G. and Goudie, F. (1990) Counselling confused elderly people. In G. Stokes and F. Goudie (Eds), *Working with People with Dementia.* Bicester, Oxon: Winslow, pp. 181–190.

Teri, L. and Gallagher-Thomson, D. (1991) Cognitive–behavioural interventions for treatment of depression in Alzheimer's patients. *Gerontologist,* 31: 413–416.

Watkins, R., Cheston, R., Jones, K. and Gilliard, J. (2006) 'Coming out with Alzheimer's disease': changes in insight during a psychotherapy group for people with dementia. *Aging and Mental Health*, **10**: 1–11.

Yale, R. (1995) *Developing Support Groups for Individuals with Early Stage Alzheimer's Disease: Planning, Implementation and Evaluation*. Baltimore: Health Professions' Press.

Yalom, I.D. (1970) *The Theory and Practice of Group Psychotherapy*. New York: Basic Books.

Chapter 11

Experiential support groups for people in the early to moderate stages of dementia

Marie Mills and Elizabeth Bartlett

We're all people, without other people it would be a very lonely life.

(Group member)

Introduction

The literature suggests that experiential and support groups help many people to cope with the experience of dementia. This chapter explores why this should be so, and discusses groupwork theory, methods and practical observations. The discussion is illustrated by current experiential groupwork with people who have an early to moderate dementia. It is further augmented by the insights offered by group members who wished to help people in a similar situation. The chapter argues that support groups meet needs on different levels. Some find them very necessary, some see them as less necessary but helpful and some see them as a useful part of the services offered by the organization as a whole. The chapter concludes that experiential support groups form a useful part of the services offered to people with dementia.

Groupwork theory

Experiential groupwork with older people in the UK is a comparatively recent phenomenon. Bromley (1966) suggested that group therapy or counselling would be helpful for some older people, but with no suggestion of therapeutic interventions for people with dementia. However Morton and Bleathman (1991) Bleathman and Morton (1996) and Day (1997) found that groupwork based on Feil's (1993) validation groupwork method was beneficial for this client group. Furthermore, reminiscence groupwork with people who have dementia also appeared to lead to an improvement in well-being (Woods and McKiernan, 1995), although the Cochrane review on reminiscence work (Spector et al, 2000) concluded that there is insufficient evidence to reach any positive conclusions.

Yale (1991, 1995) began to promote the concept of supportive groupwork with people who have dementia in the 1990s. Cheston (1998) found that groupwork interventions were more prevalent than individual work. Although this could be attributed to cost effectiveness and the need to maximize resources, there are sufficient arguments to suggest that groupwork has a place in the range of therapeutic strategies for a condition that requires effective management in order to promote well-being and personhood (Mills and Coleman, 1994; Kitwood, 1997).

Furthermore, collaborative memory studies suggest that the 'group memory' is superior to individual memory (Thompson, 2002). Individual recall appears to be improved within the group (Mills, 2003), although this finding requires further investigation. Another slant on this perspective is that the group mind can help and support individual minds within dementia. Psychoanalytic groupwork theory gives some understanding of the potential of the group to support, heal and renew, although other schools of thought also add to the understanding of group processes (Miesen and Jones, 1997).

Group processes

Most theories about group processes agree that human beings learn how to 'be' in groups from very early in life, and continue to move in and out of groups throughout the lifespan (Foulkes and Anthony, 1957; Morgan and Thomas, 1996; Thomas, 1996). People learn to interact, behave and think in groups. Infants grasp the complex notion of 'turn taking' in interactions with primary care-givers, which leads to skill in communication with others. Care-givers also provide the 'scaffolding' or support to encourage safe learning (Bruner 1966, 1983; Vygotsky, 1978). Much of this is learnt through humorous play (Oates, 1994). By adulthood, people are well-experienced group members. This knowledge is part of the self and remains throughout the lifespan and for much of the process of dementia.

Groups protect, nurture, educate, shape and control (Brown, 1986; Morgan and Thomas, 1996; Thomas 1996). They assist or encourage the individual to conform to group norms and expectations, often with surprising and disturbing results (Asch, 1951, 1955; Milgram, 1974). However, experimental research on groups also indicates the positive influence of group membership. Tajfel and Turner (1979) argue that personal identity gives way to social identity, leading to a corresponding rise in self-esteem. This has important implications for people in the early stages of dementia, where a new and unwelcome identity has to be constructed.

Groups construct the social self (Burkitt, 1991). William James (1894) succinctly stresses the 'pit of insecurity beneath the surface of life', with psychodynamic theorists suggesting that all individuals tend unconsciously to defend against anxiety from an early age. These arguments perceive the individual to be unconsciously motivated, influenced by early experiences and primitive emotions and with an overpowering need to defend against anxiety. These unconscious behaviours are brought into the group process. Earlier accounts of groupwork with people with dementia indicate that anxiety ebbs and flows throughout group sessions (Cheston et al, 2002a,b).

In our own work, and as some vignettes will illustrate in part, anxiety was managed and controlled through denial, humour and redirecting it outside of the group. Bion's (1961) seminal work at Northfields gave rise to the notion of the work group or the task, and the unconscious basic assumption group, organized around the three assumptions of dependency, flight/ fight and pairing. He argues that group members can stay or move between these assumptions for some time. Participants' dialogue in Cheston's groups (Cheston, 1996; Cheston et al, 2002a,b; Watkins et al, 2006) illustrated that members frequently look to the facilitator for guidance and in some cases actually leave the group. They also engage in paired, friendly and meaningful conversation.

Group processes and pairing

The group were discussing where they had been born and the schools they had attended. James and Sean discovered that although they had been born at opposite ends of the country they had in fact attended the same boarding school. They became quite animated as they recalled the names of previous masters, the layout and the history of the school. The rest of the group listened with interest and it was good to see the two men, for a while, happily reminiscing about old times. However, their 'safe' discussion delayed other topics, which might generate anxiety, from being aired.

Group processes and challenge: an example

Not all pairing is so friendly. Occasionally a group member may challenge and 'pair' with the facilitator:

During a recent group session the topic under discussion was driving. One group member said she had had another driving test as she had recently got lost in a familiar area. Fortunately she passed her test although she said it had made her very nervous. She was also angry that her husband had made her have the test, but recognized that she had always found any test nerve wracking.

Various members then spoke about having to give up driving due to their 'condition'. Some found it hard to do this, others found it easier and did not overly miss it. However, Rob, also a group member, asked why they had given it up, saying no-one had told him he had to stop driving. Two members said they had to give it up when they were diagnosed. (They did not give the actual diagnosis.) Another member almost silently whispered 'with Alzheimer's'. Rob sat upright and looked at the facilitator

(E.B.) somewhat sternly. He said, 'What's this all about then? This is news to me!' She gently and calmly said that it was to do with insurance and explained that if your licence was withdrawn you were unable to get insurance. One needed insurance in case of accidents. He asked why one's licence should be withdrawn. E.B. said that some neurological conditions meant that it was often unsafe to drive. However, sometimes people were retested, as had just been described, and were allowed to continue driving. The group was silent and still, watching both of them intently. The second facilitator observed both the paired interaction and the group's response.

Rob then said 'Well, I've never been given a diagnosis, I've just got a poor memory'. E.B. went through a little of his past history, seeing the consultant, etc. Rob remembered this but still strongly denied he had had a diagnosis. This conversation continued for some minutes. E.B. remained calm and supportive, Rob remained challenging. Gradually other group members began to join in, siding with E.B. (perceived as the leader and one who had knowledge). The outcome from this discussion was that the group decided they should be told the diagnosis but also receive it in writing so that they could refer to it later if they wished. Anger was expressed over the fact that few of them had received written confirmation of their diagnosis. A remark was made, 'What's the point of just telling us, we forget what we're told anyway'.

The unconscious anger and anxiety felt about having dementia was directed outside the group. Rob accepted he had had a diagnosis, but had forgotten he had been told. His usual good humour returned and he was given leaflets about driving and dementia. Some time later, after a lot of discussion, Rob and his wife decided that it was unsafe for him to continue driving due to his dementia. He said 'Even if you have a bit of it, this Alzheimer's, you're not reckoned to be safe. You could have an accident and not remember how it came about. So I've sent my driving licence back to the DLVA place. Fortunately Mavis, my wife, can drive so we will be alright.'

Groups as a study of relationships

Foulkes and Anthony (1957, p.15) suggest that catharsis or relief through expression is possible in therapeutic groups, as is 'restoration' through participation and acceptance, an argument that is supported by Rogerian encounter groups (Rogers, 1961, 1975; Kirschenbaum and Henderson, 1989). Yet another theory of group processes involved attitudes and the construction of the social world through concepts, ideas and images and through talk or social discourse. Discursive psychology is also concerned with how people manage their 'interests' through discourse, i.e. they have a 'stake' in the outcome (Potter, 1996). The previous vignette offers a clear example of 'personal stake' in the outcome.

Within the psychodynamic perspective, it is recognized that attachment issues have a large part to play in understanding the experience of dementia (Miesen, 1992; Kitwood, 1997; Mills, 1998) and in experiential groupwork with people who have dementia. Building on the need of the other for survival purposes, humans have developed non-verbal and symbolic patterns of relating (Trevarthen, 1979; Stern, 1985). This is most clearly demonstrated in the attachment between mother and child, where Bowlby (1969) argues that care-giving and care-seeking attachment behaviours in the care-giver/child dyad are adaptive and instinctive and often operate outside of conscious awareness (Bretherton, 1985). Bowlby suggests that young infants' perceptions of threat to safety activate behaviours associated with loss and fearfulness, together with proximity and contact-seeking actions. However, the young infant is also 'driven' to explore their world. Attachment theory contends that the need for safety and reduction of anxiety triggers infant attachment behaviours, which are activated in times of stress.

Furthermore, psychodynamic arguments suggest that these experiences will be represented in a variety of ways throughout vulnerable periods in the lifespan. Miesen (1992, 1993) hypothesizes that the vulnerability associated with feelings of permanent loss and fearfulness in dementia will also reawaken such attachment experiences (Munnichs and Miesen, 1986). Cheston and Bender (1999) also argue that any psychological trauma may have a severe impact on physical well-being. They draw attention to the mute, withdrawn behaviour of some people with dementia who are placed in unfamiliar surroundings. This behaviour is reminiscent of studies of the influence of traumatic and strange environments in early childhood (Robertson and Robertson, 1967).

The group as a container

Group theory can also reflect this early need to belong and yet remain separate. Anxieties will be triggered concerning fear of rejection, of not being liked or accepted and of looking foolish. In the experiential groups, members are quick to reassure each other if a person feels in any way diminished by their condition or their perceived failure to contribute appropriately.

> Grace said that she did not like to speak sometimes because she forgot words or it took her longer than others to find the right words. She spoke of her frustration 'Because it just won't come . . . I know it's there, but it's like a black hole sometimes and . . . and . . . there's nothing there. I want to say it . . . it . . . myself . . . but . . . other people try . . . try . . . to say things for me then and . . . I feel silly and stupid'.

It was noticeable that other group members listened intently and waited for her to finish before sharing their own experiences of 'forgetting' with her. The rules of socially acceptable and skilled group behaviour, turn taking and holding were evident, as well as altruism and concern. Someone ended the discussion with a joke, which acted as a defence against the anxiety of memory loss and the unspoken fear of the future, as well as lightening the moment. Members often retreated into humour in difficult times but were aware they did so. The value of humour was well recognized and frequently discussed. This small vignette indicates the struggle for balance between the need to belong and the need to maintain individuality, which is an ongoing task for all persons.

Bion (1961) argues that the group can be seen as having a positive holding and containing function, similar to the maternal role where negative infant emotions (rage) can be transformed into more bearable feelings. [However, Melanie Klein (1932) suggests that infants can have powerfully negative feelings about their carers, such as anger, helplessness and dependency.] The group too can be experienced in such a way and felt to be a source of anxiety as well as a container (Hinshelwood, 1987; Thomas, 1996). Rob's vignette suggests support for this argument.

Another function of the group is to maintain its boundaries in order to keep members safe. They also create in-groups and out-groups. Anxieties from the in-group can be directed towards the out-group and, echoing the work of Tajfel and Turner (1979), thus increase self-esteem and prevent the group from becoming overwhelmed by its own primitive emotions. In stressful times boundaries are important, especially within a vulnerable group that is dealing with sensitive issues. The holding function is critically important and facilitators need to ensure that the 'nuts and bolts' of the group, such as dates, times, procedures, etc., are clearly explained and carefully adhered to, a topic that will be returned to later in this chapter.

Most theories about group processes increase understanding of the role and value of experiential support groups in dementia, yet a characteristic of well-being in dementia is the degree of support surrounding the individual. Indeed it is only the positive nature of the relationships in dementia that makes the condition bearable (Kitwood, 1997, Mills, 1998; Bartlett, 2002; Bartlett and Cheston, 2003).

Systems theory offers another explanation of the relationships in groups. The foundations of systems theory are based on the insight that a system as a whole is qualitatively different, and 'behaves' differently, from the sum of the system's individual elements. Systemic perspectives are normally used to understand family dynamics and they seek to describe the jointly constructed patterns of behaviour in relationships that begin in early life. Most family therapy philosophies offer insights into the structure and value of experiential groups. Possibly the most influential is Milan systemic therapy (Boscolo et al, 1987), which argues that the mind is social and change occurs through clarifying ambiguities in relationships.

Principles from the Milan approach (Becvar and Becvar, 1996), such as 'neutrality', in which the therapist does not side or unbalance the group but adopts a concerned and interested stance fit well with the requirements of an experiential group of this nature. The principle of circular questioning, where members' feedback influences and shapes the facilitator's response and thus jointly constructs new understanding of the situation, is also helpful in understanding the importance of this work. Some developmental stages or phases of the Milan technique are also applicable, particularly focusing on manageable tasks and strengths and the use of 'normalizing' and empathy.

The authors see that the experiential group is part of many groups, all of which seek to operate together in an organized manner to promote stability and create meaning. People are continuously in a flow of interactions. 'This focus on pattern and process has been central to systemic perspectives . . . where relationships are emergent and evolving' (Dallos, 1996, p. 140). Meaning and actions are connected, and each influences the other.

Fromm (1956) suggests that human beings need to experience relatedness and transcendence in order to encourage good mental health. This concept of relationships, dialogue and dependency is reflected in the work of Bakhtin (1929/1984) and Hermans and Hermans-Jansen (1995), among others.

Practical aspects of experiential groupwork

The setting

Group meetings took place in the Salisbury (UK) Branch of the Alzheimer's Society. Details of how the Branch group is linked to the National group are given in Box 11.1.

The experiential groups

The experiential groups conducted in this particular branch have been in existence for two years. During the first year the first group comprised six men and four women (age range 51–86). They were at different stages of dementia, although most were moderately compromised (see Box 11.2) Group attendance varied in size from 6 to 11, but averaged 8. In common with reports of other small groups, a size of 6–8 participants seemed to be particularly effective in enabling people to share deep concerns; this happened less frequently in the larger groups.

Seven of the original members still attend current groups, indicating the value of the service. Of the remaining three, one has died and two have become too frail to continue. Originally, groups were held three times a year and took place over 6 weeks. The groups have been run weekly, fortnightly and more intermittently during summer months. However, holding weekly group meetings was found to be more beneficial for both clients and carers.

Due to the increasing popularity of the service, groups are now held twice a

---

Box 11.1 Background information about the Alzheimer's Society and branch groups

---

The Alzheimer's Society for England, Wales and N. Ireland started in 1979 and now has 250 groups. Though it was initially started to help family carers, it now also actively supports persons with Alzheimer's disease or other types of dementia.

Branch employees often work closely with statutory services – especially with psychiatrists and other members of the mental health teams. However, they often maintain a more holistic approach to the problems associated with dementia.

Each branch operates to meet local needs within an agreed framework and offers a range of services, depending on the skills and interests of the management committee and the staff and resources. All branches provide information about dementia and the support available locally and support groups for carers (some branches have additional services, including: clubs for persons in early stages of dementia; support service for those with an early-onset type of dementia; information support and social groups for carers; advocacy and counselling services for people with dementia and their carers). Only a few branches offer experiential groups for people with dementia – a service that is still in its infancy.

---

week for 6 weeks three times a year. Group 1 has seven members and group 2 has nine members. The age range is 55–84 years and all participants in the second group are in a moderate stage of their illness; in total there are 11 men and 5 women in the two groups.

Recruitment and selection processes

Prior to setting up groups, other local professionals (two Old Age psychiatrists and members of the Community Mental Health Teams) were made aware of the service. People visiting the local Alzheimer's Branch Office or attending 'Dementia Day Services' were also informed of the service, if appropriate. These avenues generated self and/or family carer referrals.

Yale's (1995) guidelines for recruitment and selection processes, including the criteria for group participation, were used as guidelines for setting up these groups. Every participant had a diagnosis of dementia and the ability to communicate reasonably well to others. All who showed an interest and met the inclusion criteria received a domiciliary visit from E.B. During this visit, both a verbal and a written invitation to join the group were given, along with an explanation of the group's aims and procedures. A letter was sent after

---

Box 11.2 Group descriptive information

Participants and stages of dementia
Mild (1)
Mild/moderate (1)
Moderate (6)
Moderate/severe (1)
Severe (1)

Years since diagnosis
9 years (1)
8 years (1)
4 years (1)
3 years (1)
2 years (4)
1 year (2)

Diagnoses of dementia were not recent; most were several years ago

Marital status and living arrangements
Married and living in own home (8)
Widowed and living in own home (1)
Married and living in residential care (1)

Most lived in their own homes supported by their partners; three attended a day centre

---

each visit, repeating these points and including times, dates and venue; transport was arranged if necessary.

Sessions are well attended. Reasons for non-attendance are varied (transport for those living alone and/or increasing mental and physical frailty) but rarely due to a reluctance to return. People have still attended who have gone into long-term care.

The continuing attendance of former group members encourages a sense of stability and security among the group. They welcome each other warmly and in turn newcomers, including 'professional visitors' who are considering running a similar service. The group's permission is always sought in advance before allowing visitors to attend. An explanation of why visitors wish to attend is also given. The group is pleased (likely feeling empowered) to be asked to help and inform others.

Group process

Table 11.1 shows the protocol for group meetings. They are always on the same day and at the same time, beginning at 10.30 am and lasting for 90 min. The room is comfortably arranged with chairs in a circle and refreshments are offered on arrival.

Members, accompanied by their relatives, arrive after 10 am. Coffee and biscuits are served between 10 and 10.30 am. It is a very relaxed and highly social time. By 10.30 am, partners/carers have left and the group begins. A facilitator welcomes and thanks everyone for attending, thereafter asking if group members wish to use name labels (a readily accepted suggestion). The facilitator reads each name out and sensitively checks group recall for individual names. The second facilitator brings the labels around the

Table 11.1 Protocol for group meetings

Times of meeting	Members and their carers arrive from 10 am onwards Meetings last 10.30 am–12 midday Meetings begin and end on time There are no breaks Coffee/tea and biscuits are served on arrival
Seating arrangements	Seating arranged in a circle prior to arrival Facilitators face each other Members are individually given name badges Group recall for names is sensitively checked

Topics covered (notes taken by a facilitator)	Memory problems
	Emotions and coping strategies shared
	Sadness/worry over burden placed on partners/carers
	Common past experiences are explored. These include:
	  Places of origin
	  Childhood schooldays
	  Places visited
	  Career highlights
	  Hobbies/interests

Summary	In the last 10 min of each session, a summary of the main topics covered is given by one of the facilitators The amount of recall by the group is strongly emphasized and rich life experiences shared Amusing topics are revisited The session ends on a positive note
Departure	Spouses arrive to collect their partners Arranged transport tends to be punctual Usually all have departed 20 min after session ends
Debriefing	A short debriefing takes place between facilitators Main points of session are discussed, evaluated and used to plan future group meetings

group. Confidentiality is always stressed; members are then invited to talk about anything that has happened since they last met, and conversations begin.

In this way, the group determines what they wish to discuss (see Table 11.1) and a topic may emerge that is used for a subsequent session. (For example, Lesley said she could still bake cakes. The next week she brought in two magnificently iced sponge cakes. These were enjoyed and cooking became the subject of conversation.) Group members begin to recount their present and former interests. The following week Simon brought in some interesting stamps from his collection. Later, someone else brought in a small counting machine he had used for many years. For all, experiential groups are a constantly changing and flexible experience.

Frequently the facilitator is required carefully to pick up on a discussion point in order to reveal deeper meanings. Many discussions contain seemingly unrelated stories but at a deeper level reflect the discourse of dementia: the uncertainty, loneliness, loss, fear of ridicule and despair. Sensitively touching upon such discourse will often allow members to speak about their own worries more clearly, enabling them to benefit from the support and understanding of the group. For example:

> I think that . . . there are things you want to say to people that you don't want to say . . . you don't want to upset people in the family . . , I mean you're in the group there . . . that . . . you *know* that if you're upset about something, you can speak about it and you don't feel silly about it or anything. There's always someone there to listen to you and I think . . . I think that's what you need . . . I'm quite. . . . quite . . . happy as it goes. I know . . . I know that if I'm not happy about something I can say.

The post-meeting debriefing looks at the group process and discussion. If a sensitive topic has been under-discussed, it will either be carefully and appropriately reintroduced by one of the facilitators the following week, or E.B. would follow it up in her individual work with a group member.

The importance of humour

Humour has a major part to play in promoting well-being and managing anxiety in the groups. This was frequently alluded to:

> You can share your problems with laughter . . .
> There is freedom here . . . you can say what you like.
> You can act like a clown if you want . . .

Visitors to the group have commented on this freedom, saying that the members 'own the group' or 'it is definitely their group'. They have also commented on the lightness and laughter that are often present.

Certain topics and activities have proved popular (see Table 11.1), including places of origin, favourite places, significant memories of the self, school days, former/present hobbies and interests and celebration of special occasions (end of session, Christmas, birthdays, etc.). However, underneath the discussions, fear of dementia is never far from consciousness. The task of accepting it is intermittent but continual. We consider the struggle for acceptance, of owning this illness, as one of the major functions of the group. As in Rob's story below, the group re-examines and discusses this in a variety of ways. They often put the task to one side for a time when it becomes too overwhelming and then retreat into laughter and fellowship.

> You're just like a normal person here . . . Our group has got fun and laughter . . . It has got to be hasn't it? . . . you've only got one . . . got one . . . go at it . . . but I know sometimes I used to find that people [outside the group] always thought that I was jolly and laughing all of the time, . . . and then . . . sometimes I used to think that you don't know what feelings are inside sometimes, and . . . maybe you feel as if people don't even care if you're unhappy about something . . . You know you can go in there [in the group] and within a couple of minutes someone's laughing.

Group facilitators

Zarit and Knight (1996) and Mills and Coleman (2002) believe that counsellors and psychotherapists who work with older people should possess a variety of skills. This also applies to those who wish to run experiential groups for people with dementia. Facilitating groupwork requires skill and is emotionally demanding: on one occasion Rob challenged E.B. and the supportive role and help of the second facilitator was helpful.

Feil, in 1982, already wrote of the need for having two group workers/facilitators to conduct group work for persons with dementia. Scrutiny of our own work and subsequent discussions with fellow professionals have similarly highlighted the importance of having a 'paired facilitating relationship'. Thus, we agree that such work is more ideally accomplished with two facilitators. Working in pairs ensures that no individual is overlooked and that no quiet voices go unheard. Physical and/or emotional discomfort can also be quickly supported. Our recommendation is for group facilitators to have counselling qualifications and groupwork training and experience and they should both have knowledge of dementia and the aging process (see Box 11.3 for desirable skills).

Box 11.3 Desirable skills for paired facilitators doing experiential groupwork

- An ability to handle the uncertainty of the group process and group anxieties.
- Mutual trust and 'intuitive understanding' of each other. Mutual support goes a long way when dealing with the uncertainty inherent in this work. Mutual respect for each other's professionalism and abilities is also important and allows the group to be held more effectively.
- The ability for one to lead and the other to observe, but to permit roles to change when appropriate for the discussion.
- Sufficient understanding of group members to encourage everyone to participate at some point in the group. Prior knowledge of the participants is deemed to be of great importance. Having knowledge of personal histories, strengths and sensitive areas means that members can participate safely and not be overwhelmed by the task.
- One of the strengths of having two facilitators is to observe the whole person, noticing changes in body language as well as verbal contributions. The one who is observing the interactions can often pick up such cues and involve the participant in the discussion when appropriate. Further, the joint debriefing that follows every session will occasionally highlight instances when subtle body language has been missed. These insights can inform future sessions.
- The recognition of when people disagree, or do not wish to be included or supported. It is necessary at times to stand back and allow group members to struggle to express themselves, or to cope with their feelings.
- The ability to interpret if the person with dementia has difficulty in expressing what he/she is trying to say, but always to check that they have understood correctly. This is always explored tentatively and tactfully.
- A shared willingness to step back and allow members to offer support to each other. We find that the group does not allow anyone to become too overwhelmed, but it can cope with tears, grief and anger more readily than might at first be imagined. Group members do not always need our support. This can be a difficult task to learn when dealing with very vulnerable people.

Outcomes

Participants say that they enjoy attending the groups. People who have been coming for nearly 2 years report that the group continues to be a positive experience. Tensions are relieved, concerns aired and happier humorous memories are shared. Social interactions are positive, and social skills remain high among participants.

Some aspects of recall seemed to be reinforced by group attendance. For example, at the end of the first year the final group meeting looked at the significant life experiences that had been remembered by the group. Being long-term memories, these were still well-remembered (Mills, 1998) and contained both content themes and details (shown in Box 11.4).

Box 11.4 Overall topics recalled at end of the first year

Childhood	Stories of childhood and schools attended
Places of origin/interest	All recalled where they had been born and countries/places they had visited in some detail
Experienced historical events	World War II experiences were recalled in detail. Not all memories of war were negative. Some of the countries visited had been enjoyable as were new experiences
Careers	All recalled their work, including what their work entailed
Hobbies/interests and activities	These remained constant and included stamp collecting, gardening, walking and cooking. However, increasing problems with memory were having greater impact on performance
Coping with a poor memory	Practical methods were still in evidence. These included 'getting into the habit' of writing things down/keeping a diary and having a notebook with you at all times
Relationships	The group frequently discussed the impact their illness had on their carers. They often felt a burden. They were conscious that their repetitiveness and forgetfulness was annoying and hard to live with. They made jokes about these issues but their anxiety was evident

Feedback from partners and participants

Following the conclusion of the first series of groups, one of the facilitators visited members to gain feedback about the service. Four of the participants and their partners reported that they thought the service was 'essential' for their well-being. Four thought of them as being 'helpful' and two saw them as 'a useful part' of the services offered by the organization as a whole. Thus, needs were met on different levels. Feedback from current groups is similar. Participants describe the groups as 'enjoyable, great fun, interesting and helpful'.

Difficulties in running experiential groups

As with many other specialist services, the key difficulties include procuring funding, a shortage of specialist staff, locating appropriate locations and transport.

The importance of a suitable location for the group (non-threatening emotionally and where there are no interruptions) cannot be overestimated. Older Care Facilities are traditionally short of space for activities, especially activities requiring calm and being protective of confidentiality. Providing transport for people with dementia can also create problems beyond its funding; finding a service-provider who is sympathetic to and has understanding for persons' needs is also important.

Overall, there is still insufficient research into the cost effectiveness of experiential groupwork in dementia to attract more funding. Research on the effects of experiential groupwork on ability to remain functional and on specific aspects of memory ability has yet to be done, though encouragingly Cheston et al (2002a,b) found less anxiety and depression among group members, together with improved self-esteem.

What our study has shown is that experiential groupwork can contribute to the network of support felt by persons with dementia and their carers. We suggest that experiential groupwork skills, which include knowledge of groupwork and counselling, should form part of the syllabus for specialist training in dementia care. The value of counselling services for people with dementia is positively acknowledged (Bartlett and Cheston, 2003).

The way forward

There are encouraging signs that experiential and other types of support groups for people with dementia are playing an important part in encouraging well-being both in the UK (Cheston et al, 2002a,b) and elsewhere (Yale, 1995; Snyder, 2003). However, more work remains to be done. Snyder (2003) grapples with the issue of measures of group evaluation to demonstrate their efficacy.

The need for specialist training, not only in dementia-care courses but also for specialist groupwork training in many gerontological and professional and healthcare professional courses, is strongly acknowledged. (Gerontology is also under-represented in most traditional groupwork courses.)

This chapter is not solely concerned with groups, but also with the multi-layered nature of relationships that support and enrich life when someone has dementia (Coleman and Mills, 2001). In a Winnicottian sense, it is about enabling life to be 'good enough' (Winnicott, 1965). The accounts given in this work indicate that such relationships can be found by those who choose to come to experiential support groups for people who have dementia. Such groups are a positive response to the call to encourage well-being in people with dementia, in whatever ways are possible.

Acknowledgements

We wish to thank the group members and partners for their participation in this work (all names have been changed).

References

Asch, S.E. (1951) Effects of group pressure upon modification and distortion of judgements. In H. Gurtzkow (Ed.), *Groups, Leadership, and Men*. Pittsburg: Carnegie Press, pp. 177–190.

Asch, S.E. (1955) Opinions and social pressures. *Scientific American*, **193**: 31–55.

Bakhtin, M. (1929/1984) *Problems with Dostoevsky's Politics*, edited and translated by C. Emerson. Minneapolis: Minneapolis University Press.

Bartlett, B. (2002) *Even if I forget my facts, I remember my feelings*, Alzheimer's Society, July 2002.

Bartlett, E and Cheston, R. (2003) Counselling people with dementia. In T. Adams and J. Manthorpe (Eds), *Dementia Care*. London: Arnold, pp. 86–102.

Becvar, D.S and Becvar, R.J. (1996) *Family Therapy: a Systemic Integration* (3rd edn). Boston: Allyn and Bacon.

Bion, W.R. (1961) *Experiences in Groups and Other Papers*. London: Tavistock Publications.

Bleathman, C. and Morton, I. (1996) Validation therapy: a review of its contribution to dementia care. *British Journal of Nursing*, **5**: 866–869.

Boscolo, L., Cecchin, G.F., Hoffmann, L. and Papp, P. (1987) *Milan Systemic Family Therapy*. New York: Basic Books.

Bowlby, J. (1969) *Attachment and Loss, Volume 1. Attachment*. London: Hogarth Press.

Bretherton, I. (1985) Attachment theory, retrospect and prospect. In I. Bretherton, I. and E. Waters (Eds), *Growing Points in Attachment Theory and Research. Monographs of the Society for Research in Child Development*, **50**: 209.

Bromley, D. B. (1966) *The Psychology of Human Ageing*. Harmondsworth: Penguin.

Brown, R. (1986) *Social Psychology* (2nd edn). New York: Free Press.

Bruner, J. S. (1966) *Toward a Theory of Instruction*. Cambridge, MA: Belkapp Press.

Bruner, J. S. (1983) *Child's Talk: Learning to Use Language*. New York: Norton.

Burkitt, I. (1991) *Social Selves: Theories of the Social Formation of Personality*. London: Sage.

Cheston, R. (1996) Stories and metaphors: talking about the past in a psychotherapy group for people with dementia. *Ageing and Society*, **16**: 579–602.

Cheston, R. (1998) Psychotherapeutic work with people with dementia: a review of the literature. *British Journal of Medical Psychology*, **71**: 211–231.

Cheston, R. and Bender, M. (1999) *Understanding Dementia; the Man with the Worried Eyes*. London: Jessica Kingsley.

Cheston, R., Jones, K. and Gilliard, J. (2002a) Forgetting and remembering: group psychotherapy with people with dementia. In T. Adams and J. Manthorpe (Eds), *Dementia Care*. London: Edward Arnold, pp. 136–147.

Cheston, R., Jones, K. and Gilliard, J. (2002b) The impact of group psychotherapy on people with dementia. *Ageing and Mental Health*, **6**: 452–461.

Coleman, P.G. and Mills, M.A. (2001) Philosophical and spiritual perspectives. In C. Cantley (Ed.), *The Handbook of Dementia Care*. Buckingham, PA: Open University Press, pp. 62–76.

Dallos, R. (1996) Creating relationships: patterns of actions and beliefs. In D. Miell and R. Dallos (Eds), *Social Interaction and Personal Relationships*. London: Sage/Open University Press, pp. 102–156.

Day, C.N. (1997). Validation therapy: a review of the literature. *Journal of Gerontological Nursing*, **23**: 29–34.

Feil, N. (1993) *The Validation Breakthrough: Simple Techniques for Communicating with People with Alzheimer's Type Dementia*. Baltimore: Health Professions' Press.

Foulkes, S.H. and Anthony, E.J. (1957) *Group Psychotherapy*. London: Penguin Books.

Fromm, F. (1956) *The Sane Society*. London: Routledge.

Hermans, H.J.M. and Hermans-Jansen, E. (1995) *Self Narratives: the Construction of Meaning in Psychotherapy*. New York: Guilford Press.

Hinshelwood, R.D. (1987) *What Happens in Groups*. London: Free Association Books.

James, W. (1894) The physiological basis of emotion. *Psychology Review*, **1**: 516–552.

Kirschenbaum, H. and Henderson, V. (1989) *The Carl Rogers Reader*. Boston: Houghton Mifflin.

Kitwood, T. (1997) *Dementia Reconsidered: the Person comes First*. Buckingham, PA: Open University Press.

Klein, M. (1932) *The Psychoanalysis of Children*. London: Hogarth Press.

Miesen, B.M.L. (1992) Attachment theory and dementia. In. G.M.M. Jones and B.M.L. Miesen (Eds), *Care-giving in Dementia: Research and Applications*, vol. I. London: Routledge, pp. 38–56.

Miesen, B.M.L. (1993) Alzheimer's disease, the phenomenon of parent fixation and Bowlby's attachment theory. *International Journal of Geriatric Psychiatry*, **8**: 147–153.

Miesen, B.M.L. and Jones, G.M.M. (1997) Psychic pain re-surfacing in dementia: from new to past trauma? In L. Hunt, M. Marshall and C. Rowlands (Eds), *Past Trauma in Late Life: European Perspectives on Therapeutic Work with Older People*. London: Jessica Kingsley, pp. 142–154.

Milgram, S. (1974) *Obedience to Authority*. London: The Tavistock Institute.

Mills, M.A. (1998) *Narrative Identity and Dementia: a Study of Autobiographical Memories and Emotions*. Aldershot: Avebury Series, Ashgate Publishing.

Mills, M.A. (2003) A meeting of minds: allowing older people with dementia to share their thoughts and experiences about health and social care, using counselling skills. *Research Policy and Planning*, **21**: 33–42.

Mills, M.A. and Coleman, P.G. (1994) Nostalgic memories in dementia: a case study. *International Journal of Aging and Human Development*, **8**: 203–219.

Mills, M.A. and Coleman, P.G. (2002) Reminiscence and life review interventions with older people. In A. Maercker (Ed.), *Psychotherapy with the Elderly and Clinical Geriatric Psychology*. New York: Springer, pp. 359–376.

Morgan, H. and Thomas, K. (1996) A psychodynamics perspective on group processes. In M. Wetherall (Ed.), *Identities, Groups and Social Issues*. London, Sage/Open University Press, pp. 63–118.

Morton, I. and Bleathman, C. (1991) The effectiveness of validation therapy in dementia: a pilot study. *International Journal of Geriatric Psychiatry*, **6**: 327–330.

Munnichs, J. and Miesen, B. (1986) *John Bowlby – Attachment, Life-span and Old-age*. The Netherlands: Van Loghum Slaterus.

Oates, J. (1994) First relationships. In J. Oates (Ed.), *The Foundations of Child Development*. Oxford: Blackwell/Open University Press, pp. 259–312.

Potter, J. (1996) Attitudes, social representations and discursive psychology. In M. Wetherall (Ed.), *Identities, Groups and Social Issues*. London: Sage/Open University Press, pp. 119–174.

Robertson, J. and Robertson, J. (1967) *Film: Young children in Brief Separation No.1.* 'Kate aged 2 years 5 months in fostercare for 27 days'. London: Tavistock Institute.

Rogers C. R. (1961) *Client Centred Therapy*. Boston: Houghton-Mifflen.

Rogers, C. R. (1975) Empathic: an unappreciated way of being. *Counselling Psychologist*, **5**: 2–10.

Snyder, L. (2003) The role of persons with dementia in shaping support group development and evaluation methods. Paper presented at 56th Annual Scientific Meeting of the Gerontological Society of America, 21–25 November 2003.

Spector, A., Orrell, M., Davies, S. and Woods, B. (2000) Reality orientation for dementia. *Cochrane Database of Systematic Reviews*, Issue 3.

Stern, D.N. (1985) *The Interpersonal World of the Infant: a View from Psychoanalysis and Developmental Psychology*. New York: Basic Books.

Tajfel H. and Turner, J. (1979) An integrative theory of intergroup conflict, In G.W. Austin and S. Worchel (Eds), *The Social Psychology of Intergroup Relations*. Monterey, CA: Brooks/Cole, pp. 33–47.

Thomas, K. (1996) The psychodynamics of relating. In D. Miell and R. Dallos (Eds), *Social Interaction and Personal Relationships*. London, Sage/Open University Press, pp. 157–213.

Thompson, E. (2002) Are two heads better than one? *Psychologist*, **15**: 616–619.

Trevarthen, C. (1979) Communication and co-operation in early infancy: a description of primary subjectivity. In M. Bullova and P. Elkman (Eds), *Before Speech: the Beginning of Interpersonal Communication*. New York: Cambridge University Press, pp. 321–347.

Vygotsky, L.S. (1978) *The Role of Play in Development*. Cambridge, MA: Harvard University Press.

Watkins, R.E., Cheston, R., Jones, K. and Gilliard, J. (2006) 'Coming out with

Alzheimer's disease': changes in insight during a psychotherapy group for people with dementia. *Aging and Mental Health*, **10**: 1–11.

Winnicott, D. (1965) *The Maturational Process and the Facilitating Environment.* New York: International Universities Press.

Woods, R.T. and McKiernan, F. (1995) Reminiscence and dementia. In B.M. Haight and J.D. Webster (Eds), *The Art and Science of Remiminiscing: Theory, Research, Methods, and Applications.* Washington, DC: Taylor and Francis.

Yale, R. (1991) *A Guide to Facilitating Support Groups for Newly Diagnosed Alzheimer's Patients.* Greater San Francisco Bay Area: The Alzheimer's Association.

Yale, R. (1995) *Developing Support Groups for Individuals with Early Stage Alzheimer's Disease: Planning Implementation and Evaluation.* Baltimore: Health Professions' Press.

Zarit, S.H. and Knight, B.G. (1996) Psychotherapy and aging: multiple strategies, positive outcomes. In S.H. Zarit and B.G. Knight (Eds), *A Guide to Psychotherapy and Aging: Effective Clinical Interventions in a Life-stage Context.* Washington, DC: American Psychological Association, pp. 1–16.

Chapter 12

Qualitative evaluation of an Alzheimer Café as an ongoing supportive group intervention

Amy Thompson

INTRODUCTION

Background

The National Service Framework (NSF) for Older People (Department of Health, 2001) reports that the number of people over the age of 65 has doubled in the last 70 years and that the number of people over 90 years old is likely to double over the next 25 years. As such we are facing the reality of an aging population and subsequent pressures on health and social services for older people. One significant result of this aging population is likely to be an increase in the incidence of dementia. In the Department of Health publication *Who Cares?* (Department of Health, 2000) it is estimated that around 6/100 people over the age of 65 will develop dementia to some degree, with this number increasing to 20/100 among people over 85. It is also estimated that as many as 17 000 people under the age of 65 may have dementia. A recent cross-sectional study of three London boroughs by Harvey et al (2003) indicated that the prevalence of dementia in people aged 30–64 years was 54 per 100 000 people. These people are likely to be referred to Older Adult Mental Health Services, putting further pressure on resources, therefore the need to identify effective systems of care for this population is paramount.

Dementia in itself can be viewed as an umbrella term used to describe the syndromes resulting from a number of brain diseases (Holden and Stokes, 2002). Although the sub-types of dementia have the common factor of producing a progressive, irreversible decline in cognitive functioning over a number of years, affecting all aspects of the sufferers' life, more specific symptoms associated with the particular type produce a complex and varied picture of the disease.

Alzheimer's disease is the most common form of dementia, most often occurring after the age of 70, and it is thought to account for between half and two-thirds of all cases (Longley and Warner, 2002a). Common symptoms of this type of dementia include word-finding and recognition difficulties. In vascular dementia, believed to account for up to 20% of cases (Holden and Stokes, 2002), a somewhat fluctuating course may be experienced with small 'strokelets' affecting specific areas of the brain but with other areas preserved. In dementia with Lewy bodies symptoms such as visual or auditory hallucinations are common, whereas fronto-temporal dementia is characterized by disinhibition or apathy and a loss of social awareness. This limited description of the most common sub-types of dementia highlights the complexity of the needs of people suffering from dementia and the specialist skills and facilities required to address these, which inevitably makes the provision of services problematic (Longley and Warner, 2002b).

The NSF for Older People (Department of Health, 2001) sets out eight standards through which to offer care. These standards cover areas of both physical and mental health and include a framework for dementia care (see Figure 12.1). The importance of person-centred care for older people is also emphasized as a standard to be met in its own right, highlighting the importance of individually tailored services and informed choice regarding the person's care. The challenge for Older Adult Mental Health Services is to offer such person-centred services for dementia in a practical and cost-effective manner. This chapter describes an evaluation of an Alzheimer Café included in the dementia care pathway in a mental health service for older adults in order to address some of these needs.

Dementia care

In dementia, services have typically followed an organic model or 'standard paradigm' as described by Kitwood (1990). This model describes the loss experienced as being one of intellectual and cognitive functioning as a direct result of neurological impairment (Cheston and Bender, 1999). Although such a model is helpful in encouraging appropriate diagnosis and identification of specific medical needs, Kitwood (1997) emphasized the fact that this model excludes any reference to the diverse backgrounds, personalities and lives of the real people suffering the diseases. Kitwood (1997) further highlights that such models do not explicitly describe the care process, leaving this vague with the assumption that nothing will improve until medical breakthroughs have been made. Dementia in this case is viewed as an inevitable part of old age, something to be managed rather than worked with proactively (Goldsmith, 1996). Such a climate led to an early culture of dementia care, based on meeting the individuals' basic physical needs and providing a 'comfortable' existence (Sixsmith et al, 1993).

The work of proponents of person-centred care (e.g. Kitwood, 1997; Stokes and Goudie, 2002) in more recent times has challenged this 'standard paradigm' and reference to the 'real life' of persons with dementia has been encouraged. This movement is highlighted by the fact that the Department of

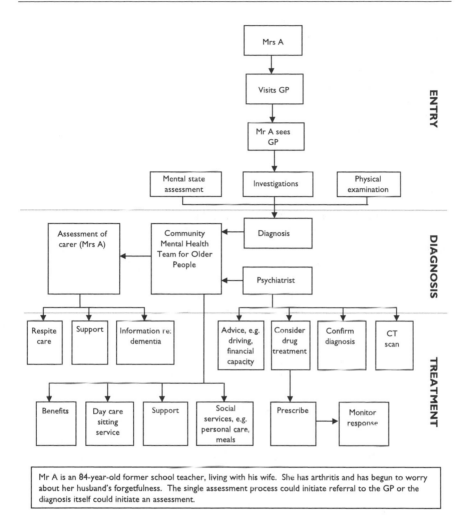

Figure 12.1 Care pathway for dementia – Standard 7: Mental Health in Older People (Department of Health, 2001).

Health's 2001 NSF for Older People sets person-centred care as Standard 2, the aim of which is proposed as:

> To ensure that older people are treated as individuals and they receive appropriate and timely packages of care which meet their needs as individuals, regardless of health and social services boundaries.
>
> (Department of Health, 2001)

Standard 7 of the NSF for Older People – Mental Health in Older People – sets out a care pathway for dementia (Figure 12.1) that incorporates these ideas.

Designed to provide adequate medical and social care and access to services, the pathway highlights the promotion of 'life' for the persons with dementia rather than focusing on degeneration.

The number of services involved in this care pathway highlights the complexities of providing dementia services. The disease has a wide impact across physical, emotional and social well-being for the sufferer as well as for their families and carers. Contact between medical and social services is essential in both initially gaining a diagnosis and in establishing an appropriate plan of care.

Carers' needs

The care of most people with dementia takes place within the community. Approximately four out of five people with dementia live outside hospital or residential settings, predominantly with a spouse or family member (Shankland, 2002). As part of the NSF dementia care pathway, the need for assessment of the carer of the person with dementia is identified. In the past, the psychological impact on individuals with dementia was overlooked and so too were the psychological effects on the carer (Kitwood, 1997). Miesen (1999) highlights the feelings of powerlessness experienced by many carers of dementing family members. In addition to the physical practicalities of caring for someone with dementia, issues around grief and loss when the person becomes more separate from their family as the illness progresses make caring for such individuals demanding and unrewarding (Parker, 1997). High evidence of stress and depression in people caring for a person with dementia has come from studies of service users and community surveys (Murray and McDaid, 2002). Such difficulties are likely to result from the fact that carers tend to become isolated from their social network of family and friends as the disease progresses and may also suffer a deterioration in their own physical health as a result of the demands of caring (Murry and McDaid, 2002). Parker (1997) identifies a number of factors as being advantageous in assisting a carer to cope better with caring for a person with dementia:

1   Helping the carer to alter their perception of the person's condition.
2   Teaching more effective management techniques for disturbed behaviour.
3   Working with the carer and person with dementia to improve their relationship.
4   Allowing carers to talk.

This presents an additional component when identifying the care needs of a person with dementia, extending to the family and carers involved with the individual, this being increasingly so as the disease progresses. Identifying ways in which to deliver such additional care is a further problem for older adult services.

The dementia care pathway in a mental health service for older adults

Figure 12.2 shows the dementia care pathway for the service involved in the evaluation described in this chapter. The service has utilized the NSF model

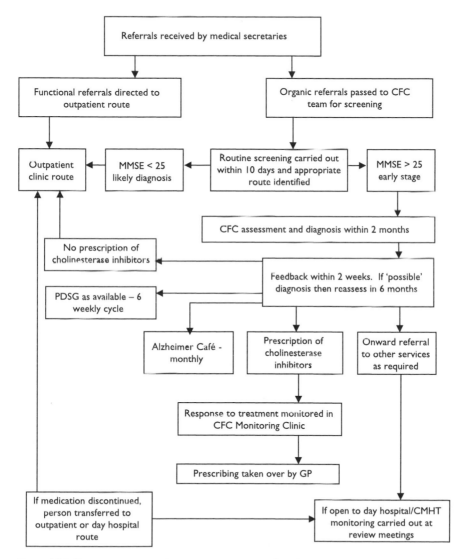

Figure 12.2 Dementia care pathway – non-urgent referrals in a mental health service for older adults. CFC, Cognitive Functions Clinic; CMHT, Community Mental Health Team; MMSE, Mini Mental State Examination; PDSG, Post Diagnosis Support Group.

and ideas relating to person-centred care to guide practice in terms of assessment and intervention for individuals with dementia.

Individuals referred to the service with difficulties stemming from organic origins are assessed through the Cognitive Functions Clinic (CFC). Based on the Memory Clinic Model (Goudie, 2002), the main function of this specialist assessment clinic is to identify organic impairment at an early stage and then to offer appropriate intervention, information and long-term support to the client and their family. As can be seen from the care pathway, the clinic operates in four stages (screening, initial assessment, feedback and follow-up) and both the person being assessed and their families/carers are involved at each stage.

The Post Diagnosis Support Group (PDSG) was piloted in July 2002 in response to a survey of individuals attending the service, which identified a need for further information and support for the persons with dementia and their family after diagnosis. This has now become an integral part of the service, offered as a time-limited group for the individual with dementia and their carer/family. Limitations for inclusion were made, however, with a Mini-Mental State Examination score of > 20 and an appropriate social behaviour prerequisite for inclusion in the group. Topics including implications for diagnosis of dementia, service structure, cognitive rehabilitation strategies and pharmacological and alternative therapies are covered in the group.

As this group is time-limited, both service providers and those involved in the care pathway identified a need for further means of support and education. As a result of this, the Alzheimer Café was introduced to the care pathway.

The Alzheimer Café (AC)

The concept of the Alzheimer Café (AC) was first introduced in 1997 by Dr Bère Miesen, Clinical Old Age Psychologist at Marienhaven, the specialist research centre for old age in Warmond, The Netherlands. The first mention of the AC, in English, was by Miesen in 1999 (translator's notes on p. ix). The AC was developed as an intervention incorporating aspects of both psychological education and emotional support for those with a diagnosis of dementia and their carers/family members (Miesen and Blom, 2001). The AC was designed to offer an all-inclusive environment where informal advice and consultation could be sought from professionals and others with dementia, and carers, in a relaxed and supportive atmosphere. The three main objectives of the AC (Miesen and Blom, 2001) are:

1   To provide information about the medical and psychosocial aspects of dementia.
2   To emphasize the importance of speaking openly about emotional problems in an atmosphere that promotes recognition and social acceptance.
3   To prevent the social isolation of persons with dementia and their families.

One of the most important aspects of the AC is the relaxed atmosphere in which persons with dementia and their families or carers can talk informally, exchanging experiences and promoting a feeling of acceptance and belonging. This philosophy is very much in line with the ideas behind person-centred care (e.g. Kitwood, 1997). The focus of the AC is on improving and maintaining the quality of life for the person with dementia, their carers and family by providing opportunities to share experiences and be part of an accepting and open environment.

To meet these objectives, the original ACs developed a standard format. Held once a month, and most successfully in the evenings, ACs lasted about two and a half hours. The evenings combined formal presentations with entertainment and refreshments and the opportunity to talk informally with other visitors. For example:

0.00   Arrivals with tea and coffee
0.30   Start of formal presentation, interview or video
1.00   Interval with music and drinks
1.30   Discussion of presentation
2.00   End of formal meeting
2.30   Informal session and departure

These initial ACs were run by a consultation or steering group, usually comprised of a wide representation of professionals involved in care-giving and local Alzheimer Society group representatives. Responsible for the planning and publicizing of the ACs, these 'core professionals' were also required to be available to provide information and advice outside of the AC should visitors need further assistance.

In the UK, Kandy Redwood and others, with joint funding from Social Services and Health Departments in Hampshire, in conjunction with the The Blackwater Valley Branch of the Alzheimer's Society, held the first AC in September 2000, with the official opening in November 2000 amidst much press interest (G.M.M. Jones, personal communication). Jones translated the Dutch document (Miesen and Blom, 2001) and set up a website for information for others wishing to start an AC (http://www.alzheimercafe.co.uk).

In November 2002, the National Alzheimer Society for England, Wales and Northern Ireland endorsed the AC concept formally, hosting a day-long workshop called 'How to set-up and Run an Alzheimer Café' (presented by Jones, Miesen and Redwood) for interested persons from the Alzheimer Regional and Branch representatives. The (patented) 'Alzheimer Café and Alzheimer Cafe UK' concepts have been established in many countries already (Belgium, Italy, Greece, Australia, USA and Japan). Miesen and Jones (2004) set out the history and purpose of the AC concept, describing it as a response to the trauma, drama and tragedy of dementia.

The 'Alzheimer Café UK' concept now extends to a dozen locations, and there are more in the planning stages. The only requirement for use of the name (logo information) is to adhere to the original aims and philosophy of the AC, accepting that local/cultural needs and practical adaptations are diverse and free to be made. (There were some initial misunderstandings about the purpose of the AC, with several groups setting them up as purely 'social events' and missing the focus of 'emotional support' through having healthcare professionals present to speak about topics linked to the annual programme of themes.)

Subsequent ACs in the UK have been held as both an adjunct to local health and social care Older Adult Services and also independently by Society members. The Older Adult Mental Health Service described in this chapter sought advice from the development officer of the Regional Alzheimer's Society in order to establish an AC as part of the 'dementia care pathway'. A group of professionals from the service, including Admiral nurses, psychologists, social workers and individuals from the Alzheimer's Society, Age Concern and 'For Dementia', as well as carers constituted the steering group and the first AC ran in September 2003 in a community centre central to the area covered by the service. Individuals who had completed the PDSG were invited to attend the AC, as well as a number of families known to the service, and it was run on a monthly basis in the evening. A number of changes to the suggested programme were made to adapt this to the population of the service. The general format of this AC is:

19.00 Arrival drinks/informal meeting time
19.30 Speaker/presentation
20.00 Refreshments
20.30 Entertainment (e.g. quiz) and informal discussion
21.00 End

Topics covered as part of the presentations at the AC have included:

- Aromatherapy
- Music
- Benefits
- Life stories
- Spirituality
- Community services

Informal feedback from persons with dementia, carers and professionals involved in the AC over the first 6 months indicated that this had been a positive addition to the service as a whole. The evaluation described in this chapter was undertaken to look more specifically at whether the AC met the objectives set out by Miesen and Blom (2001) and to identify the value of the service in terms of meeting the requirement's of the Department of Health's (2001) NSF for Older People.

Method

Procedure

Data were collected through tape-recorded, semi-structured interviews with both persons with dementia and their carers who had visited the AC. Participants were recruited through the AC, with information about the evaluation presented to visitors within the AC. Visitors were asked to volunteer to take part in the tape-recorded interviews and contact and consent sheets were distributed at the AC. It was emphasized that all interviews would be used only in the evaluation of the AC and would be treated in a confidential manner, remaining anonymous, with all personal identifiers removed prior to the writing of the report.

Those individuals volunteering were later contacted by telephone and times were arranged for the researcher to visit them in their own homes to conduct the interviews. The format of the interviews varied, with some involving both a person with dementia and their carer and others involving either a person with dementia or more often a carer alone. In instances where both a carer and a person with dementia were involved in the interview, information was collected from both parties simultaneously.

Participants

Nine families volunteered to take part in the interviews and eight were eventually interviewed. Four interviews involved both a person with dementia and their carer, three involved a carer alone and one involved a person with dementia alone. Of the persons with dementia, four were female and one was male; all were in relatively early stages of the disease. Of the carers, four were female and three were male. All carers participating in the evaluation were the spouses of the person with dementia in their care. Further demographic information was not collected because, due to the small sample and the nature of the service, it was felt that participants might have become easily identifiable. Of the families involved, two had attended all the Café's up to the time of interview (six in all). Four had attended all but one of the ACs at the time of interview. One participant could not remember how many ACs they had attended but that she had attended a number of them with her family.

Interview schedule

The interview schedule was devised in a collaborative manner by individuals involved in the running of the AC. The objectives of the AC proposed by Miesen and Blom (2001) were taken as the basis for construction of the interview. A semi-structured approach was taken, due both to the nature of the client group, with the possibility that questioning may need to be adapted to accommodate the needs of the individual, and the quality of information being sought. Smith and Osborn (2003) noted that a semi-structured interview has the advantage of producing richer data through facilitating rapport between the respondent and the interviewer, allowing a greater flexibility of coverage. Open questions were used to encourage the persons being interviewed to talk about the AC with as little prompting as possible. Prompts were used to elicit specific information about particular topics. The interview schedule used in this evaluation also incorporates the process of funnelling, described by Smith and Osborn (2003) as a process through which to gain both the respondent's general views and their ideas regarding more specific issues, e.g. the use of an initial question regarding the participant's general experience of the AC followed by more specific questioning. A number of closed questions were also included in the interview schedule to elicit specific information about components of the AC.

Analysis

Once the tape-recorded interview data had been collected, transcriptions were made of the interviews. At this point all personally identifying information was removed from the interviews. Because the evaluation was seeking to identify whether the current AC was fulfilling the objectives laid down by Miesen and Blom (2001), the interview schedule was utilized as a means of categorizing the interview material (Lindlof and Taylor, 2002). This process helped to reduce the interview data without losing the meaning of the responses that were of significance to the evaluation. Individual responses were grouped under each question heading. At this point it was evident that there was some overlap between the information gained from particular questions and it was therefore decided to condense the schedule in terms of categorizing the data to avoid repetitions. For example, when asked about how attending the AC had affected them, participants offered similar information to their general experience of the Café. Thus, information pertaining to how the experience of the AC had affected the participants was grouped with their general experience of the Café because this did not appear to be qualitatively different. This was also the case for information gained regarding participants' arrival at the AC and their descriptions of the atmosphere of the AC. Following this initial categorization, qualitative thematic analysis, as described by Boyatzis (1998), was employed in analysing the data. Themes arising under each heading were identified independently by both the researcher and a colleague involved in the AC. These themes were reviewed and a final list of themes was identified under each category.

Results

Themes arising from the responses of individuals under each category are shown in Table 12.1. These are only representative of the current sample and include the views of both the persons with dementia and their carers.

Table 12.1 Themes grouped under question categories

Category	Themes	Number of responses with theme
Experience of attending the Alzheimer Café	Enjoyable	6
	Shared experiences	8
	Supportive	6
	Education	4
	Good facilities	3
	Social	7
Atmosphere of the Café	Friendly	12
	Welcoming	7
	Inclusive	5
Structure of the Café	Enjoyable	4
	Balanced	6
	Timing difficulties	4
Café facilitators	Helpful	5
	Approachable	5
	Friendly	8
	Pro-active	10
Meeting new people at the Café	New relationships	3
	Opportunity to mix	5
Meeting outside the Café setting	Forming new groups	3
	Building friendships	2
	Limited to Café	4
Benefits of mixing with others with similar problems	Shared experiences	8
	Supportive	8
	No benefits	1
	Social	1
	Education	1
Speakers at the Café	Interesting	7
	Relevant	3
	Varied topics	2
	Concentration/retention difficulties	2
Equal inclusion for persons with dementia and carers at the Café	Inclusion	12
	Choice	3
Positive aspects of the Café	Supportive	5
	Social	9
	Shared experiences	1
Negative aspects of the Café	Generally positive	10
	More time	1
	Varying structure	3
	Expansion worries	2

Continued

Table 12.1 continued

Category	Themes	Number of responses with theme
Ending of the Café	Relaxed	6
	Sadness	6
Benefits of the Café as a whole	Social	4
	Supportive	2
	Shared experiences	3
	Relaxing	2
	Acceptance	1
	Enjoyable	2
	Not treatment	1
Barriers to attending	Openness	8
	Transport	3
	Need for support/ encouragement	3

Review of the themes indicates that a number of the categories share common themes. These categories are therefore discussed together. Additional themes arising are discussed under the relevant categories.

Experience of the Café; benefits of meeting others; positive aspects and benefits as a whole

The theme of *shared experiences* appears within all four of these categories. Participants frequently reported that meeting people who were in a similar position to themselves, experiencing similar difficulties, was an important aspect of the AC.

> Well you share a common theme really don't you, it's helpful for me to know that there are other people who have the same problems.
>
> . . . being able to meet other people in the same situation and erm it takes a bit of the stress off me . . .
>
> . . . to be able to talk to other people in the same situation and how they cope.
>
> So seeing others that have the same sort of problems and are getting on ok helps . . .

Ideas around sharing experiences and talking through issues with fellow sufferers or carers in an atmosphere of understanding were also identified.

> . . . people there in the same predicament and they understand other people's problems you know, because as I say it's so strange talking to normal people because they don't understand.

. . . nobody sits in judgement, which is lovely, because we all know we've got a problem . . .

The theme of the AC offering a *supportive* environment also appears across the same four categories. Participants referred to the supportive nature of various professionals being available at the Café.

. . . people there if you need some advice . . . and it's just nice to know that you've got that contact because initially you're given the diagnosis and you're just left to your own devices aren't you . . .

And it's like having all those different people and people from other societies, because you've got the people from the Alzheimer's society and that so all the different people are there so there's always someone to answer any questions you have or they can point you in the right direction . . .

Ideas around having a wider circle of people from whom to gain emotional support and come to terms with the diagnosis was also apparent in the responses gained.

. . . makes you realize you're not so on your own, you know. When you get told you've got theses problems you feel it's, it's like the end . . .

. . . apart from having just our family to talk to because you can always open up more to outsiders often than you do to your own family . . .

The idea of the AC providing a *social* outlet again occurred across these four categories. Participants referred to the AC providing the opportunity to meet people and socialize in an atmosphere in which they felt comfortable and accepted.

. . . I mean there's nowhere else we could go, that he [person with dementia] would feel comfortable at all . . .

Just the way we're treated as a human being and not with problems.

Within this theme the idea that the AC provided a less formal setting in which to gain support and guidance was apparent.

. . . it seemed to be the only thing that there was sort of available, where you go, while it was a erm social gathering and there were people there if you needed some advice you know and they were very nice and you could have a chat . . .

> . . . it just feels like I'm getting a night out rather than always being clinics and hospitals and doctors . . .

A number of participants also referred to the fact that the AC had re-opened social circles for them, having been isolated from existing friendships following their diagnosis.

> Well it's helped me a lot, got me out of the house, you know I'm not sitting here . . .

> I gave up work to look after S and so it meant that I'd lost all my colleagues at work if you like. Over the years that he's been getting poorly we haven't socialized so much so we've lost a lot of our you know, evenings out if you like we tend to be in more in the evenings now so I did feel if you like totally isolated you know I was just looking after S, taking him where he needs to go . . . I'd lost touch with my friends and this helped me to go and meet new friends so in that way I feel that it's lifted, it's taken me out of myself . . .

The theme of *education* arose in two of these categories. Participants expressed a feeling that the AC had helped to widen their knowledge both in terms of the medical aspects of the disease and the more personal or psychosocial implications.

> . . . we were able to get to know more about dementia.

> . . . can talk to people about her different problems then it's only by talking that you learn anything as far as I'm concerned . . .

Atmosphere

In terms of the atmosphere of the AC, the theme of *friendliness* arose frequently in the participants' responses, in reference to both the attitudes of the facilitators and those people attending the AC.

> It is a nice atmosphere. It's better than walking into just a social club, because it's not just a social club it's more than that. I find that when you get there you're among friends, you feel that you're among friends . . .

Structure

When discussing the structure of the AC the theme arising most frequently was that of a *balanced* structure. Respondents generally expressed the idea that there was a balance between the social and educational aspects of the

AC. The theme of the AC generally being an *enjoyable* experience also arose under this category.

Café facilitators

The most frequently occurring theme in this category was the idea that facilitators within the AC conduct themselves in a *pro-active* way. Participants were keen to emphasize that facilitators actively sought out contact with individuals attending the AC, integrating themselves within the group.

> . . . you can go up and ask people things if you have a question and they always mix in. I think it's erm good how the helpers move to sit with different people each time . . .

> . . . there's usually somebody at the table and then one or two others will come across and erm have a word with us which I do think is nice and erm ask how we are so that gives you the opportunity if you have got anything you know that's on your mind, that gives you an opportunity to then speak about it.

Meeting new people at the Café

In terms of meeting new people at the AC the most frequent theme arising was that of the AC providing the *opportunity to mix* with a variety of people. This referred in most part to the layout and culture of the AC, with participants feeling that they were encouraged to sit with different people within the AC and that they felt able to do so due to the inclusive feel of the AC.

> . . . you never sit on the same table, well you know sometimes you go in and your sat on another table and that so you get to know everybody anyway then, rather than just sort of everybody all sitting, oh that's my, you know, our chair or anything like that . . .

> We try and sit with different people if we can at different times like you know. And the more people that you sort of get to know it's good you see yeah.

Meeting outside the Café setting

The common theme arising from responses in this category was that contact with people at the AC did not extend beyond this setting. However a number of participants had become involved in a new group with people they had met at the AC, which they viewed as a very positive outcome.

Speakers at the Café

In relation to the speakers at the AC the theme of *interest* most frequently arose. The theme pertaining to *concentration/attention difficulties* arose in two of the participants' responses and related to the practicalities of catering for this population.

Equal inclusion for persons with dementia and carers at the Café

In this category the theme most commonly arising from the responses was that people felt the Café was fully *inclusive*, with persons with dementia, their carers and families feeling equally as involved and welcome. The theme of *choice* also arose within responses. This concerned the idea that people chose to attend the AC and that this attendance was a positive reflection on how the AC is pitched.

> Well for me it's for A to choose and he likes going and he relaxes, you know he'd be the first to dig his heels in and refuse to go if he didn't like it and if he, he felt uncomfortable . . . [Response from carer]

> Well I mean if you didn't [*feel included*] you wouldn't come along would you?

Negative aspects of the Café

Themes arising from participants' responses in this category mainly concerned difficulties in identifying negative aspects to the AC, and emphasizing its *generally positive* nature.

> I can't think of anything no, I'm just so glad that there's something. I'm just so pleased to have somewhere to go, I don't feel anything negative towards it I just think it's a very good idea and I was grateful that people had put the effort in to make it work you know.

Other themes were concerned with identifying how changes could be made. For example, within the responses of a number of the participants ideas around *varying the structure* of the Café to increase its benefits were identified.

> . . . erm but we were talking the other day though about that it would be nice to get away from the erm meeting at Alzheimer Café and go out somewhere . . .

> . . . if you had got an area where people could sit and have a coffee and chat instead of doing it when you're on your way out you could do it maybe a little bit earlier . . .

A number of the responses from participants also included the theme of concern for the future of the AC in terms of how any *expansion* of the Café may affect its current feel.

Ending of the Café

Within the responses regarding the ending of the AC, themes concerning the *relaxed* nature of the ending and participants feelings of *sadness* regarding the end of the evening were identified.

Barriers to attending

In this category a number of salient themes were identified. The theme most frequently arising in participants' responses reflected the perceived *openness* of the AC, with participants indicating that there were very few barriers to attending the AC. Another theme arising in this category referred to the possible need for *support and encouragement* in attending.

> . . . people that are by their selves then they do need encouragement to come like you know.

> . . . We wouldn't do it on our own . . . For the first time. So there could be possibilities so providing when I say transport I don't mean using a mini-bus but designating someone to pick them up and bring them.

Discussion

Outcomes

The evaluation described in this chapter was undertaken to investigate whether the inclusion of the AC within the dementia care pathway in a Mental Health Service for Older Adults enhanced the care provided and assisted in meeting the requirements of the Department of Health's (2001) NSF. In addition to this, the evaluation sought to investigate whether the AC described meets the conceptual objectives for the AC set out by Miesen and Blom (2001).

In terms of meeting the objectives laid down by Miesen and Blom (2001) it can be seen from the themes arising from the interviews that the AC described here does appear to meet these criteria. The first objective refers to providing information regarding medical and psychosocial aspects of dementia. From the analysis themes regarding the educational nature of the Café, the sharing of knowledge and the promotion of contact with professionals are apparent.

The second objective of the AC laid down by Miesen and Blom (2001) emphasizes the importance of speaking openly about problems in an atmosphere that promotes recognition and social acceptance. Review of the themes identified from interview responses indicates that this objective is fulfilled within this AC. Themes regarding the opportunity to share experiences and discuss problems within the AC are apparent within the analysis. Themes regarding the social aspects of the AC are also emphasized, with reference to participants feeling that they are accepted within the AC and their difficulties are recognized but not emphasized.

The final objective for the AC offered by Miesen and Blom (2001) regards the prevention of isolation of persons with dementia and their families. Again, review of the themes arising from the interviews highlights that this AC is seen to provide a positive social outlet, enabling persons with dementia, their carers and families to develop new relationships.

As discussed earlier, the objectives and culture of the AC are reflective of a person-centred approach to dementia care as described by Kitwood (1997). It is the aim of person-centred care to empower the person with dementia through encouraging the creation of relationships, autonomy, competence, identity and intimacy (Bryden, 2002). The findings of the evaluation described here indicate that the inclusion of the AC in the dementia care pathway for this service does indeed promote such opportunities and outcomes for persons with a diagnosis of dementia. Involving this additional resource in the dementia care pathway therefore contributes to the fulfilment of Standard 2 of the NSF for Older People – person-centred care.

In terms of adhering to the care pathway for dementia (Figure 12.1) set out in Standard 7 (Mental Health in Older People) of the NSF for Older People, the inclusion of the AC in this service can be seen to offer a resource at the treatment level of the care pathway, providing support for both the person with dementia and their carers. The opportunity for carers to be involved in the AC is of great value and is identified as a requirement in terms of an effective plan of care. The social nature of the AC provides a relaxing atmosphere for both persons with dementia and their carers, and this is likely to lead to a reduction in strain and burden, improved morale and more positive interactions between care-givers and the persons with dementia (Woods, 1999).

The AC described in this chapter also represents a medium through which advice and education can be distributed and its multi-disciplinary nature provides an environment of cohesion and communication between the various agencies both within and outside of the service. This was an area identified as particularly important for the sample of visitors to the AC involved in the evaluation. Jones and Miesen (1992) suggest that the establishment of a multi-disciplinary 'core curriculum' for professionals working with persons with dementia and their families is vital in providing care. Working as a multi-disciplinary team in the environment of the AC is likely to promote the sharing of information across disciplines, working towards a cohesive model of care. Involving a range of professionals in the provision of the AC is therefore beneficial, but it must be ensured that no one profession becomes too heavily involved because then the benefits of this multi-disciplinary context may be lost.

An additional advantage of the AC for the service described in this chapter is likely to be the impact that this has on those staff facilitating the AC. It is widely recognized that staff retention and recruitment into older adult services is problematic, and this is so for both nursing and psychology staff (Woods, 1999). The nature of this work, particularly in the field of dementia, is associated with a high degree of staff burnout as a result of the emotive experiences likely to be encountered (Astrom et al, 1991). Being involved in the AC with its emphasis on providing a positive, supportive experience within a social setting is likely to alleviate some of the stressors associated with everyday contact with such clients and promote the idea of what Britton and Woods (1999, p. 22) describe as 'adding life to the years' for older clients.

Limitations of the current evaluation

In the publication *The Health of the Nation* (Department of Health, 1992) it is stated that everyone who provides or purchases services has a duty to consult both service users and carers on the planning and monitoring of community care plans and to ensure that service users are involved in their own health and social care to the best of their ability (Goldsmith, 1996). The evaluation described here, although seeking to follow such guidelines, has been limited. Those people volunteering to take part in the evaluation were predominantly regular attendees of the Café and are thus likely to have a positive view of the AC and are not fully representative of the client group.

In relation to this, a major flaw of the current evaluation can be seen in the difficulties experienced with acquiescence within the interview process. The researcher was known to the participants, being a member of the team of facilitators at the AC, and it is likely that he was keen to offer positive comments on the AC and therefore his views may have been skewed in a positive direction. It may be helpful in future research to investigate the views of individuals who have chosen not to attend the AC and to use interviewers not known to those attending the AC.

The influence of the researcher's views of the AC, also being positive as a result of experience, may have further influenced the evaluation at the point of analysis. Giorgi and Giorgi (2003) noted that one of the vulnerabilities of any form of qualitative research is the fact that the process is dependent on the researcher's subjectivity. Involving persons not involved with the AC at the point of interview and analysis may serve to reduce these biases.

Involving both persons with dementia and their carers was important for this evaluation. In this case those persons with dementia who were interviewed had expressed the view that they would not feel comfortable being interviewed alone, as such they were interviewed with their partners/carers. Interviewing these participants simultaneously, however, may have resulted in some loss of information, with couples tending to agree with one another rather than expressing individual views. Further research may wish to gain information on an individual basis to avoid such loss of information.

In relation to this, the semi-structured nature of the interview may have led to further loss of information. Despite having a number of advantages with regard to the personally relevant information gained from such an interview, the unstructured nature does reduce the control that the researcher has over the interview (Smith and Osborn, 2003). During the evaluation there were instances when the interview strayed from the area under investigation, covering more personal information that was not relevant for the investigation and would potentially lead to the identification of individuals. Efforts to maintain the confidentiality and focus of the interview through prompting may ultimately have led to some information being lost. Using a more structured format may help to alleviate some of these difficulties.

Conclusions

The results of the evaluation described in this chapter indicate that the inclusion of the AC within the service provided by this Community Mental Health Team for Older People is seen as a positive and valuable resource for this sample. The main benefits of this resource are in the provision of a supportive and socially inclusive environment promoting the sharing of knowledge and experiences for persons with dementia, their carers and families. The philosophy and structure of the AC are in line with ideas presented in the Department of Health's National Service Framework for Older People and therefore can be seen as a positive inclusion in the service's dementia care pathway.

Special note on the purpose of the evaluation

The evaluation of the Alzheimer Café described in this chapter was conducted as a small-scale research project for the Clinical Psychology Doctorate Course at the Universities of Coventry and Warwick. The small-scale research project comprises part of the mandatory research assessments within the first two years of the course.

References

Astrom, S., Nilsson, M., Norberg, A., Sandman, P. and Winblad, B. (1991) Staff burnout in dementia care – relations to empathy and attitudes. *International Journal of Nursing Studies*, **28**: 65–75.

Boyatzis, R.E. (1998). *Transforming Qualitative Information*. London: Sage Publications.

Britton, P.G. and Woods, R.T. (1999) Introduction. In R.T. Woods (Ed.), *Psychological Problems of Aging: Assessment, Treatment and Care*. Chichester: John Wiley, pp. 1–26.

Bryden, C. (2002) A person-centred approach to counselling, psychotherapy and rehabilitation of people diagnosed with dementia in the early stages. *Dementia*, 1: 141–156.

Cheston, R. and Bender, M. (1999) *Understanding Dementia: The Man with the Worried Eyes*. London: Jessica Kingsley Publishers.

Department of Health (1992) *The Health of the Nation*. London: Department of Health.

Department of Health (2000) *Who Cares? Information and Support for the Carers of Confused People*. London: Department of Health.

Department of Health (2001) *National Service Framework for Older People*. London: Department of Health (http://www.doh.gov.uk/nsf/olderpeople.htm).

Giorgi, A. and Giorgi, B. (2003) Phenomenology. In J. Smith (Ed.), *Qualitative Psychology: a Practical Guide to Research Methods*. London: Sage Publications, pp. 25–50.

Goldsmith, M. (1996) *Hearing the Voice of People with Dementia: Obstacles and Opportunities*. London: Jessica Kingsley Publishers.

Goudie, F. (2002) Attitudes to dementia: a decade of change. In G. Stokes and F. Goudie (Eds), *The Essential Dementia Care Handbook*. Bicester: Speechmark Publishing, pp. 2–10.

Harvey, R.J., Skelton-Robinson, M. and Rossor, M.N. (2003) The prevalence and cause of dementia in people under the age of 65 years. *Journal of Neurology, Neurosurgery and Psychiatry*, **74**: 1206–1209.

Holden, U. and Stokes, G. (2002) The 'dementias'. In G. Stokes and F. Goudie (Eds), *The Essential Dementia Care Handbook*. Bicester: Speechmark Publishing, pp. 11–21.

Jones, G.M.M. and Miesen, B.M.L. (1992) The need for and interdisciplinary core curriculum for professional working with dementia. In G.M.M. Jones and B.M.L. Miesen (Eds), *Care-giving in Dementia*, vol. 1. London: Routledge, pp. 437–453.

Kitwood, T. (1990) The dialectics of dementia: with particular reference to Alzheimer's disease. *Aging and Society*, **10**: 177–196.

Kitwood, T. (1997) *Dementia Reconsidered – the Person comes First*. Buckingham: Open University Press.

Lindlof, T. R. and Taylor, B.C. (2002) *Qualitative Communication Research Methods* (2nd edn). Thousand Oaks, CA: Sage.

Longley, M. and Warner, M. (2002a) Alzheimer's disease: an introduction to the issues. In M. Warner, S. Furnish, M. Longley and B. Lawlor (Eds), *Alzheimer's Disease: Policy and Practice Across Europe*. Oxford: Radcliffe Medical Press, pp. 1–10.

Longley, M. and Warner, M. (2002b) The national policy context across Europe. In M. Warner, S. Furnish, M. Longley and B. Lawlor (Eds), *Alzheimer's Disease: Policy and Practice Across Europe*. Oxford: Radcliffe Medical Press, pp. 11–25.

Miesen, B.M.L. (1999) *Dementia in Close-up*. (trans. by G.M.M. Jones). London: Routledge.

Miesen, B.M.L. and Blom, M. (2001) *The Alzheimer Café: a Guideline Manual for Setting One Up*. Translated and adapted from the Dutch Alzheimer Society Document by G.M.M. Jones: http//www.Alzheimercafeuk.org.uk.

Miesen, B.M.L. and Jones, G.M.M. (2004) The Alzheimers Café concept: a response to the trauma, tragedy and drama of dementia. In G.M.M. Jones and B.M.L.

Miesen (Eds), *Care-giving in Dementia*, vol. 3. Hove: Brunner-Routledge, pp. 307–333.

Murray, J. and McDaid, D. (2002) Carer burden: the difficulties and rewards of care giving. In M. Warner, S. Furnish, M. Longley and B. Lawlor (Eds), *Alzheimer's Disease: Policy and Practice Across Europe*. Oxford: Radcliffe Medical Press, pp. 61–68.

Parker, G. (1997) Coping with caring for a person with dementia. In S. Hunter (Ed.), *Dementia: Challenges and New Directions*. London: Jessica Kingsley Publishers, pp. 121–135.

Shankland, M.C. (2002) Supporting families of people with dementia. In G. Stokes and F. Goudie (Eds). *The Essential Dementia Care Handbook*. Bicester, UK: Speechmark Publishers, pp. 212–222.

Sixsmith, A., Stillwell, J. and Copeland, J. (1993) Dementia: challenging the limits of dementia care. *International Journal of Geriatric Psychiatry*, **8**: 993–1000.

Smith, J. and Osborn, M. (2003) Interpretative phenomenological analysis. In J. Smith (Ed), *Qualitative Psychology: a Practical Guide to Research Methods*. London: Sage Publications, pp. 51–80.

Stokes, G. and Goudie, F. (2002) *The Essential Dementia Care Handbook: A Good Practice Guide*. Bicester: Speechmark Publishing.

Woods, R.T. (1999) Psychological 'therapies' in dementia. In R.T. Woods (Ed.), *Psychological Problems of Aging: Assessment, Treatment and Care*. Chichester: John Wiley, pp. 311–344.

Part IV

Family and professional care-givers

Chapter 13

The Meeting Centres Support Programme model for persons with dementia and their carers: aims, methods and research*

Rose-Marie Dröes, Franka Meiland and Willem van Tilburg

Introduction

In this chapter the Meeting Centres Support Programme (MCSP) – a collaborative model for providing care for persons with dementia living in the community and for their carers – is described. After an introduction into the aims and content of the MCSP model, the theoretical background and methods of support are explained in more detail and illustrated by a case history.

The second part of the chapter summarizes the research that was carried out on the MCSP: In the programme developmental phase, the effect of the integrated MCSP in the first four 'Amsterdam-based' meeting centres (MCs) was evaluated and compared with regular 'day care' in nursing/residential homes for persons with dementia. The MCSP proved more effective in diminishing behaviour problems in the persons with dementia and in delaying their admission into a care setting, as well as in increasing the feeling of competence of their carers. Because of the proven 'surplus value' of the MCSP, an implementation study into the conditions of successful nationwide implementation of the MCSP model was conducted in eleven MCs in different regions of The Netherlands. In this multi-location comparison study, the original effect of the Amsterdam study was replicated.

Aim and content of the programme

In the past decades various programmes, such as Day Care and Family Support Groups, were developed to support persons with dementia living in the community and their carers. In 1993, the Department of Psychiatry of the Vrije (Free) University in Amsterdam started the MCSP (Dröes and Breebaart, 1994; Dröes et al, 2002, 2003a). The MCSP model stands for a system-oriented, long-term comprehensive support programme of collaboration between the many services providing support for persons with dementia

* Parts of this chapter were published previously in Dröes et al (2002, 2003a).

and their carers: home care, welfare services, Regional Institute for Ambula-tory Mental Welfare, home nursing services, general practitioners (GPs), memory clinics and homes for the elderly. It was initiated to counteract the fragmentation of care and support for this target group and it combines the support for persons with dementia and their carers, gives insight into the support offers and gaps in the support offer in a region and stimulates the collaborating professional partners to create a continuum of care and welfare.

Its main goals are to make it easier and less threatening for persons with dementia and carers to find information and practical, emotional and social support, and to prevent psychosocial and health problems by means of timely interventions. This is why the support for patients and carers is integrated and long term, why the programme is offered in low-threshold local community centres or public centres for the elderly and why the decision was taken to opt for a small number of permanent professional staff who are able to build up a relationship with their clients and offer case management. In the past 11 years, 21 such MCs were set up in 10 regions of The Netherlands.

The support activities for the persons with dementia consist mainly of a social club, 3 days a week, where they can participate in several types of creative and recreational activities and psychomotor therapy (Droes, 1997a). In addi-tion to the support that is given to the persons with dementia, the programme offers information and long-term practical, emotional and social support to the family carers by means of informative meetings, discussion groups, a weekly consulting hour and by organizing social activities. Every 6 weeks all participants and the professional staff come together in a 'centre meeting' to share their experiences and to discuss the programme and planned activities. The participants (persons with dementia and their carers) are assisted indi-vidually and in group settings by a small group of professionals (a psycholo-gist, an activity therapist and a nurse assistant) who collaborate intensively with psychiatric and psychogeriatric outpatient services, including community nursing, home care and GPs, according to a collaboration protocol.

The *general goals* of the support programme are to:

1   Allow the carer and the person with dementia to experience emotional support from other people who are in the same situation.
2   Assist and support the person with dementia in adapting to and coping with the disabilities and deterioration, the ultimate goal being to improve the quality of life of the person with dementia.
3   Inform the carer about dementia and coping strategies, so that he or she learns to cope with changes in the behaviour of the person with dementia.
4   Increase the social network of the carer and the person with dementia, thereby increasing the support of the social environment.
5   Give the carer some time off and rest during the week to reduce the great burden that they bear.

Theoretical background

The support programme for the person with dementia is based on the so-called 'adaptation-coping' model (Dröes, 1991; Finnema et al, 2000), which was derived from the coping theory of Lazarus and Folkman (1984) and the crises model of Moos and Tsu (1977). In the adaptation-coping model, behaviour problems in dementia patients are partly explained as reactions to or (in)adequate ways of coping (obviously due in part to the dementia) with the stress caused by a number of general 'adaptive tasks' (see Box 13.1).

Not every person with dementia will automatically have problems with all of the adaptive tasks mentioned. A difficult task for one person may present no problem to another. In the support programme a 'support plan for the person with dementia' is made for each participant based on the *psychosocial diagnosis*. This indicates which adaptive task the person appears to have difficulty with. The support strategy is attuned to the diagnosis and varies from giving information to trying to reactivate, resocialize and/or optimize the emotional functioning of the person. Combinations of strategies are also possible (see Support plan and strategies).

The 'support programme for the carer' is based on the Model of Determinants of Experienced Burden by Carers (MDEBD; Dröes et al, 1996), in which the above-mentioned adaptive tasks are central: almost all of these adaptive tasks can also be problematic for the carer but from a different perspective, e.g. the carer not only has to deal with the disabilities of the person with dementia but also has to maintain an emotional balance and social contacts. Other aspects that are mentioned in the MDEBD are a feeling of competence, coping strategies, personal factors, health, material and social factors and received/experienced objective support. The support strategies for the carer vary from giving information and practical help to offering emotional support and stimulating them to increase their social network (see Support plan and strategies).

Box 13.1 Some general adaptive tasks for the person with dementia

- Dealing with own disabilities
- Preserving an emotional balance
- Maintaining a positive self-image
- Preparing for an uncertain future
- Developing and maintaining social relationships
- Dealing with the environment and treatment procedures
- Developing an adequate relationship with the professional staff

---

Method of support

Recruitment and admission criteria

The people with mild to moderately severe dementia and their carers who participate in this programme (maximum of 15 persons with dementia and 15 carers in each centre) are recruited via professional referrers and via (local) newspapers, posters (e.g. at the GP's office and the pharmacies) and brochures. Admission takes place after an intake procedure by the Regional Indication Organization and the MC on the basis of the diagnosis ('dementia syndrome' and the level of severity of the dementia: mild to moderately severe). For this purpose the criteria as described in the Dutch Standard for General Practitioners (Wind et al, 1998) and the DSM-IV (American Psychiatric Association, 1994) are used, as well as the Dutch version of the Global Deterioration Scale (GDS; Reisberg et al, 1982; Muskens, 1993). Persons with (very) severe dementia ('middle' and 'late' dementia in the terms of the GDS) are not admitted to the programme because the MCs lack the facilities and personnel to provide proper care for these persons. The diagnosis is always made by a medical doctor (GP), the doctor of the psychiatric outpatient service or the psychiatrist or neurologist in a memory polyclinic. Admission criteria for the carer are that s/he should be motivated to care for the person with dementia at home and to participate in the support programme as well.

Programme activities

The social club and other activities for the persons with dementia

In the 'social day club' (which in most MCs is open on Monday, Wednesday and Friday from 10 am till 4 pm) the person with dementia can participate in activities ranging from domestic (assisted shopping or washing dishes) through to creative and recreational activities (listening to music and reading the newspaper). Most centres also offer psychomotor therapy (Dröes, 1997b) for 1 h three times a week (Dröes and van Tilburg, 1996; Dröes, 1997a). Excursions are organized several times yearly for the person with dementia and their carer. There are always two professional helpers and one or more volunteers present in the social club (see below). The main goal there is to assist and support persons with dementia to cope with the consequences of the illness and to offer them pleasant activities on a regular basis to increase their quality of life (see Table 13.1).

The persons with dementia can also utilize the 'consulting hour' for individual support and advice, once weekly.

Social club activities are comparable with those offered in regular Day Care Centres in The Netherlands but with several differences, e.g. the social

Table 13.1 The Meeting Centres Support Programme and its goals

Programme	Goals
For the person with dementia	
Social club	Assistance and support in coping with the consequences of the dementia
Psychomotor therapy	Offer pleasant activities
For the carer	
Informative meetings	Education
Discussion group	Emotional and social support
For both	
Consulting hour	Individual support and advice
Case management	Practical support
Monthly meeting where staff and participants meet	Attuning the programme to the needs of participating members and optimizing communication between staff and participants
Recreational activities	Expansion of social network
Excursions	

club is situated in 'low-threshold' general community centres or public centres for the elderly instead of in isolated rooms in residential/nursing homes. This means that participants in the social club meet other guests (young and old) from the neighbourhood who visit the centre, and that their carers are always welcome too. In some cases this leads to new friendships, integrated activities with other clubs in the centre and even the enlistment of volunteers who want to offer their help on one or more days. Another aspect in which the social club differs from day care is that the latter offer multi-disciplinary care if needed, whereas the 'MCs' do not offer multi-disciplinary care themselves; such care can be organized when needed, according to the collaboration protocol set up with the care and welfare services in the neighbourhood.

Activities for the family carers: informative meetings

The carers are given special information during 'informative meetings' and supported emotionally and socially through discussion groups. Carers can utilize the weekly 'consulting hour' for more personal support and advice, and participate in social activities organized by the centre to expand their social network (see Table 13.1).

'Informative carer meetings' are organized once every two weeks (a total of 8–10 meetings). Themes discussed include: the diagnosis of dementia, different types of dementia, handling behaviour problems, the anticipatory mourning process, psychopharmacotherapy, offers of care and welfare services in the region, legal and ethical aspects of caring. The informative meetings are public, which means that people who do not participate in the MCSP are also welcome.

A 'discussion group' also meets every two weeks. Carers can participate as long as they feel the need to do so. Both the informative meetings and discussion groups last about 2 h. The programme coordinator organizes both. Professionals (psychologist, neurologist, social worker, etc.) are invited to the informative meetings to speak on the particular theme of that meeting.

The 'consulting hour', which also has a public function, is held by the programme coordinator at a fixed time once a week for 2 h. Participants and other persons who are interested (or want specific information on, for example, dementia and support services) can visit the centre or contact the centre by telephone during that time. Some MCs do not limit themselves to one consulting hour, but offer consultation whenever the centre is open (see also Dröes et al, 2004a).

Some joint activities are organized for the carer and the person with dementia (the monthly centre meeting, recreational activities and excursions) (see Table 13.1).

The 'monthly centre meeting' is aimed at attuning the programme to the needs of the participants and optimizing the communication between staff and participants.

Support plan and strategies

The structure of the support programme is such that it offers mostly emotional and social support to the people with dementia and to the carers; besides this it also offers practical support and information. For both groups the individual emphasis is on offering support in learning to deal with one or more specific 'adaptive tasks'.

When a client–carer dyad applies (or is presented by a referrer) to one of the MCs, the MC staff first determine the *general request for support*: is this a sudden crisis situation that requires immediate support measures, or is it a question of a somewhat precarious balance that could perhaps be stabilized with a little support? A third possibility is that carers indicate they have been going from one problematic situation to another for quite a while, and they are afraid they will not be able to cope with caring for the person with dementia much longer without some outside help. In that case one can speak of a downward spiral that external support and intensive counselling might possibly break.

The moment the person with dementia starts utilizing the social club marks the start of a 1-month introductory period. During this month the programme coordinator gathers *information* about the person with dementia from the person in question and the carer. The coordinator also checks with the person with dementia, as well as the carer, whether they experience problems with particular '*adaptive tasks*'. The information on the person with dementia concerns personal background, material and social circumstances and medical information. This information is collected on the basis of a so-called client information form. Interviews with the person with dementia and the carer, along with behaviour observation during activities in the social club, discussion group and informative meetings, are used to inventorize which adaptive tasks are problematic. Based on this inventory, a team (the programme coordinator, the activity therapist and carer) draws conclusions about the way the person with dementia and the carer handle the various adaptive tasks, and if relevant which tasks seem to be most difficult for them. Based on this conclusion, also known as the '*psychosocial diagnosis*', preliminary support plans are drawn up for the person with dementia and the carer. These preliminary support plans are discussed with the carer (and with the person with dementia if possible) and subsequently a final plan is agreed on for a fixed period of time. Usually the validity of the 'plans' is reviewed every 6 weeks; or more often if currently needed.

The person with dementia can visit the social club two or three days a week and, if the carer needs this, home care can be arranged to help wash and dress the person. Furthermore, agreements are reached with the carer about participating in the other services and activities. Carers are encouraged to participate in social and cultural activities in the community or elsewhere to maintain their social life and increase their social network.

Depending on which adaptive tasks are most problematic, the support plan for the person with dementia will include the support strategies shown in Box 13.2.

Various approaches and techniques are used, including reality orientation, validation, behaviour therapy and insight-oriented techniques, such as thematic discussions in peer groups and discussions on experiences during exercises in the psychomotor therapy sessions.

The support plan for the person with dementia is discussed with the carer so that they can use similar techniques at home.

Location, required space and personnel

The support activities for both the persons with dementia and the carers are offered in the same building (general sociocultural community centres) by the professional helpers and volunteers. The programme coordinator has at least a higher vocational education (e.g. a psychologist) and has 70% input, the activity therapist has 30% input and the nurse assistant has 30% input. This balance allows support for both carer and the person with dementia.

Box 13.2 Possible individual or combination support strategies	
Support strategy	Aim
Reactivation	Preventing or reducing excessively regressive ways of coping with own disability and the environment by stimulating the remaining cognitive ability regarding memory, perception and action
Resocialization	Preventing or reducing isolated, passive behaviour and encouraging social relationships between the participants in the social club by stimulating communication with others in their environment
Improvement of affective functioning	Increasing or restoring the person's sense of control and identity and experiencing success and joy. The ultimate goal is to improve the emotional balance and achieve a positive self-image in the person with dementia. The expectation is that people are better able to accept the future if they are more content in the present (van der Wulp, 1986; Dröes, 1991).

The MCSP requires the following spaces:

For persons with dementia

- On three days a week (i.e. Monday, Wednesday, Friday) a collective cosy space of about 60 m² with tables and chairs in a local MC.
- Three times a week (on the same days), a cleared room large enough for psychomotor therapy, preferably a small gymnasium or room that can be used like one. It must be possible to do ball games in this room.

For the carers

- Two hours each week on a fixed morning or afternoon in a room where 15–20 persons can attend informative meetings and discussion groups.

Other space needed

- Once a week (preferably on Monday, Wednesday or Friday; not coinciding with the time of the discussion group), a room for the consulting hour (a telephone and a table are also needed).
- Once a month, a space large enough for the monthly meeting attended by carers, personnel and the persons with dementia.

Case history

During a visit to the GP, Mrs Berg complained about being nervous all the time and having frequent headaches. The GP felt that she had become over-burdened due to caring for her husband, whom she had cared for since his diagnosis of dementia. A recent added strain for both Mr and Mrs Berg was the deterioration of his eyesight in the past year. The GP therefore advised Mrs Berg to get in touch with the MCSP. It was hoped that both could receive support at the same time, since they would not agree to being separated during the day to have traditional 'respite' such as day care.

At the MC it was felt that Mr Berg could participate in the social club for three days a week, whilst Mrs Berg could join the carer programme to receive both emotional support and information on how to cope with the daily caring problems. If Mr and Mrs Berg liked the MC, she would also be able to have some 'respite' on the other two days that her husband attended the centre.

Initially Mr and Mrs Berg had a period of familiarization; she liked the small size, the relaxed atmosphere and the individual attention that staff gave to the participants. She thought that the opportunity to listen to classical music would interest her husband, now that his vision was poor. The first time that she participated in the discussion group with other family members, she reported feeling a bit lost, but she was soon able to explain in her own words her experience of how she was struggling with 'gradually losing her husband'. This sharing opportunity to describe her feelings enabled her to experience the relief of shared support. During one meeting, it dawned on her that the somatic complaints that she sometimes experienced were connected with the sorrow and fear of losing her husband.

When Mr Berg attended the MC without his wife, she filled her time with housekeeping and shopping. Initially, she found it difficult to do things that were 'totally for herself'; she would think of her husband and feel guilty. However, at the MC there was the opportunity to have a cup of tea with others, after the discussion group. Mrs Berg met another lady of her own age, whose husband also had dementia; gradually they became friends. By spring-time they decided to take a course in flower-arranging together. They had fun and after every meeting they would have a cup of tea or coffee at the social club. Her husband was observed to beam with happiness when he heard her cheerful voice – 'Jo is still the best!' Contented, they went home at 4 o'clock.

The intervention study during the developmental phase

Since the start of this project in April 1993 until October 1996, approximately 70 couples have participated in the support programme in four MCs (Dröes and Breebaart, 1994; Dröes, 1996). Most couples consisted of spouses (75%);

70% of carers were female and 30% were male. Of the persons with dementia, half were female and half were male. The severity of dementia, as measured with the Brief Cognitive Rating Scale (Reisberg et al, 1982), varied mainly from mild to moderately severe.

The intervention study conducted between 1994 and 1996 (Dröes et al, 2000) focused on the effects of the MCSP on: the behaviour problems and mood of the persons with dementia; the feelings of burden and mental health of the carer; and *determinants* of feelings of burden of the carer (feeling of competence, coping skills and strategies). A quasi-experimental design was used with two matched groups: the Amsterdam MC group ($n=33$) and a regular day care control group ($n=23$). Matching was done on the basis of the severity of dementia, the person's need for care and on feeling of competence of the carer. Measurement took place before the intervention and after 7 months.

Standardized questionnaires and assessment scales were used to measure the following variables for the persons with dementia: initiative and aggressive, unsociable, inactive, depressed and dissatisfied behaviour; for the care-givers: feelings of stress, satisfaction, mental health, feeling of competence, coping behaviour, experienced social support and loneliness. Analysis of covariance (ANCOVA) was conducted on the 7-month data. The baseline data were included as covariate in the analysis.

After 7 months the persons with dementia who participated in the MCSP demonstrated significantly less behaviour problems than the persons with dementia in the control group ($F(1,36)$, $p=5.79$; effect size 0.75), as measured with the Behaviour Observation Scale for Intramural Psychogeriatrics (Verstraten and van Eekelen, 1987). This effect was found for all behaviour problems, but for two in particular: *inactivity* ($F(1,42)=4.46$, $p=0.02$; effect size 0.66) and *unsociable behaviour* ($F(1,42)=3.29$, $p=0.04$; effect size 0.61). No effect was found on mood of the persons with dementia.

Another effect found was that after 7 months only 8% of the persons in the MC group had been admitted to a residential/nursing home facility, whereas in the control group 30% had already been admitted. None of the mentioned effects could be explained by longitudinal changes in severity of dementia, physical limitations or disease of the person with dementia, nor by use of other services or special life events. The only aspect that may have influenced the admission rate was that the Amsterdam MC group contained more spouses than the control group. However, other research has shown that the effect of the type of relationship between the person with dementia and his carer on admission rate is only limited (Vernooij-Dassen, 1993) and that behaviour problems are usually much more decisive in predicting admission rate (Christie and Wood, 1988).

The family carers who participated in the MCSP for 7 months felt more competent ($F(1,36)=3,4$, $p=0.04$; effect size 0.45) with regard to caring, as measured with the Feeling of Competence Scale (Vernooij-Dassen, 1993), than carers of persons with dementia who participated in regular day care. Their social network also increased, which might explain why the admission rate of persons with dementia to nursing homes was substantially lower in the MC group. In our anonymous questionnaire, completed after 7 months of participation, 37% of the carers subjectively reported that they felt much less burdened than before they entered the programme, although no objective effects of the support programme on feelings of stress and mental health of the care-giver were found with standardized measures. This discrepancy is also found in other studies (Zarit et al, 1999) and possibly has to do with retrospective assessment: at both measurements carers judge the care equally burdensome, but retrospectively some experience a comparative decrease of the burden. The subjective decrease we found in feelings of burden correlated positively with the emotional support and understanding that carers experienced from other carers.

The implementation study

Based on the positive results of the intervention study, the support programme was continued in Amsterdam on a structural basis. Several other regions in The Netherlands adopted this new type of support. To stimulate 'nationwide' implementation, the VU Medical Centre in Amsterdam (in cooperation with the University Medical Centre St. Radboud in Nijmegen and the Trimbos Institute in Utrecht) investigated the conditions of successful implementation in all regions that offered, or had started to offer, the MCSP from 2000 to 2002 (Dröes et al, 2003b). Eleven MCs in seven regions [Amstelveen/Uithoorn (2), Amsterdam (2), Groningen (2), Haarlem (1), Haarlemmermeer (2), Nieuwegein (1), Nijmegen (1)] participated in the study.
   The aims of the implementation study were to focus on:

1 Facilitating factors and barriers to the implementation of the MCs.
2 Variations in performance, characteristics of participants and usage/ attendance of the programme's support activities by participants in the different regions.
3 Effects on patients and carers.

Facilitators and barriers

To trace facilitating and impeding factors, different phases (preparation, implementation, continuation) and different levels (micro, meso and macro) of implementation were studied. These were based on a theoretical model that was developed especially for our study (Meiland et al, 2004). In addition, characteristics of the innovation and other preconditions were examined for their facilitating and impeding influence on the implementation of MCs.

Various factors proved to have facilitated successful implementation in all phases. For example: *motivated organizations and staff members*, the availability of *financial resources*, continuous and varied *public relations activities* and *sound collaboration* with other organizations. This collaboration proved relevant at several levels: both within/between organizations and at the executive/management board level. In some regions extensive cooperative relationships were already present, whereas in others they had to be developed.

Some factors turned out to be facilitators in one phase but barriers in another, e.g. waiting lists. The existence of waiting lists for other facilities for the target group (i.e. day care) at the start of the implementation had a positive influence on the demand and support for setting up an MC. On the other hand, waiting lists in the continuation phase could have an impeding effect because they kept participants from moving on to other facilities.

At the macro level, laws and regulations proved important for the financing of the MCs. Arranging the financing for both care for people with dementia and support for the care-givers was often challenging.

Characteristics of the MCs (including 'surplus value' compared to the existing support offered and availability of already existing examples) and other preconditions (such as time, finances) could facilitate or impede implementation.

Regional variations

Variations in performance

Implementation in other regions did not lead to major changes in the programme, in the characteristics of participants or in attendance (Dröes et al, 2004a). The data gathered about variations in set-up, execution, structural embedding and financing show that there are more similarities than differences between the MCs. All but one of the MCs that were established made preparations by using a 'group of initiators' comprising both healthcare and welfare organizations. Once the centres were operational, all MCs worked jointly with (mental) healthcare and welfare organizations in the region. All centres offer the already described support programme for people with mild to moderately severe dementia and their carers in an easily accessible location in the neighbourhood. The themes for informative meetings are almost identical in all centres (see Programme activities). The activities in the social club are comparable, although adapted to the preferences and abilities of the users at that time and to the local situation. Nearly all centres base their admission policy on the original criteria described. All centres have a small team and volunteers, as described. This allows the 'MCSP' model to offer well-defined integrated support.

The differences between the centres relate to the originators/initiators, the location, frequency of discussion groups/monthly centre meetings, educational background of staff, number of volunteers and the structural financing. (Some health insurance companies feel that support for family carers should be financed by the municipal authorities, whereas other health insurance companies feel that this type of 'preventative' support is their responsibility.)

Variations in participants and attendance rate

No statistically significant differences in sex, age, civil status, severity of dementia or physical disability could been found between persons using the 11 different MCs (see Table 13.2): similar numbers of men and women attend the centres, the average age varies between 75 and 80, the majority are married or cohabit and most persons have mild to moderately severe dementia and limited physical disabilities. The majority of the participants in all regions had Alzheimer's disease or some other form of dementia, although there were some differences in the other diagnoses, partly because of the admission policy used by the MCs. In all centres at least half of the participants had four or more 'psychiatric behaviour symptoms', as measured with the Neuropsychiatric Inventory (Cummings, 1994).

The family carers also show many similarities across regions; the majority of carers are female, married or cohabiting and a minority are gainfully employed (see Table 13.3). In general, they share a household with the person with dementia or they live in the same municipality. Their average age ranged mostly from 60 to 70, and the majority of carers exhibit psychological and/or psychosomatic symptoms.

Most referrals are made by the Regional Mental Welfare Institute, but a substantial number of family carers apply to the support programme on their own initiative; in some regions the Home Care organization and the Elderly Welfare Foundation are important referrers.

In most regions, carer attendance at the 'consulting hour' is consistently high.

In locations where the informative meeting was combined with the Alzheimer Café (education and support offered within a low-threshold, understanding environment in the presence of healthcare professionals, persons with dementia and their family and friends; Miesen and Jones, 2004), a relatively low attendance of carers from the MCs was recorded.

The informative meetings draw a number of external visitors. Differences between regions in terms of 'consulting hour contacts' are considerable, although the reason is still unclear. It may depend on whether they are held during variable or fixed time slots. There is regular contact with both family carers and healthcare and welfare workers; the programme coordinator initiates contact about as often as family carers and welfare workers. These contacts mostly relate to practical questions, advice and combinations of

Table 13.2 Characteristics of the people with dementia in the first meeting centres (starters) and the 'follow-up' centres in the different regions A–G

Region Characteristic	A (n=42)	B (n=18)	C (n=5)	D (n=9)	E (n=11)	Starters χ²	Starters p	F (n=14)	G (n=49)	Follow-up χ²	Follow-up p
Sex											
Male	23 (54.8%)	8 (44.4%)	3 (60.0%)	5 (55.6%)	4 (36.4%)	1.72	0.79	9 (64.3%)	33 (67.3%)	0.05	0.83
Female	19 (45.2%)	10 (55.6%)	2 (40.0%)	4 (44.4%)	7 (63.6%)			5 (35.7%)	16 (32.7%)		
Age (sd)	76.9 (7.2)	77.5 (6.8)	79.0 (4.1)	75.1 (6.4)	79.5 (5.8)	F=0.66	0.62	75.1 (3.0)	75.6 (9.6)	t=-0.20	0.84
Civil status											
Married/cohabiting	28 (66.7%)	11 (61.1%)	2 (40.0%)	8 (88.9%)	5 (45.5%)			11 (78.6%)	37 (75.5%)		
Divorced/widow(er)	14 (33.3%)	7 (38.9%)	3 (60.0%)	1 (11.1%)	6 (54.5%)	5.47	0.24	3 (21.4%)	12 (24.5%)	0.06	0.81
Diagnosis											
Dementia											
Alzheimer's disease	23 (54.8%)	10 (55.6%)	2 (40.0%)	7 (77.8%)	6 (54.5%)			5 (35.7%)	25 (51.0%)		
Vascular	4 (9.5%)	1 (5.6%)	1 (20.0%)	–	2 (18.2%)			1 (7.1%)	4 (8.2%)		
	3 (7.1%)	1 (5.6%)	–	1 (11.1%)	–			4 (28.6%)	8 (16.3%)		
Mixed type	8 (19.0%)	1 (5.6%)	–	–	2 (18.2%)	18.90	0.02*	2 (14.3%)	6 (12.2%)	3.76	0.15
	–	–	–	–	1 (9.1%)			1 (7.1%)	–		
	1 (2.4%)	4 (22.2%)	–	1 (11.1%)	–			–	1 (2.0%)		
	3 (7.1%)	1 (5.6%)	2 (40.0%)	–	–			1 (7.1%)	5 (10.2%)		

Amnestic
syndrome

Other
  Depression
  Unknown

Severity of dementia

Forgetfulness	10 (23.8%)	3 (16.7%)	–	2 (22.2%)	2 (18.2%)	17.24	0.64	3 (21.4%)	4 (8.2%)	6.38	0.27
Early confusional	11 (26.2%)	5 (27.8%)	2 (40.0%)	1 (11.1%)	6 (54.5%)			3 (21.4%)	5 (10.2%)		
Late confusional	10 (23.8%)	7 (38.9%)	2 (40.0%)	2 (22.2%)	1 (9.1%)			5 (35.7%)	17 (34.7%)		
Early dementia	9 (21.4%)	3 (16.7%)	1 (20.0%)	3 (33.3%)	2 (18.2%)			3 (21.4%)	10 (20.4%)		
Middle dementia	2 (4.8%)	–	–	1 (11.1%)	–			–	7 (14.3%)		
Unknown	–	–	–	–	–			–	6 (12.2%)		

Physical disability

0–1 mild	29 (69.0%)	(61.1%)	–	6 (66.7%)	8 (72.7%)	3.24	0.78	9 (64.3%)	–	–	–
2–3 moderate	7 (16.7%)	5 (27.8%)	–	3 (33.3%)	3 (27.3%)			5 (35.7%)	–		
4–6 severe	2 (4.8%)	–	–	–	–			–	–		
Unknown	4 (9.5%)	2 (11.1%)	–	–	–			–	–		

NPI

Total score (sd)	26.1 (15.2)	25.8 (14.0)	–	23.6 (20.5)	28.3 (15.9)	F=0.46	0.71	11.0 (6.13)	26.9 (16.28)	t=–3.54	0.01*
NPI score ≥4 Behaviour symptoms	30 (71.4%)	14 (77.8%)	–	7 (77.8%)	7 (63.6%)	1.25	0.74	7 (50.0%)	27 (55.1%)	2.41	0.12

* Statistically significant; NPI, Neuropsychiatric Inventory.

Table 13.3 Characteristics of family carers in the first meeting centres (starters) and the 'follow-up' centres in the different regions A–G

Region	A (n=42)	B (n=18)	C (n=5)	D (n=9)	E (n=11)	Starters χ²	p	F (n=14)	G (n=49)	Follow-up χ²	p
Characteristic											
Sex						4.54	0.34			0.15	0.70
Male	11 (26.2%)	3 (16.7%)	5 (100.0%)	4 (44.4%)	2 (18.2%)			3 (21.4%)	13 (26.5%)		
Female	31 (73.8%)	15 (83.3%)	–	5 (55.6%)	9 (81.8%)			11 (78.6%)	36 (73.5%)		
Age (sd)	62.4 (13.6)	60.2 (14.6)	68.5 (13.0)	74.2 (6.9)	58.6 (9.2)	F=2.55	0.05*	69.6 (13.0)	65.1 (12.2)	t=1.19	0.24
Civil status						4.13	0.39			0.50	0.48
Married/ cohabiting	38 (90.5%)	16 (88.9%)	3 (60.0%)	8 (88.9%)	10 (90.9%)			13 (92.9%)	42 (85.7%)		
Divorced/ widow(er)	4 (9.5%)	2 (11.1%)	2 (40.0%)	1 (11.1%)	1 (9.1%)			1 (7.1%)	7 (14.3%)		
Work						7.62	0.11			1.33	0.25
Gainfully employed	11 (26.2%)	1 (5.6%)	–	–	3 (27.3%)			1 (7.1%)	10 (20.4%)		
Other	31 (73.8%)	17 (94.4%)	5 (100%)	9 (100%)	8 (72.7%)			13 (92.9%)	39 (70.6%)		

Relationship with person with dementia						χ²	p			χ²	p
Partner	27 (64.3%)	7 (38.9%)	2 (40.0%)	9 (100%)	4 (36.4%)	16.23	0.04*	11 (78.6%)	37 (75.5%)		0.06
Daughter/son	12 (28.6%)	8 (44.4%)	1 (20.0%)	–	5 (45.5%)			2 (14.3%)	8 (16.3%)		
Other	3 (7.1%)	3 (16.7%)	2 (20.0%)	–	2 (18.2%)			1 (7.1%)	4 (8.2%)		
Living distance											
Shared household	28 (66.7%)	7 (38.9%)	2 (40.0pc)	8 (88.9%)	4 (36.4%)	18.40	0.10	12 (85.7%)	35 (71.4%)	1.38	0.71
Walking distance	1 (2.4%)	3 (16.7%)	1 (20.0%)	–	3 (27.3%)			–	2 (4.1%)		
Same municipality	7 (16.7%)	4 (22.2%)	–	–	1 (9.1%)			1 (7.1%)	6 (12.2%)		
Other municipality	6 (14.3%)	4 (22.2%)	2 (40.0%)	1 (11.1%)	3 (27.3%)			1 (7.1%)	6 (12.2%)		
GHQ											
Average (sd)	5.98 (5.5)	6.82 (6.2)	–	9.56 (4.9)	7.0 (5.4)	59.37	0.39	3.7 (3.5)	–	–	–
GHQ score≥5	23 (57.5%)	11 (64.7%)	–	7 (77.8%)	6 (72.7%)	9.56	0.05*	3 (21.4%)	–	–	–

* Statistically significant; GHQ, General Health Questionnaire.

information, emotional support and/or care and counselling issues. The consulting hour serves a clear 'public function' in all MCs.

Effects

Persons with dementia

The data gathered inter-regionally on behaviour and mood of the persons with dementia were compared with data from a control group of visitors to two regular day care centres (pre-test–post-test design with measurements in the first month of participation and after 7 months)(Dröes et al, 2004b). Once again, the integrated family MCSP proved to have 'surplus value' compared to regular day care with respect to managing behaviour problems. After attending the MCs for 7 months, the behaviour problems in the MCSP participants had increased less than for persons using (non-integrated) psychogeriatric day care. As in the previous Amsterdam study (Dröes et al, 2000), effects were found on *inactivity* ($F(1,89=2.77$, $p=0.05$; effect size 0.37), *unsociable behaviour* ($F(1,89)=7.26$, $p=0.004$; effect size 0.60), and the total number of observed *behaviour problems* ($F(1,89)=5.43$, $p=0.01$; effect size 0.52). Additionally, a statistically significant positive effect was found on *depressive behaviour* ($F(1,89)=17$, $p=0.00$; effect size 0.92). Contrary to expectations (increase in life satisfaction and decrease in depressive behaviour with progression of the disease; Reisberg et al, 1987; Merriam et al, 1988; Lyketsos and Olin, 2002), dissatisfaction remained almost the same and depressive behaviour increased during the experimental period in both groups. However, this increase was significantly smaller in the MCSP group. Finally, a positive effect was found within the MC group on *self-esteem* ($t=2,7$, $p=0.009$; effect size 0.43), one of the aspects of quality of life.

Carers

After 7 months, the MCSP proved more effective than partner use of regular day care in reducing the psychological and psychosomatic symptoms in carers who felt lonely. The effect was expected, because the MC offers the carer substantial social contact and emotional support. Carers who feel isolated will therefore benefit most.

The programme also had a delaying effect on nursing home placement in comparison to regular day care. The mean length of participation before placement in a nursing home was 41.2 weeks for those who were admitted from the MCs and 24.9 weeks for those who were admitted from regular day care. After 7 months, only 4% of the persons with dementia who participated in the support programme of the MCs had been placed in a nursing home, whereas the percentage in the group of persons who used regular day care was 29% at this point. Finally, a 'reduction of experienced burden' and an increase in 'experienced support from professional services' *within* the MCSP were found after a 7-month participation period (data were not collected in the regular day care group.)

The effect on 'feeling of competence' that was found in the previous Amsterdam MC study was not confirmed in this multi-centre study, although the 'feeling of competence' within the regular day care group decreased significantly during the experimental period, whereas the 'feeling of competence' within the MC group remained stable.

As in the Amsterdam study, no controlled (sub)group effects were found for the other (potential) determinants of burden – coping strategies, experienced support by professional carers, social support from family and friends and loneliness – although 87.5% of the carers in the MCs felt less burdened and 43.7% developed friendships in the MCs. For coping strategies, only a very small *within*-group effect in the MC group was found after 7 months on seeking distraction (emotion-focused coping strategy; $t=1.69$, $p=0.05$; effect size 0.14), which could be seen as an indication of feeling less stressed after participating in the programme (see also Kramer and Vitaliano, 1994). During the experimental period there was an almost significant increase in 'behaviour and psychiatric problems' ($t=-1.81$; $p=0.07$) in the persons with dementia who participated in the MCs, whereas the mean emotional impact of these problems on the carers remained stable ($t=0.32$, $p=0.75$). This in itself seems to be a favourable sign.

Conclusions and discussion

The intervention and implementation studies show that the support programme based on the Amsterdam MC model meets a number of the defined needs of people with mild to moderately severe dementia and their carers. It was also shown to be a reproducible intervention in other regions of The Netherlands and would therefore appear to be generally applicable. The positive outcome on behaviour and mood in the persons with dementia and on psychological and psychosomatic complaints and feelings of burden in the carers found in the multi-centre effect study confirms the previous effects found in the effect study during the developmental phase of the MCSP. This proves the surplus value of this integrated support programme in these aspects as compared to regular day care for the target group. Because behaviour problems are one of the main determinants of overburdening of the care-giver and of 'institutionalization' of the person with dementia (Christie and Wood, 1988; Teri et al, 1988; Steele et al, 1990; Vernooij-Dassen, 1993; Dröes et al, 1996; Pot, 1996), this is an important finding. The effects were measured after a period of 7 months of participation in the programme, which is an argument in favour of long-term support.

In terms of adaptation and coping, inactivity, unsociable behaviour, depression and self-esteem can be seen as indicators of the problems that the person with dementia experiences in coping with his or her own disabilities and maintaining social contacts on the one hand, and maintaining an emotional balance and a positive self-image on the other. One could therefore conclude that the participants in the MCSP have fewer problems with these adaptive tasks than the users of the regular psychogeriatric day care.

The variations in set-up between the MCs make it clear that adaptive implementation is desirable in each new region.

Several of the facilitators and barriers found in the implementation study have been described in other implementation studies as well. Examples are: motivation of the people involved (Wilkinson et al, 1999), problems reaching the target group (Poppelaars et al, 2003), financing problems (Mur-Veeman et al, 1994) and organizational characteristics (Berlowitz et al, 2003). We therefore anticipate that the model we developed to trace facilitating and impeding factors can also be used in other adaptive implementation projects. Using models for the implementation of care innovations is in line with the notion that implementation requires attention, because implementation does not occur spontaneously (van der Linden and Schrijvers, 1998; Hulscher et al, 2000, Grol and Wensing, 2001).

Both research and practice show that various strategies on the micro, meso and /or macro levels, such as early involvement of potential partner organizations, 'needs assessment' among the target group, acquiring the necessary funding and continuous public relations activities, can facilitate the implementation of care innovations (Nies, 1994). A combination of strategies is usually more effective than simple strategies (Grol, 1997; NHS Centre for Reviews and Dissemination, 1999; Bero et al, 1998). Grol (1997) suggests a cyclical five-step plan for the implementation of innovations. After a proposal to change is developed (1) and facilitating and impeding factors are identified (2), strategies must be tuned to these facilitators and barriers (3), an implementation plan must be developed (4) and executed and evaluated (5). Adaptation to specific situations and target groups is always necessary (Grol and Grimshaw, 2003). Since cooperation with other organizations is necessary, the strategies that one chooses when setting up new MCs will also depend on the local situation. In this type of innovation *adaptive* implementation is often preferred over programmed implementation (Boekholdt and Pepels, 1994; van der Linden and Schrijvers, 1998). It is advisable to link studies to adaptive implementation projects in order to obtain insight into the effectiveness of the strategies used and to make a contribution to 'evidence-based' implementation (Grol and Grimshaw, 1999; Wensing et al, 1998).

The insight obtained into facilitating and impeding factors in setting up new MCs may contribute to an effective implementation of integrated support programmes for people with dementia who live at home, and their carers. Partly on the basis of the variations encountered between present MCs and the facilitators and barriers found in our study, a guide including a 'toolkit' was developed for the adaptive implementation of MCs for people with dementia and their carers (Dröes and van Ganzewinkel, 2003). In addition to information and advice, this guide describes in detail implementation strategies for the different levels of organization (micro, meso, macro) and offers concrete aids to facilitate implementation (e.g. floppy disks containing forms and questionnaires, examples of applications for funding, etc.). Such aids increase the chances of successful implementation compared to merely providing information (Wilkinson et al, 1999). Furthermore, plans were prepared for the continued nationwide implementation and evaluation of MCs. In addition to the implementation guide, local initiators can use the knowledge that is available in the National Working Group of MCs, the national help desk in the Alzheimer Centre of the Vrije Universiteit medical centre and a training course developed for the staff of new MCs. In the near future an informative website will also be designed. In all, this provides a solid foundation to set up new MCs for persons with dementia and their carers.

Acknowledgements

The authors wish to thank all the participants and personnel of the MCs in the period from 1993 to 2003 for their cooperation in the different phases of the MCSP project. The project was financed by the Valerius Foundation, Association for Support of Christian Care of People with Mental and Nervous Diseases, National Fund Mental Public Health, the Health Insurance Company Amsterdam, the Municipality of Amsterdam, Dutch Health Research and Development Council, Novartis, National Fund Elderly Support, Association Sluyterman Van Loo, VSB-fund and the Provinces of Groningen, Utrecht and Gelderland.

References

American Psychiatric Association (1994) *DSM-IV: Diagnostic and Statistical Manual of Mental Disorders. Fourth edition.* Washington, DC: American Psychiatric Asociation.

Berlowitz, D.R., Young, G.J., Hickey, E.C., Saliba, D., Mittman, B.S., Czarnowski, E., Simon, B., Anderson, J.J., Ash, A.S., Rubenstein, L.V. and Moskowitz, M.A. (2003) Quality improvement implementation in the nursing home. *Health Services Research*, 38: 65–83.

Bero, L.A., Grilli, R., Grimshaw, J.M., Harvey, E., Oxman, A.D. and Thomson, M.A. (1998) Closing the gap between research and practice: an overview of systematic reviews of interventions to promote the implementation of research findings. *British Medical Journal*, 317: 65–68.

Boekholdt, M. and Pepels, R. (1994) Implementatie: het invoeren van vernieuwingen in de ouderenzorg [Implementation: introducing innovations in the field of care for the elderly]. In H. Nies and S. Kollaard (Eds.), *De Praktijk van Vernieuwingswerk in de Ouderenzorg [Innovation Work in the Field of Care for the Elderly in Practice]*. Houten/Zaventem: Bohn, Stafleu Van Lochum.

Christie, A.B. and Wood, E.R.M. (1988) Age, clinical features and prognosis in SDAT. *International Journal of Geriatric Psychiatry*, 3: 63–68.

Cummings, J.L. (1994) *Neuropsychiatric Inventory (NPI)*. Los Angeles, CA: UCLA Alzheimer's Disease Center.

Dröes, R.M. (1991) *In Beweging; over Psychosociale Hulpverlening aan Demente Ouderen' [In Movement; on Psychosocial Care for Elderly with Dementia]* (in Dutch), Academic Dissertation. Nijkerk: Intro.

Dröes, R.M. (1996) *Amsterdamse Ontmoetingscentra; een Nieuwe Vorm van Ondersteuning voor Dementerende Mensen en hun Verzorgers [Amsterdam MCs; a New Type of Support for People with Dementia and their Carers. Final Report Outcome study]* (in Dutch). Amsterdam: Thesis Publishers.

Dröes, R.M. (1997a) *Beweeg met Ons mee! Een Activeringprogrammema in Groepsverband voor Mensen met Dementie [Get Moving with Us. An Activation Programme in Groups for People with dementia]* (in Dutch). Maarssen: Elsevier/De Tijdstroom.

Dröes, R.M. (1997b) Psychomotor group therapy for demented patients in the nursing home. In B.M.L. Miesen and G.M.M. Jones (Eds), *Care-giving in Dementia*, Vol. 2. London: Routledge, pp. 95–118.

Dröes, R.M. and Breebaart, E. (1994) *Amsterdamse Ontmoetingscentra; een Nieuwe Vorm van Ondersteuning voor Dementerende Ouderen en hun Verzorgers [Amsterdam MCs; a New Type of support for people with dementia and their carers. Final Report Preliminary Study]* (in Dutch). Amsterdam: Thesis Publishers.

Dröes, R.M. and van Tilburg, W. (1996) Amélioration du comportement agressif par des activités psychomotrices [Improvement of agressive behaviour by psychomotor activities] (in French). *L'Année Gérontologique*, 10: 471–482.

Dröes, R.M. and van Ganzewinkel, J. (2003) *Draaiboek Ontmoetingscentra voor Mensen met Dementie en hun Verzorgers [Implementation Guide MCs for Persons with Dementia and their Carers]*. Amsterdam: Department of Psychiatry, VU Medical Centre.

Dröes, R.M., Lindeman, E.M., Breebaart, E. and van Tilburg, W. (1996) Determinanten van belasting van verzorgers van mensen die lijden aan dementie [Determinants of burden of carers of people suffering from dementia] (in Dutch). In R.M. Dröes (Ed.), *Amsterdamse Ontmoetingscentra; een Nieuwe Vorm van Ondersteuning voor Dementerende Mensen en hun Verzorgers*. Amsterdam: Thesis Publishers.

Dröes, R.M., Breebaart, E., van Tilburg, W. and Mellenbergh, G.J. (2000) The effect of integrated family support versus day care only on behaviour and mood of patients with dementia. *International Psychogeriatrics*, 12: 99–116.

Dröes, R.M., Breebaart, E., Ettema, T.P., Meiland, F.J.M., Mellenbergh, G.J. and van Tilburg, W. (2002) Effect of the MCs Support Programme on persons with dementia and their carers. In S. Andrieu and J-P. Aquino (Eds) *Family and Professional Carers: Findings Lead to Action, Research and Practice in Alzheimer's Disease*. Paris: Serdi, pp. 161–166.

Dröes, R.M., Meiland, F.J.M., Lange, J., Vernooij-Dassen, M.J.F.J. and van Tilburg, W. (2003a) The MCs Support Programme: an effective way of supporting people with dementia who live at home and their carers. *International Journal of Social Research and Practice*, 2: 426–432.

Dröes, R.M., Meiland, F.J.M., Schmitz, M.J., Vernooij-Dassen, M.J.F.J., de Lange, J., Derksen, E., Boerema, I., Grol, R.P.T.M. and van Tilburg, W. (2003b)

Implementatie Model Ontmoetingscentra; een Onderzoek naar de Voorwaarden voor Succesvolle Landelijke Implementatie van Ontmoetingscentra voor Mensen met Dementie en hun Verzorgers [*Implementation Model of MCs; a Study into the Conditions of Successful Nationwide Implementation of MCs for People with Dementia and their Carers*]. Amsterdam: Department of Psychiatry, VU Medical Centre.

Dröes, R.M., Meiland, F.J.M., Schmitz, M.J., Boerema, I., Derksen, E., de Lange, J., Vernooij-Dassen, M.J.F.J. and van Tilburg, W. (2004a) Variations in meeting centers for people with dementia and their carers: results of a multi-centre implementatie study. *Archives of Geriatrics and Gerontology Supplement*, **9**: 127–148.

Dröes, R.M., Meiland, F.J.M., Schmitz, M. and van Tilburg, W. (2004b) Effect of combined support for people with dementia and carers versus regular day care on behaviour and mood of persons with dementia: results from a multi-centre implementation study. *International Journal of Geriatric Psychiatry*, **19**: 1–12.

Finnema, E., Dröes, R.M, Ribbe, M. and van Tilburg, W. (2000) A review of psychosocial models in psychogeriatrics; implications for care and research. *Alzheimer Disease and Associated Disorders*, **14**: 68–80.

Grol, R. (1997) Beliefs and evidence in changing clinical practice. *British Medical Journal*, **315**: 418–421.

Grol, R. and Grimshaw, J. (1999) Evidence-based implementation of evidence based medicine. *Joint Community Journal of Quality Improvement*, **25**: 503–513.

Grol, R. and Wensing, M. (2001) *Implementatie: Effectieve Verandering in de Patiëntenzorg* [*Implementation: Effective Change in Patient Care*]. Maarssen: Elsevier Gezondheidszorg.

Grol, R. and Grimshaw, J. (2003) From best evidence to best practice: effective implementation of change in patients' care. *Lancet*, **362**: 1225–1230.

Hulscher, M., Wensing, M. and Grol, R. (2000) *Effectieve Implementatie: Theorieën en Strategieën* [*Effective Implementation: Theories and Strategies*]. Den Haag: ZON.

Kramer, B.J. and Vitaliano, P.P. (1994) Coping: a review of the theoretical frameworks and the measures used among caregivers of individuals with dementia. *Journal of Gerontological Social Work*, **23**: 151–174.

Lazarus, R.S. and Folkman, S. (1984) *Stress, Appraisal, and Coping*. New York: Springer.

Linden, B.A. van der and Schrijvers, A.J.P. (1998) Het implementeren van transmurale zorg: theorie en praktijk [Implementation of transmural care: theory and practice]. In *Handboek Thuiszorg*, G1.1.1–G1.32 [Guide Home Care]. Utrecht: De Tijdstroom.

Lyketsos, C.G. and Olin, J. (2002) Depression in Azheimer's disease: overview and treatment. *Biological Psychiatry*, **52**: 243–252.

Meiland, F.J.M., Dröes, R.M., de Lange, J. and Vernooij-Dassen, M.J.F.J. (2004) Development of a theoretical model for tracing facilitators and barriers in adaptive implementation of innovative practices in dementia care. *Archives of Geriatrics and Gerontology Supplement*, **9**: 279–290.

Merriam, A.E., Aronson, M.K., Gaston, P., Wey, S.L. and Katz, I. (1988) The psychiatric symptoms of Alzheimer's disease. *Journal of the American Geriatrics Society*, **36**: 7–12.

Miesen, B. and Jones, G. (2004) Alzheimer Café concept; a response to the trauma, drama and tragedy of dementia. In B.M.L. Miesen and G.M.M. Jones (Eds), *Caregiving in Dementia*, vol. 3. Hove: Brunner-Routledge, pp. 307–333.

Moos, R.H. and Tsu, V.D. (1977) The crisis of physical illness: an overview. In R.H. Moos (Ed.), *Coping with Physical Illness*. New York: Plenum Medical Book Company, pp. 3–21.

Mur-Veeman I., van Raak, A. and Maarse, H. (1994) Dutch home care: towards a new organization? *Health Policy*, **27**: 151–156.

Muskens, J.B. (1993) Het beloop van dementie; een exploratief longitudinaal onderzoek in de huisartsenpraktijk [The course of dementia; an explorative longitudinal study in the practice of the general practitioner]. Academic Dissertation, Katholieke Universiteit Nijmegen.

NHS Centre for Reviews and Dissemination (1999) Getting evidence into practice. *Effective Health Care*, **5**: 1–16.

Nies, H. (1994) *Innovatie in de ouderenzorg. Een methodische leidraad tot zorgvernieuwing [Innovation in the Field of Care for the Elderly. A Systematic Guideline to Care Innovations]*. Houten/Zaventem: Bohn, Stafleu Van Lochum.

Poppelaars, F.A., van der Wal, G., Braspenning, J.C., Cornel, M.C., Henneman, L., Langendam, M.W. and ten Kate, L.P. (2003) Possibilities and barriers in the implementation of a preconceptional screening programme for cystic fibrosis carriers: a focus group study. *Public Health*, **117**: 396–403.

Pot, A. (1996) Caregivers' perspectives. A longitudinal study on the psychological distress of informal caregivers of demented elderly. Academic Dissertation, Vrije Universiteit, Amsterdam.

Reisberg, B., Ferris, S.H., de Leon, M.J. and Crook, T. (1982) The Global Deterioration Scale for assessment of primary degenerative dementia. *American Journal of Psychiatry*, **139**: 1136–1139.

Reisberg, B., Borenstein, J., Salob, S.P., Ferris, S.H., Franssen, E. and Georgotas, A. (1987) Behavioural symptoms in Alzheimer's disease: phenomenology and treatment. *Journal of Clinical Psychiatry*, **48**: 9–15.

Steele, C., Rovner, B., Chase, G.A. and Folstein, M. (1990) Psychiatric symptoms and nursing home placement of patients with Alzheimer's disease. *American Journal of Psychiatry*, **147**: 1049–1051.

Teri, L., Larson, E.B. and Reifler, B.V. (1988) Behavioral disturbance in dementia of the Alzheimer type. *Journal of the American Geriatric Society*, **36**: 1–6.

Vernooij-Dassen, M.J.F.J. (1993) *Dementie en Thuiszorg: een Onderzoek naar Determinanten van het Competentie Gevoel van Centrale Verzorgers en het Effect van Professionele Interventie [Dementia and Home Care: a Study into the Determinants of the Sense of Competence of Central Carers and the Effect of Professional Intervention]* (in Dutch), Academic Dissertation. Amsterdam: Swets & Zeitlinger.

Verstraten, P.F.J. and van Eekelen, C.W.J.M. (1987) *Handleiding voor de GIP; Gedragsobservatieschaal voor de Intramurale Psychogeriatrie [Manual for the BIP; Behaviour Observation Scale for Intramural Psychogeriatrics]* (in Dutch). Deventer:Van Loghum Slaterus.

Wensing, M., van der Weijden, T. and Grol, R. (1998) Implementing guidelines and innovations in general practice: which interventions are effective? *British Journal of General Practice*, **48**: 991–997.

Wilkinson, E.K., Bosanquet, A., Salisbury, C., Hasler, J. and Bosanquet, N. (1999) Barriers and facilitators to the implementation of evidence-based medicine in general practice: a qualitative study. *European Journal of General Practice*, **5**: 66–70.

Wind, A.W., Muskens, J.B., de Bruyne, G.A., Meyboom-de Jong, B., Veltman, M.T.M., Weijtens, J.T.N.M. and Burgers, J.S. (1998) *NHG-Standaard M21 Dementie*. Utrecht: Nederlands Huisartsen Genootschap.

Wulp, J.C. van der (1986) *Verstoring en Verwerking in Verpleeghuizen [Disruption and Coping in Nursing Homes]* (in Dutch). Nijkerk: Uitg. Intro.

Zarit, S.H., Gaugler, J.E., and Jarrot, S.E. (1999) Useful services for families: research findings and directions. *International Journal of Geriatric Psychiatry*, **14**: 165–181.

Chapter 14

Couples group (psycho)therapy (CGT) in dementia

Bère Miesen

Introduction

Once it becomes evident that one partner in a couple has dementia, it is known that emotional isolation lies ahead, not to mention a range of practical problems. This risk of emotional separation applies not only to the couple with respect to their social environment, but also to the individual partners with respect to each other. In the same way as visiting the Alzheimer Café *together*, attending group (psycho)therapy *together* has the aim of preventing this emotional isolation or at least delaying it for as long as possible.

It has now become common practice to counsel *spouses* of people with dementia in a group setting. Research has shown that both partners benefit from this type of intervention in a variety of ways, at least for a while. Although group (psycho)therapy for the actual *person with dementia* is on the increase (especially in connection with grieving/bereavement counselling processes), clinical experience of 'group therapy for couples' [couples group (psycho)therapy, CGT] is still in its infancy, particularly any research into its effects.

This chapter offers a description of this type of CGT intervention, illustrated with expectations and subjective evaluations given by people with dementia and their spouses. Data are also presented from exploratory research (Huybrechtse and Kouwenhoven, 2000) based on two groups (of four couples each) over 1 year of intervention. When reviewing the data, Bowlby's Attachment Theory was found to clarify some of the results. Securely attached individuals (whether the person with dementia or their partner) appeared to benefit from this type of intervention more than insecurely attached individuals (Krouwer, 2001).

This chapter introduces CGT not only as a supplement to current interventions in the field of dementia but also as a relatively new and useful intervention for couples where one of the partners has dementia. The 'heart' of this type of intervention focuses on the problem of denial and avoidance in the couple's fight against their loss of control and security.

Background: the link between the Alzheimer Café and CGT

One of the objectives of the Alzheimer Café (AC) is 'to speak openly about the feelings behind living through the trauma, drama and tragedy of dementia. (. . .) The AC is intended to offer persons a safe place, where they express themselves and can be listened to, thus finding some comfort in their struggle of isolation and loneliness; at least for a while' (Miesen & Jones, 2004, p. 308). The AC can be described as a psychosocial intervention or approach, combining aspects of psycho-education (about the emotional processes involved in having and caring for someone with dementia) and psychotherapy (the chance to talk about, and hear voiced, discussions on the emotional responses to having dementia and caring for someone with dementia) in a low-threshold (all inclusive) social context: a Café-like situation. It is relaxed and informal, and people can always find a willing ear to listen to their story. They can also hear about other people's stories and come and go as they please. By its very nature and form, the AC symbolizes a secure base as well as a safe haven. The AC system embodies an important concept in attachment theory, i.e. that people (including people with dementia) (may) have to feel secure in order to (dare to) actually explore themselves and their life situation (see Box 14.1). After all, without security, there is fear (see also Chapter 3, p. 108).

The CGT described in this chapter is an intervention based on virtually the same ideas and approach as the AC. 'The underlying assumption is that once the illness can be named and discussed in the presence of all affected, some of the denial, secrecy and pain surrounding it lessens' (Miesen and Jones, 2004, p. 308).

Literature

In general

Research into the effects of group psychotherapy for *family members* of people with dementia on the actual members of the group is far from recent (Haley, 1983; Jones and Miesen, 1992; Cuijpers et al, 1997). The popularity of this form of help and support has spread rapidly since the end of the 1970s. It has three main objectives: to increase people's mental well-being, to improve the care that the family carers give to the person with dementia and to delay or prevent the person with dementia having to be admitted to a care facility. It is true that more attention needs to be given to examining whether delaying or preventing admission is by definition a positive or favourable objective. However, evaluations are generally positive from the members of the group, who find other positive effects on the quality of life and well-being of the family and person with dementia, as well as on the quality of how they

Box 14.1 History of the Alzheimer Café and the concepts of diagnosis disclosure and breaking through denial and secrecy

The idea of the Alzheimer Café became a reality in 1997 in a lecture room at Leiden University, The Netherlands, running in parallel as it were to recent work exploring the issue of 'closure or disclosure of the diagnosis'. Although Bamford et al (2004, p. 151) conclude that studies of the impact of disclosure indicate both negative and positive consequences of diagnostic disclosure for people with dementia and their carers, in The Netherlands in clinical practice, certainly by the beginning of the 21st century, there is general agreement about the issue of disclosing diagnosis: 'Make sure the diagnosis is clearly presented and explained as soon as possible. Try and waste as little time as possible in denial and avoidance. This is the only way of developing a perspective of the disease for the long term, with the support of others.'

In other words, the general Dutch 'response' is: 'disclosure, unless there is a very good reason not to'.

In this respect, Bowlby's Attachment Theory also plays a major and guiding role (Bowlby, 1969, 1973, 1980) as a framework for explaining what happens during this type of intervention (see also Chapter 3). The CGT in dementia described in this chapter is an intervention based on virtually the same ideas and approach as the AC. 'The underlying assumption is that once the illness can be named and discussed in the presence of all affected, some of the denial, secrecy and pain surrounding it lessens' (Miesen and Jones, 2004, p. 308).

interact (Marriott et al, 2000), albeit for a limited period of time. Other positive effects of group psychotherapy include aspects such as improved morale and a greater knowledge of dementia.

Research into the effects of group psychotherapy for *people with dementia* on themselves dates back to the early 1990s and is still at an early stage, 'although psychotherapeutic work with older people with a cognitive impairment has been described since the early 1950s' (see Chapter 10). The results are nevertheless promising, especially in terms of coping positively with their illness (Snyder et al, 1995; Mapes, 2004): an increase in solidarity, knowledge and openness, as well as a means of relaxing and being able to share feelings and experiences (Huybrechtse and Kouwenhoven, 2000, pp. 29–30). Since the early 1970s in The Netherlands it has been part of the daily work of psychogerontologists to give people with dementia support and assistance in dealing with the disease from a psychodynamic perspective, especially in their clinical work, on a one-to-one level as well as in group sessions (Miesen, 2004).

In this context (i.e. effects on the people with dementia), Huybrechtse and Kouwenhoven (2000, p. 30) explicitly state that: 'the experience of Snyder and colleagues shows that a "mixed" group enables the person and healthy partner to discuss key issues and take decisions together. Apart from having the opportunity to discuss their own problems in separate sessions and get things off their chest, it is also important to have the option of attending group therapy sessions, so that communication between person with dementia and partner can be enhanced and the distress shared.' This is also the author's (clinical) experience as a group therapist and (discussion) leader of a large number of Alzheimer Café meetings (Miesen, 2002). It is therefore interesting that a literature search (as of 2004: Ovid MEDLINE®; APA ONLINE; PsychLit) into group psychotherapy (including *couples* in which one of the partners has dementia) produces only one research project (Haupt et al, 2000).

Specific

Haupt et al (2000) refer to research into the effects of an open, uncontrolled group therapy approach in 32 families (eight groups of four 'couples' or pairs), i.e. people with dementia and their family carers. The people with dementia had an average age of 72 and a moderate level of dementia: a Mini Mental State Examination (MMSE) score of 15 on average (Folstein et al, 1975); the majority of them were married (72%). Approximately 50% were female and had had dementia for at least 2 years. The average age of family members was 61, nearly three-quarters of them were female and approximately 90% of them were married. Thus, although it is clear that the groups were not made up entirely of couples, it is not known exactly how many couples there were.

The group therapy (intervention) involved weekly sessions over a 5-month period. Each session devoted a certain amount of time to performing motor exercises, sensory and cognitive activities and relaxation exercises. Each participant was able to put forward their own topics for discussion relating to their social environment, keeping the person with dementia at home and their personal experiences. Problems in dealing with dementia were approached interactively in the group by making people aware of the residual skills of the person with dementia. The family was also given the opportunity to discuss various issues, if necessary *apart from the group*. A group session was organized once a month for family members only, to discuss 'important problematic everyday situations' *without the person with dementia* being present.

Apart from stability in the behaviour, mood and activities of daily living (ADL) functions of the person with dementia, the results demonstrate 'a significant improvement of communication abilities among the patients and a significant reduction of coping problems and of care burden with respect to the caregivers'. According to the researchers, the stability referred to above is particularly noticeable because this phase of dementia usually entails a (rapid and significant) decline if there is no intervention. They explain the improvement in communication between the pairs during the weekly sessions as being a result of stimulating brain reserve capacity.

Although the researchers are aware of the methodical restrictions in their research, they conclude that this type of intervention seems to reflect the generally positive effects of group work with the family as well as (coping) groups for people with dementia. Their group therapy approach reinforces the family's mutual relationships and their ability to withstand the burden, which in turn means that the person with dementia can generally remain in their familiar environment (home) for longer. Finally, they conclude that systematic support of the person with dementia, as well as their family, throughout the course of the disease forms a necessary component of the overall treatment for dementia. 'In addition to medication, all necessary measures must be taken in future to ensure that people with dementia are also given psychotherapeutic support and that their partners and families are competently given information and advice on resolving problems in everyday care' (Haupt et al, 2000, p. 514).

Apart from the value of the content of the above statement, the way it is worded suggests an approach similar to the Dutch Meeting Centres investigated by Dröes (see Chapter 13) rather than what is meant here by CGT. Furthermore, the results in terms of the person with dementia are explained from a more 'organic perspective', whereas the results of our research (see below) are explained from a 'psychodynamic perspective'. In our opinion, it is the openness, i.e. the avoidance of denial, that instigates the process of actually coping with the illness. The feeling of security that this creates stimulates the person with dementia in particular to positively explore their situation and illness.

Couples group (psycho)therapy in dementia

Definition of the intervention

The intervention is aimed in particular at the coping ability of the person with dementia and their partner through meetings attended by both partners together. The primary focus is placed on counselling. Where necessary, psycho-education is also provided. During the meetings, couples are given the opportunity to share various (personal) experiences on a practical as well as emotional level. The mutual giving and taking of support and understanding forms a fifth aspect of the group phenomenon (see also Yalom, 1975, 1980; Cheston, 1998).

Each meeting starts off with a catching-up session, when each couple is given a chance briefly to say how things have been going for them. A topic always emerges from this, which is important or typical for most couples. At the end of each meeting, everyone is given the opportunity to briefly sum up the discussion and/or say what they thought of the meeting. Table 14.1 gives an overview of intervention topics, divided into counselling, psycho-education, sharing tips and support.

Hypothesis

It has been shown and argued elsewhere (e.g. Miesen, 2004) that the dementia illness has a considerable impact on the person with dementia as well as their partner. Both spouses are confronted with a drastic and shocking event that becomes chronic in the long term. We have called this a 'Type III Trauma' (Miesen and Jones, 2004, p. 311). The dementia illness creates a situation of increasing isolation for both partners: a situation of (double) separation.

Table 14.1 Overview of general topics: one year of couple (group) psychotherapy

Counselling	Psycho-education	Sharing tips	Support
	Medication	Experiences with medication	
Dealing with the outside world	Learning to understand and accept the illness	Dealing with a lack of support from the outside world	Support and understanding
Being open about the illness	Self-care	Practical solutions	Sexuality and intimacy
Taking responsibility			
Planning activities for the day at home		Experiences with planning activities for the day	
Day care	Day care		Day care
Dealing with aggression	Aggression		Perceived feelings
Fear of the future	The future		Expectations and desires
Death of the person with dementia			Between hope and despair
Communication problems	Ways of communicating	Disappointment and expectations in contact	

This is extremely stressful (e.g. Pot, 2004). Couples group (psycho)therapy is expected to have a positive effect on the ability of both 'parties' to deal with this painful situation. The research referred to examines the extent to which there is a correlation between attachment and the (ways of) coping adopted by the partner of a person with dementia. In concrete terms, it is assumed that (having) a secure attachment leads to a more effective ability to cope than another (insecure) attachment (Clulow, 2001).

Method

At the end of the 1990s, research was carried out into the effect of specific 'couples counselling' as a psychosocial intervention in several groups, each made up of four couples (Huybrechtse and Kouwenhoven, 2000; Krouwer, 2001). There was no logic or argument behind the 'choice' of having both male and female groups; this just happened by chance and spontaneously. Analyses were carried out on two groups who met in the course of 1998/1999. The meetings took place once a month over a period of 10 months, and lasted for 2 h (i.e. participants arrive, 3/4 h, break, 3/4 h, participants leave). Measurements were taken before and after the series of meetings. A control group was not available. Comments and interactions were noted down by two psychology students: per individual, per couple and a general impression per session (see Boxes 14.2 and 14.3). The meetings were led by the author.

Box 14.2 Example of a meeting for couples in which the husband has dementia

---

In this meeting, men and women are split up and seated opposite each other. The session kicks off with the chance to 'catch up': some are doing better than others. Many enjoy getting together again. It is fun and enjoyable. You can forget about your troubles and worries for a while. It is interesting that today a lot of compliments and tips are exchanged. They seem to be bolstering each other. A few men go to the same day care unit; they spend a lot of time with each other there as well.

The women in particular say that they are getting better at dealing with their husbands' dementia. They find it easier to accept their behaviour than they used to: 'We've learned to put aside our fears and anxieties a bit more'. Which means there are fewer arguments and conflicts. The women are aware that they have to allow more time for themselves. They are not so worried that their husbands will not be able to manage on their own without them being there. They now go out more. Their husbands do not like this: 'These few hours feel like an eternity'.

Discussion then moves on to the reactions of other people. People often ask the women: 'How is your husband?' or 'Has your husband got dementia? You wouldn't know it, would you!' This just tends to wind them up. Mrs James' husband actually thinks it is quite nice: 'At least it means I'm treated like a normal person'.

With people around you realizing what is going on, fewer contacts are lost than expected. 'But you have to keep working at it', believe Mr Lawson and Mr Forrester. Mr Forrester explains how he always tries to help compatriots in distress at day care who find it difficult to express themselves. This earns him a spontaneous round of applause. Mrs Forrester is visibly moved. 'I'm happy to see this side of my husband again. At the moment he only makes jokes about his illness. It's difficult to get him to ever talk seriously about it.'

They then speak about their experiences with their family doctors who lack expertise or understanding or who seem indifferent. It makes them really angry and most also feel hurt by it. It upsets Mrs James in particular. Mr Lawson is the first to point out that it also makes them more responsible for their own lives. Especially with dementia, you have to stand up for yourself and ask everything you want to know. 'Before you simply accepted everything a doctor or pastor said to you, because you looked up to these people.' But it is now becoming clear that these people are just ordinary human beings who do not (and cannot) know everything; especially not in the field of dementia. 'I've since given my doctor all the information he needed', says Mrs James.

Mrs Lawson remarks that her husband is far more active at the day care unit than at home. Other women have noticed this too. 'Perhaps it's because they're all equals there. If they do something wrong there, it's not commented on as much as it is at home. It's also perhaps easier to accept criticism from strangers rather than from your partner.'

Results of the eight people with dementia

General criteria

Average age 65.5 (sd 5.8); average age of group with four men 63.8 (2.8) and average age of group with four women 67.3 (7.9). Most were educated to intermediate or lower vocational education level; three were educated to degree level. Most had senile dementia of the Alzheimer type and two had multi-infarct dementia.

Box 14.3 Example of a meeting for couples in which the wife has dementia

At this meeting, the spouses spontaneously go and sit opposite each other, the men on one side and women on the other. This means that the men speak to each other more – which is what the wives do as well – so in a way they are two individuals rather than a couple.

The discussion starts with what has happened over the last month. Mrs Mcdonald's day care unit moved from Leiden to Warmond. Mrs Green was already there. Both women find it pleasant and enjoyable. Day care means that their partners have more time to themselves and that the situation at home is slightly more balanced. For the two other couples, little had changed. Both husbands wonder whether their wives (both just 60) are perhaps too young for a day care setting. They are reassured when they hear that 'the more intensively people interact with each other, the less age plays a (negative) role'.

People ask each other how they should plan activities for the day to make things enjoyable for the person with dementia. This is not so difficult for the husbands, but the wives tend to be bored. Several husbands say that they have to go out at least once a day, either to go shopping or to visit friends and children. This breaks the day up. They also find it good to do household chores together as far as possible. They can then sit down together and listen to music or dance. 'At any rate, we need to use and try and build on the things we both find fun.'

'Nowadays, the atmosphere at home is far more affected by our mood than it used to be', find the husbands. If they are really happy, this automatically makes their wives happy. The same can be said if they are feeling in a bad mood. The wife used not to be so affected by what mood her husband was in, but now the way the husband feels has a direct impact on the atmosphere at home, they find. If there is a quarrel or confrontation, it takes much longer than before to patch things up or clear the atmosphere. The husbands find it particularly difficult not to lose patience. This happens often and the wives take it very badly 'because they themselves can't do much to change the situation'. Luckily for most of them, the following saying still applies: 'The best thing about arguing is making up'.

Feelings of love and tenderness have also changed somewhat between the husbands and their wives with dementia. For some, the love is stronger because the dementia has made them more closely involved with each other. For others, the love has changed into affinity and compassion.

Level of cognitive functioning

Values are means (and ranges), with no levels of significance given because the number of people was too small:

	Pre-measurement	Post-measurement
Nine words test/recall	1.8 (0–5)	3.1 (0–8)
MMSE[a]	20 (12–29)	22.5 (8–30)
Raven's CPM(A)[b]	10 (4–12)	10 (3–12)
Seven objects test/recall	2.6 (0–6)	3.5 (1–7)
Word fluency	8 (0–13)	8.8 (1–15)

[a] Mini Mental State Examination (Folstein et al, 1975).
[b] Coloured Progressive Matrices (Part A) (Raven et al, 1977).

In general the scores are 'bad' compared with people of the same age who do not have dementia, but over half of the people with dementia either kept the same score or managed to improve them.

Background variables

Based on the Intimate Bond Measure (Wilhelm and Parker, 1988), a self-report measure assessing underlying intimate relationships in terms of 'care' and 'control', it is possible to conclude that both the men and women express care emotionally and physically, but that, in comparison with the women, the men found the behaviour of their healthy partners to be more dominant, more critical and more authoritative (Huybrechtse and Kouwenhoven, 2000, p. 60).

The NEO-FFI, a short-form personality instrument in Dutch based on the NEO tests (Costa and McCrae, 1985), which are self-report measures assessing individual personality based on the 'Big Five' factors, revealed that the men behaved more extrovertly, assertively, actively and optimistically than the women, who preferred to be on their own or did not feel comfortable in company (Costa and McCrae, 1985, p. 61).

Coping variables

Values are means (and standard deviations), with no levels of significance given because the number of people was too small:

	Pre-measurement	Post-measurement
Impact of Event Scale[a]		
Intrusion	15 (4.9)	14.8 (5.7)
Denial/avoidance	15.9 (8.9)	11.3 (6.4)
Total	33.3 (11.7)	27.9 (8.9)
Self Esteem Scale	22.1 (3.4)	22.4 (5)
Mood	13.1 (3.1)	9.9 (5)

[a] A Dutch translation of the Impact of Event Scale was used: the SVL (Schok Verwerkings Lijst); see Kleber and Brom (1992).

In general, the coping response scores have gone down but the post-measurement total shows that they are still considered as 'serious' (> 26). The intrusion of the (diagnosis of) dementia is just as strong as it was at the start, whereas denial/avoidance has decreased (Horowitz et al, 1979). As far as self-esteem is concerned, there seems to have been little or no change (Self Esteem Scale: Rosenberg, 1989). In terms of mood, the results show that the (small) degree of depression has disappeared (Brink et al, 1982).

Results of the eight partners

General criteria

The average age of the partners (four men and four women) was 64.1 (sd 3.8). There is a wide range of education, varying from secondary school to university education. Five out of the eight partners are educated to lower or intermediate vocational level.

Background variables

From the Intimate Bond Measure, it can be concluded that the men express care emotionally and physically better than the women, but compared to their female companions in distress they act more dominantly, critically and authoritatively (Huybrechtse and Kouwenhoven, 2000, p. 49).

The NEO-FFI reveals that the men behaved more conscientiously, persistently, ambitiously and with greater focus than the women (Huybrechtse and Kouwenhoven, p. 49).

Coping variables

Values are means (and standard deviations), with no levels of significance given because the number of people was too small:

	Pre-measurements	Post-measurement
Impact of Event Scale[a]		
Intrusion	8.9 (7.6)	10.6 (6.9)
Denial/avoidance	5.4 (5.0)	9.5 (6.7)
Total	14.3 (11.7)	20.1 (12.2)
Self Esteem Scale	18.3 (1.9)	15.8 (1.9)
Mood	7.8 (5.7)	6.5 (4)

[a] A Dutch translation of the Impact of Event Scale was used: the SVL (Schok Verwerkings Lijst); see Kleber and Brom (1992).

In general the coping response scores have gone up, although the final level cannot be classified as 'serious' (total > 26). The intrusion of the (diagnosis of) dementia also increased, as did denial/avoidance. Self-esteem went down. As far as mood is concerned, the small degree of depression remains almost at the same level.

By comparing the pre- and post-measurements using the Utrecht Coping List (Schreurs et al, 1984), the SCL-90 symptom checklist (Arrindel and Ettema, 1986) and the Sense of Competence Questionnaire (Vernooij-Dassen, 1993), it was possible to conclude that they felt less positive towards the care that the person with dementia showed them and that they felt less able to care for them. Although this did not seem to have led to an increase in (existing) symptoms, a decrease in self-esteem was apparent.

Interpretation and practical relevance

The (first) study (Huybrechtse and Kouwenhoven, 2000) generally shows that the coping ability, measured objectively, of the *(healthy) partners* had not undergone significant change. However, the coping ability of the *people with dementia* did seem to have changed (for the better). In the subjective evaluation of the intervention (based on all the individual cases), *all* spouses – people with dementia and their partners – clearly showed that their ability to cope with dementia had improved.

General expectations before

All participants shared the hope of gaining a better understanding of the disease of dementia and accepting it. They wanted to find out about other people's experiences.

The (healthy) partners primarily hoped to find support in this difficult situation in their lives. They want to know how best to deal with their partner, the person with dementia. They also wanted to be able to support their partner in such a way that they would continue to get along well, i.e.

preventing or delaying any emotional isolation towards each other. Above all, they wanted to improve communication with their partners and maintain this communication for as long as possible. They find it particularly hard that they increasingly have to take decisions on their own. They also were finding it difficult to speak to outsiders about the illness, and did not want to burden their children with it (to any great extent). There were mixed feelings and scepticism among the husbands in particular. They found the fact that their 'partners with dementia' always wanted to have them around particularly hard to deal with. They also found it hard seeing their partners and not knowing how to deal with their fear and powerlessness. They were really concerned about their loss of freedom and social contact, because they were forced to spend more time than before with each other (social isolation). The sharp increase in household chores and having to assess the risk of a particular action or situation are also sources of concern, especially if their partner with dementia gets angry if they are forbidden or stopped from doing certain tasks.

The partners with dementia are apparently pleased to observe (in due course) that they are not the 'only' ones with Alzheimer's disease and that they will get the opportunity to speak with 'companions in distress'. Most couples together give vent to their worries that they may lose each other through the consequences of the disease.

General evaluation after

The meetings were felt to be supportive. Everyone knows exactly what is going on in each other's lives. They find that their feelings of sorrow, anger, powerlessness, etc. are understood, and 'you can be yourself, and you don't have to deal with it all on your own'. The main thing people have learned is how *not* to deal with their partner (for instance, learning not to always correct their mistakes). This gives strength; it is easier to deal with them and you learn to accept the situation. There is a strong desire to stay in contact with each other; people want the group to stay together forever, as it were.

All (healthy) partners observe that they feel very satisfied and involved, and believe they have benefited from all the information. Social contact has increased or improved. They find that communication has significantly improved not just with the person with dementia but also with their (social) environment. Although they still find actual contact with the person with dementia difficult, they have learned different ways of communicating. They are also pleased to have learned how to speak to others about the situation more easily. This provides some form of relief and stops them feeling so embarrassed. It is easier for them to ask for more help. They find it easier to accept (the deficits of) the person with dementia because the process of dealing with them is running more smoothly. They no longer have the feeling that they are 'on their own', in that they now know all about each other's feelings of sorrow, anger and frustration. This provides comfort and support for everyone. Sharing practical tips was also found to be useful. Last but not least, all spouses found that their partners with dementia were able to express their feelings more effectively, especially at the meetings.

The people with dementia particularly appreciate the companionship with each other. The main thing they have learned is how to speak to their partner as well as to other people about their problems and worries. Because they were together with people in the same situation, they felt it easier to get things off their chest.

Attachment

Because the results suggested that attachment could affect coping, a second study was carried out (Krouwer, 2001) to extend the (analysis of the) sample survey to a group of six couples. Attachment was measured among other things using a self-assessment questionnaire known as the Relationship Questionnaire (see Bartholomew and Horowitz, 1991). The clear conclusion from the results was that the coping ability of the *(healthy) partners* was less affected by the burden on themselves due to the dementia of their partners (the consequences of the disease of dementia) than by their attachment, and the same applies for the ability of the *person with dementia* to cope with their own dementia. Insecurely attached people (whether the person with dementia or their partner) are more bothered by coping problems than securely attached people (Krouwer, 2001, p. 79). In other words, the 'suffering' or burden felt by individuals with a secure attachment is less than those with an insecure attachment.

In practical CGT in dementia, consideration should be given to at least two sorts of couples in terms of (in)secure attachments. This has been highlighted previously by Clulow (2001), who recently edited *Adult Attachment and Couple Psychotherapy*. This book 'looks at what is meant by (in)secure couple attachment, describes how theory and research have been applied to practice (and how practice has added to understand the complex problems that couples bring to therapy)' – for example, following on from the death of their own child (as a stressor) – 'and examines the significance of training and the organization of work for effective practice with couples'. In parallel to Bowlby's work on (in)secure individual attachment, Clulow examines (in)secure couple attachment. And just as it is possible to describe three distinct patterns of insecure individual attachment, it is also possible to distinguish three patterns of insecure couple attachment. This chapter will only focus on the distinction between secure and insecure individual attachment.

When dementia is involved (as a stressor), the effect of CGT differs for the two types of couple because they have a different starting point (basis). On the one hand, there is someone with a secure attachment partnered with a person with dementia who has an insecure attachment. On the other hand, there is someone with an insecure attachment, partnered with a person with dementia who has a secure attachment. The aim of the therapy for partners with a secure attachment could be to learn a certain degree of avoidance, while just the opposite could apply for partners with an insecure attachment, i.e. they could learn how to stop avoiding so strongly. The effect on the person with dementia is that, in both cases, there is more scope for learning how to deal with the disease in their own way, because if a person with an insecure attachment learns to be less 'egocentric' they can devote more essential attention to what the person with dementia is experiencing and going through. If partners with a secure attachment learn to function a bit more 'egocentrically' (thus giving the person with dementia more 'room to breathe'), then it will become more apparent or obvious to them what this person is actually experiencing and going through. In this way, the person with dementia gets more 'impartial' attention, i.e. attention involving less counter-transference. An insecurely attached partner learns to listen out more for the people with dementia rather than themselves, and vice versa with a securely attached partner (i.e. they learn to listen out for themselves more rather than the person with dementia). If couples (group) psychotherapy is generally divided into psychotherapeutic and psycho-educational elements, partners with a secure attachment benefit most from the psycho-educational elements and partners with an insecure attachment benefit most from the psychotherapeutic elements.

Comparable results are revealed in recent research (Van Wunnik, 2004) into the relationship between the attachment of partners ($n = 28$) and their perceived usefulness of visiting the AC based on a sample survey of 70 ACs running at the beginning of 2004 in The Netherlands. Just as in Krouwer's research (2001), Van Wunnik used the Dutch translation of the Relationship Questionnaire (Bartholomew and Horowitz, 1991), translated by Kakoyannis, Miesen and Jones (see De Groot and Kakoyannis, 2001), to measure their attachment. The perceived usefulness of visiting the AC for partners was primarily found to be contact with people in the same situation and psycho-education. Partners with a secure attachment found contact with people in the same situation the most important thing, with the emphasis being on conviviality, whereas partners with an insecure attachment attached equal importance to psycho-education and contact with people in the same situation, with the emphasis being on supporting these people.

The most striking thing about this research carried out on people who regularly visit the AC with their partners who have dementia is the relatively large number of partners with an insecure attachment, i.e. 65%. In normal populations, this figure is usually only one-third (compared to two-thirds of individuals with a secure attachment) (see Cowan and Cowan, 2001, p. 67). According to Van Wunnik (2004), partners with an insecure attachment could well prefer the anonymity of the context of AC (40–100 visitors each session) to the openness of a CGT setting (8–12 persons each session). In either case, it is important for counsellors to realize in advance that insecurely attached people are generally more vulnerable in dealing with a shocking event and this makes them eager to seek support among people going through the same thing without the emphasis necessarily being on conviviality. In other words, a more neutral environment in which partners with an insecure attachment (at the beginning at least) are able and allowed to maintain their 'distance' and are not 'crowded' by the professional care-giver right from the start is perhaps a particularly favourable climate for them to explore and make a start on coping with their situation.

Case histories

We mentioned earlier that when all spouses (people with dementia and their partners) gave their subjective evaluation of the intervention (based on all individual cases) they clearly stated that their ability to cope with dementia had improved. The reason behind this improvement possibly lay in the heterogeneity of the individual expectations, so these expectations needed to be examined in more detail.

Individual expectations before

Mr *McDonald* wants to be able to talk to his wife more easily about her disease. *His wife* denies that she has got Alzheimer's disease, and certainly does not want to talk about it. 'I've come with my husband for the company.'

Mr *Farmer* wants to find out how he can best support his wife. *His wife* finds that it is hard for her to express herself, that she is not able to manage housework and that she gets bored.

Mr *Green* finds it really difficult to accept his wife's illness. He says he does not understand anything about it. *His wife* finds it difficult that her social contact is getting more limited and thinks that they spend too much time with each other.

Mr *Sparrow* finds it difficult to deal with his wife's illness without getting angry. He wants to learn how to stop doing this. He wants to have more time to himself. *His wife* knows that she has dementia. It is hard for her to remain optimistic. 'I know what's in store for me, as my mother also had dementia.'

Openness is important for Mr and Mrs *Lawson*. Both say what is on their minds and speak plainly. They find that they do not need to be embarrassed because everyone understands what is going on. Mrs *Lawson* does not have any particular expectations. She comes to these meetings 'for him'. *Her husband* finds that he does not always manage to deal with his illness very well, because it all seems to be happening too quickly. 'Things that used to be no problem are now really difficult for me.'

Mrs *James* finds it difficult often having to hold her husband back or prohibit him from doing something, for instance driving the car. She also finds it hard when he flies into a rage. She is not sure to what extent she should be understanding and tolerant. *Her husband* does not expect a lot from the meetings, but he does hope that he will learn something from them. 'I've become like this because of surgery that went wrong. I just can't accept that.'

Mrs *Forrester* finds it difficult to see her husband declining, to see him sometimes really struggling with it and especially to know that nobody understands because it often does not look like anything is wrong with him. *Her husband* says there are many things that he cannot do. He finds it difficult to try to resolve these things together with his wife, because that entails a risk. 'It doesn't make it any easier. And I don't want to risk our love.'

Mrs *Lofters* has no difficulty in telling others. 'If they don't get it, that's their problem.' The main thing she wants to know is what to expect in the next few years. *Her husband* knows that he is getting forgetful. 'I find I'm not doing so well. If I can't do something or if I don't know something, I get angry.' His disease has created problems within the family and he finds that painful.

Individual evaluations after

Mr *McDonald* found the (first) year to be a year of 'learning': 'I learned how to talk and to listen. I learned to stop feeling embarrassed and reserved'. He looks forward to this fixed day in the month. 'It's not threatening. I can say what I want and everyone knows what I'm talking about.' According to Mr McDonald, *his wife* feels 'great in the group', and the added value for her is that she has stopped denying she has dementia. They have since been able to speak about it together. Mrs McDonald laughs a lot and pays compliments to the others.

Mr *Farmer* finds the most important thing is that he does not have to feel embarrassed in the group, and that there have never been any conflicts in the group despite the many different participants. 'I'm happy they didn't see us as pitiful, even though my wife's the worst one affected in the group.' *His wife* speaks more than she used to. She often responds directly and appropriately to members of the group with brief comments, even if they were not addressing her in particular.

Mr *Green* appreciated the new mutual friendships most, as he had lost many acquaintances due to his wife's illness, because he had had to give up many of his hobbies and also because she put people off with her (mistrustful/suspicious) behaviour. 'I feel better, in spite of the ups and downs. But I'm still worried when she goes out on her own.' *His wife* finds the most important thing is the actual people in the group: 'It's really fun and enjoyable seeing everyone again'. When she is in the group, she speaks calmly about her problems. 'And I now even dare to watch TV again. That wasn't possible before. I wanted to learn how to let go of my husband a bit more, so that he could spend a bit more time doing his own hobbies (playing tennis).'

Mr *Sparrow* appreciated the regularity and continuity of the meetings: 'I always really looked forward to them'. As soon as her husband speaks, *his wife* agrees with what he says. An example of their conversation:

WIFE:	I think you want to be cremated. But I'm not sure.
HUSBAND:	We've talked about that. That's what we both want.
WIFE:	That's good, but not for quite a few years yet.
HUSBAND:	If we didn't have support, we would've had a lot more problems. But I've never given euthanasia a second thought.
WIFE:	I always feel happy. I try not to think of the future. But sometimes I can't get away from it.
HUSBAND:	If you're having trouble dressing, and I have to help you, what do you say then?
WIFE:	Ugly words!
HUSBAND:	What do you think then?

While his wife is speaking about this, he says that he is sometimes at his wits' end. If he mentions in passing that he met Mr H, his wife responds: 'Did you? He's got what I've got'.

The main thing that Mrs *Lawson* has learned is how to control herself if her husband causes problems. 'I find it very hard when he wakes me up in the middle of the night. I usually get really angry. I now find it easier to control myself.' She feels that it is easier for her now to accept her husband's illness. 'I have to watch out that I don't go too far the other way and become too resigned and passive. I now accept he won't get better. And I know how it can affect my life. It boils down to the fact that people with dementia no longer have things they've got to do, because they simply can't do them. That's the consequence of the illness.' She also says that it annoys her when her husband speaks to other people about his illness more openly than with her. *Her husband* says that he has become less negative and rebellious. He has 'got an awful lot' out of the group. He sees the difficult things in the other people too and shows his sorrow more. 'I may be a bloke, but I no longer hide my tears. I feel I can be myself in this group. I find it easier to express myself.'

Mrs *James* indicates that her husband 'has now more or less accepted he's got this illness. I live my life now with more awareness. I focus a lot more energy than I used to on "the two of us".' She allows others to do things for her and finds it easier to accept the support she gets from various quarters. 'And it is now easy to talk to my husband about the disease and the situation we find ourselves in.' *Her husband* says he has got a lot of support from the group and finds it easier to express himself. 'I can still be a hothead. But I've learned to control myself a bit better.' His biggest problem is driving the car, which has always been his passion. 'I now only drive around where I live, I don't go further afield.' Instead of driving, he travels in the train and bus with his wife, for example to go and visit the children.

Mrs *Forrester* found the meetings particularly good 'because I got the feeling I wasn't alone'. And she finds that she can now get on better with her husband, although some problems still remain. 'My husband is often down and wanders around a lot especially at night.' She now takes more time to do her own things. At the same time 'we're trying to go out together as much as possible'. When describing her husband, she says: 'He's become calmer and often has more "lucid" moments'. Having said that, she thinks this is mainly due to him taking Exelon. *Her husband* perceives the group as 'positive'. When asked what he means by this exactly, he says: 'It works well, although I often feel lonely. I know I'm taking Exelon, because I'm calmer than I used to be.'

Mrs *Lofters* has learned a lot from the discussions, especially practical things: 'You hear about solutions other people have found'. She feels she is luckier than most because her husband is 'the best in the group'. 'I now see why he quickly "flies off the handle" and sometimes reacts nastily and angrily.' She is also aware of his powerlessness: 'Sometimes he gets furious with himself if something's not going the way he wants.' *Her husband* sometimes feels bad when he comes to the meetings. 'I hear so many things from the others that may also happen to me.' This makes him sad when he is at home. He agrees that he gets angry more quickly than he used to. Despite this, he finds that he is doing very well. He is not sure if he wants to carry on going to the group sessions for another season.

Epilogue

The 'male partners' of the CGT recently invited me out for a meal in Delft to catch up, because when I left my previous job they carried on meeting each other as an independent group. After the meal, I invited them back to mine for coffee. Their partners had since all been admitted to various care facilities. Some visited them more often than others. What struck me the most was that they were all able to speak about their ups and downs, both emotionally as well as with a certain detachment, about the good and bad things that happened from their point of view in the daily care of their wives. Mr Farmer was the first to leave after the coffee. He visits his wife in the care facility twice a day. It is he who puts her to bed at night. The professional care-givers have since come to rely on this, and his wife does too.

Although I always used to worry if the family visited 'too often', I was now touched and happy not just for Mr Farmer but for them all. They had found peace with how things were going. They were no longer victims of the disaster that was happening to them, but survivors. They had become 'partners in care'.

Acknowledgements

I owe a big vote of thanks to my former dedicated students: Petra Huybrechtse, Christine Kouwenhoven, Majonne Krouwer and Nitsa Kakoyannis. Through their intensive (and often verbatim) notes, as well as reports for their doctoral theses, they gave me the opportunity to devote my full attention to the group meetings and focus on the (therapeutic) processes between the couples, participants and myself.

References

Arrindel, W. A. and Ettema, J. H. M. (1986) *Klachtenlijst: SCL-90*, Nederlandse vertaling. Lisse: Swets & Zeitlinger.

Bamford, C., Lamont, S., Eccles, M., Robinson, L., May, C. and Bond, J. (2004) Disclosing a diagnosis of dementia: a systematic review. *International Journal of Geriatric Psychiatry*, **19**: 151–169.

Bartholomew, K. and Horowitz, L. M. (1991) Attachment styles among young adults: a test of a four category model. *Journal of Personality and Social Psychology*, **61**: 226–244.

Bowlby, J. (1969) *Attachment and Loss Volume 1: Attachment*. London: Hogarth Press.

Bowlby, J. (1973) *Attachment and Loss Volume 2: Separation: Anxiety and Anger*. London: Hogarth Press.

Bowlby, J. (1980) *Attachment and Loss Volume 3: Loss: Sadness and Depression*. London/New York: Hogarth Press/Basic Books.

Brink, T. L., Yesavage, J. A., Heersema, P. H., Adey, M. and Rose, T. L. (1982) Screening tests for geriatric depression. *Clinical Gerontologist*, **1**: 37–43.

Cheston, R. (1998) Psychotherapeutic work with people with dementia. A review of the literature. *British Journal of Medical Psychology*, **71**: 211–231.

Clulow, C. (2001) *Adult Attachment and Couple Psychotherapy. The 'Secure Base' in Practice and Research*. London: Brunner-Routledge, p. 228.

Costa, P. T. and McCrae, R. R. (1985) *The NEO Personality Inventory Manual*. Odessa, FL: Psychological Assessment Resources.

Cowan, P. and Cowan, C.P. (2001) A couple perspective on the transmission of attachment patterns. In C. Clulow (Ed.), *Adult Attachment and Couple Psychotherapy. The 'Secure Base' in Practice and Research*. London: Brunner-Routledge, pp. 62–82.

Cuijpers, P., Hosman, C. and Munnichs, J. (1997) Carer support groups: change mechanisms and preventive effects. In B. Miesen and G. Jones (Eds), *Care-giving in Dementia. Research and Applications*, vol. 2. London: Routledge, pp. 233–247.

De Groot, B. and Kakoyannis, N. (2001) De partner centraal. Een onderzoek naar de invloed van hechting, copingstijl en sociale steun op het psychisch welzijn van partners van dementerende ouderen. PhD Thesis, Universiteit Leiden.

Folstein, M. F., Folstein, S. and McHugh, P. R. (1975) Mini-Mental State: a practical method for grading the cognitive state of patients for the clinician. *Journal of Psychiatric Research*, **12**: 89–198.

Haley, W.E. (1983) A family-behavioral approach to the treatment of the cognitively impaired elderly. *Gerontologist*, **23**: 18–20.

Haupt, M., Siebel, U., Palm, B., Kretschmer, J. H. and Jänner, M. (2000) Behandlungs-seffekte einer paartherapeutischen psychoedukativen Gruppenarbeit mit Demenz-kranken und ihren pflegenden Angehörigen. *Fortschritte der Neurologie und Psychiatie*, **68**: 503–515.

Horowitz, M. J., Wilner, N. and Alvarez, W. (1979) Impact of Event Scale: a measure of subjective stress. *Psychosomatic Medicine*, **41**: 209–218.

Huybrechtse, P. and Kouwenhoven, C. (2000) Coping met dementie. Een onderzoek naar het effect van echtpaarcounseling bij partner en patient. PhD Thesis, Universiteit Leiden.

Jones, G. G. M. and Miesen, B. M. L. (1992) *Care-giving in Dementia. Research and Applications*. vol. 1. London/New York: Tavistock/Routledge.

Kleber, R.J. and Brom, D. (1992) *Coping with Trauma: Theory, Prevention and Treatment*. Amsterdam/Lisse: Swets & Zeitlinger, p. 317.

Krouwer, M. (2001) Gehechtheid en coping met dementie. Een exploratief onderzoek naar de rol van gehechtheid op het effect van echtparen-counseling. PhD Thesis, Universiteit Leiden.

Mapes, N. (2004) Memory groups: Facilitating open dialogue between persons with dementia. In G. G. M. Jones and B. M. L. Miesen (Eds), *Care-giving in Dementia. Research and Applications*, vol. 3. Hove: Brunner-Routledge, pp. 138–154.

Marriott, A., Donaldson, C., Tarrier, N. and Burns, A. (2000) Effectiveness of cogni-tive–behavioural family intervention in reducing the burden of care in carers of patients with Alzheimer's disease. *British Journal of Psychiatry*, **176**, 557–562.

Miesen, B. (2002) *Het Alzheimer Café*. Utrecht/Houten: Kosmos-Z&K Uitgevers/ Bohn Stafleu van Loghum.

Miesen, B. (2004) Towards a psychology of dementia care: awareness and intangible loss. In G. G. M. Jones and B. M. L. Miesen (Eds), *Care-giving in Dementia. Research and Applications*, vol. 3. Hove: Brunner-Routledge, pp. 183–213.

Miesen, B. M. L. and Jones, G. G. M. (2004) The Alzheimer Café concept: a response to the trauma, drama and tragedy of dementia. In: G. G. M. Jones and B. M. L. Miesen (Eds), *Care-giving in Dementia. Research and Applications*, vol. 3. Hove: Brunner-Routledge, 307–333.

Pot, A. M. (2004) The care-giving stress process. In G. G. M. Jones and B. M. L. Miesen (Eds), *Care-giving in Dementia. Research and Applications*, vol. 3. Hove: Brunner-Routledge, pp. 287–306.

Raven, J. C., Court, J. H. and Raven, J. (1977) *Coloured Progressive Matrices*. London: Lewis & Co.

Rosenberg, M. (1989) *Society and the Adolescent Self-Image* (reprint edition). Middletown, CT: Wesleyan University Press.

Schreurs, P. J. G., van de Willige, G., Brosschot, J. F., Tellegen, B. and Graus, G. M. H. (1984) *De Utrechtse Copinglijst: UCL, Omgaan met Problemen en Gebeurtenissen*, Herziene Handleiding. Lisse: Swets & Zeitlinger.

Snyder, L., Quayhagen, M.P., Shepherd, S. and Bower, D. (1995) Supportive Seminar Groups: an intervention for early stage dementia patients. *Gerontologist*, **35**: 691–695.

Van Wunnik, L. (2004) Ervaringen met het Alzheimer Café. De relatie tussen gehecht-theid van mantelzorgers en het ervaren nut van het Alzheimer Café. BSc Thesis, Universiteit Leiden.

Vernooij-Dassen, M. J. F. J. (1993) *Dementie en Thuiszorg. Een Onderzoek naar*

Determinanten van het Competentiegevoel van Centrale Verzorgers en het Effect van Professionele Interventie. Lisse: Swets & Zeitlinger.

Wilhelm, K. and Parker, G. (1988) The development of a measure of intimate bonds. *Psychological Medicine*, **18**: 225–234.

Yalom, I. D. (1975) *The Theory and Practice of Group Psychotherapy*. New York: Basic Books.

Yalom, I. D. (1980) *Existential Psychotherapy*. New York: Basic Books.

Part V

Education and ethics

Improving end-of-life care for people with dementia – the benefits of combining UK approaches to palliative care and dementia care

Neil Small, Murna Downs and Katherine Froggatt

Introduction

In the years after World War II, first in the UK and subsequently in many parts of the world, a new way of responding to the care needs of people who were dying began to take shape. This new approach informed what became the modern hospice movement, palliative care and the pattern of bereavement care we now see in many countries. Pioneers began to shape a new heuristic that accepted the importance of embracing appropriate advances in medical science in the context of an ethical commitment to the importance of the self. Each individual should be supported to live as fully as possible until they died.

We will examine how far a body of theory and practice developed in response to end-of-life care, primarily in its early years for people with cancer, has relevance for dementia care. We want to put modern hospice care, and subsequent developments in palliative care, alongside current practice in dementia care to see what each might learn from the other.

Further, examining the historical development and current assumptions of palliative care and dementia care offers an insight into underlying patterns of social change, including changing formulations of how we perceive the self and changing understandings of the place of illness in society.

The first part of the chapter concentrates on a historical approach to examining the place of disease in society. It begins with a consideration as to whether at any time in history there is a prevalent 'dread disease'. What is identified is that this is shaped not just by the extent and severity of that disease but also by its function as signifier, and metaphorical encapsulation of, the preoccupations of that society. Considering what constitutes the dread disease helps provide a map to chart a shift from early modern via modern to postmodern society. It is this shift in society that provides the context for the development of both palliative care and dementia care. From these more conceptual considerations we will move on to sketch a history of developing thinking about dementia care and, in more detail, hospice and palliative care.

In the second part of the chapter we will shift from the historical to the comparative – we will show similarities between palliative care and dementia care and we will demonstrate the potential for enhancing care at the end of life through combining these understandings and approaches.

In the final part of the chapter we will return to examine the underlying assumptions inherent in the various areas of activity we have presented. In particular we will emphasize the importance of having a robust concept of the self and a recognition that 'being with' and 'doing for' are complementary parts of the way we should engage with the needs of those with life-limiting illness. We will consider the way ethics reflect approaches to the relationship of the self and society, and we will indicate the importance of shifts in prevailing assumptions about autonomy and care.

Central to the argument we wish to develop is a similarity between palliative care and person-centred dementia care, and in Box 15.1 we offer definitions

---

Box 15.1 Definitions

Palliative care	Person-centred care
Palliative care is an approach that improves the quality of life of patients and their families facing the problem associated with life-threatening illness, through the prevention and relief of suffering by means of early identification and impeccable assessment and treatment of pain and other problems, physical, psychosocial and spiritual. Palliative care:	An approach to caring for people with dementia that seeks as its aim to affirm continuing 'personhood' (and that, in so doing, challenges a previously prevalent 'malignant social psychology'). Person-centred care:

Palliative care (cont.):
• provides relief from pain and other distressing symptoms;
• affirms life and regards dying as a normal process;
• intends neither to hasten nor postpone death;
• integrates the psychological and spiritual aspects of patient care;

Person-centred care (cont.):
• affirms the value of a person and their life regardless of disability;
• recognizes that people actively cope with dementia;
• recognizes that people actively cope with dementia;
• Seeks to minimize the impact of cognitive, functional and behavioural impairments on a person's quality of life;
• addresses physical, emotional, spiritual and social aspects;
• recognizes the role of life history and personality;
• insists that each person be treated as an individual;

- offers a support system to help patients live as actively as possible until death;
- offers a support system to help the family cope during the patient's illness and in their own bereavement;
- uses a team approach to address the needs of patients and their families, including bereavement counselling if indicated;
- will enhance quality of life, and may also positively influence the course of illness;
- is applicable early in the course of illness, in conjunction with other therapies that are intended to prolong life, such as chemotherapy or radiation therapy, and includes those investigations needed to understand better and manage distressing clinical complications.
(World Health Organization, 1996)

- recognizes that family and staff play a key role in maintaining personhood and quality of life;
- recognizes that family and care staff need support.
(Kitwood, 1997a)

of these terms. Many of the developments in palliative care in the UK have emanated from the model of care that emerged in hospices. In the 1960s and 1970s a modern hospice movement was taking shape in the UK; it was essentially 'a particular sort of social movement, focussed on a single issue – the improvement of the care of the dying' (Clark et al, 2005, p. 3). First via inpatient units and then in day care, home care and in hospital teams the hospice movement was seeking to combine best medical care and care for the whole person, tailored to their individual needs. Its assumptions and evolution are described in more detail below.

The dread disease as signifier of social change

In this section we will argue that examining prevalent fears in any society provides a forensic tool to facilitate an examination of the changing

Table 15.1 The dread disease as signifier of social change

Phase	Defining characteristic	Prevalent fear(s)	Dread disease
Early modern	Industrialization/ urbanization	Enforced proximity Being unproductive Being cast aside	Tuberculosis
Modern	Promise of science/ technology; reason and progress intrinsically linked	Being out of control/the irrational/not being able to solve problems	Cancer
Postmodern	Acceptance of contradictions	Loss of intellectual capacity and capacity to choose	Dementia

Source: Patterson (1987).

characteristics of that society. Table 15.1 offers a template that proposes a link between the defining imperative of a historical period and an identification of its most feared disease.

One historical phase does not replace another in a simple chronological sense, for example a move to postmodernity does not occur 'in the sense of displacing and replacing modernity, of being born only at the moment when modernity ends or fades away, of rendering the modern view impossible once it comes into its own, but in the sense of implying . . . that the long and earnest efforts of modernity have been misguided, undertaken under false pretences and bound to – sooner or later – run their course' (Bauman, 1993, p. 10). Likewise, one dominant fear does not eliminate others. We still get fears about infectious disease. In the West it is only recently that it became clear that HIV was not going to assume the status of dread disease and there are regularly other infectious diseases to scare us. Also, cancer is ever more present and more of us are likely to have it and to die from it, or die with it. For many it has become a chronic disease, something to live with and not to assume we will die from. We are now able to have a more nuanced appreciation of knowledge and reason – we can, for example, distinguish between scientific optimism and therapeutic caution. We can see how it is possible to know much about what happens in any cellular process but not why it happens in a specific case. We can consider what living with cancer might involve. This allows us to escape from defining metaphors of cancer that are punitive or sentimental, most significantly constructions of our relationship with cancer that rely on military metaphors – a war on cancer, fighting cancer. Susan Sontag has argued that 'illness is not a metaphor, the healthiest way of being ill is the one most purified of, most resistant to, metaphoric thinking' (Sontag, 1977, p. 1).

Cancer no longer takes centre stage in defining the social metaphors of fear and suffering – the contemporary fear (postmodern fear) is a loss of autonomy. While modernity emphasized individualism, in contrast to the ordered traditionalism of a customary way of life that preceded it, postmodernism makes a priority of the exercise of choice as a person shapes a narrative of their own lives. This narrative would be informed by a new concern with the validity of the subjective self. The loss of capacity to live with a reflective sense of the self, and to make choices, combine to shape dementia into the quintessential dreaded loss for the postmodern person.

The breakdown of the monolithic structure of modernity allowed the emergence of hybrids such as hospice care and person-centred dementia care, and their emergence in turn illustrates that such a social change has occurred. These new approaches draw where they can on science and they aim to utilize many professional disciplines in collaborative ways, emphasize the centrality of the individual and their choices, call on different philosophies and allow for change through both the exercise of reason and the commitment of belief. They recognize that there are many different ways to live until one dies.

In their implementation, these new forms of care may depart from this formulation and in relation to hospice care, for example, there have been critiques of the emergence of 'routinization' (James and Field, 1992), medicalization (Biswas, 1993), institutionalization (McNamara et al, 1994) and narrowness of focus (Seale, 1991).

Brief histories of dementia care and palliative care

Dementia

Approaches to dementia care before the 1950s were characterized by segregation and therapeutic pessimism, a sense that nothing could be done. This was countered by research and practice innovation in six main areas:

1   A developing understanding of the brain. This began to make a generalized dismissal of all therapeutic possibilities less sustainable. There was now a more nuanced understanding of how the brain functioned. Developments in neurobiology and neuropsychology allowed for the identification of new sub-types of dementia, a better understanding of memory, perception and attention and a closer understanding of what abilities were destroyed, compromised or left intact. A recognition emerged of the role of enriched environments in promoting nerve cell growth and of the inhibiting effects of impoverished environments (Diamond, 1988). The availability of antidementia drugs has engendered a sense of therapeutic optimism and offered a justification for early diagnosis.

2   A series of interventions aimed at improving cognition and functioning in the present. These included interventions such as reality orientation

(Woods and Britton, 1985) and behaviour modification. People with dementia could still learn from, and participate in, present reality (Folsom, 1983; Dröes, 1997).

3   An emphasis on addressing and meeting the emotional needs of people with dementia. This allowed a debate as to the relative value of a focus on maximizing the possibility of engagement in the present reality, as defined by those caring for people with dementia (the cognition approach), and an approach that accepted that people with dementia were more likely to be emotionally in the past. This could be reframed as, 'engaging in active life review'. Thus reminiscence and validation therapy were developed as therapeutic tools (Feil, 1982). This active involvement of people with dementia in life resolution led Kihlgren et al (1994) to describe 'integrity-promoting care' as that which supported people in their life review work.

4   This interest in the emotional world was further developed by Kitwood (1990), who argued that attending to a person's social and emotional needs could arrest pathological processes. Kitwood (1990) referred to this interplay between neurobiology and the social environment as the *dialectical process of dementia.* This strengthened the recognition that care was not simply about custodial containment for those of no value to society but could be utilized to improve well-being. Rader et al (1985), Kitwood (1997b) and Stokes (1986, 1987, 2000) argued that behaviours, rather than being symptomatic of neuropsychiatric disease, were attempts at communication and at meeting emotional or social needs. Kitwood's contribution, broadly referred to as person-centred care (Kitwood, 1997c; Morton, 1999; Brooker, 2004) will be considered further below.

5   There was also more recognition of the 'hidden victims' of dementia, the family context of care and specifically the burden of care, how it changed over time and how it might best be ameliorated (Zarit et al, 1985). This has led to an emphasis on service development designed to give carers a break and, more recently, to an emphasis on the need for partnership working between professionals and carers (Adams and Clarke, 1999).

6   There were the beginnings of personal accounts of living with dementia. As such, the subjectivity of the experience was considered not only worthy of exploration (Lyman, 1989; Downs, 1997) but essential to a full understanding and appropriate care provision, service development and evaluation (Cotrell and Schulz, 1993; Kitwood, 1997c).

The results of this body of accumulated work were to facilitate changes in how care could be delivered. 'Collaborative, multidisciplinary research and care-giving has only become a realistic goal with the recent advances in diagnostics' and to change the focus in terms of the perception of the person with dementia so that one could 'assume that the behaviours exhibited in dementia still express meaning, symbolically if not explicitly' (Jones and Miesen, 1992,

p. 3). The studies were now providing a focus for care-givers, including guidance about how to stimulate the least affected abilities and to assess the impact of what one does. This enables a member of care staff to have the sense that there were achievable goals and that care could not just contain but enhance self-actualization and help maintain the quality of life.

Hospice and palliative care

Four background factors contributed to shaping the development of hospices (Small, 2000):

1　The changing demographic and morbidity picture in the UK. By the beginning of the 1960s life expectancy in the UK had increased to 66.2 years for men and 71.2 for women and has continued to increase. Death from infectious disease had almost disappeared and most deaths were from circulatory or respiratory disease or from cancer (OPCS, 1985).
2　Emerging treatments that had an impact on the typical client group of the hospices. From the 1950s clinical pharmacology and pain research were able to make considerable advances. Important articles on pain were published in the late 1950s and early 1960s (Clark, 1998: Scymour et al, 2005).
3　A growing body of research and anecdotal evidence that was critical of existing practice in the care of older people and of the dying. A series of studies identified the poor quality of care for older people and for people with cancer, and continued revelations from the early 1950s until the 1980s underlined the intractability of the problem (Mellor and Shilling, 1993). These studies included one that found many cancer patients 'living on their own, or with equally old or infirm relatives, often in appalling housing conditions and often short of the right sort of food, warm clothing and bedding'(Marie Curie Memorial Foundation, 1952).
4　A shift in the way we understand death and bereavement in society. The range of critical scholarship about death and dying expanded in the post-war years (Mulkay and Ernst, 1991; Corr, 1993, Small, 2000). Gorer (1955) described society as manifesting an increasing distance from death as a natural reality. Glaser and Strauss (1965) reported people left alone in hospital beds as they approached death as first suffering from a 'social death'. Aries (1974) identified five basic patterns in attitudes towards death in Western society from the middle ages to the present. He categorized the last of these as 'forbidden death' in which the subject is perceived as socially unacceptable and is removed from social view, for example into institutions.

These background factors were necessary, but not sufficient, to effect the change that hospice and palliative care heralded in the way we care for the dying. The vision and tenacity of the pioneers was the additional factor. This was inspired by an understanding of what was necessary, what was now possible and a vision of what was desirable. The birth of the modern hospice movement is widely linked with the opening of St Christopher's Hospice in South London in 1967. The opening of St Christopher's was not the beginning of the story but only a significant milestone on the route (Clark, 1998). Dame Cicely Saunders identified the origin of her ideas, which came to fruition in St Christopher's, in her clinical work in the 1940s.

Others were also contributing innovative work. In the USA in 1969 Elizabeth Kübler-Ross published what became an international best-selling book, *On Death and Dying*, based on more than 500 interviews with dying patients. She subsequently summarized her thinking both about society and institutional care: 'We live in a very particular death-denying society. We isolate both the dying and the old, and it serves a purpose. They are reminders of our own mortality' (Kübler-Ross, evidence to US Senate Special Committee on Ageing 1972: www.nahc.org/HAA/history).

America's first hospice, The Connecticut Hospice Inc in Branford, Connecticut, opened in 1974. Subsequently there was a considerable emphasis on home care in the USA. In Europe there was a significant early history of hospice care in France and Ireland (Clark, 2000), but in terms of the modern hospice movement it was the late 1970s and particularly the 1980s that saw significant growth. A home care service opened in Sweden in 1977 and in Italy in 1980. An inpatient unit started in Cologne, Germany, in 1983, a palliative care unit in Santander, Spain, in 1984, a home care and inpatient unit in Belgium in 1985 and an inpatient hospice in The Netherlands in 1991 (Clark, 2000).

But the spread and impact of hospices goes wider. Its enthusiasts would have it identified as 'a philosophy not a facility' (Corr and Corr, 1983). 'The central point about hospice is the outlook, attitude, or approach it represents, not the building or structure in which it may be housed.' Hospice is best understood 'not as a noun but as an adjective' (Corr et al, 2004, p. 227). If we accept this, influences can be identified in a wide range of activity from palliative medicine and bereavement care to a propagation of multi-professional working and a holistic approach to responding to need.

In this section we have considered the history of hospice and palliative care and identified trends similar to those observed in dementia:

- A prevalent approach that segregates those with dementia and the dying from mainstream services and excludes them from the agenda of medical and other innovation. They do not fit into the prevailing paradigm of the optimism of reason and the promise of science.
- Pioneers that redefine the construct of science such that care (rather than cure) is legitimized and then build evidence via, in the main, the example of small-scale innovation, often led by the insights of practitioners and patients.

- A recognition that there is not just one approach and one dominant profession but that these are the arenas for multi-professional and multi-disciplinary collaborations and a variety of care modalities.
- The development of an ethic of care that is based on privileging the person in need at the heart of the intervention, that argues that the self is maintained even when the intellect is compromised and that says that the challenge is to build appropriate responses based on this ethic.

At a 'Caring for Cancer' Conference in London (20 April 1998), Dame Cicely Saunders reminded people that the hospice movement 'grew by listening' and embodied the basic philosophy that 'you matter because you are you' and that people should be 'helped to live until they die' (Saunders, 1998).

Contemporary practice and possible connections

Disease progression and the possibilities for palliative care

The trajectory of different illnesses varies and this shapes the possibilities for response. Most hospice and palliative care developed with a focus on cancer. A person with cancer may have a lengthy period of relative stability, or only slight decline in terms of physical functioning, followed by a period of rapid decline that is, relative to the whole illness's history, brief and in many cases of somewhat predictable duration. People with dementia can spend many years with limited functional abilities and continue to show a slow but steady deterioration, with then a small drop at the end of their life (see Lynn and Adamson, 2003).

This pattern of characteristic decline influences both the extent to which packages of palliative care can be assembled and, in some countries, the willingness of health service organizations to fund them. If palliative care is directed at the terminal phase then a clear recognition of when that is likely to begin, and what signs herald it, helps. However, it has been argued that palliative care, as a component of comprehensive supportive care, can play a part at all stages of disease. In many cases, there is an overlap of curative and life-prolonging therapy and then a further overlap as life-maintaining priorities take over. At all stages there is a place for supportive care, defined as including palliative care but with a broader scope, including contributions from psychologists, rehabilitation, physiotherapy, occupational therapy, dietetics, complementary therapies as well as pain specialists, social workers and chaplains (see Ahmedzai and Walsh, 2000).

If we use this approach, seeing palliative care as having a contribution – within a supportive care framework – even when curative or life-prolonging therapy is the first priority of clinicians, then the contribution of palliative care to dementia care becomes more relevant throughout the illness. Further, it is now recognized that palliative care can be given in three ways (National Council for Hospices and Specialist Palliative Care Services, 1995):

1   General palliative care – should be used by every doctor or nurse caring for a person nearing the end of a chronic illness, it is an integral part of all clinical practice. Applicable everywhere – at home, through general practice, hospitals, nursing and residential homes.
2   Palliative procedures and techniques – mostly performed by specialists in other disciplines e.g. radiotherapy, chemotherapy, psychosocial care.
3   Specialist palliative care – done in and by units with palliative care as their core speciality, with accredited staff. Found in inpatient units, hospital palliative care teams, day care, specialist community services, hospices.

The first two should be readily available for people with dementia, with some modification with regard to psychosocial care. Specialist palliative care, and the contribution that it can and should make, is more widely discussed below.

A problem in people with dementia accessing palliative care

Specialist Palliative Care Teams and Hospices are under-used by older people and by people with non-cancer diagnoses, including dementia (Lloyd-Williams, 1996; Addington-Hall and Higginson, 2001). In general, palliative care has had difficulties when prognosis is uncertain and when dying is potentially protracted (Hanrahan and Luchins, 1995). Palliative care units have often not known how to respond to cognitive and behavioural problems (Luchins and Hanrahan, 1993; Volicer et al, 1994). It is a situation in which an eminent head of a French regional palliative care service was able to say, in a plenary at a European conference, that: 'as a rule, patients suffering from dementia and wanting to be managed by a palliative care unit ought to remember to develop some form of cancer' (Wary, 2003, p. 29).

Barriers to people with dementia accessing Hospice and Specialist Palliative Care include a failure to recognize dementia as a terminal illness. In the UK it is only since the 1990s that palliative care literature has recognized that 'diseases manifesting a dementia syndrome are terminal illnesses' (Black and Jolley, 1990, p. 1321). The majority of palliative care teams, even by the mid 1990s, did not include dementia as falling within their remit. In the USA the admission of people with dementia into hospice programmes has been promoted since the early 1980s (Volicer, 1986), which resulted in 2002 figures indicating that 7% of 885 000 individuals admitted to the primarily home-based US hospice provision have Alzheimer's disease as their primary diagnosis (National Hospice and Palliative Care Organization, 2003). Other barriers include a concern that staff (and volunteers and financial supporters) would perceive dementia care as less rewarding (National

Council for Hospice and Specialist Palliative Care Services and Scottish Partnership Agency, 2000).

There is a need to acquaint palliative care staff with the progress that has been made in identifying the range of needs that people with dementia will have and their changing nature (see contributors to this volume). Death can occur at any time from age-associated conditions such as atrial fibrillation, heart failure and myocardial infarction. With increased immobility, weakness and swallowing difficulties the likely presence of a life-threatening physical illness increases (Burns et al, 1990; Jolley and Baxter, 1997).

An area of ongoing discussion within the dementia field concerns the inevitability and orderliness of deterioration in dementia and the value of seeking to encapsulate this process in a stage-based model. There are parallels in palliative care. For example, in debates about progression for people with HIV infection there was a remorseless shift from HIV-positive status via AIDS-related syndrome to 'full blown' AIDS early in the epidemic. Critics of stage-based models of decline questioned how far such formulations reflected day-to-day experience, or helped the people themselves, their carers or the immediate professionals involved in care (Treichler, 1992). Rather, these models were understandable as attempts to create social constructions of reality that allowed us to contemplate distressing and frightening phenomena in ways that promised *us* a route to understanding and management (see Berger and Luckman, 1967). A postmodern approach offers a route out of the paradox of a mismatch between lived experience and social construction/ prevailing metaphor. We examine this in our conclusions.

The quality of end-of-life care for people with dementia

The final cause of death for many people with dementia is not known. Death certificates rarely record deaths as being caused by dementia, and autopsies are rare. There are also no reliable figures on the number of people who have dementia plus a terminal illness such as cancer (de Vries, 2003, pp. 115–116). The most commonly recorded cause of death is aspiration pneumonia (Jolley and Baxter, 1997) linked to dysphagia. As well as the presence of physical illness there is also a high incidence of fractures, which also increase the risk of premature death (Hermans et al, 1989). The most commonly reported symptoms during the last year of life are mental confusion, urinary incontinence, pain, low mood, constipation and loss of appetite (McCarthy et al, 1997).

The experience prior to death for many people with dementia who are admitted to hospital is one of an interventionist regime, including tube feeding, laboratory tests, the use of restraints and intravenous medications. The result is not good quality care even when defined within a narrow medical paradigm. There is evidence of pressure ulcers, constipation, shortness of breath and pain (Mitchell et al, 2004). One specific finding in a New York study was that 51% of patients with advanced dementia received a new feeding tube during a terminal hospitalization compared with 11% of patients with metastatic cancer. 'This wide spread practice of tube feeding in end-stage dementia is concerning amid growing empirical data and expert opinion that the intervention has no demonstrable health benefits in this population and may be associated with undesirable outcomes, such as the use of restraints' (Mitchell et al, 2004, p. 325). It is for these reasons that the Alzheimer's Society in England and Wales and the US Alzheimer's Association have posited statements advising against the use of feeding tubes.

But most people with dementia do not die in hospital, they live and die in facilities that provide long-term care that encompasses personal and/or nursing care (in the UK these are Nursing and Residential Care Homes, now known as Care Homes). For the people with dementia living in these facilities the evidence points to:

1   Poor pain control.

    i   Residents with cognitive impairment and hip fracture are less likely to receive analgesics (Feldt et al, 1998).

    ii Forty per cent of residents with pain do not receive analgesics (Williams et al, 2003).

    iii The under-use of analgesics (Cohen-Mansfield, 2000, 2003) may be linked with an over-use of psychotropic medication.

2   Dehydration and malnutrition. Among residents with cognitive impairment Williams et al (2003) found that 54% had low food intake and 51% had low fluid intake.

3   Emotional and social neglect. Observation of interaction and activity of 218 residents with dementia in 19 nursing homes found that 'no home showed even a fair standard of care' (Ballard et al, 2001a, p. 426).

4   Absence of spiritual care. A survey of 644 nursing homes found this to be poorly understood, insufficiently resourced, given a low priority, with a lack of external support and lack of training (Orchard, 2002).

5   There is evidence that family carers are excluded from involvement in the relative's care (Nolan et al, 2001; Woods, 2001).

6   Staff caring for people with dementia at the end of their lives report being expected to hide their own grief reactions; they are disenfranchised as people who might legitimately experience loss from such deaths and there is no place, time or legitimacy for grief resolution (Moss, 2001; Moss et al, 2003).

This is a very negative picture and is not the whole story. There are examples of good practice and, overall, one may argue that, just like most hospitals and hospices, any institution is likely to encompass good and bad practice and have good and not so good employees. Indeed, there are dangers in negatively labelling care homes, not least for the morale of staff and for the impact on people needing care for themselves or their relatives.

What palliative care could offer to people with dementia

People with dementia do have a condition that is not responsive to curative treatment. Many aspects of the care they currently receive at the end of life is of poor standard. Techniques and protocols developed in palliative care could be adapted to dementia care. In this section we will consider three ways in which end-of-life care in dementia could be enhanced. We will then consider the more conceptual advances linked with hospice and palliative care and how they might be adapted to dementia care.

Reducing unnecessary interventions

There are things that adopting a palliative care paradigm would inhibit. For example, admissions to acute units could be reduced if there was a recognition that aggressive treatments might not be in the interests of the individual but rather might be responding to an anxiety of the healthcare professional. A simple question about how far an action maximizes the person's interests is a useful yardstick for planning. Volicer (1986) and Post (2000) have argued that if dementia care used a palliative care approach then some of the difficult ethical issues in the end stage, including hydration and feeding, would be considered differently. Volicer et al (1994) also argued that costs would decrease and patient comfort would increase if a palliative care approach were adopted. Such considerations have led the US Alzheimer's Association and the Alzheimer's Society of England and Wales to posit statements advocating a palliative response to difficulties with feeding and swallowing, one that promotes comfort rather than invasive procedures (http://www.alz.org/AboutUs/PositionStatements/overview/asp, accessed 31 March 2005; http://www.alzheimers.org.uk/News_and_campaigns/Policy_Watch/palliativecare.htm, accessed 31 March 2005).

Specific 'technical' interventions

The use of palliative care protocols in key areas could improve the quality of life, e.g. utilizing assessment tools for ascertaining levels of pain and the effectiveness of prescribed pain relief. If pain is consistently untreated or under-treated then the guidance offered via the 'Analgesic ladder' (World Health Organization, 1996; www.who.int/hiv/topics/palliative/PalliativeCare) is useful. This emphasizes oral medication given at fixed times and offers guidance whereby both the type of analgesic and the dose are increased gradually, and with consultation, according to the severity of pain. There have been pain assessment scales developed and validated in palliative care and used with people with dementia (Lefebvre-Chapiro et al, 2001). Other palliative care protocols and procedures, e.g. attention to nutrition and hydration, mouth care regimes and non-invasive treatment of infection, can also be transferred to the advantage of people with dementia.

Assessing and managing problems in ways that allow the views of the person to be privileged and their carers to be supported

This involves both imaginative ways of seeking the views of people with dementia and informed ways of inferring meaning from the significance of their actions. One challenge is to try to respect the *now* of a person and not seek to attribute judgements or choices that one assume for the *then* (Jaworska, 1999). People in the early stages of dementia can relate their feelings and experiences (Logsdon and Albert, 1999). In the later stages there is research evidence that meaningful information can be obtained, although this might take some time and require a range of ways of eliciting, or inferring, the nature of experiences they are having (Sabat and Harré, 1992; Russell, 1996; Normann et al, 2002; Norberg et al, 2003). Beard (2004) reports the increasing input of people who are at an early stage in their Alzheimer's disease, informing research, practice and policy. While organizations advocating on their behalf are committed to enhancing the voice of people with Alzheimer's in all available contexts, there is significant resistance encountered. We will consider just three areas in which a different approach to the role of people with dementia and carers as partners in care could improve dementia care:

1   Diagnosis and prognosis. There is a wide variation in how and how many people are told of their dementia diagnosis (Downs, 1999). Palliative care has included a considerable focus on truth telling in diagnosis, discussion of prognosis and the implications of decline. There has also been a recognition of the need to engage family and carers in the time approaching death and then in the bereavement phase. With dementia, even when people are told the diagnosis there may be no real discussion of prognosis (Bamford et al, 2004). If carers are told, there is a considerable majority – 83% according to a study by Maguire et al (1996) – who do not want to tell their relative with dementia. As well as ethical issues about withholding information, there is evidence that: people with dementia suffer trauma associated with the separation and displacement that illness progression can precipitate and that trauma might be ameliorated by forward planning and open communication (Miesen, 1997); people with dementia and carers planning together can exacerbate any guilt felt by carers that they might be betraying a previously made pledge, e.g. to care for a person at home (Shucter and Zisook, 1993); and knowledge of diagnosis and prognosis can make practical planning – the preparation

of a will, advance directives, power of attorney, planning ideal living arrangements – more likely (Pitt, 1997).

2   Improved support for family carers. A study in the USA of 217 family care-givers to persons with dementia during the year before and in the months after the death of the patient found that half of the care-givers reported spending at least 46 h per week assisting with activities of daily living. More than half of the care-givers in the study reported that they felt 'on duty' 24 h a day. The study identified, using standardized assessment instruments, high levels of depressive symptoms in care-givers up to the patient's death. These levels improved significantly and speedily after the death (Schulz et al, 2003).

3   Developing quality-of-life measures that are appropriate and useful. Making quality-of-life measures central in assessing the efficacy of an intervention, rather than more specifically cognitive or functional measures, in itself makes possible a paradigm change in the way we understand what we are seeking to do in dementia care. Lawton (1995) has devised a model for assessing the quality of life for persons with dementia, assembled from four domains: psychological well-being, including anxiety, depression, agitation and positive affect; behavioural competence, including physical health, functional ability and cognition; the objective environment – events and architecture; and perceived quality of life. The fourth domain reflects recognition that, in advanced dementia, it may not be possible for people to verbalize their experience. Observational approaches such as Dementia Care Mapping (Kitwood, 1997b; Ballard et al, 2001b; Brooker, 2006) and the Apparent Affect Rating Scale (Lawton et al, 1999) can assist in this domain.

Conceptual advances

We have described above that hospice and palliative care sought to be a 'philosophy not just a facility'. It drew on emerging debates about understanding death in society and about the meaning of care and the importance of the self. Many of these debates have resonance for understanding the individual impact and social significance of dementia and for shaping service provision. We will use the example of developing conceptualization of the bereavement process and the potential for bereavement care to illustrate.

Bereavement care in the modern hospice movement was shaped by an early encounter between Cicely Saunders and Colin Murray Parkes (Clark et al, 2005, pp. 159–160). Dr Parkes was working with John Bowlby and John Bowlby is described in the dedication in Volume 1 of *Care-giving in Dementia* as the person 'who unknowingly provided the concept of attachment history which turned out to be a fundamental key to be able to relate to the inner world of the demented elderly' (Jones and Miesen, 1992). A number of landmark developments in understanding bereavement can also be used to help understand the challenges of dementia care and the impact of progressive dementia:

- Glaser and Strauss (1965) spoke of the emotional awareness of terminally ill patients about their condition. This emotional awareness may also be evident in people with dementia. Miesen argues that 'even demented persons experience and feel threatened losses' (Miesen, 1992, p. 39).
- Rando, originally in 1986 and then in a more refined form in 2000, developed the understanding of anticipatory grief/anticipatory mourning (Rando, 1986, 2000). She portrayed mourning as a 'reaction and response to all losses encountered in the past, present or future of a life-threatening illness'. This describes the everyday reality for many people with dementia, and for people caring for someone with dementia, as they watch successive losses and anticipate those losses to come (Doka, 2004, p. 2).
- A paper by Kalish (1966) presented the concept of 'psychological death' – a loss of individual consciousness in which a person ceases to be aware of self. 'Not only does he not know who he is – he does not know that he is' (Kalish, 1966, p. 247). Doka and Aber (2002), in relation to dementia, consider how family members experience 'the death of the person who once was' and spouses, they argue, may become 'crypto widows'. The consideration of psychological death is problematic because of its assumptions about the nature of the self, and we will return to this below.
- Doka (1989) has argued for the importance of recognizing the existence of disenfranchised grief. Specifically in relation to dementia, we can see the exclusion of care staff as legitimate grievers. There is a culturally prevalent belief that the death of a person with dementia is a release, for the carer and the person with dementia – that they are old and a 'burden' and that death must be 'welcomed'. Unlike hospices where a person may only have been an inpatient for a short period of time before their death, nursing home staff may have known a person with dementia for some years. Katz et al (2000) identified the need for bereavement support for the staff involved in long-term care relationships. There is evidence that a relationship can develop between care staff and the person with dementia that exhibits what Miesen calls transference and counter-transference. This is a terminology borrowed from psychoanalysis, indicating that 'the professional bond is affected by more than the attributes of the present situation' (Miesen, 1999, p. 171). Events from there and then affect the here and now interactions, i.e. old behaviour patterns and conflicts are re-enacted both by the person with dementia and their carer. For this to happen a considerable degree of emotional attachment is required, a process Miesen seeks to capture in his description of staff members 'adopting' individuals they care for (Miesen, 1999, pp. 137–149). This is an evocative concept that describes a process replete with potential

dangers: there may be conflict with the person with dementia's family, e.g. they may be trying to take leave of the person and find evidence of their being 'replaced' problematic; and it may be difficult for the 'adopter' to be clear about appropriate boundaries in the subsequent care relationship, e.g. they may believe they know better than their colleagues or better than the family what is best for the adoptee, and they certainly might feel considerable loss and grief when the person dies.

• The debate that is most prominent in bereavement scholarship in recent years is the one that contrasts an idea that one must 'move on' from loss, establishing a new identity shaped without continuing reference to the person who has died, and an approach that affirms the importance of 'continuing bonds' – the dead continuing in an ongoing role in the lives of the living (see Klass et al, 1996; Walter, 1996; Small, 2001). The significance for the losses associated with the progression of dementia is that the 'continuing bonds' approach suggests that one can continue to engage with the person that *was* while not denying the challenges of living with the person that *is*.

The contribution that palliative care could make to dementia care includes technical skills and procedural practices, but it is primarily one that reinforces the message of person-centred care in recognizing the needs of the whole person and responding with a multi-disciplinary regime. Palliative care and person-centred dementia care are both inclusive and optimistic approaches, recognizing that something should be done to retain and sustain the quality of life right up to death (and to care for the bereaved after the person's death) and that there are things that can make a significant difference (Downs et al, in press). Consultation, forward planning and, most especially, an approach to care that puts the person with dementia and their needs at the centre would make a considerable difference to the many problems in end-of-life care discussed above.

While we have explored in some detail what palliative care could contribute to dementia care, there are areas of experience developed in the more general care for older people, including those with dementia, that offer much to palliative care. Relevant strengths include:

• Expertise across many diseases.
• Ability to respond to multiple pathologies.
• Experience in developing programmes for long-term engagement with people.
• Engaging individuals who have no verbal abilities.
• Working with cognitive and behavioural problems.

More generally: 'Geriatrics stresses the importance of doing (such as ability to walk, to wash, to eat by oneself), whereas palliative care is rather focused on being. Being autonomous is to be ruled by one's own choices, but doing and being can be combined so as to avoid both fatalism and over-treatment' (Wary, 2003, p. 29).

Person-centred care

In our introduction we suggested similarities between palliative care and person-centred care. We will now consider, in a little more detail, conceptual assumptions underpinning person-centred care. These assumptions share the critique of modernity and the possibilities of postmodernism discussed above. While person-centred care has been widely accepted as a significant contribution to conceptualizing, designing and evaluating care (Morton, 1999), it has also been criticized for what is seen, erroneously, as its assumptions about the importance of an ethic of autonomy (Nolan et al, 2004). We will examine these criticisms and seek to reconcile autonomy and care by utilizing postmodern ethics.

Kitwood writes from a position that recognizes the exclusion of the old, the demented and the dying from society, a situation in which 'one can be a human being, and yet not be acknowledged as a person' (Kitwood, 1997a, p. 4; Kitwood and Bredin, 1992). In this context, caring has been transformed from a verb into a noun – carer – someone who is assigned the role of caring to enable others' lives to go on without them having to engage with that particular demand/burden. Kitwood locates the dynamics of this shift in the pursuit of rationality – 'all that smacked of disorder must be suppressed'. This suppression is implemented via segregation and the subjugation of the non-rational, first by moral correction and then by medical categorization and treatment (see Foucault, 1967).

For Kitwood the alternative construction is one illuminated in Buber's identification of the *I and Thou* mode of relating, making contact with the pure being of another, with no distinct purpose save the affirmation and confirmation of personhood. This is contrasted to the 'I and It' encounter that is characteristic of much of our interaction. This sort of encounter exhibits coolness, an information getting objectivity, an instrumentality and an engagement without commitment (Buber, 1970).

Kitwood identifies three characteristics necessary if one wishes to enhance 'personhood' – a recognition of uniqueness and an acceptance of both subjectivity and relatedness (Kitwood, 1997a, p. 10). All three characteristics call into question established tenets of modernity and all are consistent with postmodernity, which does permit and, indeed fosters a new humanism. 'We are faced with the task of creating environments in which caring feels natural, and so, eventually, bringing about a new culture of care' (Kitwood, 1997a, p. 3).

The emphasis of modernity and postmodernity on individual choice and self-determination (see Table 15.1) presents a problem in that it suggests the elevation of a concern with achievement. There can appear to be an imperative to 'make oneself'. While emphasizing achievement can be a useful counterforce to a deficit model of aging (aging as decline), having to construct for oneself a successful aging presents a new burden, or barrier, for some. Seale (1995) has discussed the presence of scripts for proclaiming heroic self-identity in the face of death, either from the person dying – who struggles to gain knowledge, demonstrate courage – or from the carer – who enshrines a 'heroics of care, concern and emotional expression'. That is, dying can be 'successfully incorporated into the process of reflexive formation of self identity' (Seale, 1995, p. 598). There is a danger here that we have to 'do' aging, or even dying, and we cannot just have 'the courage to be' (Tillich, 1962).

Hospice, palliative care and person-centred dementia care do not have to be about achievement. They can be constructed around an ethic of the present – of the moral worth of humanness, not of human action (Post, 1995; Jennings, 2004, p. 251). Tillich called this the riddle of the present – neither the past or the future – a place to celebrate our 'presence' (Tillich, 1959, p. 36). (T.S. Eliot, in the opening of *Burnt Norton*, was considering the same riddle, published in *Four Quartets* by Faber in 1944.) For the carer it reminds us of the value of *being with* rather than assuming we have to be *doing for*. Cicely Saunders (2003) uses Christ's request to his disciples in the garden of Gethsemane to summarize the hospice approach. As he contemplated his own imminent suffering and death, he asked them to 'watch with me', which they found difficult to fulfil because they kept falling asleep, illustrating that *being with* is not an easy request to meet (Matthew: chapter 26, verse 38).

'O, reason not the need'

Considering the ethical assumptions of our various modes of response to dementia creates challenges, even for an ethic of care based on *I and Thou* interactions or on *being with*. Buber's *I and Thou* has a 'dialogical character the anticipation of a dialogue; *I–Thou* has an address and response structure' (Bauman, 1993, p. 49), i.e. I treat you as *thou*, rather than *it*, because I expect/require you to do the same to me, perhaps at a near point in the future. *Being with* also has the same dialogical assumptions, 'I am with the other in so far as we are in it together' (Bauman, 1993, p. 49). We are side by side. But if the other is a baby, a person who is unconscious and unlikely to recover consciousness or a person with advanced dementia who cannot act on an understanding of what remains as self and what is other, then we have to look for an ethic before the reciprocal. *Being for* does this. Bauman has developed an argument, building on Kant's position that morality is guided solely by the concerns of the other for the other's sake – that there is a 'mystery of mortality inside me' – for a morality that 'precedes the emergence of the socially administered context'. 'Being for the Other before being with the Other is the first reality of the self, a starting point rather than a product of society' (Bauman, 1993, p. 13). We will briefly pursue the implications of this approach both for palliative care and dementia care. In particular we will look at the recent debates in dementia care that have contrasted 'an obsession with autonomy' with a 'perception based ethic of care' (Hertogh, 2004a).

While it is agreed that a concern with autonomy might have been welcome as a part of a democratization of service provision – as a counterforce to paternalism – there is a danger that if autonomy is seen to override other concerns it might result in inadequate care. A person is not always the best judge of what they need. The usual situation in a palliative care setting sees the likelihood that an agreed approach to care can be achieved based on respect for the autonomy of the person. Where a person is likely to lose the ability to communicate there is the possibility of the precedent autonomy of a 'living will' being evoked. In contrast, with dementia we have to consider the possibility of an absence of a shared sense as to the nature of the challenge being responded to (an absence of illness insight; a break in the sense of a consistent autonomous self), i.e. a person with dementia may not recognize the person they were and who made autonomous decisions as being the person they are now, and a person for whom the elevation of autonomy (of being able to make choices) is now a fiction principally serving the ethics of the staff and far removed from the person with dementia's overwhelming wish to be made to feel safe and cared for (see Hertogh, 2004b).

There is here a conflict between rights and needs. 'Rights language offers a rich vernacular for the claims an individual may make on or against the collectivity, but it is relatively impoverished as a means of expressing individuals' needs for the collectivity' (Ignatieff, 1984, p. 13). Ignatieff argues that we are more than rights-bearing creatures and more than our rights need to be respected. For example, in our hospitals an individual might have his rights respected but he 'may still feel the silent contempt of authority in a glance, gesture or procedure' (Ignatieff, 1984, p. 13).

What Ignatieff is arguing for is a new sort of discourse about needs – one that moves beyond rights. 'It is because fraternity, love, belonging, dignity, respect cannot be specified as rights that we ought to specify them as needs and seek, with the blunt institutional procedures at our disposal, to make their satisfaction a routine practice' (Ignatieff, 1984, pp. 13–14).

We can then reframe the debate about autonomy and care into a new morality, a postmodern one. To cite Bauman again: 'Few choices (and only those which are relatively trivial and of minor existential importance) are unambiguously good. The majority of moral choices are made between contradictory impulses. Most importantly, however, virtually every moral impulse, if acted upon in full, leads to immoral consequences (most characteristically, the impulse to care for the Other, when taken to extreme, leads to the annihilation of the autonomy of the Other, the moral self moves, feels and acts in the context of ambivalence, and is shot through with uncertainty)' (Bauman, 1993, p. 11). If this is the case we cannot reconcile the contrasting pursuit of autonomy and care, save by preceding it with the morality of *being for* the other. This approach undermines any conflict that poses autonomy against care by saying that such conflicts are inevitable and are second-order phenomena enacted in a social domain that is preceded and superseded by being for the other, whatever their capacity for independence or autonomy.

Ignatieff looks to the plight of William Shakespeare's *The Tragedy of King Lear* (Cambridge University Press, 1992) to illustrate the fragility of natural and social obligation. Lear begins to sense the change in the way others see him when two of his three daughters respond to his expression of needs by asking him to give reasons. His reply, 'O, reason not the need' (Act 2, scene 4), reflects not just an intimation of his own powerlessness but also a sense that if others ask him for reasons then this presupposes that he lacks the capacity to know his own mind. The father is being made the child. He has to reconcile what he calls his needs, but are in fact his wants (the powerful assume what they desire is also what they need), with the realization that he has when he finds himself cast out on the heath in the natural world, that an unaccompanied man is no more than a 'poor, bare, forked animal' (Act 3, scene 4). He only learns what is enough by having less than enough. The tragedy for Lear and for his youngest daughter, Cordelia, is that he does not recognize in her telling him 'I love your majesty according to my bond, no more or less' (Act 1, scene 1) that this is enough – it precedes rights and needs – it is *being for*.

Ignatieff comments that today: 'Old men whom their daughters abandon now get their pension and a home visitor . . . But there is still a heath: it is in the vast grey space of state confinement . . . Needs are met, but souls are dishonoured. Natural man – the "poor bare, forked animal" is maintained; the social man wastes away' (Ignatieff, 1984, pp. 50–51).

Conclusions

We have examined the historical and social context of palliative care and dementia care and have considered how the practices of the former could be directed towards the needs of the latter (Hughes et al, 2004). Figure 15.1 offers a summary of the areas explored.

A prevalent theme throughout the chapter is that postmodernism offers an opportunity to both think and do things differently. We have avoided any precise definition of our understanding of postmodernism. We have hoped to suggest its meaning via the way we have used the concept as a critical and descriptive term. But it beholds us, as we finish, to be more precise. The most common definitions are negative ones; postmodernism shows an 'incredulity towards metanarratives' (Lyotard, 1984, p. xxiv) or it proclaims that 'there is no knowledge without discourse' (Lacan, 1977). But we offer Bauman's more positive reading. Postmodernity is 'modernity without illusions, the illusions in question boil down to the belief that the "messiness" of the human world

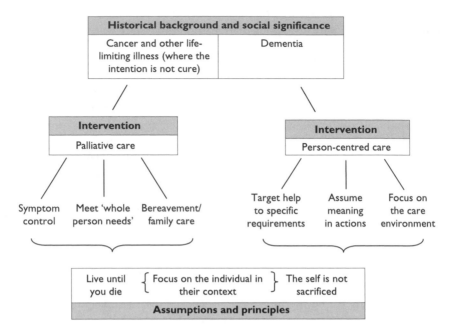

Figure 15.1 The areas considered in palliative care and dementia care.

is but a temporary and repairable state, sooner or later to be replaced by the orderly and systematic rule of reason. The truth in question is that the "messiness" will stay whatever we do or know, that the little orders and "systems" we carve out in the world are brittle, until-further-notice, and as arbitrary and in the end contingent as their alternatives' (Bauman, 1993, pp. 32–33). For Bauman, this change opens the possibility that we can become re-enchanted with the world, we can return dignity to emotions, indeed to all that is irrational, we can enjoy mystery, respect ambiguity and appreciate actions without purpose. To us this sounds like the sort of world where people with dementia will be better understood.

We have argued that a widespread challenge to the precepts of modernity makes space for the innovations that characterize hospice and person-centred dementia care. Postmodernism legitimizes a concern with subjectivity and variety, but there is also a need for the active agency of committed individuals, driven by both a critique of existing practice and a vision of what can be better – that vision is shaped by a philosophy of the self that challenges instrumentalism and utilitarianism. People matter as individuals, for who they are and not what they can do.

References

Adams, T.L. and Clarke, C.L. (1999) *Dementia Care: Developing Partnerships in Practice*. London: Ballière Tindall Royal College of Nursing.

Addington-Hall, J. and Higginson, I. (2001) *Palliative Care for Non-Cancer Patients*. Oxford: Oxford University Press.

Ahmedzai, S.H. and Walsh, T.D. (2000) Palliative medicine and modern cancer care. *Seminars in Oncology*, **27**: 1–6.

Aries, P. (1974) *Western Attitudes Toward Death: From the Middle Ages to the Present*. Baltimore: Johns Hopkins University.

Ballard, C., Fossey, J., Chithramohan, R., Howard, R., Burns, A., Thompson, P., Tadros, G. and Fairbairn, A. (2001a) Quality of care in private sector and NHS facilities for people with dementia: cross sectional survey. *British Medical Journal*, **323**: 426–427.

Ballard, C., O'Brien, J., James, J., et al (2001b) Quality of life for people with dementia living in residential and nursing home care. *International Journal of Psychogeriatrics*, **13**: 93–106.

Bamford, C., Lamont, S., Eccles, M., Robinson, L., May, C. and Bond, J. (2004) Disclosing a diagnosis: a systematic review. *International Journal of Geriatric Psychiatry*, **19**: 151–169.

Bauman, Z. (1993) *Postmodern Ethics*. Oxford: Blackwell.

Beard, R.L. (2004) Advocating voice: organizational, historical and social milieux of the Alzheimer's disease movement. *Sociology of Health and Illness*, **26**: 797–819.

Berger, P.L. and Luckman, T. (1967) *The Social Construction of Reality*. Harmondsworth: Penguin.

Biswas, B. (1993) The medicalization of dying. In D. Clark (Ed.), *The Future for Palliative Care*. Buckingham: Open University Press, pp. 132–139.

Black, D. and Jolley, D. (1990) Slow euthanasia? The deaths of psychogeriatric patients. *British Medical Journal*, **300**: 1321–1323.

Brooker, D. (2004) What is person-centred care for people with dementia? *Reviews in Clinical Gerontology*, **13**: 212–222.

Brooker, D. (2006) Dementia care mapping: a review of the research literature. *Gerontologist*, **45**: 11–18.

Buber, M. (1970) *I and Thou* (first published in German in 1923). Edinburgh: Clark.

Burns, A., Jacoby, R., Luthert, P. and Levy, R. (1990) Cause of death in Alzheimer's disease. *Age and Ageing*, **19**: 341–344.

Clark, D. (1998) Originating a movement – Cicely Saunders and the development of St Christopher's Hospice 1957–1967. *Mortality*, **3**: 43–63.

Clark, D. (2000) Common threads? Palliative care service developments in seven European countries. *Palliative Medicine*, **14**: 479–490.

Clark, D., Small, N., Wright, M., Winslow, M. and Hughes, N. (2005) *A Bit of Heaven for the Few?* Lancaster: Observatory Press.

Cohen-Mansfield, J. (2000) Approaches to the management of disruptive behaviours. In M. Powell, M.P. Lawton and R.L. Rubinstein (Eds), *Interventions in Dementia Care: Toward Improving Quality of Life*. London: Springer Publications.

Cohen-Mansfield, J. (2003) Nonpharmacologic interventions for psychotic symptoms in dementia. *Journal of Geriatric Psychiatry and Neurology*, **16**: 219–224.

Corr, C. (1993) Death in modern society. In D. Doyle, G. Hanks and N. Macdonald (Eds), *The Oxford Textbook of Palliative Medicine*. Oxford: Oxford Medical Publications, pp. 28–36.

Corr, C. and Corr, D. (1983) *Hospice Care: Principles and Practice*. London: Faber and Faber.

Corr, C.A., Corr, K.M. and Ramsey, S.M. (2004) Alzheimer's disease and the challenge for hospice. In K. Doka (Ed.), *Living with Grief. Alzheimer's Disease*. Washington, DC: Hospice Foundation of America, pp. 227–243.

Cotrell, V. and Schulz, R. (1993) The perspective of the patient with Alzheimer's disease: a neglected dimension of dementia research. *Gerontologist*, **33**: 205–211.

Diamond, M. (1988) *Enriching Heredity: the Impact of the Environment on the Brain*. New York: Free Press.

Doka, K. J. (1989) *Disenfranchised Grief: Recognizing Hidden Sorrow*. Lexington, MA: Lexington Books.

Doka, K.J. (2004) Grief and dementia. In K. Doka (Ed.), *Living with Grief: Alzheimer's Disease*. Washington, DC: Hospice Foundation of America, pp. 131–144.

Doka, K.J. and Aber, R. (2002) Psychological loss and grief. In K. Doka (Ed.), *Disenfranchised Grief: New Directions, Challenges and Strategies for Practice*. Champaign, IL: Research Press.

Downs, M. (1997) The emergence of the person in dementia research. *Ageing and Society*, **17**: 597–607.

Downs, M. (1999) How to tell? Disclosing a diagnosis of dementia. *Generations (Journal of the American Society on Ageing)*, **23**: 30–34.

Downs, M., Small, N. and Froggatt, K. (in press) Person-centred care for people with severe dementia. In A. Burns and B. Winblad (Eds), *Severe Dementia*. London: Arnold Press.

Dröes, R.M. (1997) Psychosocial treatments for demented patients. In B.M.L. Miesen and G.M.M. Jones (Eds), *Care-giving in Dementia*, vol. 2. London: Routledge, pp. 127–148.

Feil, N. (1982) *Validation: The Feil Method* (1st edn). Cleveland: Feil Productions.

Feldt, K.S., Ryden, M.B. and Miles, S. (1998) Treatment of pain in cognitively impaired compared with cognitively intact older patients with hip fracture. *Journal of the American Geriatrics Society*, **46**: 1079–1085.

Folsom, J.C. (1983) Reality orientation. In B. Reisberg (Ed.), *Alzheimer's Disease*. New York: Free Press.

Foucault, M. (1967) *Madness and Civilization*. London: Tavistock.

Glaser, B. and Strauss, A. (1965) *Awareness of Dying*. Chicago: Aldine.

Gorer, G. (1955) The pornography of death. *Encounter*, **5**: 49–52.

Hanrahan, P. and Luchins, D.J. (1995) Access to hospice programmes in end-stage dementia: a national survey of hospice programmes. *Journal of the American Geriatrics Society*, **43**: 56–59.

Hermans, D., Lisaerde, J. and Triau, E. (1989) Sense and non-sense of a technological health care model in terminally ill demented patients. The first international conference on the palliative care of the elderly. *Journal of Palliative Care*, **5**: 39–42.

Hertogh, C. (2004a) Between autonomy and security: ethical questions in the care of elderly persons with dementia in nursing homes. In G.M.M. Jones and B.M.L. Miesen (Eds), *Care-giving in Dementia*, vol. 3. Hove: Brunner-Routledge, pp. 375–390.

Hertogh, C. (2004b) Autonomy, competence and advanced directives: the physician proposes, the patient disposes? In G.M.M. Jones and B.M.L. Miesen (Eds), *Care-giving in Dementia*, vol. 3. Hove: Brunner-Routledge, pp. 391–403.

Hughes, J.C., Hedley, K. and Harris, D. (2004) The practice and philosophy of palliative care in dementia. *Nursing and Residential Care*, **6**: 27–30.

Ignatieff, M. (1984) *The Needs of Strangers*. London: Chatto and Windus.

James, N. and Field, D. (1992) The routinization of hospice: charisma and bureaucratization. *Social Science and Medicine*, **12**: 1363–1375.

Jaworska, A. (1999) Respecting the margins of agency: Alzheimer's patients and the capacity to value. *Philosophy and Public Affairs*, **28**: 105–138.

Jennings, B. (2004) Alzheimer's disease and the quality of life. In K. Doka (Ed.), *Living with Grief: Alzheimer's Disease*. Washington DC: Hospice Foundation of America, pp. 247–258.

Jolley, D. and Baxter, D. (1997) Life expectation in organic brain disease. *Advances in Psychiatric Treatment*, **3**: 211–218.

Jones, G.M.M. and Miesen, B.M.L. (1992) *Care-giving in Dementia*, vol. 1. London: Routledge.

Kalish, R.A. (1966) A continuum of subjectively perceived death. *Gerontologist*, **6**: 73–76.

Katz, J., Sidell, M. and Komaromy, C. (2000) Death in homes: bereavement needs of residents, relatives and staff. *International Journal of Palliative Nursing*, **6**: 274–279.

Kihlgren, M., Hallgren, A., Norberg, A. and Karlsson, I. (1994) Integrity promoting care of demented patients: patterns of interaction during morning care. *International Journal of Ageing and Human Development*, **39**: 303–319.

Kitwood, T. (1990) The dialectics of dementia: with particular reference to Alzhiemer's disease. *Ageing and Society*, **10**: 177–196.

Kitwood, T. (1997a) The concept of personhood and its relevance to a new culture of dementia care. In B.M.L. Miesen and G.M.M. Jones (Eds), *Care-giving in Dementia*, vol. 2. London: Routledge, pp. 3–13.

Kitwood, T. (1997b) *Dementia Reconsidered: The Person comes First*. Buckingham: Open University Press.

Kitwood, T. (1997c) The experience of dementia. *Ageing and Mental Health*, **1**: 13–22.

Kitwood, T. and Bredin, K. (1992) Towards a theory of dementia care: personhood and well-being. *Ageing and Society*, **12**: 269–287.

Klass, D., Silverman, P.R. and Nickman, S.L. (1996) *Continuing Bonds, New Understandings of Grief*. Washington, DC: Taylor & Francis.

Kübler-Ross, E. (1969) *On Death and Dying*. London: Tavistock.

Lacan, J. (1977) *Ecrits: a Selection*. London: Tavistock.

Lawton, M.P. (1995) Quality of life in Alzheimer's disease. *Alzheimer's Disease and Associated Disorders*, **8** (Suppl. 3): 138–150.

Lawton, M.P., van Haitsma, K., Perkinson, M. and Ruckdeschel, K. (1999) Observed affect and quality of life in dementia: further affirmations and problems. *Journal of Mental Health and Ageing*, **5**: 69–81.

Lefebvre-Chapiro, S. and the DOLOPLUS Group (2001) The DOLOPLUS 2 Scale – evaluating pain in the elderly. *European Journal of Palliative Care*, **8**: 191–193.

Lloyd-Williams, M. (1996) An audit of palliative care in dementia. *European Journal of Cancer Care*, **5**: 53–55.

Logsdon, R.G. and Albert, S.M. (1999) Assessing quality of life in Alzheimer's disease: conceptual and methodological issues. *Journal of Mental Health and Aging*, **5**: 3–6.

Luchins, D.J. and Hanrahan, P. (1993) What is appropriate health care for end stage dementia? *Journal of the American Geriatrics Society*, **41**: 25–30.

Lyman, K.A. (1989) Bringing the social back in: a critique of the biomedicalization of dementia. *Gerontologist*, **29**: 597–605.

Lynn, J. and Adamson, D.M. (2003) *Living Well at the End of Life*. Santa Monica: Rand Health.

Lyotard, F. (1984) *The Postmodern Condition*. Manchester: University of Manchester Press.

Maguire, C.P., Kirby, M., Coen, R., Coakley, D., Lawlor. B.A. and O'Neill, D. (1986) Family members attitudes towards telling the patient with Alzheimer's disease their diagnosis. *British Medical Journal*, **313**: 529–530.

Marie Curie Memorial Foundation (1952) *Report on a National Survey Concerning Patients Nursed at Home*. London: Marie Curie Memorial Foundation.

McCarthy, M., Addington-Hall, J.M. and Altman, D. (1997) The experience of dying with dementia. A retrospective study. *International Journal of Geriatric Psychiatry*, **12**: 404–409.

McNamara, B., Waddell, C. and Colvin, M. (1994) The institutionalisation of the good death. *Social Science and Medicine*, **39**: 1501–1508.

Mellor, P.A. and Shilling, C. (1993) Modernity, self-identity and the sequestration of death. *Sociology*, **27**: 411–431.

Miesen, B.M.L. (1992) Attachment theory and dementia. In G.M.M. Jones and B.M.L. Miesen (Eds), *Care-giving in Dementia*, vol. 1. London: Routledge, pp. 38–56.

Miesen, B.M.L. (1997) Awareness in dementia patients and family grieving: a practical perspective. In B.M.L. Miesen and G.M.M. Jones (Eds), *Care-giving in Dementia*, vol. 2. London: Routledge, pp. 67–79.

Miesen, B.M.L. (1999) *Dementia in Close-up*. London: Routledge.

Mitchell, S.L., Kiely, D.K. and Hamel, M.B. (2004) Dying with advanced dementia in the nursing home. *Archives of Internal Medicine*, **164**: 321–326.

Morton, I. (1999) *Person-centred Approaches to Dementia Care*. Bicester: Winslow.

Moss, M. (2001) End of life in nursing homes. In M. P. Lawton (Ed.), *Annual Review of Gerontology and Geriatrics: End of Life: Scientific and Social Issues*. New York: Springer Publishing, pp. 224–258.

Moss, M. S., Moss, S. Z., Rubinstein, R. L. and Black, H. K. (2003) The metaphor of 'family' in staff communication about dying and death. *Journal of Gerontology: Social Sciences*, **58B**: S290–S296.

Mulkay, M. and Ernst, J. (1991) The changing profile of social death. *Archives of European Sociology*, **XXXII**: 172–196.

National Council for Hospices and Specialist Palliative Care Services (1995) *Occasional Paper 8. Specialist Palliative Care: a Statement of Definitions*. London: NCHSPC.

National Council for Hospices and Specialist Palliative Care Services and Scottish Partnership Agency (2000) *Positive Partnerships. Occasional Paper 17*. London: NCHSPC.

National Hospice and Palliative Care Organization (2003) *NHPCO Facts and Figures*. Alexandria, VA: NHPCO.

Nolan, M.R., Davies, S. and Grant, G. (2001) *Working with Older People and their Families: Key Issues in Policy and Practice*. Buckingham: Open University Press.

Nolan, M.R., Davies, S., Brown, J., Keady, J. and Nolan, M. (2004) Beyond 'person-centred' care: a new vision for gerontological nursing. *International Journal of Older People Nursing*, **13**: 45–53.

Norberg, A., Melin, E. and Asplund, K. (2003) Reactions to music, touch and object presentation in the final stage of dementia: an exploratory study. *International Journal of Nursing Studies*, **40**: 473–479.

Normann, H.K., Norberg, A. and Asplund, K. (2002) Confirmation and lucidity during conversations with a woman with severe dementia. *Journal of Advanced Nursing*, **39**: 370–376.

Office of Population Census and Surveys (OPCS) (1985) *Mortality Statistics, 1841–1980*, Series DH1 No. 15. London: HMSO.

Orchard, H. (2002) Spiritual care in care homes: perceptions and practice. In J. Hockley and D. Clark (Eds), *Palliative Care for Older People in Care Homes*. Buckingham: Open University Press, pp. 66–85.

Patterson, J.T. (1987) *The Dread Disease*. Cambridge, MA: Harvard University Press.

Pitt, B. (1997) You've got Alzheimer's disease': telling the patient. *Current Opinion in Psychiatry*, **10**: 307–308.

Post, S.G. (1995) *The Moral Challenge of Alzheimer Disease*. Baltimore: Johns Hopkins University Press.

Post S. (2000) *The Moral Challenge of Alzheimer's Disease: Ethical Issues from Diagnosis to Dying*. London: John Hopkins.

Rader, J., Doan, J. and Schwab, M. (1985) How to decrease wandering, a form of agenda behavior. *Geriatric Nursing*, **6**: 196–199.

Rando, T.A. (1986) *Loss and Anticipatory Grief*. Lexington, MA: Lexington Books.

Rando, T.A. (2000) *Clinical Dimensions of Anticipatory Mourning: Theory and Practice in Working with the Dying, their Loved Ones and Caregivers*. Champaign, IL: Research Press.

Russell, C.K. (1996) Passion and heretics: meaning in life and quality of life of persons with dementia. *Journal of the American Geriatrics Society*, **44**: 1400–1402.

Sabat, S. and Harré, R. (1992) The construction and deconstruction of self in Alzheimer's disease. *Ageing and Society*, **12**: 443–461.

Saunders, Dame C. (1998) In *Information Exchange*, 25 June. London: National Council for Hospice and Specialist Palliative Care Services, pp. 6–7.

Saunders, Dame C. (2003) *Watch with Me*. Sheffield: Mortal Press.

Schulz, R., Mendelsohn, A.B., Haley, W.E., et al (2003) End-of-life care and the effects of bereavement on family caregivers of persons with dementia. *New England Journal of Medicine*, **349**: 1936–1942.

Seale, C. F. (1991) Death from cancer and from other causes: the relevance of the hospice approach. *Palliative Medicine*, **5**: 12–19.

Seale, C. (1995) Heroic death. *Sociology*, **29**: 597–613.

Seymour, J., Clark, D. and Winslow, M. (2005) Pain and palliative care: the emergence of new specialities. *Journal of Pain and Symptom Management*, **29**: 2–13.

Shucter, S.R. and Zisook, S. (1993) The course of normal grief. In M.S. Stroebe, W. Stroebe and R.O. Hansson (Eds), *Handbook of Bereavement*. Cambridge: Cambridge University Press, pp. 23–43.

Small, N. (2000) The modern hospice movement. In J. Bornat, R. Perks, P. Thompson and J. Walmsley (Eds), *Oral History, Health and Welfare*. London: Routledge, pp. 288–308.

Small, N. (2001) Theories of grief: a critical review. In J. Hockey, J. Katz and N. Small (Eds), *Grief, Mourning and Death Ritual*. Buckingham: Open University Press, pp. 19–48.

Sontag, S. (1977) *Illness as Metaphor*. Harmondsworth: Penguin.

Stokes, G. (1986) *Wandering*. Bicester: Winslow Press.

Stokes, G. (1987) *Aggression: Common Problems with the Elderly Confused*. Bicester: Winslow Press.

Stokes, G. (2000) *Challenging Behaviour in Dementia: a Person-centred Approach*. Bicester: Speechmark Publishing.

Tillich, P. (1959) The eternal now. In H. Feifel (Ed.), *The Meaning of Death*. New York: McGraw Hill.

Tillich, P. (1962) *The Courage to Be*. London: Fontana.

Treichler, P.A. (1992) AIDS, HIV, and the cultural construction of reality. In G. Herdt and S. Lindenbaum (Eds), *The Time of AIDS*. Newbury Park: Sage, pp. 65–98.

Volicer, L. (1986) Need for hospice approach to treatment of patients with advanced progressive dementia. *Journal of the American Geriatrics Society*, **34**: 655–658.

Volicer, I., Collard, A., Hurley, A., et al (1994) Impact of special care unit for patients with advanced Alzheimer's disease on patients' discomfort and costs. *Journal of the American Geriatrics Society*, **42**: 597–603.

de Vries, K. (2003) Palliative care for people with dementia. In T. Adams and J. Manthorpe (Eds), *Dementia Care*. London: Arnold, pp. 114–135.

Walter, T. (1996) A new model of grief: bereavement and biography. *Mortality*, **1**: 7–25.

Wary, B. (2003) Geriatrics and palliative care: the best of both worlds. *European Journal of Palliative Care*, **10** (Suppl.): 29–31.

Williams, C., Sloame, P., Zimmerman, S., Boustani, M., Preisser, J. and Reed, P. (2003) Pain in nursing home and assisted living residents with dementia: how assessment, treatment and staff perceptions relate to resident report. Paper presented at the *Annual Scientific Meeting of the Gerontological Society of America*, November.

Woods, R.T. (2001) Discovering the person with Alzheimer's disease: cognitive, emotional and behavioural aspects. *Ageing and Mental Health*, **5**: 7–16.

Woods, R.T. and Britton, P.G. (1985) *Clinical Psychology with the Elderly*. London: Croom Helm.

World Health Organization (1990) *Technical Report*, Series 804. Geneva: WHO.

World Health Organization (1996) *Cancer Pain Relief* (2nd edn). Geneva: WHO (www.who.int/hiv/topics/palliative/PalliativeCare).

Zarit, S.H., Orr, N. K. and Zarit, J.M. (1985) *The Hidden Victims of Alzheimer's Disease: Families under Stress*. London: New York University Press.

Chapter 16

Death comes in the end

A palliative perspective of caring for people with dementia

Marinus van den Berg

Introduction

Having dementia can be described as a continuous loss, as fighting a losing battle and as saying goodbye agonizingly slowly, saying goodbye to life as it used to be with everything it meant and finally saying goodbye to life itself. Death comes in the end. In this chapter, the terms 'the threatened self', 'the lost self', 'the submerged self' and the 'withdrawn self' are used to describe the dementia process (Verdult, 1998). They are equivalents to Behavioural Stages 1–4 in Jones (2004).

Dementia is about experiencing loss on many fronts: loss in terms of time, people and place, as well as loss of independence, relationships and meaning. A variety of different strategies are used to cope with this process of loss. Fighting a losing battle is experienced differently from one person to the next, and this battle is fought by the dying person but also by those close to them who have an emotional bond with them. This may even be the professional care-givers who enter into a process of adoption and attachment over the period of care. For them too, death comes at the end of the caring. In this battle with grief, a battle with suffering, the topic of death exists in a number of guises. Death comes not just in the end but also during the battle. It may be something hoped and wished for by the person with dementia. It may be something hoped and wished for by the next of kin. Wishing for death brings its own wave of ethical dilemmas. Death may also be a growing awareness on the part of the person with dementia or family and care-givers or care staff as we approach the final phase of this suffering. We call this final phase the terminal phase.

In this chapter, we will look at dementia and the terminal phase of dementia from a palliative viewpoint. We will examine what this palliative viewpoint entails and what it can mean for those with dementia, for their families and for care-givers and staff. We will also examine what this palliative viewpoint means in the terminal phase.

This chapter will not focus on medical and somatic aspects of dementia, but will approach the subject from a *psychosocial* and *spiritual dimension*.

This viewpoint means that we cannot begin to understand a person's life and the way in which that person deals with the suffering they are going through if we do not have insight into their *life history* and *life events* and the way in which these events are *interwoven* into their life history. *By spiritual dimension, we mean a person's entire conscious and subconscious interpretation and perception of life*: the people, ideals and aspirations of significance in their lives and how these people and things have stimulated them or held them back. The spiritual dimension may also refer to faith, religion, church and philosophy of life – these things may be a source of strength providing individual significance in the battle with grief, or else they may become a source of suffering in themselves and have a negative impact on someone's battle with grief (e.g. traumatic experiences as a result of particular beliefs or events).

When we refer to the palliative viewpoint of care, we take into account the physical, psychological, social and spiritual dimension of a person's life. Palliative care aims to lighten and, where possible, remove the burden of suffering as a result of suffering from dementia. This suffering is felt by the person with dementia but also by those who have an emotional bond with them. The focus is not on how to cure the disease but on the disease itself. Dementia is an irreversible disease with a whole host of secondary phenomena, creating a burden for some people and suffering, all of which requires relief.

In the first section we will look at dementia as a terminal journey, a way of continuously saying goodbye until the end. The second section will discuss the terminal phase of dementia.

Dementia as a terminal journey

Introduction

The idea of finiteness, dying and death relates not only to the actual end of someone's life but also to the course of the disease or trauma of dementia. It is important to refer to dementia as a trauma for a number of reasons: not only does it reflect the psychological impact but also the seriousness of the grief that is suffered.

Chronic condition

Dementia can be considered as a chronic condition – it unfolds over a period of time and lasts for life's duration. It is not very easy to identify exactly where it begins and ends. It usually lasts for a long to a very long period of time, during which the lives of all those directly affected are upturned. When speaking of time, it is important to distinguish between 'time' in terms of calendar time and 'duration' in terms of the perceived time. The years during which the disease manifests itself and develops can be perceived as a very long time. Days may suddenly feel like 36-h days.

The insidious onset

It is possible to differentiate between various phases or periods of time that overlap one another by identifying a specific sort of suffering in each. First and foremost, there is the unclear and uncertain onset. It is an insidious onset. The person may be forgetful, without it being clear whether this is normal forgetfulness or the result of depression or another condition. They may also exhibit changing behaviour that may be put down to stress or relationship problems. Furthermore, these initial changes are often intermittent and may not be perceived at the same time by others. Apart from differences in when these changes are actually perceived, there are also differences in how they are interpreted. You can compare it to a jigsaw puzzle made up of thousands of pieces and many colours. Slowly the puzzle begins to lose its colour and the pieces no longer fit together properly. The smooth radiance of life begins to fade and things sometimes get rough, which never happened before. Hairline cracks start appearing in the walls of your life, as it were.

Specific suffering

The specific suffering referred to here can be described as experiencing feelings of uncertainty, sensing that you are losing control of things that are sometimes perfectly obvious. There may be non-verbalized fears, a lack of comprehension, misunderstandings, accusations and unnoticed feelings of loneliness. It is like a ship sailing out of the harbour of life without telling anyone when and where it is leaving. Loved ones begin to lose contact with each other without it being noticed. Different people can experience the same suffering in different ways. If someone lives on their own and does not share their daily life with someone else, their specific suffering will perhaps go unnoticed for longer. The misunderstandings and conflicts that arise over this initial period of uncertainty may lead to feelings of guilt at a later stage, once they realize what it was all about. Families have been heard to say 'if only I'd known . . .'.

Concealed suffering

As seen so often with a life-threatening disease, denial is one of the first reactions. 'We all forget things at times.' The person undergoing the insidious onset of the disease tends to play it down and conceal it, and so do their nearest and dearest. In the insidious onset phase, they are practically unable to perceive whether it is occasional forgetfulness or whether the gaps are bigger than is apparent. They continue to play hide-and-seek in order to give each other peace of mind. This is called concealed suffering. Privately there is suffering because of the uncertainty.

Understanding and lack of understanding

The initial period, which can increasingly be likened to the phase of the lost self, when someone feels they are lost, typically involves a lack of understanding. This is felt not just by the person with dementia who does not understand what is going on but also by their family and the professional care-givers. Many find that the first signs are not taken seriously by the family doctor and they feel fobbed off with empty words. This can raise a significant barrier to people approaching a care-giver for help. It often takes a long time before going to the doctor and it is usually the partner or next of kin who makes the move, because the person with dementia does not have any insight into the disease and does not understand why he or she should need a doctor.

It is increasingly apparent to me that people with an irreversible condition and their families are in need of psychospiritual education. The main aim of this education is to show them a way out of the chaos. People with dementia and their families find themselves in a maze of chaos. First of all, the experiences and stories of the next of kin must be carefully listened to. The next stage is to examine the person and provide information. This helps pave the way from the pre-diagnosis phase to the actual diagnosis.

Diagnosis from a palliative perspective

A fundamental aspect of looking at dementia from a palliative perspective is to adopt a multi-dimensional, multi-disciplinary and interdisciplinary approach. The diagnosis is made by examining the person via a number of 'disciplines', but interdisciplinary support is required to convey the results of these examinations to the people involved. Psychosocial and spiritual support is needed in addition to help given via medication. It is not just one person who is suffering, but a number of people in a number of respects.

We assume that people with dementia are also told about the diagnosis – this is not always done as a matter of course. They are steadily losing control of their own lives, so it is all the more important for them to receive as much information as possible to try to curb this loss of control. We do not assume that people with dementia have no knowledge of the changes going on in their lives but, on the contrary, that they are perfectly aware of these changes, are depressed about them, feel despair and desperation and are looking for something to hold on to and people to latch on to. We assume that they are more aware and have more knowledge about what is going on than we want to acknowledge. All too often, people think that suffering can be relieved by avoiding it – by not talking about it – but the only way to relieve this suffering is to bring it out into the open and share it. A wound needs careful attention.

We also assume that people with dementia have their own coping styles to face any difficulties presented in life.

The trauma of dementia (a better word than the disease of dementia) may also evoke earlier traumatic experiences, acting as a trigger. By telling a person what the diagnosis is, they are given more of a chance to be a co-partner in the battle against grief and not just a victim who looks on helplessly. This viewpoint is usually shared from the beginning, and explained to the next of kin who is most likely to take on the role of volunteer carer. They have just as little knowledge and experience of this disease or trauma as the person with dementia and so have equal need of the psychospiritual education referred to above. It is therefore not just a question of giving the diagnosis, or telling 'the truth', but also of providing as much information and support as possible for the future. Examples of such support include the work of the Alzheimer Association and the Alzheimer Café: initiatives that meet the need for information and support in different ways.

Between recognition and denial

As with other irreversible diseases, disbelief and denial may be the first reaction when a diagnosis is given. A second opinion may be requested or hopes placed in alternative medicine or reports of a possible cure. The various people involved seldom react in the same way. It dawns on people in different ways and at different times that they have got to adapt to a changing situation. Dementia also affects family and social life and can bring about a whole host of changes in existing relationships. The established roles and family positions have to change and all sorts of new tasks are presented. A new way of communicating is needed. Old and unspoken latent tensions may suddenly flare up, but this may also strengthen the mutual bond, creating a high degree of solidarity with each other. Together the couple or family will tackle the consequences of the disease; it is possible to differentiate who the person is from the disease. 'I still see my father in him – someone who's done so much for me in the past, who I can now help in return by giving security and support.'

People often become aware of the changing situation in different ways and also at different times. For instance, one person may reproach another for being all doom and gloom, because that person may have different experiences and perceptions of the person with dementia. Often it is only a few family members who are open to receiving the information and support referred to above, with others believing that they do not need it. As the dementia progresses and situations become more complex (e.g. feelings of mistrust, getting lost when away from home, anger and highly depressive episodes), the psychological ability of the voluntary carers and family to 'carry the burden' risks being undermined at the very time when it is vital for them to form a united front.

Suffering from loss

The person with dementia and their family live in a world turning into chronic grief. It is as if they are 'slowly saying goodbye'. There is a long list of people and things that have to be left behind. From no longer being able to drive, to no longer being able to go to the toilet on one's own without encountering additional problems. There is also a sense of losing oneself, no longer knowing who one has become, returning to the past and losing the ability to interpret things. Persons with dementia no longer know how to fill their time usefully.

It is also possible to look at this grief from the perspective of psychological processing. For instance, someone who has knowledge of the approaching end to their life, who consciously and subconsciously looks back at their life, takes stock of things, wants to set their house in order, think about the way they will die, say goodbye to those around them and draw their life to a close. In the process of doing this, important spiritual topics sometimes come to the fore, such as unresolved conflicts, guilt, sin or evil, or gratitude and greater awareness of who has been the most supportive; people who mean an awful lot right now or who may be missed. Everyone will process these things from the point of view of their own life history and lifestyle.

Various tasks can be distinguished in the grieving process: growing awareness of the loss suffered; experiencing all sorts of feelings that trigger the feeling of missing a person; getting to know the 'new' person; and reorienting and adapting oneself to the changing situation. Periods of restlessness can be seen in dementia, as well as periods of tranquillity in which the person appears to be at rest and to have found their own way.

Suffering, especially during the periods of restlessness, can be relieved by analysing the topics that come up as if they are current and full of meaning now, and not rejecting them as things that have been and gone, things in the distant past. 'I spend most of my time looking back', said a very old lady with vascular dementia. She was looking back at her life and, in doing so, saying goodbye to her life. Her increased physical reliance on support and a small family network meant that she had to live in a nursing home.

Awareness of death

As with an incurable disease, the awareness of the definitive goodbye (the awareness of death) plays its own role in the background, just like a drum rolling in the distance. Focus is on the here and now, enjoying the good times, doing what you are still able to do, going off on holiday together and enjoying any children and grandchildren. But sometimes the awareness of 'temporariness' cannot be repressed, so again it is necessary to listen to what the persons with dementia have to say and explore their questions.

The person may refer to their awareness of their pending death. They may wish to die. The subject of wishing their life to end may even be broached by the persons themselves, without them being able to say exactly when they want this to happen. I attended an Alzheimer Café when people in the early stages of dementia brought this topic up for discussion, and I realized they were not so much asking for their lives to end but were looking for dignity and care for their partners. They were very worried about being a burden. When discussing these issues, it is important not so much to examine the ability of the person to give informed consent, but their underlying fears and questions about support and dignity. They are asking for support and not for a discussion about their destiny, and for relief from the burden of suffering rather than an end to their lives.

The topic of death can also be of significance for the next of kin. You may hear them say things like 'it should be possible to do something, this is no longer dignified'. The topic of death can take on a growing significance, especially when the disease is further advanced, when the person is at the stage of the 'lost self', when feelings of both despair and hopelessness increase – their ability to live independently lessens, supplementary care begins to take over, communication is more difficult, speech is harder, day-time and night-time routines are more frequently disrupted and the need for permanent 'supervision' is greater. Or when the person is at the stage of the 'submerged self' in which they withdraw more and more frequently into their own world that is becoming inaccessible to others.

It is a topic that is shocking to some people. There is still a great taboo surrounding wishing someone to die or being so desperate that you want to assist in the death of the person with dementia. Research has shown that there is a close correlation between abuse and the feelings of powerlessness of family carers or care-givers. Death should therefore be taken out of the realm of taboo and treated as a normal topic. It is not unusual or strange for thoughts of death to emerge. In fact, it is strange if they do not emerge. Nor do these thoughts signify the opposite of concepts such as love, care and attention. They are very closely linked. 'I wouldn't wish this upon my husband', I often hear people say. 'I wouldn't wish this upon my worst enemy.'

With the palliative approach, death is very much a topic for discussion. It teaches you to look and listen out for questions behind the questions. Thoughts of wanting to die are transmitted via signals that have to be inter-cepted and decoded. They may be interpreted as the intense depression of a spouse who has to live in a dual world in which their partner is still there and yet at the same time is no longer there. So they feel like a widow or widower, although they are not one yet. The loss of a partner or parent to dementia is often an underestimated loss. Contact with 'companions in distress', who can recognize and acknowledge the way you feel, is often a good way to relieve the burden of grief.

Allowing the topic of death to be openly talked about, even though the person is not yet in the terminal phase, also means that the opportunity is there to discuss a number of things together while it is still possible. For the next of kin, it is often important for concrete arrangements to be decided – for instance if the person wants to be buried or cremated, if they want a church service or not, if they want to lie in state, the choice of music and many other things – so that they reflect the wishes of the deceased. Many want to be able to say: 'that's how he/she wanted it'.

By openly discussing the topic of death while both parties are still alive and not necessarily nearing the end of their life, it is also possible to let each other know and feel what they mean and have meant to each other. It also gives the opportunity to put into words the things that were, and still are, good and worthwhile. It gives the opportunity to celebrate their life together. Celebrating means festivity and letting go.

The care-giver and death

Whether the topic of death and end of life can be discussed and explored in depth in the course of the dementia also depends greatly on the care-givers and what they are able or dare to convey. If they do not hear (or pretend not to hear) the topic, they can reinforce the taboo through their behaviour. It can be fatal to say things like 'we shouldn't go thinking of that yet'. The topic of death often cannot be discussed in family relationships. This is why it is important that they *are* able to talk about it in contact with other people and away from home. What I have seen and heard in a few Alzheimer Cafés has shown me how much this opportunity to talk frankly is wanted and how satisfying it can be. Café participants, and in particular their family members, continue to draw support from these open discussions for a long time afterwards.

The various care-givers involved should observe and bring into the open the topic of death. For instance, if doctors do so they can ascertain in good time where the desirable limits lie in medical treatment. Not all treatable diseases have to be treated. Because these limits are not always generally evident and have to be clarified in each individual situation, this topic has to be discussed in good time. In this respect, pro-active and anticipatory vision and views are needed, not just reactive ones. Reactive treatment may lead to a person's life being prolonged against their will and to reproaches from the next of kin. 'I know he'd never have wanted this.' Care-givers must also know where they themselves stand on the subject of life and death and have the necessary skills to communicate with persons and their family about the issues involved. This requires a knowledge of oneself and good communication skills.

But there are also other care-givers who have to watch out for the topic of death and be aware of their own abilities and limits. Just as signs of pain have to be observed, so too must the 'life pain' that makes death a desirable option for some people. Care-givers and nurses have different skills and tasks than psychologists, pastoral counsellors or voluntary carers. Each will have to find out what their individual tasks are from the point of view of their own profession.

If a person with dementia and their next of kin have to call upon support and care from a care facility, the vision and views of that facility are very important with regard to what their stance is with respect to issues of finiteness and how they envisage care in the final phase of life.

Palliative care in the final phase of dementia

Introduction

It is first of all important to note that the end does not always come exactly when planned or expected. It is not always the dementia that causes the death – there may be other causes, such as heart failure or brain disease. And this may mean that death comes suddenly. It may come during the phase I have referred to as the 'lost self', or during the phase of the 'submerged self'. The initial reaction of the family will be surprise and then possibly relief, as both the person with dementia and the partner are spared possible suffering in the future.

Another point of importance is that death or dying may take place at different locations: at home, in a hospital or in a care facility. This is to be taken into consideration because it may affect the meaning one gives to it and the organizational aspects relating to death. For many people, making the decision that care at home is no longer possible is fraught with difficulty. They may have promised the person with dementia (or themselves when a parent died) that they would continue to look after someone at home. It is not unusual for the family to hope for the person to die before they are admitted to a home. Admission to a nursing home or, as a last resort, to hospital may give rise to feelings of guilt and may sometimes even signify a new crisis in family relationships. The one who had to relinquish the person with dementia to a home or hospital may want them to lie in state at home once they have died. This can be comforting to them.

To make sure that care at home can be sustained, much attention needs to be paid to the organizational aspects of care. It is nearly always necessary to get home care help and sometimes to call upon volunteers for support (especially volunteers who are able and want to take on the task of watching over the person).

The expected end

The end may also come when it is expected. It is obviously easier in retrospect to see when the last few days and hours have come and yet there are signs indicating the last phase. Signs such as increasing tiredness, sleeping more, withdrawing further and further away, diminishing response to contact, refusal to eat and drink and no longer being able to swallow medicines. Even the effect of the medicine may diminish. Refusing to eat or drink by keeping one's mouth shut is understood as a sign that the person with dementia no longer wishes to live. Sometimes they may also have pneumonia, in which case a general weakening and decline is even more common.

The end may come when expected and wished for. The overall decline and refusal to eat can be considered as a purposeful wish on the part of the person. Whoever knows and has known them will also be able to recognize this. It may coincide with the partner's own wish for the death to come soon. *The palliative perspective refers to an end of life that is neither accelerated nor delayed.* Inserting a drip feed tube is somewhat at odds with this perspective. A person has to be given the opportunity to die. Even the treatment of pneumonia in this phase can be a moot point.

An aspect unique to dementia is that people find themselves in a situation in which their ability to express themselves is seriously impeded. It is the task of the care team and care-givers to learn to watch out for signs that indicate pain and/or discomfort. Signs such as moaning during care and unexpected physical movements may indicate pain and restlessness. Palliative care in the last phase of life is aimed at the general comfort of the person.

Contact with family

Another unique aspect of this palliative time is contact with the family. In the first place, it is important to know whether they share the same outlook of the person's situation, so attention must be paid to the 'awareness context'. There may also be an issue here of people being 'aware' at different times and in different ways. Some or all members of the family may hope that this is a crisis that will not carry on forever. 'The end' is either not wanted or absolutely not wanted. There is sometimes such a bond between the dying person and a relative that the relative resists any possible severance of this bond until the very end. It is not unusual for this to cause disagreement between care-givers and the family, where the family's wishes become demands they want to enforce. The doctor (and sometimes other care-givers) adopts the role of the bearer of bad tidings – which can meet with considerable aggression. This may prevent the care-givers from fulfilling their role as supporter or companion, and from looking out for the psychological and spiritual needs of this phase. The situation may be easier if no relationship of trust has built up and you are seen as a total stranger. Religious or cultural backgrounds may also play an important role and be another area in which care-givers and the family do not see eye to eye. Recognizing beforehand that this unwanted power struggle is brewing may help you to take preventative action. The guiding principle for care-givers' actions and support should be to ensure that the interests of the person are met and that the family is involved in deciding what policy to adopt.

Crisis in family

Attention should also be paid to the 'awareness context' of the care-givers involved (we will come back to this point). Taking the family into consideration is important because we see the death as something that may be wanted (a release and relief) as well as a crisis that was underestimated rather than overestimated. The end is approaching but it often takes a long time, giving rise to a multitude of problems and a considerable amount of care. We have called this grief a slow process of saying goodbye. The literature refers to this as 'anticipatory grief': saying goodbye before the end actually comes. Or perhaps we are mistaken in thinking this, because the family have not said goodbye at all yet. It is also necessary to work out what is actually meant by saying goodbye. Dying can evoke incredibly strong feelings of grief. In the years in which the person is being cared for, the emotional bond may well go through change but this will not affect the intensity of the bond. 'She'll always be my mother.' I have seen people dying and their children still clinging to painful memories of them – children who were barely to be seen while the person was living in the nursing home – and then suddenly, in the days leading up to the person's death, their personal accounts of wounds would open up. There were days when these family members would need extra care and attention. They were grieving about what the person could have been or what they could have meant, but never about what they became and would now definitely never be again. Such family members were grieving about the definitive failure of dreams, wishes and expectations.

Dying can also be experienced as a crisis, because the last thing of meaning for a surviving family member has gone away. 'She was my only sister. Neither of us married. I visited her every day and cooked her a meal each day.' The death of a parent is often the death of the last parent and means that the children become orphans in a sense. A distinctly new phase in the family tree begins, and so also with the relationships between the surviving relatives. Over the long period in which the person with dementia is cared for, relationships can either get stronger or become estranged. There may be resentment towards some people who have given little or no support, and towards those who never visited. Sometimes a decision is made not to tell these relations of the approaching end, not even to tell them that the person has died or about the funeral arrangements.

Task of care-givers

By care-givers we mean the doctors, nursing staff and care staff forming the core team, supplemented by paramedics, psychologists, social workers, occupational therapists, pastoral counsellors and sometimes also volunteers. In palliative care, attention must be given to the many dimensions of life and death and this also calls for an interdisciplinary approach. In every situation, an assessment is made of who is to play an active role and who is to have a more background role.

The primary task of care-givers is to provide good care: good physical and psychological care. Good physical care (ensuring people are in a comfortable position, preventing wounds, treating bedsores, making sure their beds are clean and comfortable) can also be considered as psychological care. It is about providing technically good care and calling upon your skills and expertise. It is also about the way in which care is given. It is about the art of care: consideration, patience, scrupulousness, being attentive and perceptive. It is also about love, about caring about what you are doing. A person with dementia in the terminal phase becomes increasingly dependent; it becomes increasingly difficult for them to say what they want or to perform any self-care.

If a person with dementia is not in the phase of the 'submerged self' and has moments of lucidity, extra care and consideration needs to be taken when addressing and speaking to them. Even in the phase of the 'submerged self', it is a sign of dignified care to still speak to the person with dementia, to use their name, to say hello to them, to touch them gently or even explain to them about what you are doing. This way of interacting is important for all parties – for the person and for the next of kin, who will remember this dignified treatment, and for the care-givers, who benefit from treating fragile persons like real people instead of objects.

Mediating in care

If persons have moments of lucidity, they may also be aware of their approaching death. They may be afraid without knowing what this fear relates to: it may suggest a general fear of death or of the unknown; it may also be related to the person's religious life history or to their experiences and life events. Knowledge of their life story and history can be of help in this respect. Care-givers should watch out for signs of fear and restlessness (as well as pain) and act as an advocate in addressing these fears. It may be meaningful for the person to see a pastor.

Information

One of the core tasks of care-givers in the terminal phase is to provide information to the family, the person's contacts. If the person is going to die at home, it is often the family who give information to the professional care-givers about what they have seen or heard in the evening or night-time, when they were alone with the person. If the person is going to die in a care facility, these roles are reversed and it is the family who wants to hear from the care-givers how the person's night was and whether they responded to anything, etc. The family will have to be kept informed of a whole string of things. We have already referred to this as the 'awareness context', but more accurately it is the growing awareness that the person has entered the terminal phase. This has to be shared with the next of kin. It is important to discuss (again) with the family what policy of care and treatment they want to be followed. It is preferable to have already discussed this at the time of admission, but sometimes that is not possible. Sometimes the period between admission and dying is very short. It is also important to discuss with the family about what they may expect over the next few weeks and months. No-one can say exactly how long it will be before a person dies. Those who live life at a fast pace will have to get used to living life more slowly; dying takes its own time.

Information about possible ways of alleviating any pain and fear needs to be shared with family. Explanations about the use of morphine should be given, because it is often shrouded in myth and misunderstanding. Details should also be discussed about the place where the person is going to die: whether alone or in a room with other persons. Decisions should be made with the family about whether they want to keep vigil with the dying person during the last days and hours. If so, arrangements for them to rest or sleep at the care facility also need to be planned for.

The significance of dying

It is not just the information that has to be discussed, but also the significance that it holds for the person concerned. 'How are you feeling now that your husband or mother is approaching death?' Such a question may provide an opportunity for emotions to be expressed, and also for sharing thoughts and stories. This is often when the family members themselves look back at their own life history and run through the film of their own lives. Family carers may say that this time of saying goodbye can play an important and even valuable role for the family as well, and it is important to devote enough time to it. Family carers may speak of the significance of keeping vigil with the person, as well as rituals of saying goodbye. Dying is also a ritual with rites of passage. Care-givers should also be aware that memories of how the person died can affect the grieving process of the family and therefore their mental health.

Rituals

Rituals may refer to all kinds of activities and events. For instance, gathering the closest family members together in a circle to pay their respects to the dying person, to get things off their chest, to thank the dying person for what they have done, to hold each other once more in a circle, to be quiet together and to look at each other. This does not have to be religious in nature. If someone has a religious life history, words and gestures from the past may have a certain value to them: singing a song, anointing, saying a prayer, reading favourite passages from the Bible.

Some rituals (such as anointing of the sick) require preparation and need to be led. They take on a fairly fixed form and order of events. The family may request this kind of ritual for their own needs. Care-givers can ask whether the family would like this. Sometimes the family will say that their father or mother attached greater value to this kind of ritual than they personally did, but that they still wanted to be present for it. The person leading the ritual, a pastor or maybe someone else, may opt for a particular form or content of the ritual so that the family feel it is also meaningful for them.

There are also other informal but no less important rituals. For instance, offering coffee and tea or something to eat to those keeping vigil by the dying person's bed, regularly popping in to see how things are and reminding family members that they can always come and ask anything they want to know. Care-givers must be aware that the family of a dying person have a heightened and intense level of awareness. They are sensitive to attention and detail. It is as if they are making a film, recording every little detail. Offering them a coffee or tea is significant because it makes them feel they are real, visible and not a burden, that someone is looking out for them. It symbolizes hospitality.

Care-givers must also realize that dying is a unique event for some people – something they are experiencing for the first time. 'Father died all of a sudden, so we weren't able to be with him in his last few moments.' It is also unique because every relationship has a special significance and value, even if the value was limited.

Death and being with a dying person in their last few hours are not everyday experiences. Many people have images of dying in their heads, perhaps romanticized images, but these are often unrealistic or even wrong. The images may well be based on an earlier memory of death. They may be reassuring ('my mother also died here and I knew she was well cared for') but they may also have been traumatic, so information should be given about common phenomena in people who are dying, such as changes in breathing patterns and their sometimes gasping for breath. Families often worry that the person is suffocating or in pain, so they need explanations of what happens and to be told what is being done to ensure a peaceful death. There are frequently misunderstandings about the palliative sedation in the terminal phase. If this is not explained satisfactorily, family may get the impression that a person's life is deliberately being ended more quickly, whereas it actually involves relieving pain and restlessness. Care-givers need to explain what they have and have not done in this palliative time.

Unexpected nevertheless

Death may not be unexpected but the exact moment frequently comes at an unplanned time. It is not unusual (in my experience in over 50% of cases) for the person to die when no-one is with them. 'I was just having a chat with his brother. I'd just popped home. I was just having a rest.' The family will find it unexpected nevertheless. This subject should also be broached beforehand and discussed. It will help prevent any unnecessary feelings of guilt about not being present at the actual moment of death. Many people seem only to be able to die if they are on their own. Others die once someone they were expecting has come. The time of death is a singular time. It is as if the clock has stopped. The life calendar of the family, who have become the bereaved, now includes a before and an after, a new date in their history.

The moment of death is a ritual moment as well, requiring attention to specific details or procedures. Such details include closing the eyes, the first care given after the person has died, informing (often referred to as warning) family members who still want to come, saying a ritual prayer or burning a candle, washing and clothing the body (sometimes called administering the last care) and deciding who would, could and should do this. When a person dies in a nursing home, the family are left alone with them usually, so that they can pay their last respects in private. This also involves looking after the person's remaining belongings: rings, jewellery, photos and clothing. It can be very painful to family if any of these possessions go missing.

Care for the professional care-givers

The professional care-givers also have to say goodbye to the person they have cared for. A stronger bond than the care-giver first realizes may have formed. Just as for family members, their awareness context and what the death meant for them should be noted. They also have to be told about the policy to be adopted and they may need to discuss this policy. For instance, withholding treatment to someone they have become attached to may not come so naturally to them. There should also be a clear way of informing them of the death of the person they have cared for; this may even include the staff who provided care by cleaning the room or distributing linens. Managers have the additional task of keeping a watchful eye on how a care-giver may be affected by someone's death. Care for the care-givers should be an intrinsic part of the overall vision of palliative care. A specific vision and policy, as well as a programme of care, should be adopted for the family carers.

After-care

And finally we come to 'after-care' – the days between the person dying, the funeral and the period immediately after this. Relatives should be given the option of having a final meeting to discuss things and to review the care provided. It is not always possible for staff to attend the funeral, although a condolence card is always sent. Care-givers may sometimes write their own 'in memoriam', which they give to the family or may be read at the memorial ceremony. In an increasing number of care facilities, memorial services are held once or several times a year. The names of those who have died are read out at these services. Many care facilities have a meditation centre or chapel with a book containing the names of all those who have died. The UK hospice movement in particular has an established formal after-care service. It offers support to the bereaved by providing individual grieving support or holding group sessions.

Conclusion

Most experience of palliative terminal care thus far has been acquired with persons dying of cancer. The process of dying from chronic conditions such as dementia has its own individual features, yet a lot of knowledge, learning and skills gained in the field of palliative terminal care for persons with cancer has been translated into appropriate knowledge and skills for those having a chronic illness. This translation of skills involves looking at the specific aspects of a given illness. More targeted research could be done in future, to help further refine palliative care for dementia. This includes a more conscious focus being placed on the topic of death and dying as an integral part of support and care for people with dementia. Death comes in the end, but the thought of it comes much sooner.

References

Jones, G.M.M. (2004) The loss of meaningful attachments in dementia. In G.M.M. Jones and B.M.L. Miesen (Eds), *Care-giving in Dementia* vol. 3. London: Brunner-Routledge, pp. 261–284.

Verdult, R. (1998). *Dement Worden: een Kindertijd in Beeld* (3rd edn). Baarn, The Netherlands: De HBuitgeverij.

Chapter 17

Care-giving in dementia: moving ahead together

Review and perspectives

Bère Miesen

Introduction

What may be obvious for care-givers in dealing with persons with dementia may not necessarily be obvious for the family. A number of things are completely different for the family than for professional care-givers (see Miesen, 1999).

Professional care-givers

For professional care-givers, a number of aspects about the situation are considerably different than for the family. Care-givers start working in a family without there being an emotional bond with the person with dementia. It is not a matter of a long-term relationship ending for them. The care offered by the care-giver has a different context because they are unable to make comparisons with what the dementia-sufferer was like before. The likelihood of success is greater, because the patient's failings compared to what they were able to do before are not taken into account. Care-givers are able to gain from the situation. In this respect, it is often a matter of gain and building up. The care-giver starts with a clean slate   with an unknown third party. Because there is no material that can be used to make comparisons with how this person was before, they can only get to know this person better and more intimately. Care-givers have usually opted to carry out this line of work and have made it their profession to deal with people with dementia. Because they have trained for it and have the necessary expertise, they do not feel powerless so quickly. They usually try to apply what they have learned. It is their aim to try and turn the tide to a certain extent. Because they do not have the pain of the loss, they are more easily able to focus on the individual deficits as they arise, and try to find solutions or make changes or give support. Care-givers do not have to detach themselves from someone with whom they have had an emotional bond or who was very well known to them. They are even spared going through the lack of certainty that makes it really difficult to deal with loss through dementia, in the same way as it is with someone who is missing, as we will discuss later.

Family care-givers

As a family member, you always have to deal with the fact that an emotional bond is threatening to end. The care provided by the family takes on little or no context in light of everything that the person with dementia used to be able to do: in this respect, the family gains little from it. It is always a matter of loss and deterioration. As time goes by, they find themselves increasingly in the role of carer – a situation that they could not have chosen but has nevertheless landed on them. At a certain point in time, they are right in the middle of it. They obviously clearly see the individual deficits developing in the dementia-sufferer, but it is primarily the consequence of these deficits, the overall change, that causes them pain. The family often feels powerless: the tide cannot be turned. A loved one is slowly changing, becoming a different person, a stranger. Although they seem to be slipping away and slowly disappearing from family life, they remain very much a part of it for quite some time. Just as if they were in a coma or had gone missing, the lack of certainty persists about whether the person is still there. The family is facing the emotional problem of having to deal with an unclear and invisible loss. It is difficult for them to detach themselves from such a situation and create the necessary distance to be able to survive emotionally.

Family and professional care-givers: a perspective with and without pain

In short, right from the outset, care-givers have a favourable start in all aspects of their work with people with dementia. They already have a certain professional expertise and are also able to apply this knowledge without being hampered by the pain of having to slowly say goodbye to someone you love. While the family finds it difficult to achieve a distance, care-givers get steadily closer. Basically, everything is at stake for the family, certainly from an emotional point of view, whereas care-givers can only gain from the situation, even from an emotional viewpoint.

Care-giving in dementia: a brief psychology of the family's perspective

Together but alone

For the healthy partner, dementia means they are losing their mate. The process of dementia in the one affects the other at the very core of their unity together. As far as the outside world is concerned they are still living with each other, but from an emotional and psychological point of view they are no longer really together. The healthy partner feels left in the lurch and alone, and because they feel like this it is increasingly difficult to get help from people who sometimes try to cheer them up saying things like 'you should be happy she's still there'. But in fact they are living without their partner, even though the partner is physically still there. It is an absurd situation in which the status of the family is unclear, as illustrated in the following advertisement that appeared in the newspaper 'NRC Handelsblad' on 31 October 1992:

> Spontaneous man (acad., 1.72), open, friendly and 60+ to his amazement, misses his wife, who was admitted to a nursing home a few years ago (permanently) with a mental illness. He feels he is single, but does not wish to consider a close 'relationship' under these circumstances. He is therefore looking – and feels he is free to do so – for a female companion with a kind and warm personality, so that they can give a lot to each other and support each other, someone to talk to openly about what you're actually doing and with whom to do nice things. I am looking for someone from a good background and I would really prefer someone around 40 years of age. I play a lot of piano (mainly classical), have various hobbies, and do not do any sport. I live in the western central part of the Netherlands. Please write a letter under no. 247847549 to the newspaper's offices. A photo would be welcome.

One's own life and the future at issue

Because the person with dementia is always there, and given the amount of care and attention they require from the family member, the family member's own life comes to a standstill in a manner of speaking. There is no longer any time to visit friends, sing in the choir or go swimming with the grandchildren. Even holidays usually go by the board. Looking after the dementia-sufferer may well be a task that lasts for years, 24 h a day. One's own view of the future also hangs radically in the balance: 'All the plans I had to do up the attic once I retired . . . and for us to go to the caravan more often. I may as well just forget it all!' It is not uncommon for a crisis to occur in interpreting the meaning of one's own life ('What am I actually living for?'), which sometimes develops directly into a crisis of faith or depression.

Past together under scrutiny

It is not just the future that is at issue. The past, and especially the time spent together, is placed under scrutiny. This shared past affects the acceptance of the family member ('Why is this happening to me?') as well as their motivation for providing care. The mutual relationship and emotional bond are crystallized as it were. The verdict or outcome of the time spent together not only has an impact on the extent of the loss experience but also on the burden felt. On the one hand, a strong emotional bond may make it very hard for someone to accept the decline of the person with dementia. If the child or partner has always been really fond of the dementia-sufferer, they also have a lot to lose. On the other hand, this bond may make someone monopolize the care provided and find it unacceptable to allow any assistance from outside, thus putting considerable strain on their ability to bear the burden. These family members play for time if help is offered, but continually complain that it is all getting too much. At the same time, they are able to provide care over a long period of time, because they can look back on a good relationship and are grateful to the other one for what they had in the past. However, there may also be a considerable degree of unresolved conflicts in the relationship. If the other person has never taken any notice of you and is now constantly making demands on you, caring for them may well be a bitter pill to swallow. Dementia also means that the other person can no longer be held responsible and that it is no longer possible to deal with the unresolved conflicts that exist between the two.

Like a missing person

The family is confronted with a process of slowly saying goodbye. Over the course of time, the person with dementia gradually becomes a lesser person than they used to be. This enforced parting from someone close to you forms a loss experience entailing all the behaviour and feelings of a normal grieving process: protest, despair, detachment, guilt, shame, insecurity; numbness, denial, anger, sorrow; hope, perplexity, searching, desire, distress, despair. But what is a loss for one person may not be a loss for another. Losing someone through dementia does not necessarily have to be the same for everyone. It makes a considerable amount of difference if you are losing your partner or your father or mother. It also matters if you are really fond of someone, or if you both always led your own lives and did not spend much time together even when the person with dementia was fit and well. Besides these individual differences in loss experience, losing someone through dementia in general seems particularly difficult to deal with because of the invisibility of the loss.

It may be enlightening in this respect to compare this experience with the situation of a family of someone who has disappeared without trace. For as long as the loss remains intangible and indefinite, the family cannot start to grieve and deal with the loss. There is always hope. Without proof that, for example, someone's body is found somewhere, the family members do not know where they stand. Their feelings swing between hope and despair. With dementia, just as with a missing person, the situation remains unclear for a long time. The outside world usually looks elsewhere rather than at the family members. For an outsider, it looks as if you have both still got each other, you are still a couple, you still have your parents. But you know better yourself:

the other person may well be there, but actually they are not. In reality you feel you have to continue through life like a widow or widower or an orphan without any parent. No wonder that stubborn disbelief from the outside world sometimes drives family members to despair.

Apart from the fact that the type of family relationship between the person caring and the dementia patient, the personality of the family member, the emotional bond with the patient and the existence of unresolved conflicts can make it particularly difficult to deal with the loss, the invisibility of the loss adds to the difficulty. The parting only becomes final once the person with dementia has actually 'disappeared'. As long as they are still alive, family members are not sure how things stand. You are still their next of kin, but then again, you are not. The dementia-sufferer no longer sees you as their partner or child. Sometimes the next of kin is something familiar or trusted to them, sometimes they seem like a distant acquaintance and often they are simply a stranger. The family member slowly disappears out of the life of the dementia-sufferer. It is as if you do not belong together any more. It is therefore hardly surprising that family members sooner or later start wishing for the person with dementia to die. On the other hand, the hope that they will get better or improve keeps going for a long time and abandoning this hope is felt to be a form of unfaithfulness or betrayal.

Help can also be a problem

Help around the house or for looking after the person with dementia generally provides relief for the family. In the first place, it helps them resolve all sorts of practical problems. It generally makes providing care a less heavy burden to bear.

The advantages for the family of getting help from care-givers are clear: a helping hand, time and opportunity at last to go somewhere else, company and a listening ear. But there are also disadvantages: it is now all too clear how things are looking, it is a tangible sign that there are problems, the feeling of having failed, been defeated. On top of that, situations may arise that could be threatening for the family. By their very presence, care-givers are entering into the intimate atmosphere of the family. They are bursting into the existing situation. The next of kin has usually asked for the help, but did not immediately realize what it would be like to have someone in the house every day or a couple of times a week. For instance, a woman could well have asked for help in looking after her husband because he can be so difficult to take care of. But she will not be so keen to see that the care-giver is managing to take care of him without any problems, or that her husband and the care-giver immediately seem to have a much better rapport than she has had with him over the last few months. It is therefore no surprise that she is sometimes really jealous of the care-giver.

Review

Part I: Models and theories

It is hard to believe that the focus on the 'perceptual world' of persons with dementia has been underestimated to a certain extent in favour of their 'experiential world' for example. *Gemma Jones and her colleagues* prove that this focus is incomplete, and their contribution (Chapters 1 & 2) analyses, among other things, normal age-related visual changes and the visuoperceptual pathology in Alzheimer's disease. From this perspective, they stress the necessity for professional care-givers to have sufficient understanding of these changes. Not only to model their own care-giving relationships with individual persons with dementia, but also to shape the necessary environmental adjustments instead of projecting 'cosy' ones.

From the very stage at which persons with dementia are losing control of the situation, a special assessment of their visual capacities is more than ever crucial for interpreting the way in which they are coping and trying to maintain their 'handhold on life'. *Gemma Jones and her colleagues* clarify the (still) huge amount of misunderstanding surrounding visual phenomena in Alzheimer's dementia. By distinguishing between hallucinations, illusions, misperceptions and misidentifications, the authors hone a number of tools aimed at individual care-giving. At the same time, they pave the way ahead for general educational curricula on care-giving in dementia.

After presenting a brief review of Attachment Theory, *Bère Miesen* (Chapter 3) demonstrates the richness of Bowlby's theory in a variety of clinical areas. The concepts 'attachment behaviour' and 'attachment history' in particular seem to have a broad explanatory value. Many researchers and clinicians already consider Bowlby's Attachment Theory as a framework of concepts that can be used to understand the meaning of a variety of behaviours of persons with dementia, their family and professional care-givers.

Since the early 1980s, awareness has been considered a core element in clinical work performed by psychologists in dementia, certainly in The Netherlands. *Linda Clare and her colleagues* (Chapter 4) present a biopsychosocial model of awareness based on research of neurological, psychological and social aspects. There is no doubt that in a framework of coping with the chronic trauma of dementia it is crucial to assess the complex phenomenon of awareness of dementia. Their contribution towards understanding how people with dementia think, talk, feel and behave will also increase awareness about dementia.

Part II: Interventions in care facilities

Based on many years of clinical experience, *Will Blake and his colleagues* (Chapter 5) stress the importance of humour as a special tool for communicating with people with dementia. After exploring its origin and theories, they also tackle the concept of using humour in an exclusive way. By providing relief in the pain of coping with dementia, the inclusive use of humour becomes a substantial part of a palliative perspective on care-giving in dementia: reaching the patient and sharing the moment, albeit only just.

The fact that 'people in the latter stage of the dementia process' and care-givers mutually benefit from using sensory stimulation has been expressed in a number of ways and is considered common knowledge. *Lesley Ann Wareing* (Chapter 6) underpins this theory by applying several sensory stimulation techniques within the framework of occupational therapy practice. Because the aim of care-giving in dementia is always to optimize communication, she points out that occupational therapy practice in the latter stages of dementia focuses more on relationship aspects than tools.

Building Community through Arts (BCA) is another contribution aimed at improving communication with people with dementia. *Jill Anderson and her colleagues* (Chapter 7) show that by using simple arts media skills within a context of awareness, care-givers/staff can be trained to move away from focusing on basic physical care towards adopting a relationship perspective. However, they also stress that such a change in care-giving attitudes needs commitment at management level. Bonding (attachment) between care-givers/staff and management is therefore a prerequisite.

In his reflective/critical contribution, *Cees Hertogh* (Chapter 8) analyses in detail the place of nursing home medicine in The Netherlands against the background of how medical expertise has developed in medical care for chronically ill elderly people, including people with dementia. He observes that this specialism is so unique that there is a certain reticence in applying it to the (organization of) healthcare for elderly patients in other countries. In addition to substantiating this specific expertise, he points out that it can be practised in diverse settings.

As with the terror of any other catastrophe in human society, dementia in itself is meaningless. The contribution of *Peter Speck* (Chapter 9) helps foster meaning by assessing the spiritual needs of people with dementia, in addition to their various other functions and needs, in order to understand their search for meaning under the painful condition of this disease. Awareness of persons' spiritual needs makes care-givers realize that people with dementia have to, in one way or another, feel related or attached to them to make their condition bearable.

Part III: Topics related to care-giving issues

For a long time, dynamic psychotherapy with people with dementia has been a contradiction in terms. The contribution from *Rik Cheston and his colleagues* (Chapter 10) provides strong evidence for Bowlby's assumption that 'people who don't feel safe, don't (dare to) explore their condition'. As with the Alzheimer Café, group psychotherapy can function as a safe haven. It offers people with dementia the opportunity to reflect on their painful feelings. In this way the strength of their awareness is applied to overcome their denial, concealment and avoidance.

Groupwork with people with dementia is increasing in clinical practice, although it is done with a certain reluctance. At individual level, the benefits of such groupwork, measured qualitatively, are clearly positive. *Marie Mills and Elizabeth Bartlett* (Chapter 11) describe what 'the group' psychologically has to offer to individuals coping with early and moderate dementia, and then outline that experiential support groups are useful aspects of care-giving in dementia. At the same time they stress the paucity of specialist groupwork training, which, for example, should underline the importance of the concept of attachment.

Simple qualitative research can underpin and advance new ideas. Through careful analysis of semi-structured interviews with people with dementia and their carers, *Amy Thompson* (Chapter 12) presents a first evaluation of the Alzheimer Café concept in the UK. She shows that this supportive group intervention still meets the original Dutch philosophy, structure, format and objectives. She also proves that the Alzheimer Café UK merits substantial recognition in the National Health Service's dementia care pathways.

Part IV: Family and professional care-givers

Generally speaking, people with dementia and their families want to live as long and as normally as possible in the community. The Meeting Centres Support Programme model of *Rose-Marie Dröes and her colleagues* (Chapter 13) goes a long way towards helping them to meet this wish. In this chapter the authors present aims, methods and research relating to this model in The Netherlands. In addition to describing and evaluating how the model is implemented nationwide, they are able to demonstrate numerous benefits for people with dementia themselves as well as for their carers.

By means of simple quantitative and qualitative exploratory research on clinical practice, *Bère Miesen* (Chapter 14) makes a plea for Couples group (psycho)therapy to be taken as a serious method in tackling the disadvantages of denial and avoidance at an early stage. In addition to improving practical and emotional coping with dementia at an individual level, this intervention seems to be successful in delaying the emotional isolation between husband and wife while living 'together' under one roof.

Part V: Education and ethics

Palliative care is already well established in many countries outside the UK. *Neil Small and his colleagues* (Chapter 15) challenge the comparison between the care needs of people who are dying and those of people with dementia. They examine prevalent 'dread diseases' and consider them historically within different social contexts. By way of similarities between palliative care and modern attitudes in dementia care, the authors describe a number of ethical issues in care-giving in dementia, with the aim of better understanding individuals with dementia and their care needs.

Marinus van den Berg (Chapter 16) considers the overall journey of dementia, including the terminal part of it, from a palliative perspective. He offers us materials to really understand the specifics of the suffering of people with dementia and their family members. Even the family's often strong longing for the death of the patient can be both heard and empathized. 'Death comes in the end, but the thought of it comes much sooner.'

In this chapter (Chapter 17), *Bère Miesen* underlines the necessity – both for researchers and professionals – to be constantly aware of the main differences in perception of care-giving in dementia between family and professionals. Before briefly reviewing all the chapters in the book, he outlines a brief psychology of the family's perspective in care-giving in dementia. He then puts forward a number of psychological themes that both 'parties' have to become aware of and overcome in order to be able to move ahead together and become 'partners' in care-giving in dementia.

Perspective: moving ahead together

From working to caring

It is not possible to expect family members immediately to be able to deal with the person with dementia in exactly the right way. They need time to process the situation before they can face it and deal with it. Care-givers must be aware of how they themselves react to advice from well-meaning bystanders in situations of loss and sorrow. Care-givers who find themselves in both situations – working with a person with dementia and having a member of the family with dementia – know from experience that they respond completely differently in the two situations and also know which situation is more difficult.

Adoption

As far as the family is concerned, care-givers sometimes seem to become too quickly settled and comfortable in their work situation. This is why care-givers should make sure that they do not tell the family too quickly what they think about the behaviour of the person with dementia while they are working with them. If Mrs Zuidman was struggling for months with the behaviour of her husband, it is obviously difficult for her to hear Marijke enthusiastically tell her on her first day of work that her husband is 'a dear'. The 'favourable reports' given by the care-giver about the person with dementia are, in a way, transmitted on a different wavelength than those being received by the family. The family may initially receive such 'favourable' reports with a feeling of pain in their heart and may even take it as a form of rebuke that they could not accomplish the care for 'the dear'. It is therefore sometimes better to hold back on any judgements about the behaviour and intentions of the family members. Certainly in the very beginning it is nearly impossible to gauge how aspects of coping, acceptance and motivation in a specific situation determine the burden felt, and so too the behaviour of the family.

The care-giver can find this out by showing interest in what the family is feeling and going through under such difficult circumstances. This makes it less likely that the family and care-giver will disagree with each other, instead of sharing the care of the dementia-sufferer. Asking questions about and showing an interest in what the partner, father or mother was like before can help in this process, not just about practical things such as what their hobbies used to be or what their favourite food was, but also about certain habits or how they used to respond to disappointment. In many cases, talking about this can also signify a symbolic emotional transfer for the family. It helps them because it gives recognition to and strengthens their special bond with the person with dementia, and above all gives them the opportunity to convey a bit of themselves and of their own care role.

Power

It is important for care-givers to realize that their success in dealing with the person with dementia will not be met with gratitude in the beginning. There are often understandable feelings of envy and jealousy. A complete stranger may succeed in doing on the very first day what the family has not managed to achieve for some time now. Care-givers may possess this power, but they have not actually been given it yet. In the relationship with the family member, the power always has to be earned. The best way to ensure this is for the care-giver to share the powerlessness of the family. This can be done, for instance, by talking to the family about one's own powerlessness ('I'm no superhuman who can do everything') and by having sympathy for the family's feelings of powerlessness ('It really is very difficult sometimes'). Only then can the family 'empower' the care-giver, giving them the freedom to be involved and take responsibility.

Transference and counter-transference

There is a well-known saying along the lines of, 'in times of adversity you learn who your friends are'. In the same way, people get to know each other better in crisis situations. It may sometimes be a let-down or alternatively may lead to a deeper understanding of that person. One thing is for sure, in situations like these people usually react 'purely', i.e. as they actually are or how they have become. In times of crisis, someone's personality crystallizes: you react as the person you have become. At the same time, the rewards of your emotional bond with someone (i.e. what has become of your relationship) will also crystallize.

From a practical as well as emotional viewpoint, the process of dementia is usually pretty radical for the life of the family members of the patient. The impact may even lead them to ask meaningful questions such as 'What has become of me and my life (with the other person)?' It is not uncommon for family members to take stock of their life together. The outcome of this process is very important for the motivation of family members to be able to keep providing care. If the outcome tips towards the negative end of the scale, there is a likelihood that they will project the resultant feelings, which they have not been able to deal with or have not been able to deal with satisfactorily, onto the care-giver.

For care-givers this primarily means that they must be careful in how they judge the comings and goings of the family of the person with dementia. Their behaviour may stem from experiences with the person with dementia or from other things in their past about which the care-giver is (still) unaware. Secondly, it is important for care-givers to recognize their restricted knowledge of transfer processes. Their main role is to indicate such things and they should not be afraid of calling in advice from specialists.

Intimacy

It is therefore not necessarily the case that the family will initially be delighted about the more intimate care-giving activities and at a later stage about the possible growing understanding between the care-giver and the person with dementia. In this respect, it is an important guiding principle for care-givers to behave in such a way that family members do not get the impression they are trying to take over their position. This can only be done by continually gauging how the partner or child feels about what they are doing. A good way to start is by getting the family member to help with a job that has to be done and, in doing so, always asking their advice or opinion. In this way, the family have some time to get used to the idea that the person with dementia is going to become attached to a 'stranger'. The outsider care-giver therefore becomes an acquaintance of the family. After all, it is less painful for the family if someone they know deals intimately with the partner, father or mother. The opposition becomes a supporter. The stranger becomes a companion in the house.

Aggression

It is important for care-givers to realize that aggressive behaviour on the part of a person with dementia will create a conflict of loyalties for the family in particular, because they often cannot or will not give up their bond with the patient. Sometimes care-givers also find themselves facing the same conflict if an attachment has already been formed between themselves and the person with dementia. However it is generally easier for care-givers to distance themselves from a patient's aggressive behaviour than for the family. It is also easier for care-givers to literally get the person with dementia out of the way. Aggressive behaviour on the part of the family towards the dementia-sufferer is often not tolerated, but care-givers can probably try to understand this behaviour as a possible signal that the family is going through a particularly difficult process of dealing with the disease.

Conclusion: becoming 'partners' in care-giving in dementia

Dealing with people with dementia also means dealing with the close family at the same time. It is important to note that the family experiences and perceives the situation from a different perspective than the care-giver. The essential point is that care-givers are busy providing the care and do not have to detach themselves from any kind of emotional bond built up in a life history shared together. If the family are providing care they are often compelled to do this. In many respects it has an impact on their behaviour, both with respect to the person with dementia and towards the care-giver. Professional care-givers who forget this perspective when dealing with the family run into problems, which is why it is important for care-givers to think about what they do, say or do not say in terms of the process of dealing with loss on the part of the family.

Because dealing with loss is an extremely individual thing, it is difficult to generalize it. Nevertheless, it is possible to point out a few signals that care-givers can use to gauge where the family stands in the process of dealing with loss. These signals include the following:

* *Signals of normal grieving*: being prepared to take on various roles in order to share the person's own perception of the world at that time; being able to cuddle readily; a good relationship with the care-giver gradually forms; the family gradually hand over care; being able to see the funny side of certain situations; enjoying the small things together; daring to ask for help without feeling ashamed or guilty; daring to be

open about the heaviness of the burden; standing up for oneself and admitting to being sad and feeling let down.

- *Signals of grieving made complicated*: always trying to bring the person with dementia back to reality; somatization disorders; always asking the patient to remember situations from the past instead of waiting for the patient to recognize them; behaving as if nothing is wrong; immediately acting and talking for the other person; not moving on from a sense of injustice, anger or feeling left in the lurch; finding fault with everybody and everything; always complaining; nearly 'going to pieces' yet still not being able to hand over care; always blaming others; just acting as if it is not serious; if a 'good' relationship with the care-giver forms really quickly, does not form at all or only forms with difficulty.

Everyone has experience of feelings of loss. Sooner or later, care-givers themselves or someone close to them will have to deal with feelings of loss. Grief teaches you how to deal with grief. Your own past experiences of loss can be beneficial when working with people with dementia and their families. It means that care-givers keep an eye out for personal circumstances, experiences and feelings of the family. In this respect, no one family member is the same as another. There are many individual variants. One person experiences the burden differently to another and there may be all sorts of reasons for this. We want to avoid the situation in which care-givers feel guilty because they used to suspect the family of evil intent, laziness, complaining, selfishness, of visiting too much or too little and then have to say 'If only I'd known . . .'

Reference

Miesen, B.M.L. (1999). *Dementia in Close-up. Understanding and Caring for People with Dementia* (translated by G.M.M. Jones). London/New York: Routledge, p. 232.

Index

Note: page numbers in *italics* denote references to figures and boxes.

Aber, R. 380
acetylcholine 67
achromatopsia *33*
ACs *see* Alzheimer Cafés
'active life review' 370
'active treatment' 234, 235
Activities of Daily Living (ADLs):
  couples group therapy 344–5; nursing
  home medicine 229; occupational
  therapy 182, 195; residential dementia
  unit environmental changes 41;
  visuoperceptual-cognitive deficits 8, *9*
acuity 23, 36, 50, 67, 85
AD *see* Alzheimer's disease
adaptation-coping model 317
adaptive tasks 231, 317, 321
ADLs *see* Activities of Daily Living
affective functioning *322*
affective lability *115*, 117
after-care 407–8
ageing 141, 227, 233, 383
aggression *115*, 117, 124, 420
Agich, George 229
agnosia 10, *33*; apperceptive *33*, 36;
  associative *33*; hallucinations 85, 95,
  96, 98, 99; Tectal Pathway 31
agnosognosia 261
agnosticism 249–50
agraphia *33*
Ainsworth, Mary 109, *110*, 119
alexia *33*
Almiron, N. 83
Alzheimer, Alois 61
Alzheimer Cafés (ACs) 127, 292,
  296–310, 397, 416; atmosphere *301*,
  304; attachment of partners 355;

barriers to attendance *302*, 307;
couples group therapy comparison
341, 342; discussions about death 399,
400; ending *302*, 307; facilitators *301*,
305; history *343*; image of dementia
125, 129; inclusivity *301*, 306;
limitation of evaluation 309–10;
Meeting Centres Support Programme
327; meeting new people *301*, 305;
negative aspects *301*, 306–7; outcomes
307–9; positive aspects *301*, 302–4,
302; research method 299–300;
speakers *301*, 306, structure *301*,
304–5; themes *301–2*, 307–8
Alzheimer's disease (AD): awareness
135–7, 142, 264, 265; Braak stages *22*;
diagnosis 262, 274; emotional memory
178; group psychotherapy 259, 261,
264–5, 267; hallucinations 59–104,
414; hospice care 374; humour 159;
identity loss 247; indirect
consequences of disease 231; language
deficits 71–4; Meeting Centres Support
Programme 327; multi-factor
causation of disability *35*; Netherlands
112; patient input 378; psychiatric and
behavioural disturbances 61–3;
residential dementia unit study 37–50,
51–2; sensory functioning 179; shame
260; symptoms 291–2;
visuoperceptual-cognitive deficits
3–57, 60, 61–2, 63, 86, 414
Alzheimer's Society 135, 136, *278*;
  Alzheimer Cafés 297, 298; palliative
  care 377; tube feeding 376
amnesia 118

analgesics 376, 377
Anderson, Jill 187, 195, 199–217, 415
Andremann, F. 80
anger 274
anomia *33*
Anthony, E.J. 274
anticholinergic medication 60, *64*, 84
antipsychotic medication 60–1, *64*, 75,
   81, 84
anxiety *115*, 116–17, 118, 121;
   attachment theory 275; group therapy
   259, 263, 273, 274, 275–6, 285;
   psychodynamic theory 272; separation
   109, 114
anxious/ambivalent attachment *105*, *108*,
   109, *110*, 117
anxious/avoidant attachment *105*, *108*,
   109, *110*, 118
apathy *115*, 117–18, 180, 292
APES *see* Assimilation of Problematic
   Experiences Scale
Apparent Affect Rating Scale 379
apperceptive agnosia *33*, 36
apraxia 10, *33*
Aries, P. 371
Aristotle 159, 162
aromatherapy 181–2, 189
arousal *145*
art 187; *see also* Building Community
   through Arts
assessment: awareness 146–7; care
   pathways *293*, *295*, 296; hallucinations
   72, 74–5, 86–92; spiritual need 244–5,
   250–1; vision 85; *see also* diagnosis
assimilation model of psychotherapeutic
   change 262
Assimilation of Problematic Experiences
   Scale (APES) 262, *263*
associative agnosia *33*
atheism 249–50
attachment 105–32, 414; Alzheimer
   Cafés 342, *343*; behaviour 63, *105*,
   107–8, 114–18; concept 108–9; coping
   with dementia 120–5, 347; couples
   group therapy 341, 354–6; figures *105*,
   124; history 105, *105*, 111–12, 114,
   119–21, 128, 379; nurture-seeking 247;
   occupational therapy 182; patterns
   105, 108, 109–11, *110*, 121–3, 126–7,
   128; in practice 125–9; psychodynamic
   perspective 275; summary of theory
   105

auditory hallucinations 94, 95–8, *96*, *97*,
   99, 100, 292
auditory stimulation 177
autonomy 229, 242, 384–5; fear of loss
   369; functional 225, 226, 236, 237;
   person-centred care 382
avoidance: couples group therapy 341,
   351, *351*, 352, *352*, 355; shame 260–1
AWARE project 133, 148
awareness 133–51, 261, 414; Alzheimer's
   disease 135–7; Assimilation of
   Problematic Experiences Scale 262,
   263; biopsychosocial model *138*, 145,
   148; death 398–400; emotional 380;
   evaluating 146–7; group
   psychotherapy 264, 265, 266; levels of
   145; neurological aspects 137–40, 148;
   objects of 146; phenomenology 147–8;
   psychological aspects 140–2, 148;
   social aspects 142–5, 148
'awareness context' 63, 114, 142–3, 402,
   403, 404–5, 407
AWBZ *see* General Act on Exceptional
   Medical Expenses

Badley, E.M. 230, 231
Baker, R. 190
Bakhtin, M. 277
balancing concept 180–1
Balint's syndrome 3, 10, 32, *33*
Ballard, C. 83, 376
Bamford, C. *343*
BAP *see* beta-amyloid plaques
Bartlett, Elizabeth 268, 271–89, 416
Barton, R. 241–2
Bastiaans, J. 124–5
Bauman, Z. 368, 383, 384, 385–6
BCA *see* Building Community through
   Arts
Beard, R.L. 378
Beattie, J. 160
Becker, P.M. 227, 229
Behaviour Observation Scale for
   Intramural Psychogeriatrics 324
Behavioural Staging Model *22*, 185
belief 245, 249–50
Bender, M. 275
Benson's syndrome 10
bereavement 81, 95, *367*, 371, 379–80,
   381; *see also* grieving; loss
Bergson, H. 160–1
Berk, R.A. 155, 156

beta-amyloid plaques (BAP) 4, 27, 30, 67
Bion, W.R. 273, 276
biopsychosocial model of awareness *138*, 145, 148
bipolar illness 81
Blake, Will 155–74, 415
blame culture 202, 215
Bleathman, C. 271
blindness *39*
blindsight 31
Blom, M. 298, 299, 300, 307–8
body language *283*; *see also* non-verbal communication
Borge, Victor 155, 171–2
Bower, H. 180
Bowlby, John 105–11, 124, 125, 414; attachment behaviour 107–8; attachment history 379; danger 120, 122; loss 110–11; safety 275, 416
Boyatzis, R.E. 300
brain: Alzheimer's disease 3, 27; awareness 137, 139, 145; developments in understanding 369; primary visual cortex 27–30, *28*, *29*, 79–80; right side 205; visual damage 67
Bredin, K. 242–3
Bremmer, J. 161
Brief Cognitive Rating Scale 324
Bright, Ruth 171
Britton, P.G. 309
Bromley, D.B. 271
Buber, M. 382, 383
Buddhism 248–9
Building Community through Arts (BCA) 199–217, 415; arts intervention 205–6, 209, 216; cooperative inquiry 201–2, 206, 215; evaluation 210–15; financial viability 215–17; future directions 216–17; review stage 206–9; Weaver's Triangle 203–5, *203*
Burns, A. 62, 99
business partnerships 216
Byatt, S. 120–1

calling out *115*
Campbell, S. 21–6
cancer 368, *368*, 369, 373, 408
Cardoso, S. 159
care homes: attachment theory 123; Building Community through Arts 200–1, 217; death of person with dementia 401, 407–8; end-of-life care

376; humour 162–3; Meeting Centres Support Programme 324, 325, 332; negative labelling 376; sensory stimulation 179–80, 181; supportive care 237; visual environment *11*, 36–7, 37–50, 51–2; *see also* nursing home medicine
'care' medicine 222–3
care-givers 125, 409–10, 417–21; aggression 420; attachment theory 122–4, 275; awareness of dementia 134; Building Community through Arts 199, 201, 202–3, 204–11, 213–16, 415; care management strategies 143; communication with family 417–18; death of person with dementia 393, 400–1, 402, 403–4, 406, 407; definition xxiv; grief 376, 380, 421; help for family 413; humour 157, 162, 163–9, 170–1; intimacy 419–20; lack of understanding 183; 'malignant' social psychology 162, 242; palliative care 374–5; person-centred care 200; power issues 418; rehabilitation 237; research developments 370–1; sensitivity 243; sensory stimulation 178, *183*, 188, 194; spiritual care 244–5, 252, 253, 254, 415; training 199, 200, 202–3, 205–6, 208–9, 211, 215–16; transference and counter-transference 419; understanding 396; visuoperceptual-cognitive deficits 414; *see also* health professionals
carers: Alzheimer Cafés 296, 297, 299, 308; attachment theory 122, 124, 130; couples group therapy 341–62; definition xxiv; exclusion from care 376; 'experienced burden' 317, 324, 325, 332–3; family perspective 410–13; 'feeling of competence' 324–5, 333; Meeting Centres Support Programme 316, 319–21, 324–5, 327, *330–1*, 332–3; needs 294; sensory stimulation 189–90; service development 370; spiritual care 254; support for 325, 327, 332–3, 379; *see also* family
cataracts 21
catharsis 274
CDR *see* Clinical Dementia Rating Scale
cerebral lesions 79, 80
cerebrovascular accident (CVA) patients 227, 235, 236

Cernin, P.A. 36
CFC *see* Cognitive Functions Clinic
CFF effect *see* critical flicker fusion effect
CGT *see* couples group (psycho)therapy
Chapman, A.C. 156
Charcot, Jean-Martin 224
Charities Evaluation Services 203, 204
Charles Bonnet syndrome 36, 70, 78, 80, *82*, 83
Cheston, Rik 120–1, 259–70, 271–2, 273, 275, 285, 416
children 106, 107–8, 109–10, *110*, 111, 122
Chomsky, N. *107*
Christianity 248, 250, 251–2
circular questioning 277
claiming behaviour *115*, 118
Clare, Linda 133–51, 414
Clark, D. 367
Clinical Dementia Rating (CDR) Scale 171
clinical geriatrics 220, 223, 225, 226
CLSM (Continuous, Long-term, Systematic, Multi-disciplinary) care 220
Clulow, C. 354
Cobb, M. 244
cognitive abilities: Alzheimer's disease 8, 9, *9*, 21; coping with dementia 120; couples group therapy 350; sensory stimulation 177; *see also* visuoperceptual-cognitive deficits
Cognitive Functions Clinic (CFC) *295*, 296
Cohen, C.I. 121
Cohen, H.J. 227, 229
Coleman, Peter 123, 155–74, 282
collaborative approaches 202, 315–16, 326, 370; *see also* multi-disciplinary approaches
colour: cues 36; discrimination 30; hyperchromatopsia 78; saturation 3, *23*; visual deficits *33*, 49, 67
Coloured Progressive Matrices (CPM) *350*
communication: couples group therapy 345, 353; hallucinations 85; non-verbal 168, 178, *182*, 194, 252; sensory stimulation 178, 181, *182*, 190–1, 194; skills 204–5
Community Mental Health Teams for Older People 310

Compensating Balance Framework 175, 190, *192*, 193
compulsive behaviour *115*
concealment 261, 395–6
confidence 111, 206, 208, 210–11, 262; *see also* self-esteem
Conroy, C. 189–90
consulting hour 316, 319–20, *319*, 327, 332
containment 275–6
contrast sensitivity 12, *19*, *25*, *33*, 36, 67; testing 50, 85; ventral path 30, 31
controlling behaviour 116
cooperative inquiry 201–2, 206, 215
coping 113, 120–5, 127, 128, 130; adaptive tasks 231, 317; attachment 347, 354–5, 356; awareness of dementia 147–8; couples group therapy 345, 350–2, 354–5, 356; Meeting Centres Support Programme 316, 333–4
Coppola, S. 184–5
Corbin, S.L. 85
Corr, C. 372
Corr, D. 372
counselling 128, 285, 320; bereavement *367*; couples group therapy 127, 345, *346*
counter-transference 123, 129, 355, 380, 419
couples group (psycho)therapy (CGT) 127, 341–62, 416; Alzheimer Cafés 342; attachment 354–6; definition 345–6; examples *347–8*, *349*; expectations 352–3, 356–7; individual evaluations 353–4, 357–9; intervention method and results 345–54; literature 342–5
CPM *see* Coloured Progressive Matrices
creativity 215
Critchley, M. 78
critical flicker fusion (CFF) effect *25*, *34*
Cronin-Golomb, A. 10, 63
Crow, R.W. 32
CVA patients *see* cerebrovascular accident patients

Dallos, R. 277
Davis, J.M. 160, 161
day care 188–9, 315, 318, 332
Day, C.N. 271
daydreams *65*

de Ruiter, C. 106–7, 111, 121
deafness *39*
death 124, 253, 372, 393, 401–8, 417;
after-care 407–8; awareness of
398–400; care-givers 400–1, 403–4,
406, 407; causes of 375; hospice care
371; information sharing 404–5;
'psychological' 380; rituals 405–6;
significance of dying 405
decision-making 202
defences 116, 140, 164
delirium 61, 77, 81, *115*
delusions xxiii, 62, 66–7, 71, 77, 94
dementia: adaptive tasks *317*, 321; ageing
population 291; Alzheimer Cafés 125,
127, 129, 292, 296–310, 416;
attachment theory 114–16, 118–30,
414; autonomy 384–5; awareness
133–51, 261, 414; beliefs and
knowledge about 141–2; Building
Community through Arts 199–217,
415; care pathways 293–4, *293*, 295–6,
295, 308; care services 292–4; care-
giver perspectives 409–10, 417–21;
carers' needs 294; 'catastrophe of' 125;
'coming to terms with' 261, 262;
coping 120–5, 127, 128, 130; couples
group therapy 341–62, 416; death 393,
398–401, *417*; diagnosis 125–6;
disturbed behaviour 116–18; 'dread
disease' concept 367–9, *368*; emotional
isolation 341; end-of-life care 365,
375–7, 381, 401–8; experiential
support groups 271, 272, 273–4,
275–6, 277–86, 416; family
perspectives 410–13; hallucinations
and other visual phenomena 59–104,
414; history of care 369–71; humour
155, 156–7, 159, 162–71, 415; Meeting
Centres Support Programme 315–39,
416; multi-disciplinary definition
113–14; nursing home medicine 221,
415; palliative care 365, 372, 373–5,
376–82, 385–6, 394, 417; personhood
242–3; as 'problematic experience' 262;
psychological trauma 113;
psychotherapeutic groups 259–70, 416;
sensory stimulation 175–98, 415; social
stigma 260–1; society's attitude 124–5,
129, 141, 142, 144; spiritual care 241,
242, 246, 253, 254, 415; 'stage' models
171; stress 112; supportive care 237; as

terminal journey 394–401;
visuoperceptual-cognitive deficits
3–57, 414
Dementia Care Mapping 379
Dementia Voice group psychotherapy
project 259–70
dendropsia 78
denial 116, 118, 120, 125, 127, 397;
awareness of dementia 140, 141;
concealed suffering 395–6; couples
group therapy 341, 351, *351*, 352, *352*;
groupwork 261, 273
depression *115*, 118, 121; absence of joy
156; carers 294, 379; couples group
therapy 351, 352; group therapy 259,
268, 285; Meeting Centres Support
Programme 332, 333–4; problematic
experiences 262
Deprivation Hypothesis 79
depth perception *5*, 6, 12, *25*, *34*
diabetes 233
diabetic retinopathy 80
diagnosis: awareness of dementia 134;
care pathways *293*, *295*; clinical
geriatrics 225; consequences of disease
229–32; coping styles 147; dementia
125–6; disclosure *343*; early 369; group
therapy 273–4, *279*; hallucinations *72*,
83, 85, 86, 94, 100; Meeting Centres
Support Programme 318; openness
125; palliative care 378, 396–7;
psychological well-being 262;
psychosocial 317, 321; social stigma of
dementia 260–1; written confirmation
274; *see also* assessment
dialectical process of dementia 370
Dickerson, A.E. 188
disabilities: ICIDH model 230;
reactivation 234; rehabilitation 232–3,
234, 235, 236; subclinical 235–6
discrepancy score approach 146
discursive psychology 274
discussion groups 316, 319–20, *319*, 321,
322, 323; *see also* group therapy
disease 224, 227; diagnosis of
consequences 229–32; indirect
consequences 231–2; traditional
medical paradigm 229; vision
alterations *65*
disinhibited behaviour *115*, 138, 292
disposition theory 162
Doka, K.J. 380

dorsal path 30, 67
Downs, Murna 365–92
'dread disease' concept 365, 367–9, *368*
dream states *65*, 78
driving 137, 144, 273, 274, 358
Dröes, Rose-Marie 231, 315–39, 416
Dukes, C. 244
Dunne, T.E. 36
DVDs 171

early-onset Alzheimer's disease (EOAD)
    9, 10
Eastwood, M.R. 85
eating *115*
education: Alzheimer Cafés 304, 307,
    342; couples group therapy 345, *346*,
    355; psychological 127;
    psychospiritual 396; visual
    phenomena 86
emotional awareness 380
emotional memory 178, 188
emotions: 'active life review' 370;
    attachment patterns 111; health
    professionals 129; humour 156
Enabling, Person-led, Failure-free
    Approach (EPFA) 178
encounter groups 274
end-of-life care 365, 375–7, 381, 401–8
'engagement in occupation' 184, 185,
    185, *186*
EOAD *see* early-onset Alzheimer's
    disease
EPFA *see* Enabling, Person-led, Failure-
    free Approach
epilepsy 80
ethical issues: end-of-life care 365;
    humour 170, 171; palliative care 377;
    prognosis 378; reactivation 234–5; *see
    also* morality
ethology *107*
Exelon 359
existential meaning 246–7, 250, 251
experiential support groups 271–89, 416;
    see also group therapy
extracampine hallucinations 60, 95, *96*,
    97, 98, 99, 100
eye movements 3, *22*, *25*, 31, *33*, *34*, 67

facial recognition 3, 31, *33*, *34*, 50, 67, 85
falls 21–6, 36
family 121–2, 128, 130, 381, 397, 410;
    aggressive behaviour 420; awareness

context 142, 143, 402, 403, 404–5; care-
    giver communication with 417–18;
    couples group therapy 341–62; crisis
    403; death of person with dementia
    399, 401, 402–3, 404–5, 406, 407;
    exclusion from care 376; grieving
    420–1; intimacy 419–20; perspective of
    410–13, 420; powerlessness 418;
    sensory stimulation benefits 189–90;
    spiritual care 253–4; systemic
    perspectives 276; transference 419; *see
    also* carers
family therapy 276
fantasy *65*
fear xxiii; of death 404; group
    psychotherapy 264–5; hallucinations
    86, *96*, 98; re-living past trauma 7
Feeling of Competence Scale 324–5, 333,
    352
Feil, N. 62, 171, 271, 282
Ffytche, D.H. 75, 77, 78–9, 80–1, 84,
    98
figure background contrasts 3, 4, 12, *19*,
    34, 67
finance issues 215–17, 326, 327
Finkel, S.I. 77
Flint, Hilda 199–217, 252
floaters *23*
Folkman, S. 317
Folstein, M.F. 171
forgetfulness *115*, 118, 395; *see also*
    memory
Foulkes, S.H. 274
Frankl, V. 155, 246
Freud, Sigmund 164
Froggatt, Katherine 365–92
Fromm, E. 277
fronto-temporal dementia 292
fruit-tasting *189*
functional autonomy 225, 226, 236, 237
functional geriatrics 225, 226–9, 230
functional status 226–7
Fusiform Face Area 31

Galton, C. 10
gardens 181
GDS *see* Global Deterioration Scale
General Act on Exceptional Medical
    Expenses (AWBZ) 220
'geriatric network' model 223
geriatrics 223, 224–5, 381; clinical 220,
    223, 225, 226; functional 225, 226–9,

230; rehabilitation 232, 233, 235, 237; social 225–6
geriatrification 220
gerontology 286
Gerstmann's syndrome 33
Gilliard, Jane 259–70
Giorgi, A. 309
Giorgi, B. 309
Glaser, B. 371, 380
glaucoma 21, 80
Global Deterioration Scale (GDS) 318
Global Rating of Awareness in Dementia (GRAD) 146
goal-directed behaviour 145
goal-setting 204, 208
God 248, 249, 251
Goffman, E. 241–2
Goldsmith, M. 246
Golledge, J. 185
Gorer, G. 371
Gottlieb-Tanaka, D. 200
GRAD see Global Rating of Awareness in Dementia
grieving 110–11, 213, 398, 405; anticipatory grief 403; care staff 376, 380, 421; signals 420–1; support sessions 408; visual phenomena 65, 76; see also bereavement; loss
Grol, R. 334
group therapy: assimilation of problematic experiences 263–7; beneficial effects 342–4; containment 275–6; Dementia Voice project 259–70; difficulties 285; experiential support groups 271–89, 416; facilitators 281, 282, 283; feedback 285; group processes 272–4, 280–1; groupwork theory 271–2; humour 276, 281–2; limitations 267–8; Milan approach 276–7; outcomes 284; practical aspects 277–85; relationships 274–5; see also couples group (psycho)therapy; discussion groups
'guardian angel syndrome' 123
guided imagery 252
guilt 251, 378, 401, 407

hallucinations 39, 59–104, 115, 292, 414; assessment difficulties 72, 74–5; association with Alzheimer's disease 61–3; classification 78–9; content 79, 83; defining 69, 70; duration 75–7;

explanations for 79–81; extracampine 60, 95, 96, 97, 98, 99, 100; lighting impact on 36; medical/psychiatric research 61; opthalmic/perceptual research 61; over-reporting 70–1; Palette Theory 75, 80–1; questionnaire for assessment 86–92; range of 64–6, 65; Reminiscing Disorientation Theory 62; reported frequencies 81, 81–2, 92–3, 94–100; stories reported as 75, 76–7; thought chains 64; types of 77–8
handicaps 230
Harding, Jeremy 3–57, 59–104
Harvey, R.J. 291
Hasselkus, B.R. 184–5
Haupt, M. 344, 345
health professionals 155–6; Alzheimer Cafés 298, 303, 308; attachment theory 122–4, 128–9; awareness of dementia 144–5; Meeting Centres Support Programme 316, 320, 321, 327; nursing home physicians 219–20, 221, 223, 225–6; occupational therapists 182–3, 186, 187, 195; see also care-givers
hemianopsia 33
Hermans, H.J.M. 277
Hermans-Jansen, E. 277
Heron, John 199, 201, 202, 212, 215
Hertogh, Cees 219–39, 415
Hobbes, Thomas 159, 162
Hof, P.R. 10, 79
Hoffman, S. 178
home care 401
home concept 51
home-like visual cues 36, 37, 38, 43, 49, 50, 52
homeostatic cylinder model 227, 228
Hosking, C. 200
hospice care 365, 367, 369, 371–3, 374, 383; see also palliative care
hospital care 241–2
hospitalization 247
Howard, R.J. 78–9
Hughes, J. 252
humour 155–74, 415; as defence mechanism 164; definition 158–9; exclusive 158, 159, 162–3, 164–5; group therapy 276, 281–2; incongruity 160, 165; intersubjective 158, 158, 162, 169; negative inclusive 158, 165–6; negative uses 161–3; origins 156–8;

positive inclusive *158*, 166–9; theories 159; as therapeutic tool 169–71
Huybrechtse, P. 344
hyperchromatopsia 78
hypnagogic vision *65*, *72*, 78
hypnapagogic vision *65*, 78
hypnopompic vision *65*, *72*, 78
Hyvarinen, L. 30, 61, 66–7, 85

ICIDH *see International Classification of Impairments, Disabilities and Handicaps*
identity 246, 247, 261; heroic self-identity 383; personhood 242, 243; social 272
Ignatieff, M. 384, 385
illusions 59, 60, *68*, 83, *115*; education to minimize 86; hallucination distinction 70; misperception of *69*; opthalmic/perceptual research 61; reported frequencies *82*, 93, 94–5, *96*, *97*, 98, 99; thought chains *64*
illusory visual spread 78
Impact of Event Scale *351*, *352*
impairments 230, 235–6
inactivity 324, 332, 333–4
inertia *115*
informative meetings 316, 319–20, *319*, 322, 326, 327
Ingebretsen, R. 121–2
insight 261
internal working models *105*, 110, 120
International Classification of Impairments, Disabilities and Handicaps (ICIDH) 230
intimacy 419–20
Intimate Bond Measure 350, 351
Islam 253
isolation *115*, 247, 294, 296, 304, 308, 353
Izard, C. 156

James, William 272
Jeste, D.V. 77
Johnson, S.E. 183–4
jokes 160, 170
Jones, Gemma M.M.: Alzheimer Cafés 297, 308, 342, *343*; attachment history 379; dementia behaviours 370; hallucinations and other visual phenomena 59–104, 414; staff communication 178; visuoperceptual-cognitive deficits 3–57, 414
Jones, Kerry 259–70

Jones, Sidney 200–1, 212
joy 156, 159
Judaism 253–4

Kalish, R.A. 380
Kant, I. 160, 383
Katz, J. 380
Keady, John 133–51
Kempenaar, L. 189
Kihlgren, M. 370
kinaesthetic stimulation 177
King, M. 246
Kitwood, T.: celebration 162, 167; dialectical process of dementia 370; person-centred care 308, 370, 382; personhood 155, 199, 242–3, 382; 'standard paradigm' of care 292
Klein, Melanie 276
Kline, L.W. 156
Kluver, H. 78
Knight, B.G. 282
Koenig Coste, J. 71
Koenig, H.G. 245
Kouwenhoven, C. 344
Kübler-Ross, Elizabeth 372

Laatu, S. 12
Langer, K.G. 141
language 205
language deficits 71–4, 89
late-onset Alzheimer's disease (LOAD) 9, 10
laughter 156, *157*, 159, 160–1, 171, 282
Lawrence, R.D. 159
Lawton, M.P. 379
Lazarus, R.S. 317
LBD *see* Lewy body dementia
Leuba, G. 32
Lewy body dementia (LBD) 9, *39*; diagnosis *72*; hallucinations 59, 60, 81, *82*, 83, 93, 94–100; symptoms 292
Liederman, P.H. 180
life-review therapy 268
lighting 3, 4, 7, 35–6; normal age-related visual changes *24*; residential dementia unit study *40*, *41*, *42*
'living wills' 124, 246, 384
Lloyd-Lawrence, Kitty 199
LOAD *see* late-onset Alzheimer's disease
loss 110–11, 275, 381, 398, 410, 412–13; *see also* bereavement; grieving
Lowis, M.J. 252

MacDonald, Colin 200
McFadden, S.H. 250
MacKinlay, E. 162, 250
McNamara, C. 189
macropsia 78
macular degeneration 61, 80, *82*
Magai, C. 121
Maguire, C.P. 378
maintenance rehabilitation 235, 236–7
malnutrition 376
management staff 208
Manford, M. 80
Marková, Ivana 133–51
Marmysz, J. 160
MARS *see* Memory Awareness Rating
  Scale
May, H. 185–7
MCs *see* meeting centres
MCSP *see* Meeting Centres Support
  Programme
MDEBD *see* Model of Determinants of
  Experienced Burden by Carers
meaning 246–7, 250, 251
medical paradigm 229
medication 26, *26–7, 72,* 87–8;
  antipsychotic 60–1, *64,* 75, 81, 84;
  Exelon 359; neuroleptic 60, 83, 100;
  pain relief 376, 377–8, 405
meeting centres (MCs) 315–39, 345
Meeting Centres Support Programme
  (MCSP) 315–39, 416; activities
  318–20; adaptive implementation
  334–5; aim and content 315–16; goals
  319; implementation study 325–33,
  334; intervention study 323–5;
  recruitment and admissions 318;
  support plan and strategies 320–1;
  theoretical background 317
'meeting of the minds' 184, *184*
Meiland, Franka 315–39
memorabilia *40, 41, 43,* 48
memory: ageing 141; Alzheimer's disease
  3, 136, 137; awareness of dementia
  138, 142, 143, 144, 146; colour cues 36;
  delusion xxiii; emotional 178, 188;
  group therapy 261, 264, 265, 267, 272,
  284; laughter benefits *157;* self-
  knowledge 139; traumatic 7; visual 62;
  see also forgetfulness
Memory Awareness Rating Scale
  (MARS) 146–7
Memory Clinic Model 296

Memory Insight Questionnaire 146
Mental Health Services 60, 291, 292, 298,
  307
metaphorical speech 73
Michels, J.J.M. 222
micropsia 78
Miesen, Bère: Alzheimer Cafés 296–7,
  298, 299–300, 307–8, 342, *343;*
  attachment 63, 105–32, 247, 275, 379,
  414; care staff 380; care-giving 409–21;
  carers 294; couples group
  (psycho)therapy 341–62, 416;
  dementia behaviours 370; emotional
  awareness 380; PoPFID theory 62;
  professionalism 155
migraine 79, 80
Milan systemic therapy 276–7
Mills, Marie 123, 155–74, 268, 271–89,
  416
Mini Mental State Examination
  (MMSE) 171, 268, 296, 344, *350*
mirrors 5, 6, *13, 16, 18,* 36; illusions 86;
  residential dementia unit study *41, 42,
  46,* 48
misidentifications 59, 60, 71, 83;
  hallucination distinction 70; reported
  frequencies *82,* 93, 94; thought chains
  64
misinterpretations 94, 95, *96, 97, 98,* 99
misperceptions 59, 60, *69, 72,* 83, *115;*
  clinical examples *76;* education to
  minimize 86; hallucination distinction
  70; reported frequencies *82,* 93, 94–5,
  96, 97, 98, 99; thought chains *64*
Mitchell, S.L. 376
MMSE *see* Mini Mental State
  Examination
mobility aids 49, 236
Model of Determinants of Experienced
  Burden by Carers (MDEBD) 317
modernity 368, *368,* 369, 382, 386
Moffat, N. 176
mood: Building Community through
  Arts 211–12; couples group therapy
  349, 351, *351,* 352, *352;* Meeting
  Centres Support Programme 332, 333;
  sensory deprivation 179
Moos, R.H. 317
morality 383, 384–5; *see also* ethical
  issues
Moreall, J. 159, 162
morphine 405

Morse, J.M. 164
Morton, I. 271
motion perception *34*
mourning 247, 380
movement therapy 234
Muller, R. 160
multi-disciplinary approaches 308–9,
    319, 370, 373, 396; *see also*
    collaborative approaches
multi-sensory rooms 176–7, 200
multiple sclerosis 63
Munnichs, J. 112
music 177, *187–8*, 252

naming difficulties 60, *64*, 71–3
narcolepsy 80
narratives 265–7
National Service Framework (NSF) for
    Older People 291, 292–4, 295–6, 298,
    307, 308, 310
needs 294, 384, 385
NEO-FFI 350, 351
neurofibrillary tangles (NFT) 4, 27, 30,
    67
Neuropsychiatric Symptom Inventory 71
neutrality 276–7
NFT *see* neurofibrillary tangles
night vision *24*
NMC *see* Nursing Midwifery Council
Nobili, L. 67
non-adapting strategies 143
non-verbal communication 168, 178,
    182, 194, 252; *see also* body language
Norberg, A. 157, 159, 168, 177
normal retinal vision *65*, *68*
novelty activity 188
NSF *see* National Service Framework for
    Older People
nursing home care 221, 222–3
nursing home medicine 219–39, 415;
    diagnosis of consequences 229–32;
    functionality 226–9; geriatric
    principles 224–5; negative definitions
    222–4; rehabilitation and supportive
    care 232–7; social geriatrics 225–6; *see
    also* care homes
Nursing Midwifery Council (NMC) 244
nurturing strategies 143
nurturing style *108*, 109

object recognition 3, 30, 32, *33*, *34*, 67
occipital seizure 80

Occupational Process Model (OPM)
    184–5
occupational roles 183–4
occupational therapy 175–6, 180,
    182–91, 195, 415
ocular dysmetria *33*
Ohayon, M.M. 78
old age 112
Older Adult Mental Health Services 60,
    291, 292, 298, 307
olfactory stimulation 177
Oostvogel, F.J.G. 222
OPM *see* Occupational Process Model
organic perspective 345
Osborn, M. 300

Padrone, F.J. 141
pain relief 376, 377–8, 405
pairing 273
Palette Theory 75, 80–1
palliative care 365–7, 371–82, 385–6, *386*,
    394, 417; access to 374–5; autonomy
    384; death 399, 401–8; diagnosis 378,
    396–7; historical development 371–3;
    person-centred care comparison
    366–7; specialist 374
Pankow, L. 61
parent fixation 119–20, *119*, 126
Parker, G. 294
Parkes, Colin Murray 379
Parkinson's disease dementia (PDD) 9
Parkinson's disease (PD) *39*, *44*, 233;
    hallucinations 60, 80, 81, *82*, 83–4, 93,
    94–100; mobility restriction 231
participative decision-making 202
Passman, V. 121
pathology: hallucinations 78; visual 3, 8,
    9, 21, *28–9*, 61, *65*, *72*; *see also*
    psychopathology
patterned surfaces 10–12, *11*, 36–7, *41*, *42*
PBD *see* psychiatric and behavioural
    disturbances
PD *see* Parkinson's disease
PDD *see* Parkinson's disease dementia
PDSG *see* Post Diagnosis Support
    Group
peduncular lesions 80
perception 8–9; delusions 66–7; eyes
    closed *68*; hallucinations 70; time 73–4
perceptual analysis *145*
peripheral vision *11*, *24–5*
Perrin, T. 185–7

perseveration 78
person-centred care xxiv, 200, 242, 370, 382–3; Alzheimer Cafés 297, 308; holism 254; National Service Framework for Older People 292–4, 296; palliative care *366–7*, 381, *386*; social change 369
personality instruments 350
personhood 242–3, 247; change in culture of care 199; humour 155, 162, 170; person-centred care *366*, *367*, 382
pneumonia 402
polyopia 78
PoPFID theory 62
Post Diagnosis Support Group (PDSG) *295*, 296
Post, S. 377
post-traumatic stress disorder 127
posterior cerebral infarct 80
postmodernism 368, *368*, 369, 382, 385–6
power issues 418
powerlessness 120, 124, 125, 127; caregivers 123, 418; carers 294, 353, 399, 410
preventive rehabilitation 235–6
primary visual cortex 27–30, *28*, *29*, 79–80
Primary Visual Pathway 4, 27, 32, 67
problem solving 10, 32
prognosis 378
proposagnosia *33*
prosopometamorphosia 78
proximity-seeking behaviour 114, 117, 275
pseudohallucinations 78
psychiatric and behavioural disturbances (PBD) 60–1, 62–3
psychoanalysis 79, 272
psychodynamic perspective 272, 275, 343–4, 345
'psychological death' 380
psychological testing 126
psychomotor therapy 316, 318, *319*, 321, 322
psychopathology 78, 108, 121; *see also* pathology
psychosis 62, 63
psychosocial diagnosis 317, 321
psychosocial factors 227, 231
psychotherapy: Alzheimer Cafés 342; assimilation of problematic experiences 262, 263–7; Dementia

Voice group project 259–70, 416; limitations 267–8; *see also* couples group (psycho)therapy; group therapy

quality-of-life measures 379

Rader, J. 370
Rando, T.A. 380
Raven, J.C. *350*
reaction times 8
reactivation 222, 234–5, *322*
reality orientation 62, 268, 321, 369–70
Redwood, Kandy 297
referrals *295*
reflections 4, *5*, 10
reflective phase 186
reflex phase 187
rehabilitation 219, 220, 224, 225, 229, 232–7
Reisberg Descriptive Scale 171
Relationship Questionnaire 127, 354, 355
relationships: adaptive tasks *317*; group therapy 274–5, 277, *284*, 286; resocialization *322*; spirituality 247–8
relaxation therapy 252, 344
religion 244, 245, 248–50; *see also* spiritual care
reminiscence therapy 252, 268, 271, 370
Reminiscing Disorientation Theory 62
reminiscing vision *65*
repetitive motion *22*
reserve capacity 227, *228*
residential care *see* care homes
resocialization *322*
responsiveness 108, 109
restlessness 398, 402, 404
retinal degeneration 61
retinal vision *65*, *68*
Ribbe, M.W. 223
rights 384, 385
rituals 252, 254, 405–6
Ro, T. 31
Robinson, V. 159
Romero, Barbara 133–51
Ross, L. 245
routines *41*
Rumney, N. 35
Rusted, J.M. 188

saccades *33*; *see also* eye movements
Sacks, Oliver 231
Saini, K. 32

St Christopher's Hospice 372
Sannita, W. 67
Saunders, Dame Cicely 372, 373, 379, 383
Saunders, P.A. 261
SC *see* Superior Colliculus
schizophrenia 63, 81
Schreuder, J.T.R. 229, 234
screening *295*
Seale, C. 383
seating arrangements 4, *11*, *40*, *43*, *46*, *47*, 48
secure attachment *105*, 106, 107, 109, *110*; nurturing style *108*; partners 121, 122, 128, 341, 347, 354–5; proximity-seeking behaviour 117
sedation 406
self 365, 366; ethic of care 373; 'lost' 399, 401; postmodernism 369, 386; 'submerged' 399, 401, 404
self-actualization 371
self-awareness 138–9, *145*, 170
self-esteem: Building Community through Arts 201; couples group therapy 351, *351*, 352, *352*; groupwork 272, 276, 285; Meeting Centres Support Programme 332, 333–4; negative use of humour 162, 163; sensory stimulation 178, 182, 184, 187; *see also* confidence
self-knowledge 139
sensorimotor phase 187
sensory deprivation 62, *65*, 79, 178–9, 180, 182
sensory loss 179
sensory overload 179–80
sensory stimulation (SS) 175–98, 415; benefits for relatives 189–90; communication 178, 190–1, 194; equipment 188–9; multi-sensory rooms 176–7, 200; non-verbal activity 178, 188, 194; novelty activity 188; Occupational Process Model 184–5; occupational therapy link 180–2; overload 179–80; Perrin and May's model 185–7; research 191–4
separation: anxiety 109, 114; attachment patterns 111, 122
Serby, M. 83
shadows 6, 10, *11*, *14–15*, *16*
Shakespeare, William 385
shame 251, 260–1, 264–5

Shamy, E. 250
shared experiences 302–3, *346*
Shaver, P. 127
Shaw, George Bernard 160
Sheehy, P.C. 156
simulated presence therapy 120–1
simultanagnosia *33*
Sipsma, D.H. 227
sleeping *115*
Small, Neil 365–92, 417
Smith, J. 300
Snoezelen techniques 175, 17-9, 200
Snyder, L. 285
social change 365, 367–9
social clubs 316, 318–19, *319*, 320–1, 322, 326
social geriatrics 225–6
social interaction: Alzheimer Cafés 303–4; Building Community through Arts 209; seating arrangements 4, *11*, *40*, 44
social isolation *115*, 247, 294, 296, 304, 308, 353
social networks 316, 317, *319*, 325
Solem, P.E. 121–2
Sonas approach 177, 187
Sontag, Susan 368
spatial localization 30, 67
spatial palinopsia 78
special rehabilitation 235
Speck, Peter 241–56, 415
spiritual care 241–56, 376, 393–4, 415; assessment of need 244–5, 250–1; meaning 246–7; personhood 242–3; philosophical belief systems 249–50; psychospiritual education 396; relationships 247–8; responding to perceived need 251–2
spirituality 244–8
SS *see* sensory stimulation techniques
staff *see* care-givers
stage-based models of decline *22*, 171, 185, 375
'standard paradigm' of care 292
Stokes, G. 370
'strange situation' 109, 119
Strauss, A. 371, 380
stress: carers 294; laughter benefits *157*; multi-sensory rooms 176; old age 112; visual phenomena *65*
stroke *64*, 247, 267

suffering 395–6, 398
suicide *115*
Superior Colliculus (SC) 31–2
support: Alzheimer Cafés 296, 298, 303, 397; carers 325, 327, 332–3, 379; couples group therapy 343–4, 345, *346*; experiential support groups 271–89, 416; Meeting Centres Support Programme 316, 320–1, *322*, 325, 332–3; palliative care *367*; supporting strategy 143
supportive care 225, 229, 237, 373
suspicion *115*, 117, 121
Sweet, R. 63, 86
symbolic phase 186
systems theory 276

tactile stimulation 177, 251–2
Tajfel, H. 272, 276
task modification 236
taste stimulation 177, *189*
teasing 163
Tectal Pathway 4, 31–2, 67
tense errors *72*, 73, 85
tessellopsia 78
Teunisse, R. 83
theatrical humour *161*
thinking errors 8, 94
Thompson, Amy 291–312, 416
Tillich, P. 383
time perception 73–4
time-disorientation *22*, 50, 52; attachment behaviour 63; hallucinations 62; language difficulties *72*
Tinetti, Mary 227
toilet use 6, 7, *16*, *17*, *18*, 77
training: attachment theory 123, 129; Building Community through Arts 199, 200, 202–3, 205–6, 208–9, 211, 215–16; groupwork 282, 285, 286, 416; nursing home physicians 219–20, 223; sensory stimulation 178
transference 380, 419; *see also* counter-transference
trauma: coping with 113, 122; diagnosis 397; impact on well-being 275; prognosis 378; re-living 7; visual changes *65*
Tsu, V.D. 317
tube feeding 375–6, 402
Turner, J. 272, 276

uncertainty 395, 396
unsociable behaviour 324, 332, 333–4
'unstable equilibrium' 227
urinary tract infections 61, 62
Utrecht Coping List 352

validation therapy 62, 268, 271, 321, 370
Van den Berg, Marinus 393–408, 417
Van der Eerden-Rebel, William 3–57, 59–104
Van der Wulp, J.C. 231
Van Dijken, S. 106
Van Ijzendoorn, M.H. 111
Van Oers, Johan 113–14
Van Rhijn, S.J. 12
Van Tilburg, Willem 315–39
Van Wunnik, L. 355
vascular dementia 81, 94–100, 260, 292
ventral path 30, 31, 67
Verdult, R. 124
Verhey, Frans 133 51
Verhofstadt-Denève, L. 110
Verwoerdt, A. 116
victimization 158, 161
videos 171
vision 3, 8–9, 50; difficulties 10–12, *12–20*; medication effect on 26, *26–7*; normal age-related changes 21, *23–5*, *65*; pathological 78; sensory stimulation 177; testing 3, 50, 85; *see also* hallucinations; visuoperceptual-cognitive deficits
visual attention *14*, 32, 50
visual images 61, *69*
visual palette pathways 80–1, *80*, 84, 86, 90, 98, 99
visuoperceptual-cognitive deficits 3–57, 414; dorsal path 30, 67; education 86; examples 4–7, *12–20*; facial recognition 31; hallucinations 60, 61–2; neuroscientific advances 63; order of loss and progression of symptoms 32–5; Primary Visual Pathway 4, 27, 32, 67; residential dementia unit environmental changes 37–50; Tectal Pathway 4, 31–2, 67; ventral path 30, 31, 67; *see also* cognitive abilities; vision
vitreous detachment *23*
Volicer, I. 377
volunteers: Building Community through Arts 199, 201, 202, 209,

214–15, 216, 217; home care 401;
Meeting Centres Support Programme
319

Wang, Michael 133–51
Wareing, Lesley Ann 175–98, 415
Warners, I. 179
Warren, Marjory 224
Wary, B. 374, 381–2
Watkins, R. 264
Watson, M.E. 12
Watts, V. 161, 171
Weaver's Triangle 203–5, *203*
Weinstein, E.A. 140
well-being: couples group therapy 342;
   diagnosis of dementia 262; group
   therapy 286; occupational therapy
   182–4, 185, 188; quality-of-life
   measures 379; sensory stimulation 178,
   179; social and emotional needs 370;

spiritual 250, 251; support 276; trauma
   impact on 275
Whitfield Grundy, J. 35
WHO *see* World Health Organization
Wilcock, A.A. 182–3
Williams, C. 376
Williams, M. 8
wills 124, 384
withdrawal 116, 180
Wood, P.N. 230, 231
Woods, Robert 133–51, 309
World Health Organization (WHO) 226,
   232, 237

Yale, R. 271, 278
Yalom, I.D. 265

Zarit, S.H. 282
Ziegler, J.B. 159
Zuckerman, M. 179